Schooling and Society

SCHOOLING AND SOCIETY

The Politics of Education in Prussia and Bavaria 1750–1900

KARL A. SCHLEUNES

BERG
Oxford / New York / Munich
Distributed exclusively in the US and Canada by St Martin's Press, New York

For my sister Ellen
who has played a central role in my own education

First published in 1989 by

Berg Publishers Limited
- Editorial Offices -
77 Morrell Avenue, Oxford OX4 1NQ, UK
165 Taber Avenue, Providence, RI 02906, USA
Westermühlstraße 26, 8000 München 5, FRG

British Library Cataloguing in Publication Data

Schleunes, Karl A.
Schooling and society:
the politics of education in Prussia and
Bavaria, 1750–1900.
1. Germany. Education. Political aspects,
1750–1900
I. Title
379.43

ISBN 0–85496–267–0

Library of Congress Cataloging-in-Publication Data

Schleunes, Karl A.
Schooling and society: the politics of education
in Prussia and Bavaria, 1750–1900 / Karl A. Schleunes.
p. cm.
Bibliography: p.
Includes index.
ISBN 0–85496–267–0 : $52.50 (U.S.)
1. Education, Compulsory—Prussia (Germany)—History—19th century. 2. Education, Compulsory—Germany—Bavaria—History—19th century. 3. Politics and education—Prussia (Germany)—History—19th century. 4. Politics and education—Germany—Bavaria—History—19th century. I. Title
LC135.G32P787 1989
379'.23—dc19 88–25900

Printed in Great Britain by Short Run Press Ltd., Exeter

Contents

Preface

When this book was conceived its purpose, in the broadest sense, was to examine the effects of mass schooling upon the German Empire, newly unified in 1871 and, in turn, the effects of that national unification upon the course and direction of mass schooling. To make the study manageable I planned to focus upon developments in Prussia and Bavaria. Underlying the entire enterprise was the not-too-startling assumption that schooling and the society of the new German nation-state had helped shape each other, directly as well as indirectly. My purpose was to explore the nature and shape of these effects and, thereby, to learn something useful about German education and about German social and political developments. The plan was to end the study at 1914, as natural a watershed in German developments, it seemed to me then, as was 1871.

Not long after starting work, however, it became clear to me that 1871 was meaningless as a point of departure. A careful look at the sources revealed that the national unification of that year had very little effect upon the schooling of either Prussia or Bavaria. So I began to look into the decades before 1871. Only then did the events that followed 1871 begin to make sense. The conclusion was obvious: schooling after 1871 was determined more by events during the decade preceding that date than by the dramatic events surrounding the proclamation of empire. But the problem was not entirely solved: the events of that preceding decade demanded explanations of their own. And so it went on. This step-by-step process of moving backward in time did not end until I reached the mid-eighteenth century, the point when the idea of mass schooling first began to be taken seriously by German social and political reformers. Only from that base could I move forward again to address those questions I had left behind.

A word needs to be said about the documentation underlying this study. The reconstruction of the history of schooling in Bavaria is greatly hindered by the destruction of the Bavarian *Kultusministerium* records in the Allied bombing raids during the late stages of the Second World War. Fortunately, the holdings of the Bayerische Staatsbibliothek, though themselves not untouched by the bombings, allow for a reconstruction from secondary sources, most of them quite rare. For Prussia the situation is much better. The records of the Prussian *Kultusministerium* are largely intact in the archives of Merseburg and Berlin.

To the staffs of these archives and libraries (and to others mentioned in the bibliography) I am grateful for the uniformly friendly and co-operative spirit with which they met my many requests. I am grateful as well to the National Endowment for the Humanities which provided the funding that allowed me to spend a year in Germany working in these archives and libraries.

To the University of North Carolina at Greensboro, I am grateful for the research leave that allowed me to get this book off the ground. To the inter-library loan staff of the university's excellent Walter Clinton Jackson Library I am grateful for the unfailing efficiency and energy with which they filled my many – and, occasionally, very difficult – requests. One of their many successes earned them a paragraph in the Chancellor's report to the trustees. To my friends and colleagues in the history department at the university, especially to Ann P. Saab and Robert M. Calhoon, who have heard more about this book than they wanted to know and followed its sometimes fitful progress with patience and understanding, I am also grateful. I regret very much that another friend and colleague who was interested in this book, James B. MacDonald, did not live to see it come to fruition.

To my late friend in Munich, Herr Henning, I am grateful for teaching me to decipher the Gothic script in which virtually all records before the day of the typewriter were kept. To the hundreds of scribes whose handwriting I have read in the process of doing this study, I am grateful only to those who wrote legibly. To be sure, many of them wrote in the beautiful hand for which the German language provides the appropriately beautiful word, *Schönschreiben*. To Herr Henning's daughter and her husband, Margarethe and Gerhard Hellwig, also of Munich, I am grateful for assisting my family and me in dealing with the inevitable difficulties of living abroad for a year.

Finally, I am especially grateful to my wife Brenda who has read every word of the manuscript in its numerous versions and whose effective, and sometimes insistent, editorial voice has saved me from a multitude of grammatical and stylistic sins, no one of them less egregious for not being original. To my daughter Anna, whose first trip to Europe came in an early stage of this project, and whose maturing into womanhood has paralleled its own maturing and growth, I am grateful, as I am to Brenda, for inspiration.

Karl A. Schleunes

1
The Promise of a New Era

In March 1836 Calvin E. Stowe, a young professor of biblical literature at Cincinnati's Lane Theological Seminary in Ohio and a leader of his country's common school movement, was preparing for an extended trip to the intellectual centres of Europe, having been commissioned by his Seminary to purchase books for its fledgling library. The Ohio General Assembly, knowing of Stowe's interest in mass schooling and itself contemplating an educational initiative, enquired of the Seminary whether Stowe might also be allowed to 'collect, during the progress of his contemplated tour of Europe, such facts and figures as he may deem useful to the State, in relation to the various systems of public instruction in the countries through which he may pass and upon his return make report thereof'.[1] For his services the Assembly was willing to contribute $500 towards Mr Stowe's expenses. The Seminary agreed to the Assembly's proposal and Stowe was pleased to take on the additional task.

When Stowe returned from Europe late that year, he waxed eloquent about the educational conditions he had encountered. 'A new era in the history of civilization has evidently commenced', he reported to the General Assembly.[2] Everywhere he went, it seemed, educational advances were being marked by the children of the common people who were for the first time attending schools. France he found alive with the idea; Spain and Italy were considering it. England seemed to be stirring itself, as were the Sultan of Turkey and the Pacha of Egypt.

The most advanced of all European countries Stowe found to be

1. Calvin E. Stowe, 'Report on Elementary Public Instruction in Europe', p. 248.
2. Ibid., p. 251.

the German state of Prussia where King Frederick William III was 'pursuing a course of instruction for his whole people, more complete, better adapted to develope (*sic*) every faculty of the soul, and to bring into action every capability of every kind that may exist, even in the poorest cottage of the most obscure corner of his kingdom, than has ever been imagined'.[3] Second only to Prussia was the southern German kingdom of Bavaria, which, Stowe reported, had been 'zealously pushing forward' in emulation of Prussia and was at the point where 'Bavarian schools begin to rival the Prussian'.[4]

Stowe's report, it must be noted, was as much calculated to embolden schooling intentions in Ohio as it was to deliver an impartial account of his findings. He was, after all, the propagandist for a cause. Most of the countries for which he made claims he had not even visited. He had, none the less, been witness to the early stages of what was to become during the course of the nineteenth century a fundamental transformation in the lives of the great mass of Europeans. By the end of the century the one experience Europeans were to have in common was that of having been to school. Most western Europeans, at least, would be able to read, write, and do minimal arithmetical calculation, accomplishments very few of their forebears early in the century would have been able to boast of. These accomplishments were the result of governments establishing during the course of the century those systems of mass, compulsory elementary education that produced the schooled society. It was no exaggeration for Stowe to characterise this new society as representing 'a new era in the history of civilization'.

What Stowe witnessed, however, was merely an aspect of a larger educational revolution of which mass schooling was only a part. This larger revolution has until recently been more remarked upon than examined. Many of the questions surrounding it go unanswered, and some of them unasked. The intention of this study is to remedy part of this situation by examining the smaller mass schooling revolution, its origins and its effects, as well as the politics that surrounded it, in those two states where Stowe thought it most advanced.

In the case of Prussia, the justifications for such a study are self-evident. Prussia's schools enjoyed an international renown

3. Ibid., p. 251.
4. Ibid., p. 253.

throughout the century. Stowe was neither the first nor the last to visit accolades upon them. In 1831, when Victor Cousin, a leading member of the French Academy, was dispatched to assess Prussia's system for educating the masses, his report became the basis in 1833 for Guizot's school bill, a landmark in the schooling of France. Forty years later, as Frenchmen contemplated their defeat by Prussian armies at Sedan, they credited Prussia's success to its schoolmasters. Educational reformers in England, pondering on their country's notoriety early in the century as 'the worst educated part of Christendom',[5] were quick to cite the Prussian example in urging their government towards reform. When Parliament finally legislated compulsory schooling in 1870, it was moved to do so largely by the promise of the economic advantages that schooling had presumably brought to Prussia. In the United States the common school movement continued to take inspiration from Prussia. Horace Mann in 1843 justified an inspection tour of European schools to his Massachusetts Board of Education on the grounds that he was going to visit Prussia, which 'among the nations of Europe has long enjoyed the most distinguished reputation for the excellence of its schools'.[6]

Bavaria's schooling efforts warrant attention, if we are to believe Stowe, because they, like those of Prussia, were far advanced. Nowhere is Stowe's hortatory intent more evident than in this appraisal of Bavarian schooling. He does not appear to have visited Bavaria and he is not likely during the course of his travels to have encountered many tributes to its schools. Perceiving the need to report yet another instance of educational achievement, it appears that he simply conjured this one out of thin air. Not that Bavarian schooling can be dismissed as a failure — far from it. Prodigious efforts had been expended by the 1830s to school the children of Bavaria's lower orders. The essential failure of those efforts for another two decades is no less instructive about the process of schooling than would be their success.

An examination of Bavarian schooling has the additional utility of resisting the temptation to see the German experience of the nineteenth century as being merely that of Prussia writ large. Among the states destined in 1871 to become part of the unified Germany, Bavaria was second in size only to Prussia. Bavaria's traditions and

5. Howard C. Barnard, *A History of English Education: From 1760*, p. 66.
6. Horace Mann, *Annual Reports* (1843), p. 240.

circumstances were very much its own. The Reformation of the sixteenth century, which left Prussia (then Brandenburg) firmly in the Protestant camp, made of Bavaria the fortress from which was launched the Catholic counter-offensive against Protestant Germany. After the Thirty Years' War both Bavaria and Prussia played for high stakes in the game of European power politics, Prussia with remarkable success and Bavaria with a failure so abject that its very continuance as a state was threatened. By the 1750s Bavaria seemed enmeshed in the threadbare fictions of the Holy Roman Empire, whereas Prussia had achieved a reputation for enlightened progressive rule. Though basically dissimilar, both Prussian and Bavarian societies managed during the eighteenth century to produce independently of each other the basis of what was to become the schooling revolution of the nineteenth century.

Prussia and Bavaria were among the first European societies early in the nineteenth century to attempt to implement mass schooling. They are, for that reason, particularly useful settings in which to examine the revolution in education in relation to the revolutionary transformations in thought, politics, demography, and social relationships that surrounded it. Was it, as some suggest, mass schooling that shaped the urban, industrial, and national forms of the nineteenth century? Or was mass schooling itself a product of these new forms? Or is the relationship of yet a different nature?

Questions of this sort have led to the production of a multitude of hypothetical constructs. Theories of modernisation, social control, political integration, social liberation — to name just the dominant ones — have been employed in great variety to explain the relationships of schooling to the world surrounding it. The heuristic value of these constructs is undeniable, and the extent to which they have influenced this study will be evident. The conclusion is, however, that schooling ultimately had all of these effects: modernising, integrating, controlling, liberating; that sometimes it had them serially and at other times simultaneously.

The utility of these constructs is often blurred by the simultaneity of the effects they are designed to clarify. It has become a commonplace, for example, to see schooling as an attribute of Europe's modernisation during the nineteenth century, whether that modernisation is conceived as being economic, political, or social, and to treat as directly related to schooling, either as cause or effect, such phenomena as industrialisation, social mobility, or the emergence of the masses into political consciousness. There is no need to deny such relationships in order to inject a word of caution. For example, immediate limitations to modernisation theories become evident when they are used to explain the origins of the mass education revolution. That revolution had its earliest implementations in places such as Prussia and, if we are to believe Stowe, Bavaria, at a time when these states were by nearly any political, economic, or social measurement less modern than France or Great Britain, where schooling was still a generation or two away.[7] Then, as we shall see, schooling in Prussia and Bavaria was often designed to keep progress in check, or even to undo it completely. In such a case, modernisation is transformed, as if by some conceptual sleight of hand, into social control, or social control into an attribute of modernisation. The notion of the school serving as an instrument of social control is a fairly modern one, although it should be noted that when Guizot sent Victor Cousin to report on Prussian schools in 1831 he was interested in them, he said, because 'the greatest problem of modern societies is the governance of minds'.[8]

How effective an instrument of social control can schooling be? The standard wisdom of those who initiated it and of many of its later proponents has been that through the spread of literacy it is a liberating social force, freeing the individual from ignorance and opening to him or her the economic and social opportunities that illiteracy precludes. In a newer version this wisdom sees literacy (and schooling) as establishing the 'cultural infrastructure' of modern industrial society.[9] The more cynical Guizot, on the other hand, thought it an essential element in the governing of men's minds. Are we to conclude that schooling can at the same time liberate and control? What are we to make of Karl Marx's prediction that literacy, no matter how much intended to govern men's minds, will inevitably lead these same men to understandings that will enable them to overthrow those by whom they are governed?

Similar ambiguities surround those understandings of schooling

7. For a discussion of these concepts as applied to Prussia see Karl A. Schleunes, 'Enlightenment, Reform, Reaction: The Schooling Revolution in Prussia'. See also Peter Flora, 'Die Bildungsentwicklung im Prozess der Staaten- und Nationenbildung' and Wilhelm Roessler, 'Bildung von Modellen in der Schulgeschichtsschreibung'.

8. Eugen Weber, *Peasants into Frenchmen: The Modernization of Rural France, 1870–1914*, p. 331.

9. Eckart Schremmer, *Die Wirtschaft Bayerns: Vom hohen Mittelalter zum Beginn der Industrialisierung*, p. 459.

that see it primarily as a force for social or political integration. Educational reformers in early nineteenth-century Prussia and Bavaria intended schooling to be an instrument for the integration of peoples acquired in the countless boundary shifts that accompanied the war of the French Revolution and Napoleon. Some successes in integration are undeniable, but the emergence in the latter half of the century of a large and revolutionary socialist movement, and the bitter resistance to integration by the Poles in Prussia's eastern provinces, signalled the failure of schools to accomplish what they had very consciously been assigned to do. The popular upheavals in both Prussia and Bavaria in 1848 attest to similar limitations. Schools were no more perfect as instruments of integration than they were as instruments of liberation or control.

The unintended and often unexpected effects of schooling preclude any easy application of the theoretical constructs reviewed here; yet these constructs point the way into the politics that have surrounded mass schooling from the very outset. All but the most naïve of its proponents saw schooling as a multi-edged sword that could cut a number of ways at the same time. Small wonder that there were those who believed the sword best left undrawn or, later, who wanted it re-sheathed.

The politics surrounding schooling in Prussia and Bavaria also sheds light upon some under-explored developments in nineteenth-century Germany. In matters of education, a society is forced to sort out its values and put them on display. It may choose to educate in order to open up opportunities or in order to close them off. In either case it is trying to give shape to itself and to its future. The knowledge it chooses to impart to some of its members and not to others, the methods by which it chooses to impart that knowledge, and the manner in which it reaches decisions on these questions reveal its inner working more clearly than any other aspect of social policy.

Care must be taken to avoid seeing society as an independent actor in this process. The term 'society' connotes, Lenore O'Boyle fears, 'a misleading degree of integration among the institutions of society and . . . takes attention away from the goals of specific groups'.[10] As the cases of Prussia and Bavaria demonstrate, the

10. Lenore O'Boyle, 'A Possible Model for the Study of Nineteenth-Century Secondary Education in Europe', pp. 237–8.

story of schooling is one of specific groups competing to select, distribute, and control the knowledge that will be imparted to other groups with the hope of thereby imposing upon their worlds certain social and political configurations. Involved in this competition are groups with a wide range of cohesiveness, power, and organisation. Some will be clearly defined, discrete, and formal; others ill-defined, amorphous, and overlapping. In the course of this book we shall see in action business groups, court factions, political parties, peasants, churchmen, women, bureaucrats, Catholics, reform associations, Poles, burghers, children, and many others. Some of these groups will be more the actors; others more the acted upon.

The basic proposition put forward in this book is that the schooling revolution in Prussia and Bavaria was generated as an idea by certain élite groups in the late eighteenth century in response to their fears that society was in danger of coming apart, and that this idea was implemented early in the next century when, at the hands of French military might, both societies did indeed come apart.

During the 1770s and 1780s governing and intellectual élites in Prussia and Bavaria saw evidence that the bonds of traditional social order were wearing precariously thin. Beggary, banditry, illegitimacy, and infanticide seemed everywhere on the rise, particularly among those whom God had long ago assigned to the world's lower estates. For those who worried about these things, the bonds of social order, their nature, and how they might be repaired or revitalised became the stuff of theory and reflection. The fears were less of violent revolution, the spectre of which did not actually haunt imaginations until well after the startling upheavals in France, than of the more primal fear of social disorder or chaos — of coming apart. It occurred to some that a means for restoring the bonds of social order might lie in education or instruction for the lower estates.

But indeed when schooling was implemented in Prussia and Bavaria in the first decades of the nineteenth century, it was after both societies had disintegrated. The final rupture was in neither case the result of domestic pressures, but of defeat on the battlefield at the hands of French armies. The old world and its order had collapsed. A new world had to be created. Here begins the actual schooling of Prussia and Bavaria.

2
The Educational Revolution of the Eighteenth Century

The 'new era in the history of civilisation' to which Stowe referred in 1837 had its origins in the transformations undergone during the eighteenth century in the ways that Europeans understood their world and their place in it. It is easy to exaggerate claims about new eras, transformations, or revolutions, but the eighteenth century was undeniably witness to remarkable changes in man's conception of himself and of his world. 'Never was there a greater contrast, never a more sudden transition than this!' So Paul Hazard has described the changes in eighteenth-century intellectual fashion. This was no ordinary swing of the pendulum, he claims: 'It was a revolution.'[1] Contemporaries certainly noticed the change. Immanuel Kant, for one, was particularly disposed to speak of the 'Copernican revolutions' taking place in the world around him.

Of these 'Copernican revolutions', the one most vital to Stowe's 'new era' was the supposition that had developed of man's educability, and not merely that of some men but that of all men, including for the first time those at the low end of the social scale. For centuries those at the top had seen those at the bottom as innately dull and brutish, just a little above the animals, a view rooted in the notion that lowly status was an attribute assigned either by God or by nature. Intellectual currents of the eighteenth century were to undermine this perception. Kant was among those to take delight in the new realisation 'that through education human nature will be continually improved, and brought to such a condi-

1. Paul Hazard, *The European Mind*, p. xv.

tion as is worthy of the nature of man'.[2]

The lower orders stood at the confluence of numerous currents in eighteenth-century thought. Economic theories that saw in agriculture the source of all wealth necessarily placed the peasant in a new light. Any increase in wealth would depend upon making him more productive. Pietists, who as part of their religious awakening questioned religious assumptions as well as social ones, came to see even the most wretched of God's creatures as being worthy in His eyes. Enlightenment thinkers who characteristically presumed man's capacity to reason were willing to extend that capacity downwards into the lowest of the social orders. Thinkers like Rousseau went so far as to posit a human nature in which goodness and virtue were inherent. The result was a revolution in social perception. Those who at the beginning of the century had been seen as pariahs could by its end be seen as patriots.[3]

Economists, religious and social thinkers, state officials, philosophers, and publicists were all by the later decades of the century feverishly exploring the implications of this transformation. Clearly, if the lower orders were educable there were possibilities for creating a new or, at least, an improved world. Equally clear was the fact that any such creation would have to begin with the education of the lower orders. Publicists by the hudreds began to occupy themselves with schemes for social improvement through pedagogy.[4] The *Erziehungsroman*, or novel of education, flourished in this setting. Hundreds of such novels appeared in the last decade of the century alone,[5] with some, like those of Pestalozzi, directly influencing the course of nineteenth-century schooling. Pedagogical theories and schools in which they could be demonstrated sprang up by the dozens. In 1774 J. B. Basedow's *Philanthropinum*, opened at the behest of the ruling prince of Anhalt-Dessau, immediately attracted European-wide attention. Basedow's personality quirks soon led to the failure of his school, but other such establishments flourished on into the next century. One of these, the teacher-training institute established in the Bishopric of Würzburg in 1771, was the product of a pedagogical roundtable discussion which had been organised at

2. Immanuel Kant, *On Education*, p. 8.
3. John G. Gagliardo, *From Pariah to Patriot*.
4. Friedrich Eberhard von Rochow, 'Geschichte meiner Schulen (1795)', p. 59.
5. Helmut Germer, *The German Novel of Education, 1792–1805*, pp. 131–3. See also Ulrich Hermann, 'Pädagogische und politische Publizistik zur Zeit der Französischen Revolution in Deutschland'.

the court of the ruling prince, the enlightened Bishop Adam Friedrich von Sensheim. Perhaps the most prominent of Prussian educators, A. H. Niemeyer (1754–1828), the director of the noted Francke Foundation charity school in Halle, spoke in 1799 of Germans approaching the new century with a 'blind enthusiasm'[6] for pedagogy.

Education for those higher on the social scale was affected as well. The revival of the university and the restructuring of the Gymnasium were also hallmarks of the eighteenth-century educational revolution. As intellectual centres the German universities had been in decline almost since the Reformation. By the eighteenth century they had become little more than repositories of religious orthodoxies and sanctuaries for student ruffians, and thus were considered by many to be enervating to the minds of the young and corrupting of their morals. Abolishing universities became a prominent feature of enlightened educational thought. For promoting advances in knowledge, officials recommended their replacement with the learned academy; for the training of professionals, with the establishment of professional institutes.

An initial step towards university revival was taken in Brandenburg-Prussia in 1694 with the founding of a university in Halle.[7] Its purpose was to train officials for the rapidly growing state apparatus of the Hohenzollerns. The philosophical curriculum was a secular one, constructed under the influence of professors like Christian Thomasius and Christian Wolff, both of whom sought to disentangle modern knowledge from theological speculation.[8] Another major step in this revival came in 1770 with the appointment of Immanuel Kant to a chair of philosophy at the university in Königsberg. Königsberg soon became, along with the University of Göttingen in neighbouring Hanover, one of the entry points into Germany for English economic and social ideas. These universities, new or revived, did not ensure the survival of the university, however. As late as 1798 Prussian educational officials were still considering their dismantling. Not until 1809 when Wilhelm von Humboldt committed the Prussian reform party to the creation of a university in Berlin was their future secured. Berlin quickly established a reputation for excellence, becoming the cornerstone of a

6. Quoted in Wilhelm Roessler, 'Pädagogik', in *Geschichtliche Grundbegriffe*, vol. IV, p. 634.
7. Charles E. McClelland, *State, Society, and University in Germany, 1700–1914*, p. 34.
8. Friedrich Paulsen, *The German Universities and University Study*, p. 44.

renewal that allowed German universities in the nineteenth century to regain the eminence they had enjoyed in the sixteenth.

University revival in Bavaria began, oddly enough, outside the electorate itself, with the naming in 1731 of Johann Adam Ickstatt (1702–76) as professor of law at the University of Würzburg. The politically independent Bishopric of Würzburg — though not to become part of Bavaria until early in the next century — was already upon Ickstatt's arrival a model state of the Catholic enlightenment and destined to affect profoundly the course of the educational revolution in Bavaria. Ickstatt himself was to become a leading figure in the enlightenment in Bavaria and an advocate of its educational reform. As a student of Christian Wolff, Ickstatt, like his mentor, sought to free the university curriculum from its roots in religious orthodoxy.[9] When he came to Würzburg in 1731 it was to assist the Prince-Bishop in breaking down the barriers that confessional separation was seen to be placing upon the expansion of knowledge.

Ickstatt's direct connection to Bavaria began in 1741 when its Elector Charles (also Holy Roman Emperor from 1742–5) called upon him to act as his adviser and to tutor his son, the Crown Prince Maximilian. When, upon his father's death in 1745, Maximilian himself became Elector, he called Ickstatt into his permanent service, commissioning him first to free Bavaria's own university at Ingolstadt from Jesuit control.[10] Ickstatt and the students he brought with him, men like Weishaupt, Obermayer, and Lori, were to be in the vanguard of the enlightenment in Bavaria, as well as in the movement for educational reform that extended far beyond the university.

Like the university, the Gymnasium, which during the nineteenth century was to become Germany's most heralded institution of secondary education, owed its reputation to reforms begun in the eighteenth century. Its leaving certificate, the *Abitur*, was regularised in Prussia by a reform of 1788. The intention was to make of it the testamur for entrance to the university.[11] As was to be the case with the university, it was Humboldt's guidance that ultimately secured

9. Max Rieder, *Geschichte der politischen Bildung in den Volksschulen Bayerns*, p. 39.
10. See 'Johann Adam Friedrich Ickstatt', in *Neue Deutsche Biographie* (*NDB*), vol. X, pp. 113–15; Richard Du Moulin Eckart, *Geschichte der deutschen Universitäten*, pp. 136–9.
11. Karl-Ernst Jeismann, *Das preussische Gymnasium*, p. 102.

for the Gymnasium its intellectual foundation in a classical curriculum and its monopoly control over university entrance.[12]

Neither the university nor the Gymnasium was in any sense new; both traced their origins back to the middle ages when they had been designed largely to educate the higher social orders. Educating the lower orders, with the brief exception represented by the era of the Protestant Reformation, was new, and not to be accomplished merely by institutional reform. The institutions for such a task had themselves still to be created. The vast majority of those in the lower orders were, and always had been, illiterate. Although literacy estimates for the eighteenth century are hardly reliable, it is unlikely that more than ten or fifteen per cent of those in the lower orders were able to read and write.[13] For the peasant, the servant, or the day labourer, what there was of formal instruction was imparted under the authority of the Church, which was generally satisfied if its charges could recite some of the hymns required for worship, or a few verses from the Scriptures that admonished them to act humbly and to attend faithfully to their duties. If in this process someone also happened to learn to read, it was a skill of so little use that it usually wasted away from neglect. Moreover, what passed for a school in the thousands of rural villages in Prussia and Bavaria was commonly the backroom of an inn, a clergyman's attic or the loft of a peasant cottage. Here a barely literate church sexton, underemployed weaver, or invalid army veteran would drill those few children who could be forced to attend in the rudiments of religion. The Church's authority in these matters was supreme, having been reaffirmed in 1648 in the Treaties of Westphalia wherein the school was described as an *annexum ecclesia*. Any change in this relationship would in itself have been revolutionary.

There were, to be sure, lower schools outside the official orbit of the Church. The most common of these were the notorious *Winkelschulen* or unauthorised private schools, located usually in the larger towns or cities. These were frequently conducted by dissident religious sects or, as was reported to Frederick II in 1768, by unemployed preachers, preacher candidates, soldiers, artisans, and women. 'Without method, without discipline, and without supervision [these schools are] undeniably a source of depravity in our

12. Lenore O'Boyle, 'Klassische Bildung und soziale Struktur in Deutschland zwischen 1800 und 1848'.
13. Rolf Engelsing, *Analphabetentum und Lektüre*, pp. 61–2.

children . . .' the report informed him.[14] Other schools, such as *Armenschulen* or charity schools, were commonly the outgrowth of a pietistic concern with the plight of the poor, without, however, denting seriously either their poverty or their ignorance. In some instances, larger towns might establish their own charity schools, sometimes called *Industrieschulen*, hoping thereby to attack local poverty by instructing the destitute in some gainful occupation. After 1770 educational mania also managed to generate a sizeable number of experimental demonstration schools, established often by philanthropically-minded noblemen or, as was the case in Anhalt-Dessau, at the behest of an enlightened prince.

It was the transformed image of the peasant, however, that provided the basis for the educational revolution. Physiocrats and cameralists alike saw an attack on poverty possible only if peasants and manual workers could be made more productive. Neither importuning nor browbeating, both of which had been tried in abundance, had managed to bring about such an increase. The connection between physiocratic thought and schooling is most clearly illustrated by the Swiss philanthropist Issac Iselin (1728–82), who was as energetic in producing physiocratic economic tracts as he was in promoting expansion and improvement in the lower schools of his home city of Basel.[15] Iselin's influence was to be felt in the schooling of both Prussia and Bavaria. J. B. Basedow and his Prussian counterpart, Eberhard von Rochow, were inspired by his educational efforts, as was the Weimar philosopher, J. G. Herder. Pestalozzi was eventually to become one of his many protégés. In Bavaria, Ickstatt, in imitation of Iselin, coupled his own efforts for educational reform with tracts on physiocratic economic theory.

Religious thought, too, contributed to tranforming the image of the peasant. The Pietistic awakening of the eighteenth century assumed from the outset that preparation for the next life was enhanced by education in this one. No more respectful of social than of religious orthodoxies, the Pietists stressed the inherent worth of even the poorest and most unfortunate of God's creatures. Improving their earthly lot, therefore, became one of the most characteristic of their self-imposed duties. Charitable foundations in great

14. Ludwig Geiger, *Berlin 1688–1840*, vol. I, p. 569.
15. Gagliardo, *Pariah to Patriot*, pp. 37–9; Alfred Rach, *Biographien zur deutschen Erziehungsgeschichte*, pp. 138–9.

variety became the institutional fruits of this conviction. Among the first was an orphanage founded in 1695 in Halle by the Pietist leader A. H. Francke (1663–1727). The Francke Foundation was to become the great ornament of German Pietism's social concern. By 1700 it comprised, in addition to a publishing facility, various charitable schools and a free school for some 600 orphans.

The wider influence of Pietism seemed evident as early as 1717 when Prussia's Frederick William I (1713–40) ordered parents in his kingdom to send their children to school, wherever it was possible, because reports had reached him of children being 'grossly ignorant . . . of those things that are most necessary for their welfare and eternal salvation'.[16] When in 1763 Frederick II (1740–86) undertook to encourage school patrons and estate owners in their support of peasant education by promulgating a set General School Regulations for the Rural Schools,[17] he chose as their author J. J. Heckar (1707–68), a Berlin educator and theologian who had studied with Francke and who was already widely known for the modern secondary *Realschule* he had founded in Berlin in 1748. Given the nature of Prussia's governance, these General Regulations applied only in the Protestant provinces. None the less, when a similar set of regulations was promulgated two years later for Catholic Silesia,[18] their author, Johann Ignaz Felbiger (1724–88), the Augustinian Abbot of Sagan, was deeply influenced by Heckar's earlier Protestant version. Felbiger, moreover, was interested in reforming the schools of his own abbey and had for that reason come to Berlin in 1762 as an observer at Heckar's school. Eventually he was to send three of his own pupils to Heckar to be trained as teachers. During the next two decades Felbiger was to become the most influential spokesman for educational reform in Catholic Germany. Through him were filtered into the Bishopric of Würzburg and the Electorate of Bavaria many of the educational ideas from the Protestant north.[19]

It would be incorrect to see in Frederick's General School Regulations evidence of a deep altruistic concern for the lower orders. He

16. Frederick William I quoted in Robert Ergang, *The Potsdam Führer*, p. 142.
17. For Frederick II's *General-Land-Schul-Reglement* see *Das Elementarschulwesen in den Königlich Preussischen Staaten*, ed. F. W. Niedergesäss, pp. 9–14.
18. See the 'Katholische Schulreglement für Schlesien', in *Die Preussische Volksschule*, ed. E. von Bremen, pp. 52–70.
19. See 'Johann Ignaz Felbiger' in *NDB*, vol. V, pp. 65–6; see also in *Allgemeine Deutsche Biographie* (*ADB*), vol. VI, pp. 610–11.

harboured neither illusions about their perfectibility nor ambition for their social elevation. Frederick's motives are for these reasons still debated. One student of his policies has seen military considerations as the key to his interest in schooling, and the fact that the first of his Regulations came immediately after the Seven Years' War lends credence to this interpretation. Frederick had come within a hairsbreadth of defeat. Only the fortuitous death of the Tsarina Elizabeth had allowed him to turn almost certain defeat into victory. Not one to count on such miracles, Frederick may have seen possibilities for greater military effectiveness if the lower orders could have been counted upon to supply him with better prepared non-commissioned officer material.[20] Another view attributes Frederick's interest in schooling to more purely economic motives: his desire, for example, for a more productive peasantry.[21] Above all, care must be taken not to overestimate Frederick's interest in schooling. He appears to have forgotten the provision of his own Regulations within a year of having promulgated them. Neither did he have overblown expectations for what the peasants should learn. In a famous order of 1779, he made it clear that he considered it quite sufficient 'if they learn a little reading and writing, for if they learn too much they will run off to the cities to become secretaries or some such thing'.[22]

Frederick perceived risks as well as benefits in the prospect of schooling. To educate the lower orders might be to awaken in them social ambitions that would be inimical to political stability. Frederick's world still required peasants, labourers, soldiers, and non-commissioned officers as well as noblemen and educated élites to provide leadership. Yet enlightened thinkers, of whom Frederick was one, were themselves raising the kinds of questions that served to undermine the very world view, or *Weltbild* as Dilthey called it,[23] that had for centuries held in place the social relationships Frederick wanted to preserve. Frederick and his compatriots no longer believed in God, or at least not in one who troubled himself with socially useful tasks. Neither did they believe that the world had been divinely divided into those who fought, prayed, and worked.

20. Ferdinand Vollmar, *Die preussische Volksschulpolitik unter Friedrich dem Grossen*, pp. 47, 299.
21. Andreas Flitner, *Die Politische Erziehung in Deutschland*, p. 17.
22. For Frederick II's Cabinet Order of 9 September 1779 see Vollmar, *Die preussiche Volksschulpolitik*, p. 217.
23. H. A. Hodges, *The Philosophy of Wilhelm Dilthey*, pp. 85–6.

Here was the opening for schooling. If God would no longer fashion the needed social divisions, Frederick might have to do it himself. Peasants might well have to be taught to be — and to stay — peasants.

Quite the opposite view was taken by Frederick's contemporary, Rousseau, who sought to destroy the barriers between social orders that so much of the enlightenment was seeking to shore up. Rousseau's novel *Émile*, published in 1762, was to become the century's most influential work on education, and it had profound social implications. In it Rousseau portrayed as contrary to nature any attempts to limit the development of the personality. His ideas took German intellectuals by storm, more so even than they did in France.[24] *Émile* was one of the first books Frederick II read upon his return from the Seven Years' War. Understandably, he was not impressed.[25] Immanuel Kant, on the other hand, is reported to have been so preoccupied with *Émile* that for the first time in his adult life he missed his habitual walk.[26] Its publication, he was to proclaim later, was equal in importance to the French Revolution.[27]

Rousseau's *Émile* opened a new dimension to the schooling discussion in Germany. The novel gave no specific prescription for constructing a system of education, other than to remove from the child's environment the artifices of civilisation, but the implications in its vision of human nature disclosed a social potential that was eagerly explored in the *Erziehungsgespräch* of the following decades. If Rousseau was right in his assessment of human nature, there was no reason any longer to doubt the educability of anyone. The fruits of Rousseau's thinking were everywhere evident by the end of the century: in novels of education, in educational schemes and experiments, and in the chancelleries where schooling policies were being considered.

Rousseau's most direct influence upon the course of German schooling was his effect upon the thought and work of the great Swiss educator, J. H. Pestalozzi (1746–1827). Pestalozzi's thought was to shape the entire course of schooling in Prussia. Its effect in Bavaria, though less dramatic, was to be felt as well. Although he eventually came to characterise *Émile* as an 'unpractical dream

24. Frank E. Manuel, *Shapes of Philosophical History*, pp. 71–2.
25. G. P. Gooch, *Frederick the Great*, p. 145.
26. Willibald Klinke, *Kant for Everyman*, p. 123.
27. Jean Jacques Rousseau, *Émile*, trans. Allan Bloom, p. 4.

book',[28] Pestalozzi was an early champion of Rousseau's pedagogical ideas. He attempted to raise his first son, whom in a fit of enthusiasm he named Jean Jacques, according to the principles outlined in *Émile*. His life's work, trying to improve the lot of the poor through education, is difficult to imagine without the influence of Rousseau.

Pestalozzi's most lasting contribution to pedagogy was his insistence that education be shaped to fit the child. This insistence grew out of a formal, if rudimentary, conceptualisation which ascribed to the child not merely educability, but a nature intrinsically different from that of an adult. Recognition of such a nature was in itself an intellectual milestone, marking both the discovery of childhood as a distinct stage in human development and the establishment of a new foundation for pedagogical theory. Pestalozzi conceived of the human personality as developing in stages. When in 1797 he published the results of a decade of his observations in *My Inquiries into the Course of Nature in the Development of Mankind*, he offered a three-stage conception of that development. The first stage, an instinctive or animal one, he argued, was succeeded in the normal course by a second stage, the social one. A third, or moral stage, was also achievable, but not inevitably so, and therefore its development required special cultivation. Without substantial improvements in education Pestalozzi doubted if many people would ever reach this highest stage. He had long since abandoned any easy assumptions about an inevitable unfolding of goodness in human nature. For one thing, his efforts to educate little Jean Jacques according to Rousseau's precepts had failed miserably.[29] The primary function of education, therefore, had to be to bring larger numbers of people to the moral stage in their development. It was the apparently successful demonstration of these principles in a series of experimental schools which in the 1790s brought Pestalozzi to the attention of the European world, and which was shortly to make him that world's most sought-after educator.

However essential the changing assumptions about human nature and childhood were to the educational revolution, they must not be mistaken for the revolution itself. Very few peasants or their children were affected for either good or ill by any of the changes in their

28. Pestalozzi quoted in Kate Silber, *Pestalozzi*, p. 10.
29. Pestalozzi's son was also retarded.

image. In fact, the improved image of the lower orders seemed to be accompanied by a noticeable increase in their poverty and by a simultaneous decrease in the stability of the social environment in which they lived. The idea of their schooling was born and nurtured within the womb of gathering social crisis. Those who proposed schooling for Prussia and Bavaria did so in response to that crisis, not merely because of the notion that peasants had suddenly become educable.

Notions of crisis are as problematic as those of revolution. Any historian worth his salt should be able to find one, Leonard Krieger has warned.[30] Particular caution must be taken regarding the late eighteenth century not to imbue it with premonitions of the great upheaval to come. Yet it is true that by the late century contemporaries did perceive a crisis and that they did begin to act accordingly. In neither Prussia nor Bavaria were those in charge of the social and political order at all sanguine about its future. Social dislocations in both states contributed to the questioning of long-held political and social assumptions. The ultimate question of what it was that held society together drew the attention of an ever-widening circle, reaching far beyond those who ordinarily reflected upon such matters.

In Prussia the crisis was given its shape largely by a population explosion, a rapid growth in numbers that became noticeable around mid-century and that by late century had become, in Malthus's terms, a 'flood of life'. For reasons that are not at all clear, the population of Prussia appears to have doubled during the course of the eighteenth century, a rate much higher than that of many other regions in Germany. Bavaria, for example, appears to have experienced no growth at all until the beginning of the next century. The social and political consequences of Prussia's remarkable growth are only now being studied. The growth in numbers, because it was not accompanied by a growth in production, defined for Prussia a period of protracted social and political instability that came to be manifested in the increase of such social ills as beggary, illegitimacy, child abandonment, infanticide, vagrancy, thievery, and banditry. The political consequences, noted one contemporary, were 'a propensity toward disobedience and disloyalty'[31] within the lower orders.

Because it was the lower orders whose numbers were so much on

30. Leonard Krieger, *Kings and Philosophers, 1689–1789,* p. 139.
31. Gossler, 'Uber die höchstnothwendige Verbesserung des Zustandes der untern Volksklassen', p. 404.

the increase, the attending dislocations were chiefly rural. Some eighty-five per cent of Prussia's population lived in the rural villages, a rural-urban distribution that was not to change significantly until well into the following century. Rapid population growth placed extraordinary pressures upon the institutions of rural life. Family, Church, guild, peasant farmstead, and noble estate were all affected, and none of them was able to contain the problems being generated.

The irony is that at the beginning of the century Prussia's leaders had seen population increase as the solution to their economic and social difficulties, not as the problem. Gottfried Leibniz, the first president of its Academy of Sciences, quite simply equated population growth with economic well-being. Given the devastations of the Thirty Years' War and the periodic ravages of plague thereafter (the epidemic of 1709–11 in East Prussia killed forty per cent of the population — 250,000 people — and ft empty nearly 11,000 farmsteads), Leibniz's notions, which became the staple of early mercantilist and physiocratic thought, seem not at all improbable. The repopulation policies of the Great Elector Frederick William (1640–88) and King Frederick William I (1713–40), which included inducements to settlers from France and Salzburg, must be seen in this light. The first signs of change in this population picture were observed in 1741 when one of Frederick II's statisticians observed a decline in the death rate.[32]

By mid-century the picture was clearly changing and by the 1780s dangerous signs of over-population were being noted. 'Only twenty years ago everyone was crying "population"!' wrote August Schlözer at the University of Göttingen. Now, he warned, 'It is necessary to have a care for bread as well as people. . . . Bread makes men, but the reverse is not always true'.[33] Unless the trend changed, Schlözer foresaw nothing but increases in the already alarming rates of mendicancy, thievery and violence. Twenty years later that prediction had come true. When Justus Möser lamented in 1804 that 'we are producing a generation of beggars and thieves', it was already the cry of a Malthusian age.[34]

Eighteenth-century population figures are notoriously unreliable, but it seems safe to estimate that between 1740 and 1803 Prussia's population grew from about 2.25 million people to 9.5 million. Some

32. Charles E. Strangeland, *Pre-Malthusian Doctrines of Population*, pp. 214–15.
33. Schlözer quoted ibid., p. 318.
34. Möser quoted ibid., p. 320, n. 4.

of this growth is accounted for simply by territorial acquisition. Frederick II's conquest of Silesia alone added over a million people. The three partitions of Poland added some 2.5 million Catholic Poles and at least 200,000 Jews. Another million people were added in 1803 as a result of the gains made through the Imperial Settlement (*Reichsdeputationshauptschluss*) inspired by Napoleon. A more accurate picture of population growth is revealed by a glance at the individual provinces. By 1804 Silesia's population had doubled to more than two million; East Prussia, which had had 400,000 people in 1720, had 931,000 by 1800; West Prussia grew by fifty per cent during the quarter century following its acquisition by Prussia; the population of the smaller New and Electoral Marks actually tripled during the course of the century.[35]

Had productivity kept pace with population growth there would probably have been no crisis. In fact, productivity was not to catch up until the beginning of industrialisation in the middle of the next century. Voltaire, in the meantime, thought Germany's circumstances condemned it to eternal poverty. For at least a century he proved to be right. By the 1830s, E. A. Wrigley notes, population pressures in Prussia's eastern provinces were threatening 'an adjustment of Irish severity'.[36] Wilhelm Abel has tied population growth directly to the 210 per cent increase in the price of bread grains between 1740 and 1810.[37] Rising prices frequently made market days in the towns the occasion for rioting. Rarely did wages keep up with this inflation; in some instances they were even lowered, as was the case with Berlin silkworkers who in 1775 saw their wages decreased by twenty-five per cent.[38] Noble estate owners in East Elbia, in order to maintain their economic positions, felt increasingly compelled to enlarge their land holdings. This they could do only by absorbing, either through foreclosure or outright expropriation, the surrounding peasant freeholds, measures which became frequent and were to acquire the graphic description of *Bauernlegen*. Many peasants were thereby rendered landless, reduced in status to cotters, day labourers, or worse. Poverty was everywhere in evidence. Travellers took regular note of it in their letters and diaries.

35. For the figures cited, see Erich Keyser, *Bevölkerungsgeschichte Deutschlands*, p. 300.
36. E. A. Wrigley, *Population and History*, p. 154.
37. Wilhelm Abel, *Agrarkrise und Agrarkonjunktur*, pp. 182–3, 187.
38. Artur Müller, *Die Deutschen*, p. 76.

When Thomas Jefferson toured the Rhine in 1788 he passed through the Prussian County of Cleves and spoke of the roads there being 'strung with beggars'.[39] In 1800 John Quincy Adams, American minister to Prussia, travelled through Brandenburg and Silesia. The lower orders in Brandenburg he found to be 'a ragged and pallid race of beggars', and the peasant hovels of Silesia 'generally full of children [who were] oftentimes stark naked, and loaded with vermin'.[40]

The effect of this widespread poverty upon Prussian society, writes Hanna Schissler, was to encourage the growth of 'rural underclasses (*Unterschichten*)' whose very existence 'tended to break down the social order in the countryside'.[41] Bands of beggars were a common sight by the 1780s. A village situated along a main road could expect to see thirty to forty beggars a day, reported the *Berliner Monatsschrift* in 1787.[42] To refuse them alms was to invite from them some act of vengeance. Setting fires in the village or cutting down its fruit trees became common acts of malice. Some villagers regularly had to stay at home from the fields to guard against the beggar bands. Spawned in these circumstances as well was the phenomenon to which E. J. Hobsbawm has given the name 'social banditry', a primitive, inarticulate form of social rebellion. The most notorious of these German bandit gangs, those of Schinderhannes and Matthias Klostermeyer, operated outside Prussia. However, numerous smaller bands of thieves calling themselves, significantly, *Rittenschieber* or plough-pushers did menace the Prussian countryside. These were merely lesser versions of more notorious counterparts.[43]

Other signs of social distress were no less noticeable. Illegitimacy, child abandonment, child selling, and infanticide were everywhere believed to be on the increase. There is little statistical evidence that the incidences of distress were actually rising, but it is clear that contemporaries thought them to be so. 'Child murders, if we judge by the numbers that come to our attention (and few presumably do)

39. Thomas Jefferson, *The Papers*, vol. XIII, ed. Julian P. Boyd, p. 26.

40. Adams quoted in Jerome Blum, *The End of the Old Order in Rural Europe*, pp. 179, 183.

41. Hanna Schissler, *Preussische Agrargesellschaft im Wandel*, p. 97. See also Henri Brunschwig, *Enlightenment and Romanticism in Eighteenth-Century Prussia*, for a treatment of the effect of social crisis upon literature.

42. 'Ueber das Betteln auf dem platten Lande und in kleinen Städten', p. 3.

43. Friedrich Eberhard von Rochow, *Versuch über Armen-Anstalten und Abschaffung aller Betteley*, p. 9.

are becoming more frequent daily', Issac Iselin wrote in 1788.[44] That same year saw the première in Frankfurt a. M. of H. L. Wagner's six-act tragedy, *The Child Murderess*. *Sturm und Drang* writers took infanticide as one of their major topics. Schiller addressed a poem to *The Infanticide*, and reflected sympathetically upon 'the woman's shame no art can heal', and the most famous infanticide in all German literature was that of Margarethe in Goethe's *Faust*. The Hansel and Gretel theme of child abandonment was by then already a commonplace in folklore, and child selling, though less common, was etched into the German consciousness when Daniel Chodowiecki, after having had a peasant couple in West Prussia offer to sell him their child in 1773, executed an etching on the subject.[45] As for illegitimacy, so pronounced was its rise in the late eighteenth century that Edward Shorter believes it can be accounted for only by a wholesale revolution in sexual behaviour.[46]

Social dislocations were no less severe in Bavaria, and here too they were viewed as manifestations of a crisis that was threatening to social and political stability. The crisis in Bavaria, however, cannot be linked to rapid population growth; there may have been none at all, and possibly even a slight decline in some regions during the last three decades of the century. As in Prussia, the Bavarian picture is clouded by untrustworthy statistics and frequent territorial changes. The census of 1771, although compiled with a casualness remarkable even for its day (it took ten years to complete), none the less provides some basis for comparison. In Upper and Lower Bavaria census takers counted 982,505 people; in the Upper Palatinate another 165,733. In the census of 1794 they counted only 924,243 people in Upper and Lower Bavaria, a decline since 1771 of more than 50,000. But the Upper Palatinate and Neuburg-Sulzbach, a principality that Duke Karl Theodor brought with him when he succeeded to the electoral throne in 1777, had another 300,000 inhabitants. When Karl Theodor was succeeded in 1799 by Maximilian IV Josef of another branch of the Wittelsbach family, Bavarian holdings therewith became the third largest in Germany, behind those only of Austria and Prussia. A new census in 1801 showed the new Elector to have in all of his territories a total of

44. Iselin quoted in J. M. Rameckers, *Der Kindesmord in der Literatur der Sturm-und-Drang Periode*, p. 17.
45. Robert Alt, *Bilderatlas zur Schul- und Erziehungsgeschichte*, vol. II, p. 127.
46. Edward Shorter, *The Making of the Modern Family*, p. 79.

2,328,294 subjects.[47]

Bavaria's economic difficulties were more the product of big-power ambitions that had failed than of population pressures. Like Prussia, Bavaria had early in the century seen possibilities for aggrandisement in the wars of Spanish and Austrian succession. Prussia was remarkably successful in these efforts, using the Spanish war to elevate itself to a kingdom and initiating the war with Austria to gain control over the Habsburg province of Silesia. By mid-century Prussia had become a major European power. Bavaria had been less fortunate. Duke Max Emmanuel (1678–1726) had sided with Louis XIV in the Spanish war which, as it turned out, became a war also for Bavaria. For ten years after Blenheim, in 1704, his territories were occupied by enemy Habsburg armies and he was fortunate to recover even one of them in the 1714 peace settlement.

Despite a war debt of some 25 million gulden, Max continued to harbour grandiose ambitions. These now took the form of acquiring for his son, Charles Albert, election to the Holy Roman Imperial throne which was to fall vacant at the death of its current occupant, Charles VI. Max did not sign the Pragmatic Sanction with which Charles VI sought to circumvent Salic law by securing for his daughter, Maria Theresa, the undivided succession to Habsburg holdings. Charles Albert, who in 1726 became Elector of Bavaria, was eventually elected Holy Roman Emperor in 1742 and served as Charles VII until his death in 1745. But his was not a glorious reign. On the very day of his coronation an Austrian army forced Munich into surrender. Upon his death in 1745 Bavaria was forced to conclude peace with Austria and to renounce all further pretension to the imperial throne.

Bavaria had played a dangerous game and lost badly. Among its costs was a thirty-two million gulden debt that Charles Albert bequeathed to his son, Maximilian III Josef, who was confronted in 1745 with the task of putting a chastened Bavaria back together. By mid-century poverty was every bit as endemic to Bavaria as it was to Prussia and no less fraught with social implication. Bavarian peasants probably owned less of the land they worked (around four per cent) than did their Prussian counterparts. Over half of the land

47. On Bavaria's population see W. R. Lee, *Population Growth, Economic Development and Social Change in Bavaria 1750–1850*, pp. 8–11; Ludwig Maenner, *Bayern vor und in der Französischen Revolution*, p. 18. For general background, see Hans Rall, *Kurbayern in der letzten Epoche der alten Reichsverfassung, 1745–1801*.

(fifty-six per cent) was owned by the Church, another one-quarter by the nobility, and some fourteen per cent by the Wittelsbach family itself,[48] a situation that left the vast majority of peasants to the unpredictable mercies of their clerical and secular overlords. With the movement to enclose the common fields, begun in the 1720s, those mercies became less and less tender.[49]

As it did in so many other regions of Germany, an underclass of beggars, vagrants, and criminals emerged also in Bavaria. The draconian punishments stipulated for beggary in the reformed criminal code of 1751 speak as eloquently as would statistics of the extent of the problem. Foreign beggars were to be branded and expelled for the first offence and hanged (beheaded if a woman) for the second. If Bavarian subjects, they were to be flogged and set to work and, if that failed to prevent a recurrence, sent to a workhouse for a year and a day.[50] Periodic crop failures, such as the one in 1770, merely exacerbated the problem.

Growing misery in the countryside drove many young men into the cities, although conditions there were no better. Little work, if any, awaited them. Benjamin Thompson, the American loyalist who worked in Bavaria from 1784–94 as adviser to Karl Theodor, has described 'the swarms of beggars in the great towns', their infestation of the streets and public works, and their 'practice of going into private homes; and [how] churches were so full of them, that people in their devotions were . . . frequently obliged to satisfy their demands in order to be permitted to finish their prayers in peace and quiet. . . .'[51]

Many of the destitute who remained in the countryside organised themselves into beggar bands, often with ex-soldiers as their leaders. The line between beggar band and bandit gang was from the outset exceedingly thin and often overstepped. The most spectacular of the bandit leaders was Matthias Klostermayer, the so-called Bavarian Hiesl, whose gang flourished from the mid-sixties to the early seventies when Klostermayer was captured and executed.[52] Klostermayer's gang, a small army of nearly 1,000 men, more than any

48. Ibid., pp. 18–19; F. L. Carsten, *Princes and Parliaments in Germany*, pp. 352–3.
49. Alan Mayhew, *Rural Settlement and Farming in Germany*, p. 179.
50. A. Emminghaus, ed., *Poor Relief in Different Parts of Europe*, p. 119.
51. Thompson quoted in George E. Ellis, 'Benjamin Thompson — Count Rumford', pp. 449–52.
52. Carsten Küther, *Räuber und Gauner in Deutschland*, pp. 52–4.

other captured popular imagination for its challenge to wealth and authority. Klostermayer himself became the model for the outlaw hero, Karl Moor, in Schiller's play *The Robbers*.[53] Many such gangs flourished in these decades and many were the executions of those apprehended. The Upper Bavarian city of Burghausen alone during a twenty-eight year period late in the century witnessed some 1,100 executions, many for robbery, some for beggary and some for other crimes.[54]

By the late century conditions in the countryside had become so dangerous that to maintain order the government stationed small military units in some one hundred scattered rural districts. Altogether 500 to 600 men were in these units, the first standing police troops in any German state.[55] After 1789 disruption also took the form of peasant preachers, so-called *Bauernkönige*, who roamed the countryside holding forth revolutionary visions of an end to taxes, dues and social privilege. Cartoons showing Louis XVI on trial were being circulated, as were ones of French noblemen hanging from lampposts. The sudden popularity of these cartoons and the spread of revolutionary ditties came to concern officials.[56]

After 1750 Bavaria also came to be known for having one of the highest illegitimacy rates in Europe, a reputation maintained well into the next century. At its height near the turn of the century nearly one birth in four was illegitimate, a circumstance that has been traced to restrictions on marriage and to an inheritance system that produced a landless proletariat.[57] Infanticide, too, was a problem in these circumstances; how great a problem it is impossible to say, but it is clear that a good deal of public attention came to be focused upon it. In 1781 public whippings were ordered for mothers who had given birth to an illegitimate child, the calculation being that to discourage illegitimacy would be to discourage infanticide. In 1793 the government threatened anyone convicted of child murder with beheading, a punishment peasant girls were to be reminded of from the pulpit four times a year.[58]

53. Paul F. Angiolillo, *A Criminal as Hero*, pp. 31–2.
54. Maenner, *Bayern*, p. 51.
55. Küther, *Rauber und Gauner*, p. 21.
56. Maenner, *Bayern*, pp. 156–7.
57. Edward Shorter, 'Sexual Change and Illegitimacy: The European Experience', pp. 248–9; see also Lutz Berkner and Franklin Mendels, 'Inheritance Systems, Family Structure, and Demographic Patterns in Western Europe, 1700–1900', and W. R. Lee, 'Bastardy and the Socioeconomic Structure of South Germany'.
58. Maenner, *Bayern*, p. 27.

In 1780 the Mannheim philanthropist and jurist, Baron von Lamezan, offered a prize of 100 ducats for the best essay in answer to the question: 'What are the best, most practical methods to remedy infanticide without at the same time discouraging chastity?'[59] Four hundred essays were submitted and three prizes awarded, but the most important study the competition evoked was never submitted. Its author J. H. Pestalozzi, who had had his attention called to the competition by his mentor Issac Iselin, decided the subject was too large to be dealt with in an essay, so he wrote a book instead.[60] Pestalozzi's book *Concerning Legislation and Infanticide* was published in 1783. Infanticide was simply the by-product of poverty, he argued.[61] Changes in the punishment would do nothing to attack the problem at its root. Rather the state would have to concentrate upon elevating the moral level of the lower orders. He was certain that the appropriate moral instincts existed. Even infanticide, as he saw it, rested upon a noble motive: that of a mother 'hiding her shame'.[62] If this inherent goodness were to be cultivated, the problem could be solved. Pestalozzi's book connected more directly than had any previous effort a major social problem to the idea of education.

The connection had been made before, of course, and in other settings. In Prussia in the early 1770s a philanthropic nobleman, Friedrich Eberhard von Rochow (1734–1805), had established schools on his estates in order to deal with problems he had observed among his peasants in the wake of crop failures. Rochow was to become the most influential of the Prussian philanthropic educators. The peasant schools he established became some of the most important centres for pedagogical experiment in all of Germany and the models upon which Prussia made its first effort, albeit an aborted one, to implement peasant schooling.

Rochow, the scion of a prominent Brandenburg family, had served in Frederick II's army until 1760, whereupon he returned home to manage the family estates, an occupation that left him ample time to pursue his other interests in languages, literature, theology, and history. Among the first writers to catch his attention was Rousseau. In 1762 he also became Dean of the Protestant

59. Wilhelm Wächtershäuser, *Das Verbrechen des Kindermordes im Zeitalter der Aufklärung*, pp. 34–5; Rameckers, *Kindesmord*, pp. 82–5; William L. Langer, 'Infanticide: A Historical Survey'.

60. Max Liedtke, *Pestalozzi*, p. 89.

61. Silber, *Pestalozzi*, pp. 52–6.

62. Pestalozzi quoted in Wächtershäuser, *Verbrechen*, p. 48.

Cathedral at nearby Halberstadt. Rochow was by then a proponent of the enlightened, rational theology that so eagerly adjusted Christianity to fit human reason.[63]

When unusually wet weather in 1771 and 1772 spoiled crops across much of northern Germany, malnutrition and disease became as epidemic as were beggary and banditry. Concerned for the health of his own peasants, Rochow engaged for them a learned medical doctor. But the peasants rejected the expertise of this outsider and ran instead to faith healers and quacks upon whom they had always relied. Rochow was deeply depressed by this display of ignorance. When many of these peasants died he could only conclude that the peasant is so 'entrapped in a net of prejudice and nonsense that his powers of faith and reason are useless to him. . . .' Why did the peasant behave in this way? Because he had virtually no education, Rochow reasoned; because 'he grows up as an animal among animals'.[64] If the peasant were to be changed, his inherent powers of faith and reason would have to be awakened. With this observation Rochow began his career as an educator.

By Easter of 1772 he had published a manual of pedagogical advice intended for those who would teach peasant children. The manual soon came to the attention of Frederick II's Chief for Ecclesiastical Affairs and Justice Minister, K. A. von Zedlitz (1731–93), an enlightened official who was himself interested in peasant education. His appointment in 1770 had reflected Frederick's own current interest in such matters. At Zedlitz's urging, Rochow established the first schools for the peasants on his estate.[65] Three new schoolhouses were built, and to overcome the resistance of parents the instruction for their children was made free of charge. Rochow hired full-time teachers and paid them 180 thalers a year, a salary calculated to make secondary employment unnecessary.

Rochow's schools acquired immediate fame. Visitors by the hundreds came to observe the instruction in them, hoping thereby to learn how to bring under control the dislocations attending poverty. 'Governing princes and people from all confessions, even Roman

63. See 'Friedrich Eberhard von Rochow' in *ADB*, vol. XXVIII, pp. 727–34. See also Otto Gerlach, *Die Nationalerziehung im 18. Jahrhundert, dargestellt in ihrem Hauptvertreter Friedrich Eberhard von Rochow.*

64. Rochow, 'Geschichte meiner Schulen', p. 40.

65. Zedlitz to Rochow, 17 January 1773; Rochow, 'Geschichte meiner Schulen', pp. 41–2.

Catholics and also Jews', were among the visitors Rochow noted.[66] Prince Leopold of Anhalt-Dessau visited six times, Zedlitz came twice himself, and from Berlin delegations came in a steady stream,[67] all of them to marvel at Rochow's success.

The curriculum followed in these schools had been outlined by Rochow in his schoolmaster's manual of 1772. The children were to be provided with useful information on crops and animals, diseases and their treatment, arithmetic, and the rudiments of moral and political life. Special attention was to be devoted, the manual stipulated, to 'Matters of Society and Authority, of Laws and Rewards' in which the 'Dear Children' were instructed that 'in God's world there are several estates; there are those who give orders and those who obey'.[68] Rochow's social objective was clear: peasants were to be taught to remain peasants, though more productive and obedient ones.

Rochow became one of the most influential of the publicists engaged in the *Erziehungsgespräch* of the 1780s and 90s. As time went on his claims for schooling became more and more embracing. In 1779 he suggested that the 'character and disposition of an entire people might be given direction' through education; that, if implemented on a large enough scale, it might produce for Prussia a 'common spirit' or 'national character' that would give it a decisive edge in European conflicts.[69] In 1787 in the *Berliner Monatsschrift* he wrote, though anonymously, that schooling could be the solution to the problem of beggary, and in 1795 he spoke to the Economic Society of the Electoral Mark 'On the Need for a Purposeful Development of Lower Schools in Connection with Poor Houses',[70] arguing also against the practice of giving such schools a denominational or confessional identity. Confessional schools, he argued, prepared the child only for confirmation day. It was schools of this sort that were responsible for the 'national stupidity' that had now to be dispelled if 'its inevitable companion, poverty' was ever to be eradicated.[71]

Rochow's example did inspire some imitation, most notably that

66. Ibid., p. 45.
67. Friedrich Eberhard von Rochow, *Sämtliche pädagogische Schriften*, vol. IV, ed. Fritz Jonas and Friedrich Wienecke, pp. 437–63.
68. Ibid., p. 43.
69. Friedrich Eberhard von Rochow, 'Vom Nationalcharacter', p. 5.
70. 'Ueber das Betteln auf dem platten Lande', pp. 34–9.
71. Ibid., p. 35.

of a relative, Philip von der Reck, who in 1789 established a similar school on his own estate in the western County of Mark.[72] According to one count, by 1790 sixty-four such schools sponsored by noblemen were scattered across Germany. Yet, for all the attention these schools received, they barely scratched the surface of the problem. If peasant schooling were to be effective, it would have to be implemented on a scale far more comprehensive than the one made possible by philanthropic initiative.

It was Zedlitz, impressed with Rochow's demonstration that peasants were educable, who became during the next years the most vocal proponent in Frederick's government of schooling for the lower orders. Greater social harmony and increased production were among the benefits he saw coming from such schooling. 'Popular education' (*Volkslehre*) had become a necessity, he said.[73] Despotic states might be able to survive without it because they rested on fear and force, he observed in 1777, but in a monarchical state like Prussia, governed as it was by law, every subject needed to be enlightened about his duties as well as his rights and competencies. Promoting 'the spirit of self-discipline'[74] within each individual, he believed, would tie the individual more effectively to the social whole. For the peasant specifically, Zedlitz expected that schooling would make of him 'a good and, in his class, a sensible, useful, and active man'.[75]

For schooling of that sort to be accomplished, Zedlitz was convinced that the state needed to take the initiatory role. Only when education ceased to be a poor relation of the Church could it be expected to take the form, and to be introduced on the scale, that the Prussian situation required. In 1784 the *Berliner Monatsschrift*, one of whose editors was also a Zedlitz subordinate, carried a series of articles praising the minister for his educational policies and calling for the creation of a state supervisory agency to take over authority in all matters of education.[76] Ultimately, in 1787, just before his dismissal at the hands of a new king, Zedlitz was to produce an

72. See Manfred Heinemann and Wilhelm Rüter, *Landschulreform als Gesellschafts-initiative.*

73. Zedlitz quoted in Flitner, *Politische Erziehung*, p. 22.

74. Zedlitz quoted in Kurt von Raumer, 'Zum geschichtlichen Hintergrund und europäischer Kontext der preussischen Bildungsreform', p. 55.

75. Zedlitz quoted in Gagliardo, *Pariah to Patriot*, pp. 109–10.

76. Paul Schwartz, *Der erste Kulturkampf in Preussen um Kirche und Schule (1788–1798)*, pp. 48–9.

elaborate set of 'Proposals for the Improvement of the School System in the Royal States' (of Prussia).[77] According to his plan, each estate was to have its own system of schools, rigidly separated from those of the others. There were to be lower, mostly rural, schools for the lower social levels, burgher schools for those in the middle, and learned schools for those at the upper social levels. By their separateness, these schools were to help reclarify distinctions of estate that were becoming increasingly blurred, distinctions that were at the same time being redefined also by the drafters of the new civil code.[78] Through instruction in 'religion rightly understood', Zedlitz explained how schools were to lay the moral basis for the acceptance of 'those duties that accompany the estate into which we have been appointed.'[79] In the lower schools the curriculum was to be patterned almost entirely upon Rochow's model. It was to impart understandings about life and nature that would be useful to a peasant, as well as to teach him essential vocational skills. Thus Zedlitz expected the enhancement of both social stability and economic productivity.

Frederick II was concerned with both stability and productivity, and had Zedlitz timed his proposals to coincide with one of Frederick's bursts of enthusiasm for schooling, something of consequence might have come of them. One of those bursts of enthusiasm had come in 1772 in the wake of the annexation from Poland of the province that was to be called West Prussia. To 'rescue the common man from his Polish slavishness and to lead him toward acceptance of Prussian ways',[80] Frederick had ordered the appointment of German schoolmasters. He set aside 200,000 thalers, the interest from which was to be used for school improvements in the new province and for subsidising the salaries of its schoolmasters.[81] Monies for comparable purposes were set aside also for the other provinces. By the late seventies, however, when Zedlitz's plan was ready, Frederick's interest in schooling had waned.

In Bavaria, as in Prussia, the idea of schooling for the lower orders was generated in response to widespread social dislocation. Bavaria, however, was not as strongly positioned as Prussia to deal with these

77. Zedlitz, 'Vorschläge zur Verbesserung des Schulwesens in den Königlichen Staaten'.
78. Reinhart Koselleck, *Preussen zwischen Reform und Revolution*, p. 76.
79. Zedlitz, 'Vorschläge', p. 103.
80. Frederick II quoted in Max Bär, *Westpreussen unter Friedrich dem Grossen*, p. 550.
81. Vollmar, *Die preussische Volksschulpolitik*, p. 300.

dislocations. Not only was the Bavarian state heavily saddled with debt; it had never managed to establish the financial independence gained by its Prussian counterpart during the time of the Great Elector. No Bavarian version of royal absolutism had yet been fashioned. If the monarchy were to address the dislocations in Bavarian society, it had to tap the wealth of the Church and the nobility, both of which enjoyed immunities that in Prussia had long ago disappeared. Until such time the Bavarian monarchy remained heavily dependent upon the capricious generosity of churchmen and nobles. For that reason schooling was only one of the reforms attempted after 1745 when the enlightened Max. III Josef became Elector, and one of the later ones at that.

Efforts to lay the foundation for monarchical absolutism in Bavaria, begun in the 1750s with the codification of the various bodies of law, culminated between 1768 and 1771 in a flurry of activity designed to secure those foundations. The leading figure in these efforts was Peter Osterwald (1718–76), who had in the 1760s become the Elector's closest adviser. Osterwald, like Ickstatt, was an outsider, not native to Bavaria, and a convert to Catholicism who had taken his legal studies at Protestant universities in northern Germany.[82] The Elector's appointment in 1761 of Osterwald to head the secular division of the government's Spiritual Affairs Council (*Geistlicher Rat*) signalled the beginning of the state's offensive against clerical immunities. One of the four collegial councils serving the monarchy, the Spiritual Affairs Council had been established in 1570 during the Counter-Reformation to supervise relations between Church and state and to guard against the entry of Protestantism into Bavaria. Censorship and education were placed under its control and had remained there ever since, making the Council a kind of spiritual–intellectual bodyguard of the *Bavaria Sancta*. If there were to be fundamental changes in the relationship between Church and state, control of this Council was essential.

By the time Osterwald gained that control in 1768, he had also headed a commission investigating how the state might impose taxes upon the Church and, under a pseudonym and at the Elector's behest, written a treatise calling for the establishment of an Imperial State Church that would in all but name be independent of Rome.[83] Osterwald's attack upon clerical immunities began as soon as he

82. See 'Peter von Osterwald' in *ADB*, vol. XXIV, pp. 525–6.
83. Ibid., p. 525.

took charge of the Council. A series of decrees was aimed at restricting the independence of both monasteries and the prelature. A censorship body independent of clerical influence was established and, lastly, electoral sanction, a *placetum regium*, for all Church pronouncements was required.[84]

From the outset Osterwald had also been a proponent of educational reform which, as far as secondary Latin schools and universities were concerned, meant breaking the monopoly control held by the Jesuits.[85] As for the lower schools, which served the common people in the countryside, there were so few of them that the question was less one of reform than one of creation. Yet, where such schools did exist, they were by tradition and law clearly within the jealously guarded purview of the Church.

In November 1768 Osterwald recruited to the Council a new School Commissioner, the prominent linguist and ardent anti-Jesuit, Heinrich Braun (1732–92). Braun, a Benedictine theologian, was an advocate of the use of the German language in all of Bavaria's schools, attracting thereby the enmity of the Jesuits who saw their own position threatened should Latin be displaced as the language of instruction. Although Braun's linguistic achievements are still recognised,[86] it is as 'the spiritual father of the public *Volksschule*'[87] that he made his most significant contribution to the development of modern Bavaria. Having been named to Bavaria's Academy in 1765 in recognition of his role in the stabilisation of German as a literary language, he quickly became the Academy's educational expert and its foremost advocate of schooling for that majority of Bavarian subjects whose education the Jesuits and the Church largely ignored.

Braun was charged by Osterwald's Council with developing a plan for a system of lower schools, to prepare for them the necessary instructional materials, and to draft the electoral decree whereby the plan would be implemented. He was well aware of the difficulties in trying to educate the lower orders. They were, he told Max. III Josef, for the most part so 'malicious, ignorant, lazy, and vice-ridden . . . that they really must be classified with the animals'. Yet

84. Ludwig Hammermayer, 'Das Ende des alten Bayern', pp. 1093–4.
85. August Kluckhohn, *Beiträge zur Geschichte des Schulwesens in Bayern vom 16. bis zum 18. Jahrhundert*, p. 233.
86. Eric C. Blackall, *The Emergence of German as a Literary Language, 1700–1775*, p. 145.
87. Michael Doeberl, *Entwicklungsgeschichte Bayerns*, vol. II, p. 327.

this alone was no reason for despair. 'The most damaging prejudice that could exist would be to believe that ignorance and low morals are qualities inherent in the peasantry. No!' he explained: 'They are the product of a bad education'.[88] Because it was the state that was the first to feel the evil consequences of people who lacked the knowledge required to be effective even in life's lowest stations, it was incumbent upon it to impart that knowledge. 'The better educated people are, the more moral they will be and the more amenable (*biegsam*) to obeying good laws and leaders', he assured the Elector.[89]

Braun submitted his proposal to Osterwald's Council in September 1770 and saw it effected by electoral decree in February 1771. He tells us that the chief influences upon his proposal were Abbot Felbiger's Prussian School Regulations for Silesia and J. J. Heckar's textbook prepared for his *Realschule* in Berlin. He also solicited information from other parts of Germany, 'particularly from the Protestant lands', and had combed carefully through educational publications, school reports, and the like.[90] Braun's plan resembled very much the one Zedlitz was to produce a few years later in Prussia. In Bavaria, too, each social order was to have its own set of schools. As in Prussia, the learned and Latin schools for the upper orders, and burgher schools for the artisan and commercial classes, already existed. For these Braun needed to do no more than propose that they be placed under the supervision of the state and that German be the language of instruction. In both cases the change was significant.

For the lower orders, rural and urban, Braun proposed what he called 'trivial schools' (*Trivialschulen*).[91] These were new; attendance at them was to be compulsory; they were to have a modern curriculum; and they were to be under state, not Church, supervision. Here the pupils were to be divested of their superstitions by being taught the basic concepts of nature. They were also to gain an understanding of the cause of common diseases and of their treatment, as well as to acquire the basic skills of reading, writing, and calculation, and the rules of proper behaviour towards persons of higher station. This

88. Heinrich Braun, *Gedanken über die Erziehung und den öffentlichen Unterricht in den trivial- real- und lateinischen Schulen nach den katholischen Schulverfassungen Oberdeutschlands*, p. 11.
89. Ibid., pp. 3–4.
90. Heinrich Braun, *Pragmatische Geschichte der Schulreformation in Baiern*, pp. 15–16.
91. Braun, *Gedanken*, pp. 22–3.

last instruction, Braun hoped, would enable them to recognise even subtle social signals from their betters.[92]

Braun recognised that particularly in the rural areas the need for establishing these trivial schools was immediate and great. The state would have to push hard if these schools were to exist in sufficient numbers soon. As for teacher training, here too the state would have to play a larger role. Rather than establish expensive institutions for the training of teachers, Braun recommended that certain existing schools in strategically-located cities be designated as 'normal schools'. Here teachers and teacher candidates could, at minimal expense to the state, be brought to observe the demonstration of good pedagogical practice.[93] Abbot Felbiger had been the first to propose such normal schools as an inexpensive way to train those who were to teach the children of the lower orders. For a financially straitened Bavaria, the relative cheapness of teacher training was vital. Financing for his overall plan Braun envisioned as coming from a general school fund that he expected would be created by contributions from the Church, the corporation of nobles, and the treasury of the Elector.[94] Successful implementation of his plan rested, as he saw it, upon co-operation between the monarchy and the Church, and upon the existence of good teachers.[95]

Braun's plan for the schooling of Bavaria was not to be implemented, any more than was Zedlitz's in Prussia. According to Braun himself, who later wrote a history of his educational efforts, the reasons for this failure were 'administrative and financial', i.e. Bavaria's lack of an effective bureaucracy and the lack of money.[96] To this must be added the resistance of the clergy as well as that of those who were to be schooled. Even if the lower orders had been inclined to send their children to a school, fewer than half the villages in which they lived had anything resembling one. The Church and the clergy, moreover, were little tempted to co-operate with a government that was at the same time attacking their prerogatives on this, and virtually every other, front.

The fundamental reason for the failure, however, was lack of money. Braun's own vision of a general school fund, voluntarily generated, was at best naïve. Already in 1771, in response to

92. Ibid., pp. 116–21.
93. Ibid., pp. 317–18.
94. Doeberl, *Entwicklungsgeschichte*, vol. II, p. 328.
95. Braun, *Gedanken*, p. 319.
96. Braun, *Pragmatische Geschichte*, p. 93.

Osterwald's reform decrees, the Church had reduced the size of its annual 'free gift' to the monarchy. Braun was to argue in his history that a major funding opportunity had been missed in 1773 when the assets confiscated from the Jesuits upon their dissolution were not used for the schools.[97] Ickstatt had in fact urged the Elector to set aside the confiscated 7,832,000 gulden for a special school fund.[98] Instead, most of the money had to be used to relieve the victims of the famine of 1770.

The death in 1776 of Max. III Josef and the accession to the electoral throne of his Palatinate cousin, Karl Theodor, is also often adduced in explanation for the failure of enlightened reform in Bavaria. Karl Theodor (1776–99) was to acquire a reputation as a reactionary, and at the beginning of his reign, at least, seemed to have little interest of any sort in Bavaria, to say nothing of its schooling. Twice, once in 1778 and again in 1784, he was on the verge of giving Bavaria to Joseph II of Austria in exchange for the Austrian Netherlands. Only the intervention of Prussia's Frederick II, fearful of Austrian aggrandisement in South Germany, prevented the exchange from being completed.[99] Karl Theodor's reign did ultimately produce a reaction, though one more of indifference and neglect than of conscious design.[100] While he did formally rescind numerous measures of the Osterwald era, many of those which he ignored, including the General School Mandate of 1771, had become dead letters even before he came to the throne. By 1783, when he finally came to dismantle the 1768 reform of the Spiritual Affairs Council, that body had for some time been functioning along its pre-reform lines.[101]

Most of Karl Theodor's reputation stems from his suppression after 1784 of the Illuminati, a secret reform society based at the University of Ingolstadt and whose members were purportedly conspiring to overthrow the established order so as to reconstruct a new one along totally secular and rational lines.[102] The Illuminati-

97. Ibid.; Ludwig Wolfram, 'Heinrich Braun, Ein Beitrag zur Geschichte der Aufklärungsepoche in Bayern', p. 37.
98. Doeberl, *Entwicklungsgeschichte*, vol. II, p. 316.
99. C. T. Atkinson, *A History of Germany, 1715–1815*, pp. 310–14, 318–19; Karl Bosl, *Bayerische Geschichte*, p. 197.
100. Eberhard Weis, *Montgelas, 1759–1799*, p. 32; Klaus Epstein, *The Genesis of German Conservatism*, pp. 100–4.
101. Rudolf Hindringer, *Das kirchliche Schulrecht in Altbayern*, p. 88.
102. J. M. Roberts, *The Mythology of Secret Societies*, pp. 119–22; Epstein, *German Conservatism*, pp. 87–100.

hunt of the mid-eighties did lead to the exile of a sizeable number of enlightenment figures, including numerous voices favouring education reform.

Only once, late in his reign, did Karl Theodor show a brief interest in schooling, and then under the pressures arising from domestic dislocations which after 1793 had become entangled with those associated with Bavaria's involvement in the war against revolutionary France. 'Religion, only religion, saves me', he told his chief Illuminati-hunter, Privy Councillor Lippert.[103] So that it might also save Bavaria, Karl Theodor reiterated in January 1795 the compulsory school attendance decree of 1771, with the provision that religion (*Christenlehre*) be at the centre of instruction.[104] In a countryside plagued by beggars, bandits, and *Bauernkönige*, and since 1793 also by army deserters, schools and *Christenlehre*, he thought, might be necessary for preserving social tranquillity.

Whatever schools might have done was obviated by the fact that there were few of them and because even these few were so bad. Contemporary reports of lower schools during these years yield a picture of unrelieved dreariness. In 1790 Lorenz von Westenrieder (1749–1829), one of the proponents of school reform who had not been forced to quit Bavaria in the 1780s, and for thirty years the publisher of a journal of patriotism and enlightenment, reported on school conditions in an article to which he gave the revealing title: 'Why are We so Far Behind in the Enlightenment of Burghers and Peasants and How Far Have We Come?'[105] Fewer than half of Bavaria's 8,141 rural villages, he claimed, had anything resembling a school, and many of these had only a *Wanderschule*, wherein classes were conducted only occasionally by an itinerant schoolmaster in whatever quarters could be found. Where there was a regular school, it was often conducted in the teacher's living quarters which the pupils had sometimes to share with his chickens, geese, or swine. Most teachers Westenrieder found to be 'totally useless', and many of them physically infirm and of questionable morals; few were genuinely literate. So meagre was their pay that the job attracted only the lowest types; in status their rank was often below that of

103. Karl Theodor quoted in Maenner, *Bayern*, p. 137.

104. See 'Deutsches Schulwesen im allg. Christenlehre', Vol. I, 1774–1860, Bayerisches Hauptstaatsarchiv (BHStA), MK 22876.

105. Lorenz Westenrieder, 'Warum man mit Aufklärung der Bürger und Bauern noch so weit zurück, und wie weit man gleich wohl gekommen ist', pp. 352–70.

gravedigger, shepherd, or day labourer, occupations with which teachers regularly had to supplement their incomes. Genuine improvement, Westenrieder admitted, seemed out of reach. To construct the necessary schools, he calculated, would cost 200,000 gulden annually for years to come, and an equal amount would be needed to pay for teachers' salaries, and for school fees and books that poverty-stricken parents would be unable to afford. Even in Munich the picture was not appreciably better. Here, the Spiritual Affairs Council learned in 1793, barely a third of the children were in a proper school. 'The rest are in no school at all, or in a lower, unlicensed and unauthorized *Winkelschule* with God knows what kind of instruction . . .' the Council concluded.[106] Travellers through Bavaria were regularly struck by the wholesale ignorance and superstition they encountered. 'No one can read and write and a heavy darkness has settled over the countryside', wrote a late eighteenth-century observer.[107]

In Prussia education for the lower orders was no more effectively implemented than in Bavaria. Zedlitz's schooling plans, though initially encouraged by Frederick II, were ultimately undermined by him as well. When Zedlitz proposed training for those teachers Frederick had wanted dispatched to West Prussia, the King demurred, proposing instead that any retired army sergeant who knew a little about reading and writing would do perfectly well. In fact, Frederick ordered Zedlitz to enquire about invalided war veterans who might qualify. By the time he learned that only seventy-nine of more than 4,000 such veterans were even marginally qualified in reading and writing, Frederick's interest in the matter had disappeared.[108]

Frederick's fundamental reservation about schooling was that he did not share the view that education would necessarily strengthen the bonds that held society together. Neither was he certain that schooling could be meted out in socially safe doses. In such circumstances schooling might actually accelerate the dissolution of society rather than retard it.

Frederick as king, no less than as philosopher, was deeply concerned with those things that he believed held society together. What would keep the lower orders from behaving in ways disruptive

106. Hindringer, *Schulrecht in Altbayern*, p. 100.
107. Quoted in Eckart Schremmer, *Die Wirtschaft Bayerns*, p. 463.
108. Walther Hubatsch, *Frederick the Great of Prussia*, p. 206.

of the social whole? What could keep them from begging, stealing, murdering, or running off to cities? Since 1769 Frederick had been corresponding on precisely this question with his friend, the French *philosophe*, d'Alembert. The two agreed that until recently Christianity had served as the main force for social cohesion, keeping social relationships in place by explaining them as part of God's benevolent design. Their further agreement about the impending death of Christianity raised immediately the question about the future basis of social cohesion. D'Alembert took the position that rationally-derived truth would serve that cohesive purpose, and that eradication of falsehood and superstition, among which he counted religious beliefs, would reduce the vice and crime rampant among the lower orders. Of this Frederick was not persuaded.[109] Religion, though he too thought it to be 'a system of fable more or less absurd',[110] might well be necessary for keeping the lower orders in line. Some 'system of myth', he said, was necessary to 'lead men and make them docile'.[111] After all, would enlightened peasants be satisfied to remain merely peasants? He feared not.

D'Alembert eventually persuaded Frederick to submit the problem to his Academy for one of its essay competitions. In November 1777 the Academy announced a prize of fifty ducats for the best answer to the question: 'Is it the lot of the people either to be deceived by being led into new errors, or to be maintained by those in which they find themselves?'[112]

The question itself reveals a great deal about the dilemma confronting eighteenth-century political leaders; the answers it inspired reveal much more. Thirty-three essays qualified for the final competition, of which twenty took the affirmative position and thirteen the negative. Unable to decide which position was correct, the Academy awarded a prize to the leading essayist on each side of the question.[113] Though not awarded a prize, the essay of Pastor Gebhard of Berlin's New Jerusalem Church illustrates the dilemma. Taking the position that errors could indeed have social utility, he proposed that the lower orders be allowed those that 1) are socially

109. For a discussion of the exchange see Lester G. Crocker, 'The Problem of Truth and Falsehood in the Age of the Enlightenment', pp. 596–600.
110. Frederick II quoted in Gooch, *Frederick*, pp. 294–5.
111. Frederick II quoted in Ronald Grimsley, *Jean D'Alembert*, p. 169.
112. Adolf Harnack, *Geschichte der Königlichen Preussischen Akademie der Wissenschaften zu Berlin*, p. 417.
113. Crocker, 'Truth and Falsehood', p. 597.

useful, or at least harmless, 2) socially harmful, but whose eradication would cause even greater harm, or 3) harmful, but worked to support other useful errors. Gebhard was able also to envision circumstances in which new errors might have to be introduced.[114] His conclusion was simple: if truth could not hold society together, error would have to do.

Frederick's own views on these matters were similar to those of Pastor Gebhard, leaving him less than enthusiastic about either Zedlitz's various proposals for expanded schooling, or about his call for a state supervisory agency to oversee the Church in its role as educator. Frederick's pessimism grew deeper as he grew older and finally it was fed also by the prospect of being succeeded by his nephew, the lecherous profligate, Crown Prince Frederick William.[115] Zedlitz had no cause either to rejoice at this prospect, for the Crown Prince was known for holding views decidedly unfriendly to rationalist enlightened figures like himself. The Frederick William II who succeeded to the throne at Frederick's death in August 1786 is in fact better remembered for his shortcomings than for his merits. The Comte de Mirabeau, an observer of the transition at the court, reported to Paris that 'deceit', 'irascible vanity', and 'avarice' seemed the 'three principal shades of character of the new King'.[116]

Despite these deficiencies, or perhaps because of them, Zedlitz had far greater immediate success with the new king than he had had with the old one. Not only did Zedlitz remain in Frederick William II's service for two more years, he managed also to persuade him to approve the school plan Frederick had for years ignored. When in January 1787 Zedlitz submitted his plan in the form of a lengthy 'Memorandum on the Present Situation of the School System and Proposals for its Improvement',[117] Frederick William II, of whom Mirabeau said 'no human power could induce him to read forty lines together', approved it within two days.[118]

Zedlitz appeared to be getting everything he wanted. Prussia was finally to have, it seemed, a system of schools for each estate, as well as a state agency that would take from the Church supervisory

114. Edmund Hennes, *Die Volkserziehungslehre bei Herder und bei Vertretern des gebildeten Mittelstandes des 2. Hälfte des 18. Jahrhunderts*, pp. 58–9.
115. Gooch, *Frederick*, pp. 308–9.
116. See Mirabeau's letter of 8 December 1786 in Count of Mirabeau, *Memoirs of the Courts of Berlin and St. Petersburg*, p. 272.
117. Schwartz, *Der erste Kulturkampf*, p. 50.
118. Mirabeau, *Memoirs*, p. 135.

authority over matters of education.[119] This supervisory body, which was to replace the Ecclesiastical Department created in 1763, was to be called the *Oberschulkollegium* or Superior State Board of Education. Zedlitz was to be its head. Its function, the king ordered, was to provide 'essential uniform supervision' so that 'good people and useful subjects will be trained for each estate';[120] its jurisdiction to extend over universities, Gymnasien, Knights' Academies, elementary and orphan schools. The only exclusions were to be the military schools and those for Jews and the French colony.[121] Zedlitz also was allowed to name his own associates to the board. With one exception, he selected those who shared his rational, enlightened views.

The State Board's first task was to assess current schooling conditions. Requests were sent to the provinces asking officials there to report on such things as the number of schools available, the rates of attendance at them, the nature of what was being taught, and the level of teacher-training and teachers' salaries. Responses were patchy, but they revealed conditions almost uniformly dismal. School attendance was miserably low, reported an East Prussian official.[122] Everywhere school fees were beyond the means of day labourers, shepherds, servants and the like. Salaries for schoolmasters had not risen since 1736, although the costs of many staples had in the meantime risen five-fold. Understandably very few schoolmasters could boast of any pedagogical training. The reporting official concluded that schools and teachers could be supported adequately only by a general land tax. Conditions in Berlin were no better, the Board learned. For its 120,000 people there were only 243 lower schools, and nearly a third of these belonged to the French colony. Only seventy-five were under authorised supervision of either Church or municipality. Another 102 of them were unsupervised *Winkelschulen* whose fugitive existence so irritated officials.[123]

The Board's enquiry seemed a useful beginning. For Zedlitz it also turned out to be the end. On 3 July 1788, Frederick William II

119. W. M. von Bissing, *Friedrich Wilhelm II*, p. 170.

120. Frederick William II quoted in Ludolph Beckedorff, 'Zur Geschichte des Preussischen Volks-Schulwesens', p. 83.

121. Ernst Müsebeck, *Das Preussische Kultusministerium vor hundert Jahren*, p. 8.

122. Paul Schwartz, 'Die Schulen der Provinz Ostpreussen unter dem Oberschulkollegium, 1787–1806', pp. 57–61.

123. Dietrich Rittershausen, 'Beiträge zur Geschichte des Berliner Elementar-Schulwesens; Von der Reformation bis 1836', pp. 270–1.

replaced him with J. C. Woellner (1732–1800), one of his favourites from their days together in the Rosicrucian Society and the man who would for the next ten years be the architect of Prussia's domestic policy. Klaus Epstein has called Woellner one of 'the first self-consciously Conservative politicians in German history. . . .'[124] His appointment marked Frederick William II's formal break with the enlightened officialdom of his predecessor.

Like Frederick and d'Alembert, Woellner was concerned with social cohesion and with the behaviour that everywhere seemed to be threatening it. Unlike them, however, he believed society to be held together by the Christianity of mystery and miracles, the one of dogma and orthodoxy so much denigrated by rationalist theologians. 'Just as an army cannot survive without a decisive set of regulations, so the state cannot survive without a uniform set of precepts in matters of faith and religion', claimed one of Woellner's spokesmen.[125] With those who had neglected to foster these uniform precepts lay the responsibility, Woellner believed, for the spread of unbelief among the lower orders and for the behaviour that undermined social cohesion. He was determined, he told a friend, to 'humble the apostles of enlightenment'[126] by using his authority to restore the *Weltbild* in which these apostles had lost confidence. By doing so, he believed he would also be restoring a modicum of social equilibrium.

It is a measure of the secondary role Woellner assigned to schools that it took him until 1794 to issue an order about what should, and should not, happen in them. There were, he recognised, simply too few schools to have a decisive effect upon the lower orders. Instead, it was the thousands of pastors — most of whom he suspected of being theological rationalists — who had the most direct influence upon them. His first act, therefore, was to issue on 9 July 1788, within a week of assuming office, an Edict on Religion that was designed 'to restore and re-establish in the Prussian lands the original purity and truth of the Christian religion'. Anything that would 'bring into doubt the basic beliefs' was henceforth to be avoided.[127] Confessional divisions were once again to be clarified

124. Epstein, *German Conservatism*, p. 354; see 'Johann Christof von Woellner' in *ADB*, vol. XLIV, pp. 148–58.
125. H. D. Hermes quoted in Manfred Heinemann, *Schule im Vorfeld der Verwaltung*, pp. 278–9.
126. Schwartz, *Der erste Kulturkampf*, p. 95.
127. Fritz Valjavec, 'Das Woellnerische Religionsedikt und seine geschichtliche Bedeutung', p. 386.

rather than ignored; Jews, Mennonites, Bohemian Brethren and other sects were to be tolerated only so long as they obeyed the state and refrained from proselytising. Woellner was also concerned with the nature of sermons. Might not their content be used to spread rationalism? To find out what topics pastors were selecting for their sermons, Woellner empowered a commission of enquiry. Where pastors were found to be choosing undesirable topics, the commission was instructed to assign more acceptable ones.

In the face of these measures, Woellner's 'Curricular Instructions' for the lower schools, issued in 1794, seem at most an afterthought. Schoolmasters were directed to restrict their efforts to providing their pupils with adequate practice in the catechism, acquainting them with basic doctrine, imparting 'an appropriate understanding of the Bible and assuring their memorization of a store of well-known hymns'.[128] Beyond this subjects like geography and natural history were to be de-emphasised. No deviation from these instructions was to be allowed.

Only a handful of schoolmasters was likely ever to have come close to reaching the limits that Woellner warned them not to overstep. Moreover, his instructions could apply only to such schools that existed. From reports made by a state inspection team in 1792, he knew that in East Prussia only one village in six had a school and that the ratio was even lower in West Prussia.[129] Most of the rural schools were to be found in the villages on royal estates. Schools on the noble estates were much rarer. Rochow apparently had inspired few of his compatriots into imitation.

For these obvious reasons Woellner's practical influence upon the course of Prussian schooling was limited. Just as schools, because there were so few of them, had been unable to produce the useful subject envisioned by Zedlitz, they were now unable to produce the orthodox believer deemed essential by Woellner. Whether schools in sufficient numbers could have produced either remained to be tested. Woellner was successful only in pointing those schools that did exist away from the enlightened direction in which Zedlitz had sought to steer them. His various decrees in support of religious orthodoxy were, in effect, the newly-articulated conservatism's answer to the

128. Woellner's instruction quoted in Johannes Tews, *Ein Jahrhundert preussischer Schulgeschichte*, p. 36.
129. Schwartz, 'Schulen der Provinz Ostpreussen', pp. 280–2.

question posed a few years earlier by Frederick's Academy. Society and its political and social arrangements were to be sustained by a rigid orthodoxy, not by the rationalism and scepticism of enlightenment. One major element that Woellner introduced into this consideration, however, was radical in its implication for education: religion was too important to be left to the Church.

Impatience with the failures of Prussian schooling was revealed early in the reign (1797–1840) of the new king, Frederick William III, who at the first opportunity cleared out the Rosicrucian clique that had served his father. Woellner was dismissed in March 1798; his replacement was Ernst von Massow (1750–1816), a man cut clearly out of the Zedlitz mould. At first the new monarch's interest in schooling seemed more genuine than that of any of his predecessors. The 33,000 thalers granted him by his estates as a coronation gift he turned over to local communities to build schools, raise schoolmasters' salaries, and pay the school fees of the poor.[130] But he wanted more than that. He informed Massow that 'The time has finally come to stress the meaningful education and instruction of burgher and peasant children'.[131] Massow was accordingly commissioned to devise the plan that would lead to such 'meaningful education and instruction'.

He began with what was to be the most thorough effort yet to assess the condition of Prussia's schools. He himself made a series of inspection tours that by 1802 had taken him to nearly every province. What he discovered was no less dreary than what Zedlitz had found in 1787. Particularly bad was the situation in the recently annexed Polish provinces. South Prussia, for example, acquired in 1793, had only 712 schools and even fewer teachers for its 9,400 communities.[132] Electoral Brandenburg, on the other hand, had 1,650 schools, but half of its schoolmasters earned fewer than forty thalers a year.

Massow's School Improvement Plan, finished in 1801, was the most comprehensive one to date for the schooling of Prussia's lower orders.[133] Its most prominent features were taken over directly from

130. Ludwig von Rönne, ed., *Das Unterrichts-Wesen des Preussischen Staates*, vol. I, p. 89.

131. Frederick William III to Massow, 3 July 1798, in Bruno Gebhardt, *Die Einführung der Pestalozzischen Methode in Preussen*, pp. 8–9.

132. Klewitz, 'Geschichte und Darstellung des Südpreussischen Schulwesens', p. 164.

133. Gottlieb Lüttgert, *Preussens Unterrichtskämpfe in der Bewegung von 1848*, pp. 13–14.

Zedlitz's proposals. Each estate was once again to have its own class of schools. There was to be no mixing of the orders. Such mixing, Massow feared, would inevitably lead to social confusion, leaving those in the lower orders 'unhappy and dissatisfied'. Religious instruction, again subordinated to the imparting of useful knowledge, was to be non-confessional, the spectre of which had so recently thrown Woellner into panic. Massow hoped also to drive a wedge into the longstanding practice of having individual schools supervised or inspected by the local clergyman. On this count, as on others, Massow's hand seemed greatly strengthened by the increased authority granted the state in the new civil code of 1794. The code declared schools to be 'establishments of the state' (*Veranstaltungen des Staats*), as well as making school attendance compulsory, and clarifying, at least in theory, the basis for school financing.[134]

Little of educational significance was to come of Massow's plan for the same reasons that little had come of those of Zedlitz or Woellner. The state's lack of bureaucratic reach in educational matters was again decisive. It had few means by which to execute its will. Nowhere is this lack more evident than in the way local communities spent their portion of the 33,000 thalers Frederick William III had assigned to them for their schools. Most of the money came to be used instead for local projects such as bridge building, road construction, or debt payment.[135] Also, although the civil code defined schools as 'state establishments', it stipulated that the Church and clergy were to continue to perform the major function of school supervision, although now in theory as agents of the state.[136]

Certainly the most insuperable barriers to implementing Massow's schooling proposals were financial. Prussia's economic difficulties had been recently exacerbated by the war of 1792–5 with France. The civil code specified, moreover, that schools were to be funded primarily by the Church and charitable foundations. Only if funds from these sources were unavailable would the burden fall upon the heads of households in the local communities (whether or not they had children). On patrimonial estates, should the heads of

134. See the Prussian Civil Code, Zweiter Teil, Zwölfter Titel (Von niedern und höhern Schulen), Paras 1, 12, and 29–33, in *Allgemeines Landrecht für die Preussischen Staaten von 1794* (Textausgabe), pp. 584–6.
135. Rönne, ed., *Unterrichts-Wesen*, p. 89.
136. *Allgemeines Landrecht*, Paras 12 and 17, p. 585.

households be unable to fulfil this obligation, the noble estate-owner was obliged to come to their assistance.[137] The code made no mention of state funds. Financial provisions such as these did no more than paper over the difficulties of raising the money that would have been needed to effect Massow's plan. He admitted as much when he rejected even a modest proposal for the establishment of teacher-training institutions because 'they would cost too much'.[138]

The course of Prussian schooling was ultimately affected less by the nature of Massow's proposals than by the debate they inspired. Carried on vigorously during the first years of the new century and then abandoned in the face of the disaster of 1806–7, this debate explored more fully than had any previous one the social implications of schooling. These, as it turned out, alarmed some of schooling's staunchest proponents and ultimately led Frederick William III to withdraw in confusion from his earlier commitment to its full implementation.

Four persons stand out in this debate: Friedrich Gedike and J. F. Zöllner as proponents of Massow's plan, and Friedrich Schleiermacher and B. M. Snethlage as opponents. Friedrich Gedike, the very embodiment of enlightened rationalism, had been a protégé of Zedlitz, a member of the Superior State Board of Education, a former editor of the *Berliner Monatsschrift*, and currently director of Berlin's prestigious Gymnasium of the Gray Cloister. He had also founded a journal in 1800 to advance the cause of school reform. His ally, J. F. Zöllner (1753–1804), another of Zedlitz's protégés, has been described as a 'shining light among the rationalist preachers in Berlin'.[139]

The rhetoric that came to be employed in the debate over Massow's plan reflected the anxieties of a world very much aware of the revolution that had so recently transpired in France. Social fissures that for generations had prompted nervous speculations were seen by the first years of the new century to have grown sufficiently worrisome to warrant immediate action. In 1803 the Prussian Academy asked for advice on the most efficacious means of 'leading crude nations [Poles and Lithuanians] still wallowing in error and superstition, back to a state of healthy reason'.[140] Three years later

137. Ibid., Para. 33, p. 586.
138. Massow quoted in Gunnar Thiele, *Geschichte des Preussischen Lehrerseminare*, vol. I, p. 203.
139. Schwartz, *Der erste Kulturkampf*, p. 30.
140. Horst Joachim Frank, *Geschichte des Deutschunterrichts*, p. 375.

the problems of Prussia's own lower orders were summarised in the *Berliner Monatsschrift* in an article 'Concerning the Pressing Need for Improving the Lower Orders'.[141] 'Unbelief and fanaticism', 'an immoderate propensity for physical gratification', 'beggary and poverty', and 'a penchant for disobedience and disloyalty' were widespread among these orders, the author noted.[142] These 'rapidly spreading problems', he claimed, 'were undeniably a result of the dissolution of all moral principles, of the growing insolence common in modern life, and of increasing poverty'. What laws, prison, and judicial decisions had been able to do in addressing these problems had largely been accomplished. For a solution, he said, 'something else, from another direction, will have to be done'.[143]

To Gedike and Zöllner that 'something else' obviously had to be the implementation of Massow's Comprehensive School Improvement Plan. Gedike, though by no means the first to do so, claimed that criminality was inevitably greater in localities without schools.[144] Zöllner advanced the proposition that instruction in the German language, if it replaced Polish and Lithuanian, would serve to uplift these backward peoples and promote in them the development of a Prussian national spirit.[145] The same kind of improvements might be anticipated for Prussia's native lower orders, for, as Zöllner defined it, education was the process of 'continual, intentional participation in the lives of peoples, in order to prepare them in their youth so that in their mature years they will become what they should be'.[146] This was the 'national education' that would work to narrow the fissures in Prussian society by reinforcing in it the divisions of estate.

It was this promise of a 'national education' serving to shore up the divisions of estate that in 1804 moved a young theologian from the University of Halle, Friedrich Schleiermacher (1768–1834), to subject Zöllner's proposition and Massow's proposals to a devastating critique. 'National education' for a populace divided into estates was an impossibility, Schleiermacher argued in the *Jenaischer Literaturzeitung*. Only the removal of these divisions, followed by a uniform

141. Gossler, 'Ueber die höchstnothwendige Verbesserung', pp. 401–29.
142. Ibid., p. 404.
143. Ibid., p. 419.
144. Friedrich Gedike, ed., *Annalen des Preussischen Schul- und Kirchenwesens*, vol. I, p. 410.
145. Jerry F. Dawson, *Friedrich Schleiermacher*, pp. 77–8.
146. See 'Johann Friedrich Zöllner' in *ADB*, vol. LV, pp. 423–5.

education for the entire populace, would make possible a truly 'national education'. Anyone advocating education in that sense would also be 'unavoidably the instigator of revolution'.[147]

Schleiermacher was disposed to accept such an implication. Massow and Zöllner were not. Their reservations were nurtured as well by the growing attention being paid to the pedagogical theories and practices of Pestalozzi. Pestalozzi was on the threshhold of his great fame as an educator. His main methodological work, *How Gertrude Teaches Her Children*, had appeared in 1801, and his school in Burgdorf was already a magnet for those interested in employing education to address the problems they saw in their worlds. Whether his methods could be employed without stirring up additional social dissatisfactions, however, was another question.

Doubts about the social implications of Pestalozzi's method had already been raised. B. M. Snethlage (1753–1840), a Berlin Gymnasium director who was later to play a significant role in Prussian schooling, was among the first to raise them. Snethlage doubted whether Pestalozzi's method could 'be used without differentiation for all orders in society without also being disadvantageous for the future position of these orders in the state'. From reading the *Gertrude* book, Snethlage concluded that 'Pestalozzi makes no distinction between orders; he wants one treated just like the other'.[148] The impression that Pestalozzi's methods would serve to weaken social distinctions was not Snethlage's alone. Madame de Staël, travelling through Germany in late 1803 and early 1804, gained the impression from her conversations at various German courts that 'The instruction which is acquired at Pestalozzi's gives every man, of what class soever he may be, a foundation on which he may erect, as he chooses, either the cottage of the poor man or the palaces of kings'.[149] To a world rendered acutely sensitive to social unrest and revolution such a prospect was not universally welcome.

Interest in Pestalozzi and his method did not for that reason subside. In 1803 J. H. Plamann, a young theologian from Berlin and a Pestalozzi enthusiast, borrowed money to study at Pestalozzi's Burgdorf Institute.[150] The school that Plamann opened in Berlin

147. Friedrich Schleiermacher, *Ausgewählte pädagogische Schriften*, ed. E. Lichtenstein, pp. 13–17.

148. Snethlage quoted in *Beyträge zur Berichtigung der Urtheile über Pestalozzi, seine Methode und sein Institut*, ed. F. J. Müller, pp. 76, 93.

149. Anne Louise Germaine Baronne de Staël-Holstein, *Germany*, pt. 1, p. 129.

150. See 'Johann Ernst Plamann' in *ADB*, vol. XXVI, pp. 222–3; also Ritters-

upon his return was to become the city's most prestigious boarding school for children of upper class families, and the first in Prussia to employ the new method. There was interest in Pestalozzi at the official level as well. Gedike himself planned a stopover in Burgdorf on his way to Italy during the summer of 1803. His death prevented what would have been Prussia's first high-level look at the new method being tested in Switzerland. Instead, a lesser Prussian official was dispatched to Burgdorf that same summer by Otto von Voss, the governor of the Polish-speaking province of South Prussia.[151] Voss, being directly concerned with integrating a Polish population into the life of Prussia, had on his own initiative sent a local education official by the name of Jeziorowski to Burgdorf to learn if the method could be applied effectively to the local situation. Jeziorowski's report must have been extremely favourable. In December, Voss informed the king in person that Pestalozzi's method was applicable particularly in backward regions 'because it made use of the natural talents and inclinations of crude and coarse peoples. . . .'[152]

Frederick William III was not to be convinced. Though an advocate of schooling, and still willing to back Massow's plan, he was not at all sure about Pestalozzi's method. Innately cautious — others said dull and unimaginative — he was particularly receptive to warnings that Pestalozzi's assumptions did not give proper recognition to the importance of the divisions of estate. Schooling, as conceived by Frederick William III and Massow, was seen to have utility if it served to support social foundations, not if it undermined them. Thus Frederick William III rejected Voss's proposal to introduce the Pestalozzian method into the lower schools of South Prussia. In a Cabinet Order of 31 December 1803, drafted by Massow, he warned that with lower schools, 'one must never forget that, with few exceptions, we are dealing with our precious lower class (*schatzbare Volksklasse*). . . . The children of this hard-working *Volksklasse* should become not lecturers, not chancellery officials, not mathematicians, not religion professors. They should learn to read their catechism, Bible, and hymnal, to write and calculate in accordance with their limited circumstances, to love and fear God and behave accordingly. . . .'[153] Given the king's doubts and the

hausen, *Geschichte des Berliner Elementar-Schulwesens*, pp. 285–6.

151. Klewitz, 'Geschichte und Darstellung', p. 180.

152. Voss quoted in Gebhardt, *Die Einführung*, p. 10.

153. For Massow's order, see Ingeborg Charlotte Bussenius and Walther Hu-

parsimoniousness of Massow's plans, a major commitment to schooling seemed precluded. As had been the case in Bavaria, schooling was deemed an undertaking too expensive and too dangerous to risk.

batsch, eds., *Urkunden und Akten zur Geschichte der preussischen Verwaltung in Südpreussen und Neuostpreussen, 1793–1806*, pp. 464–5.

3
New World Through Schooling 1800–1830

Nothing less than military disaster sufficed to overcome the resistance to schooling. To Bavaria that disaster came in December 1800 when her forces, along with those of her Austrian ally, were defeated by the French at Hohenlinden. To Prussia it came six years later with her defeat by Napoleon at Jena-Auerstadt in October 1806. Hohenlinden and Jena-Auerstadt signified that the worst fears of the Berlin Academy had come to be realised: the world of Germany had fallen apart; everywhere the floodtide of revolution seemed to threaten. After 1815, when the tide receded, both Bavaria and Prussia were firmly established on the road to schooling.

Defeat left Bavaria and Prussia in very different positions relative to their French conqueror. By joining forces with Napoleon, Bavaria emerged as a medium-sized German state more than doubled in territory and population. In 1806 it was even granted the status of a kingdom. Prussia, on the other hand, was left deeply humiliated by its defeat. In the Treaty of Tilsit Napoleon stripped it of half its territory and people, and imposed upon it an occupation and an indemnity, as well as membership in his Continental System. Any one of these provisions alone threatened Prussia with economic ruin. 'There was no longer unity in the state', wrote a government official from exile, 'not even real provinces any longer . . . .'

In both Bavaria and Prussia, however, reform parties emerged which took up the task of putting their worlds back together. Animated with the latest ideas in administration, economics, and law, these reform parties were remarkably optimistic about the prospects for constructing a new world. The leading figure in Bavaria was the Count Maximilian Josef von Montgelas whose vision of a renewed Bavaria was shaped by enlightenment assumptions regarding the efficacy of state absolutism. Montgelas' long tenure in office, which lasted from 1799 to 1817, earned him the reputation of being the architect of the modern Bavarian state. His counterpart in Prussia was the Baron Karl vom Stein who had no less of an impact upon his society, a fact made more remarkable by Stein's brief tenure which lasted for only a little more than one year. Stein's vision for Prussia was radically different from that of Montgelas for Bavaria. He found nothing attractive in Montgelas' notions of imposing change from above. His vision was for a Prussia rejuvenated from below by reforms that would unlock the potential inherent in the lower orders. Eventually he foresaw a Prussian society enlivened by popular participation in political and economic affairs, a Prussia that would be a model for the rest of Germany.

Though their objectives were different, the measures associated with the reforms of Montgelas and Stein were actually quite similar. They each began by dismantling the remnants of an old régime in collapse. At the highest levels of government, functional ministries were created immediately to replace the old collegial bodies. Serfdom was ended and the legal inequalities that had been the basis of traditional social and legal relations abolished. For the first time in Prussia, peasants and Jews were given, or at least promised, civic equality. The monopoly powers of guilds were rescinded, a reflection of the laissez-faire economic ideas of Adam Smith. The rule of law and reason was to be guaranteed by written constitutions. A constitution for Bavaria was promulgated in 1808. During the same year municipalities in Prussia were granted self-government as the first step in what Stein hoped would lead to the creation of a representative body for all of Prussia. Here Prussia's divergence from Bavaria was clearly evident. Montgelas' constitutional ideas had no room for representative bodies of any sort.

Both Montgelas and Stein, however, shared an extraordinary faith in the powers of pedagogy to create the social bonds that would hold their new worlds together. Montgelas had long been the champion of educational reform. In his Ansbach Memorandum of 1796, which he drew up when he learned that his princely employer was likely to inherit the Bavarian throne, he called for 'a total reorganization' of 'the elementary schools in the cities and the countryside' because it 'will be here where the capabilities of the most important class in society will be developed and where the seal of a national spirit (*Nationalgeist*) will be imposed upon it'. Prussia's reformers were equally serious about educational reform. 'The state can and must, even by force if necessary, bring about a situation in which everyone of its citizens receives a measure of education and instruction', the king was advised shortly after Tilsit. Stein explained his reason in his 'Political Testament of November 1808'. Schooling, he believed, could tie together the effects of all the other reforms, because through it alone would be made possible 'the awakening of a physically and morally powerful generation'.

When the Elector Karl Theodor died on 16 February 1799, his last-minute heroic efforts to produce an heir having been unsuccessful, his throne passed to the head of a cousin branch of the Wittelsbachs, Maximilian Josef of Zweibrücken. Four days later the new Elector, now Maximilian IV Josef, arrived in Munich. In his entourage was Montgelas, eager to implement the programme outlined in his Ansbach Memorandum. Within a week Karl Theodor's corrupt officials were replaced by a new set of ministers. Foreign, judicial, and financial affairs were each accorded their own ministry. The most immediately important task, however, was given over to a new Ministry for Spiritual and School Affairs which was commissioned to supervise the secularisation of ecclesiastical territories and properties in the hopes of replenishing an electoral treasury more than fifteen million gulden in debt.[1] The old Spiritual Affairs Council, now subordinate to this new ministry, was immediately charged with looking into how the conditions of the lower orders might be improved. Methods of training teachers who might be able to break through the coarse 'brutal natures' of the young people from these orders were to be investigated,[2] as was the advisability of moving the university from Ingolstadt to Landshut in order to protect it in the case of renewed warfare.

The renewal of the Empire's war against France seemed imminent in early 1799. One of Karl Theodor's last acts had been to commit 20,000 Bavarian troops to the anti-French alliance being organised by Austria. War did in fact break out in March, but fortunately Bavarian soil itself was spared until May of the following year. None the less, the war placed Bavaria in an extremely precarious position. Even its existence seemed in doubt. Because it was of

1. Eckart Schremmer, *Die Wirtschaft Bayerns*, p. 262.
2. Michael Doeberl, *Entwicklungsgeschichte Bayerns*, vol. II, p. 509.

great strategic importance to both Austria and France, there was no more assurance that Bavaria would be allowed to survive victory any more than it would be defeat. Long accustomed to playing mouse to an Austrian cat, a victory over Napoleon could easily lead to Bavaria's being swallowed by her bigger ally. But Napoleon, too, recognised Bavaria's importance. What did he have in mind for a defeated Bavaria? Questions like this left little time to concentrate on reform, and all progress ceased in July 1800 when Munich itself was occupied by the French. Then, on 3 December 1800, came the decisive battle at Hohenlinden.

The defeat at Hohenlinden may well have saved Bavaria from extinction; it certainly redirected the course of its political development. Napoleon proved eager to enlist it in his plans to contain Austria, and Montgelas, long before Hohenlinden, had put out secret feelers to Napoleon broaching precisely such a possibility. The Peace of Lunéville of February 1801 laid the groundwork for what was to become a twelve-year-long association between Montgelas' Bavaria and Napoleon's France. The treaty held out the prospect of territorial acquisition as well as the reorganisation of the Holy Roman Empire along lines favourable to Bavaria's political and economic interests. In August 1801 Bavaria's link to France was made formal with the signing of a treaty of friendship.

Under Napoleon's protective umbrella, Bavaria was to experience four critical years of peace, years during which it was allowed to weather and, ultimately, to profit from the revolutionary storms sweeping through Germany. In the great Imperial Resettlement of 1803 Bavaria proved by far to be the biggest gainer of any of the German states. The alliance with Napoleon was paying off. Seventeen imperial free cities, a dozen abbeys and priories, the bishoprics of Freising, Bamberg, and Würzburg, as well as parts of those of Passau and Eichstädt were incorporated into the domain of Max. IV Josef. The incorporation shortly thereafter of the territories of the imperial free knights, when added to the secularisation of monastic enclaves, made Bavaria for the first time something approaching a geographically contiguous state. The territories brought with them also 850,000 new subjects and, more importantly, the prospect of producing an annual revenue of nearly 6,600,000 gulden.

The challenge of integrating these territories and peoples into the kind of Bavaria envisioned by Montgelas was no small one. The *Bavaria Sancta* of tradition was dead. 'Between yesterday and today there is a gap of a thousand years' noted one of Montgelas' aides about the effect of the secularisations.[3] Over 700,000 new subjects were Protestant. Perhaps as many as 50,000 were Jews.[4] Neither Protestant nor Jew had before been allowed permanent residence in Bavaria. The secularisations had also severed the complicated feudal relationships between peasant and ecclesiastical landowner, producing what amounted to a form of emancipation for nearly seventy per cent of the Bavarian peasantry.[5] The need for new legal and social definitions was thereby made immediate.

Montgelas and his compatriots, of course, had full confidence in the integrative powers of pedagogy. Through it would be impressed the 'seal of a national spirit' upon Protestant, Jew, Franconian, Swabian, and peasant. Montgelas' hopes were considerably enhanced by the dissolution of the monasteries which, he said, had heretofore 'built up obstacles against the spread of enlightened principles'.[6] Thus were school affairs given a special place in the bureaucratic structure that Montgelas was creating. In October 1802 a General School and Studies Directory (GSSD), in effect an education ministry with jurisdiction over lower and Latin schools as well as over teacher-training, was created to replace the antiquated Spiritual Affairs Council.[7] To head the GSSD Montgelas named the Baron J. M. von Frauenberg, an enlightened cleric believed by his enemies in the Roman Curia to be a Deist and a one-time member of the hated Illuminati society.[8] Frauenberg's immediate task, he was told, was to steer the poor away from their penchant for immorality and towards a more productive life.[9]

The first official act of Frauenberg's GSSD came on 23 December 1802 in the form of a decree making school attendance compulsory. From September until July each year every child between the ages of six and twelve was to attend a school. Punishments for recalcitrant parents were threatened but not spelled out. Ultimately, attendance was to be ensured by the fact that a school-leaving certificate was to

3. Quotation in Eberhard Weis, *Montgelas, 1759–1799*, p. 166.

4. Adolf Kober, 'Jewish Communities in Germany from the Age of Enlightenment to their Destruction by the Nazis', p. 199.

5. Jerome Blum, *The End of the Old Order in Rural Europe*, p. 380.

6. Montgelas quoted in Klaus Epstein, *The Genesis of German Conservatism*, p. 607.

7. Michael Doeberl, 'Zur Geschichte der bayerischen Schulpolitik im 19. Jahrhundert', pp. 3–4; Heinrich Held, *Altbayerische Volkserziehung und Volksschule*, p. 262.

8. Walter Schärl, *Die Zusammensetzung der bayerischen Beamtenschaft von 1806 bis 1918*, pp. 283–4; Beda P. Bastgen, *Bayern und der Heilige Stuhl*, vol. I, p. 318.

9. Joseph Heigenmooser, *Ein bayerischer Pestalozzischüler*, p. 30.

be required for permission to marry, to purchase real property, or to begin practising a trade. The decree provided further that a weekly school fee of two kroner (about one gulden, twelve kroner per year) was to be collected from each child and that, until separate school districts could be drawn up, such districts were to coincide with the existing parish boundaries of the local church.[10] The following September a supplementary decree mandated that children of the lower orders also attend Sunday and Holiday Continuation Schools until the age of eighteen so as to ensure that what had been learned in the lower schools should not be forgotten.[11]

To extend his agency's reach, Frauenberg established in each of the provinces a commissioner for schools. In September 1804 the schools in the territories acquired in the Imperial Resettlement were also placed under the jurisdiction of such a commissioner. The integrative purpose behind these measures was clear. A decree of 1804 allowed Jews admission to both higher and lower schools for the expressed purpose of 'assimilating them with the Bavarian population'.[12] To tie together the various levels of education, the principle of allowing talented pupils to move from one level to the next was adopted.

Frauenberg soon discovered that his bureaucratic reach had severe limitations, and that the implementation of schooling could not be effected without the active co-operation of the clergy. Who else was in a position to supervise the schools and teachers at the local level, or enforce school attendance and ensure that school hours were kept? To enlist their support Frauenberg delivered to the clergy a fiery incantation on schooling as 'an indescribably beneficial step forward for Bavaria', one that would create for it a 'generation of hope'.[13]

One of Frauenberg's immediate concerns was to train a large body of teachers in the most effective teaching methods. A highly laudatory report in 1802 on the successes of the teacher-training Seminars of Bamberg and Würzburg persuaded him to establish a similar institution in Munich.[14] The implications of this decision

10. Alfons Bock, ed., *Lehrplan für die Volksschulen in Baiern, 1804–1811*, pp. 78–80.
11. Josef Heigenmooser and Alfons Bock, eds, *Geschichte der Pädagogik; Quellenbuch und Überblick*, pp. 201–4.
12. The 1804 decree is quoted in Harold C. Vedeler, 'The Genesis of the Toleration Reforms in Bavaria under Montgelas', p. 482.
13. Bock, ed., *Lehrplan*, p. 81.
14. Bayerisches Hauptstaatsarchiv (BHStA), MInn, 23973/I.

were far-reaching. School-teaching was no longer to be a skill acquired simply by apprenticeship to a schoolmaster. Seminar training, although presumably more effective, would inevitably be more expensive. Moreover, Frauenberg had not yet discovered the single most efficacious pedagogical method. In his invocation to the clergy he had urged them to prepare themselves for their new duties by reading works of educators such as Rochow, Vierthaler, and Niemeyer.

Neither Frauenberg nor anyone else in Montgelas' party was expert in pedagogy, yet his failure to recommend Pestalozzi must have been an oversight. Perhaps for that reason he was particularly receptive to a request from two residents of Passau, one a priest, the other a Lyceum teacher, for a 300-gulden subvention each to support them in a three-month stay with the master at Burgdorf. Only Montgelas, with the approval of the Elector, could grant such sums. Montgelas was quick to give his approval provided that the applicants agreed upon their return to teach the method at Munich's new Seminar. Max. IV Josef, who had recently read Pestalozzi's *Gertrude*, gave his consent enthusiastically.[15] From September to November 1803 these two young men were in Burgdorf. Their stay happened to coincide with that of Jeziorowski from Prussia.

Little came of this early brush with Pestalozzi. Neither priest nor teacher was temperamentally suited to play the roles Frauenberg had envisioned for them. The search for the right pedagogical method continued. Early in 1805 Frauenberg commissioned Josef Röckl, a teacher of pedagogy at a Lyceum in Dillingen, to make a tour through various German states investigating the teaching methods being used. Röckl set off in March, stopping off at schools in Salzburg, Vienna, Prague, Halle, Dessau, and Berlin. By the time he returned in late September, interest in what he had to report had been disrupted.[16] A few weeks earlier war had broken out. This time Bavaria was an ally of Napoleon, but an Austrian army had already crossed into Bavarian territory. The war also disrupted Frauenberg's tentative negotiations with K. A. Zeller, a Pestalozzi disciple noted for establishing courses to train teachers in the Pestalozzian method.

15. Heigenmooser, *Ein bayerischer Pestalozzischüler*, pp. 15–19; Remegius Stolzle, 'Pestalozzi und die bayerische Regierung im Jahre 1802', pp. 222–4.
16. Joseph Röckl, *Paedagogische Reise durch Deutschland*.

Fortunately for Frauenberg there seemed no need to be unduly concerned about financing either the schools or expensive teacher-training institutions. In large measure the schools were to be funded by the fee schedule adopted in 1802, but, beyond that, veritable financial magic was expected to be worked by the secularisation of ecclesiastical properties, given that fifty-six per cent of the land in Bavaria was owned by the Church.[17] The secularisation of non-immediate monasteries had alone brought twelve million gulden into the state's coffers in 1803[18] and the great spring of ecclesiastical wealth was therewith only beginning to be tapped.

The full extent of the Bavarian reform party's confidence in the powers of schooling had been revealed in the Comprehensive School Plan drawn up by the GSSD in 1804. Often called the Wismayr Plan after its chief author, Joseph Wismayr, a councillor in the GSSD, the plan stands as a monument to enlightenment pedagogical assumptions. Wismayr, like Montgelas, had been hounded out of Bavaria during the Illuminati hunts of the 1780s. Part of his exile had been spent in Salzburg where he entered into the pedagogical circle surrounding F. M. Vierthaler.[19]

The centrepiece of Wismayr's plan was the new elementary school (*Elementarschule*) which was designed to replace the old 'trivial schools' and *Volksschulen*. To this elementary school Wismayr assigned tasks more ambitious than any that had ever been given to its predecessors. For their first three years of schooling, children from all the social orders were to attend this common elementary school. Here, in a curriculum that was to be essentially utilitarian, were to be imparted those elements of knowledge deemed essential to every member of society.[20] After three years children of the upper social orders were to be sent to schools appropriate to their station. Children of the lower orders would remain in the elementary school to the age of twelve. While an organic connection between schooling levels was to open careers to talent, Wismayr did not envision great surges of upward social movement. Rather the elementary school was to provide the basis for a new social stability that would be rooted in a new Bavarian patriotism. The first crucial steps towards

17. Wolfgang Zorn, 'Sozialer Wandel im Mitteleuropa, 1780–1840', p. 317.

18. Wolfgang Zorn, 'Staatliche Wirtschafts- und Sozialpolitik und öffentliche Finanzen, 1800–1970', p. 177.

19. See 'F.M. Vierthaler', in *Allgemeine Deutsche Biographie* (*ADB*), vol. XXXIX, pp. 679–82.

20. Werner Sacher, *Die zweite Phase in der Lehrerbildung*, p. 22.

a Bavarian *Nationalbildung* were to be taken within its walls. 'The children should be educated to be state citizens and patriots rather than cosmopolitans', Wismayr wrote in acknowledgment of the integrative function performed by what he called 'love for the Fatherland'.[21] He informed teachers of their dual assignment: educating the nation and enlightening the lower orders. To prepare them for these tasks, Wismayr recommended a Seminar curriculum nearly encyclopaedic in scope. Twenty-seven different courses were to be explored in depth.[22]

Wismayr anticipated that schooling would be entirely under the aegis of the state. While the co-operation of the clergy might be enlisted, schooling was clearly to be a function of the state carried out for purposes defined by it. Legal underpinning for this assumption was provided on 26 November 1804 when Elector Max. IV Josef defined the school as an agency of the state and specified that henceforth schools were no longer to be identified with a specific confession. Aside from religion itself, his decree stipulated, there existed no Catholic or Protestant forms of knowledge, and just as there was no Catholic science or Protestant mathematics, there was no Catholic or Protestant method by which such subjects could be taught. Consequently, teachers were to be hired for their abilities, not their religious persuasion. The Churches were to be restricted to imparting instruction in religion and even here there were plans eventually to fuse Protestantism and Catholicism into one official religion governed by the state.[23]

Opposition to Wismayr's plan came most immediately from Catholic circles, especially from those elements most directly associated with the Bavaria of tradition. There were those who saw his proposal as an effort to 'de-Catholicise' or even 'de-Christianise' Bavaria.[24] To support their case they cited Article 63 of the recent Imperial Resettlement which had promised to each confession the right to its religious properties and school funds. This promise in turn was solidly rooted in the Westphalian treaties of 1648 which defined the school clearly as an extension of the Church. Protestants, who shared all the complaints of their Catholic counterparts, had an additional one of their own: they were unrepresented on Frauenberg's GSSD.

21. Wismayr quoted in Bock, ed., *Lehrplan*, p. 38.
22. Ibid., p. 22.
23. Rudolf Hindringer, *Das kirchliche Schulrecht in Altbayern.*
24. Doeberl, *Entwicklungsgeschichte*, vol. II, p. 521.

Assured of Montgelas' support, Frauenberg saw little reason to back down in the face of such opposition. To the Churchs' legal arguments, he simply pointed out that the Westphalian provisions applied only to the teaching of religion, which in 1648 happened to be almost the only thing the lower orders were taught. Now that the curriculum was being expanded to include non-religious subjects, the state was legally justified in assuming control over all but confessional religious instruction.[25] Further concessions seemed unnecessary. Only to the Protestants did he make a gesture in 1805 when he appointed one of their number as a councillor in the GSSD.

Could Wismayr's plan have been implemented? Not completely, because it was much too ambitious. But there were more immediate obstacles standing in its way as well. The most serious of these was that it underestimated the powers of the Church to resist. Reform measures notwithstanding, it was representatives of the Church in the form of individual clergymen, and not those of the state, who were established in the local communities. Until new school district lines could be drawn, moreover, the parish boundaries of the Church would constitute the school district. Non-confessional schools would be virtually impossible to create in such circumstances. With Church-state relations everywhere in a condition of upheaval, at least until the conclusion of a concordat with Rome, the Church had everything to gain by delay. In order to strengthen his position, Frauenberg in the autumn of 1805 reorganised the GSSD and renamed it the *Geheime Schul- und Studienbureau* or Privy Bureau for Elementary and Higher Studies. It proved to be no more effectual than its predecessor.

Even if the Church had presented no opposition, the lack of qualified teachers alone would have sufficed to keep Wismayr's plan from succeeding. Neither had he addressed the problem of whence the teachers would come. The religious teaching orders were being everywhere disbanded, leaving Bavaria, ironically, with fewer teachers in 1804 than it had had in 1799 when Montgelas arrived in Munich. Reports from the regional School Commissioners indicated that those teachers still in service were generally very poorly trained and in social status and income often below that of the day labourer.[26] While the Seminars were eventually to produce the new

25. Doeberl, 'Geschichte der bayerischen Schulpolitik', p. 43.
26. Heigenmooser and Bock, eds, *Geschichte der Pädagogik*, pp. 190–2.

teacher corps, they offered no solution in the short-run. The Munich Seminar, established in 1803, managed to produce only eighty teachers in its first four years of existence. In these circumstances, thought was given to recruiting women into the teaching of girls, though not of boys.

School buildings, too, or the lack of them, presented serious problems. The School Commissioners had little good to report about the physical conditions of the schools. Many of them, where they did exist, were still of the *Wanderschule* variety. In addition the Commissioners were unable to report an enthusiastic reception among villagers to the prospect of being forced to send their children to school. Parents often needed the labour of their children; rarely could they see the advantage of losing that labour and absorbing, at the same time, the added expense of paying the school fees. Compulsory schooling was not likely to meet with widespread acceptance easily.

The greatest obstacle to implementing Wismayr's Plan was the lack of money. Here Bavaria's reformers had made their most serious miscalculation. Secularisation was supposed to yield millions, and those millions were to support the various reform projects, including schooling. But of the twelve million gulden-worth of properties secularised in 1803, only 110,000 found their way to the schools.[27] Most of these monies were ultimately spent on the costs of war. The military alliance signed with France in August 1805 committed Bavaria to providing Napoleon with 2,500 men and 3,600 cavalry. Within a week of the signing Bavaria was invaded by Austria, and Max. IV Josef had fled to Würzburg. Thus even Röckl's return went unnoticed.

Fortunately the war was brief and, for Bavaria, relatively cheap; much cheaper, as it turned out, than the subsequent peace. With his victory at Austerlitz in December 1805 Napoleon was approaching the zenith of his powers, and Bavaria found itself caught up with his rise. Bavaria's gains at first glance seemed impressive; they included the right to assume the status of a kingdom as well as to acquire territory that would round out some of the gains of 1803. In the final Peace of Pressburg, however, Bavaria was forced to cede Würzburg in exchange for the Austrian Tyrol and the Italian bishoprics of

27. W. R. Lee, *Population Growth, Economic Development and Social Change in Bavaria, 1750–1850*, p. 346; see also Rudolfine Freiin von Oer, ed., *Die Säkularisation, 1803*, pp. 84–7.

Brixen and Trent. The exchange would not be to Bavaria's advantage. Würzburg had been eminently governable; the Tyrol and the Italian bishoprics would be less so. Whether they could have been successfully integrated, either by schooling or by any other means, seems doubtful. Then in 1806, when Napoleon decided to organise those parts of Germany under his control into a Confederation of the Rhine, Bavaria found herself required to provide him with a standing force of 30,000 men. Victory, secularisations, and royal status notwithstanding, Bavaria in 1808 was once again forced to borrow four million gulden from the Munich banking house of Seligman.

The momentum of schooling, so apparent before the war, was never fully regained. Although the critical debate about Wismayr's proposals was not fully joined until 1807, by then Frauenberg and his officials had come to regard as dubious the miracles his schooling programme promised to perform. Then in early 1809 Frauenberg himself was replaced as head of the Privy Bureau. His successor was one of Montgelas' most energetic compatriots, Friedrich von Zentner. The energy and ideological continuity that Zentner seemed to represent was largely cancelled out when he appointed Friedrich Niethammer as one of his new councillors in the Bureau.

It was Friedrich Niethammer, rather than Josef Wismayr, who was to become the actual architect of Bavarian schooling. A Protestant and a Württemberg native, Niethammer's studies at Jena had brought him into contact with Fichte, Goethe, and Schelling. In 1803 he was made a professor at the University of Würzburg. When Würzburg was lost to Bavaria in 1806, he moved to Bamberg as an official in its Provincial Church and School Directory. It was from Bamberg that Zentner brought him to Munich in 1807. Cantankerous and ill-tempered by nature, Niethammer considered himself an implacable foe of the utilitarian-philanthropic ideas represented by Wismayr. As a proponent of the neo-humanist rejection of utilitarianism, he insisted that the conflict with the philanthropists raised educational issues upon which 'it is more important to bring war than peace'.[28]

No two people represented more clearly the differences between the views held by the philanthropists and those of the neo-humanists

28. Friedrich Immanuel Niethammer, *Der Streit des Philanthropinismus und Humanismus*, p. 28.

than did Wismayr and Niethammer. Although the ideas of both had their origins in the intellectual ferment of the eighteenth century, and both had pedagogical objectives at the core of their thought, they disagreed in principle about the subject matter of education as well as about the social groups to whom it should be directed. The philanthropists, in the tradition of Basedow and Rochow, believed that instruction of a practical sort needed to be imparted directly to the lower orders. Education for the higher orders they did not make their concern. The neo-humanists, on the other hand, were concerned chiefly with education for an élite, although few of them would have denied the utility of some instruction for the masses.

True education for the neo-humanists resided in the study of classical antiquity, particularly that of the ancient Greeks. An intensive engagement with Greek culture and with its aesthetic and intellectual precepts, people like Niethammer believed, served to cultivate in human beings their highest capacities. Thus the study of the Greek language and its literature was offered as a means for preparing men of high cultivation for leadership in practical as well as in intellectual affairs. To this elevated form of cultivation was applied the German term *Bildung*. A world that needed to be rebuilt, the neo-humanists agreed, required leadership that only *Bildung* could provide. The educational institution with which they were concerned was the Gymnasium. Their differences with the philanthropists were, most neo-humanists believed, unbridgeable. These were the questions upon which Niethammer promised to bring war rather than peace.

War he brought. When Zentner asked each of his councillors, Niethammer included, to make an assessment of Wismayr's proposals, Niethammer's critique was devastating. He rejected as completely unworkable Wismayr's elementary school curriculum with its emphasis upon the teaching of history, geography, and the rudiments of the various natural sciences. He suggested in their place the teaching of language, arithmetic, and religion. He thought the idea of maintaining an organic connection between school levels socially unwise. Completely separate schooling for each of the social orders would be much safer. As for Wismayr's emphasis on *Nationalbildung*, he denied that this was either a possible or desirable objective for the lower schools.[29] Neither did he share Wismayr's

29. Bock, ed., *Lehrplan*, p. 113.

assumptions about the inherent educability of the lower orders, most of whom he considered comprised of those 'who by fate are neither inwardly nor outwardly particularly favoured'. He doubted whether they could be much uplifted simply by having their children schooled with those of the higher order. 'An unidealized reality teaches us that the *Volk* is not capable of such pretensions', he concluded.[30]

Niethammer's proposals eventually carried the day. Wismayr soon found himself isolated and in 1810 he left the Bureau quietly. Although his plan was never formally withdrawn, Niethammer was careful to attend to its total revision. In 1809 came the royal decree rescinding the organic connection between the various school levels.[31] The elementary school was no longer to be the possible first rung of an educational ladder; it was to be the school for the lower orders alone. Accordingly, in 1811, the name itself was changed to *Volksschule*, signalling a demotion in status both for the school and for those attending it.

Niethammer had also been critical of the nearly encyclopaedic curriculum Wismayr had devised for the Seminars. In July 1809 he issued his own General Regulations for the Organisation of Teachers' Seminars, reducing the courses required from Wismayr's twenty-seven to a mere nine, thereby freeing the pupils, Niethammer said, from a 'spiritually deadening mechanistic instruction'. The main courses in the Seminar curriculum were to prepare the teacher to teach reading, writing, and religion. The courses for his own secular edification were to be limited to geography, an introduction to natural science, and the history of Bavaria. The latter was to be taught so as to demonstrate how, in trying times, Bavarian subjects had consistently been loyal to their princes. It may have been no accident that this order came at the very moment in 1809 when peasant rebels from the Tyrol and Vorarlberg were within striking distance of Munich. Ironically, a Seminar established in Tyrol the year before had probably helped produce the rebellion. The Seminar had been financed by local secularisations, a fact that had infuriated Tyroleans loyal to the Church.

None the less, Niethammer remained committed to the idea of

30. Niethammer quoted in Max Rieder, *Geschichte der politischen Bildung in den Volksschulen Bayerns*, pp. 142–3.

31. For a discussion of the 28 January 1809 order see Sacher, *Die zweite Phase*, p. 23.

Seminar training. In 1809 Seminars were established in Nuremberg and Augsburg, promising to relieve the severe shortage of teachers in Franconia and Swabia. In 1803 the Munich Seminar had been moved north to Freising. Its place in Munich was taken by a new Seminar established to train women as teachers, the first such institution in any of the German states.[32] Niethammer's Regulations stipulated that the course of instruction in the Seminars be no longer than two years and that no one under the age of fifteen was to be admitted. He stipulated further that each pupil be instructed in organ-playing, so as to enhance his eventual utility to the local church, and in such skills as would allow the future teacher to function as clerk in the village community where he was likely to be one of the few literate persons.[33]

In May 1811, two years after the promulgation of his Seminar Regulations, Niethammer's revised curriculum for the *Volksschule* was also adopted. Its main objective, he said, was to inculcate into pupils a recognition of the eternal truths of religion and virtue and to make them receptive to the further teachings of the Church.[34] Utilitarian knowledge was to be handled very cautiously, for it was by its nature of the sort that could lead children into unnecessary and shallow 'reflection and reasoning' (*Reflektion und Räsonieren)*.[35]

The effect of Niethammer's influence was to redirect the course of Bavarian schooling. His Seminar guidelines were in effect until 1836; his *Volksschule* curriculum until the late 1860s. While his ambitions for schooling were considerably lower than had been Wismayr's, they were also more realistic. Not all of Niethammer's actions reflected reduced ambition. Like his predecessor he tried to create a bureaucratic structure that would reach down to the local level and thus make schooling enforceable. District School Councillors (*Kreisschulräte*) as well as local supervisory officials were established by a School Edict of September 1808, but once again, at the lower levels at least, very few people other than clergymen were available to fill such posts.[36] (Also in 1808 the Privy Bureau for Elementary

32. Berta Sachs, *Pläne und Massnahmen der Regierung des Königs Max I. Joseph im Mädchenschulwesen Altbayerns*, pp. 69–70; also Joanne Frances Schneider, *An Historical Examination of Women's Education in Bavaria*, p. 143.

33. BHStA, MInn, 23973 II; see also Albert Fritz, *Geschichte der Lehrerbildungsanstalt Kaiserslauten von 1818–1918*, pp. 8–9; Sacher, *Die zweite Phase*, p. 28.

34. Rainer Roth, *Politische Bildung in Bayern*, p. 36.

35. Josef Neukum, *Schule und Politik, Politische Geschichte der bayerischen Volksschule, 1818–1848*, p. 25.

36. For the School Edict of 15 September 1808, see Gustav Seiler, *Schulbedarfsgesetz*

and Higher Studies was reorganised as the Section for Instruction and Education and placed, with Zentner still as head, directly under the authority of the Interior Minister.)

Zentner's continued presence and the fact that Montgelas himself had taken over as Interior Minister, ensured that enlightenment principles would not be completely discarded.[37] In 1810, for example, the ministerial order to create school districts separate from parish boundaries was finally issued. Only then did it become possible to implement the principle enunciated in 1804 of establishing non-confessional schools. Niethammer was not pleased. By 1813 he succeeded in reversing the official endorsement of the non-confessional school principle and, by January 1815, in getting rescinded also the order requiring the independent secular school districts. Not until 1873 would state officials make a second attempt to create such secular districts.

That all of this activity in Munich was accompanied by very little advance in the actual schooling of the lower orders is not to be explained by any lack of trying. War, or the threat of war, during these years consumed inordinate quantities of Bavaria's energy and treasure. In April 1809 Austria attacked again, encouraged to do so this time by Napoleon's difficulties in Spain. Austria's hope was to spark a German-wide war of liberation against the Napoleonic yoke. It turned out to be another of Austria's disastrous miscalculations. At Wagram, in July 1809, Napoleon again defeated the Austrian forces. In the subsequent Peace of Schönbrunn Austria lost the Bishopric of Salzburg, which a year later Napoleon gave to Bavaria. Bavaria in turn had to give up the Tyrol, Ulm, and some territory in Franconia. Once again Bavaria's boundaries had shifted; again there were new territories to integrate and new costs to absorb.

In 1813 came the most critical decision in Bavaria's development since it had decided to join forces with Napoleon in 1800. As Napoleon's ally, it had been forced to provide 20,000 men for his 1812 invasion of Russia. The defeat of his Grand Army brought Bavaria face to face with a terrible dilemma. Could it risk abandoning Napoleon and joining the growing coalition against him? Or could it risk not abandoning Napoleon and joining that coalition? Montgelas, in October 1813, finally chose to join the coalition when

vom 28 Juli 1902, pp. 367–70.

37. On Zentner, see Franz Dobmann, *Georg Friedrich Freiherr von Zentner als bayerischer Staatsmann.*

its members promised to respect Bavaria's territorial integrity in any post-war settlement. Once again Bavaria's existence was at stake. Schooling, and everything else, depended upon the outcome.

By contrast, in Prussia the plans for schooling appeared by 1813 to be on the verge of completion. No sense of doubt or resignation about the efficacy of the enterprise had as yet manifested itself. Prussia's school reformers, moreover, were already critical of the direction being taken by their Bavarian counterparts. No less a figure than Wilhelm von Humboldt, the most articulate of the reformers and the one whose name was to become synonymous with educational reform, was the first to express his criticism. Humboldt had taken a first-hand look at educational reform in Bavaria in October 1808 during a stopover in Munich on his way back to Berlin from Rome, where he had been Prussia's envoy. At the time he was still uncertain whether or not he would accept Stein's offer to head an educational division in Prussia's Interior Ministry. Humboldt did not like what he saw of educational reform in Bavaria, particularly its apparent emphasis (officially at least) upon a utilitarian or vocational school curriculum and its insistence upon establishing separate school systems for each of the social orders. 'It is my conviction', he later explained to Frederick William III, 'that this is fundamentally mistaken and will make inevitable their failure to achieve the objective they have in mind'.[38] That objective, as Wismayr had defined it, was *Nationalbildung*, one the Prussian reformers set for their own schools as well, but one they believed achievable only by very different means.

Humboldt did eventually accept Stein's offer but delayed his arrival in Königsberg, Prussia's temporary capital, until April 1809. By the time of his arrival, Prussia's version of the 'good revolution from above', as the reformer Hardenberg called it, was well under way despite the fact of Stein's unexpected departure the previous November. The October 1807 Edict of Emancipation, which abolished the remnants of personal servitude, had promised most immediately to affect the peasantry, but, by abolishing the legal barriers of estate, it served at the same time to break up the whole of the traditional social order. Burghers could now own land legally, and noblemen engage in trade. Prussia, the edict concluded, was hence-

38. Wilhelm von Humboldt, *Werke*, vol. 4, Andreas Flitner and Klaus Giel, eds, pp. 217–18.

forth to be made up of an 'entirely free people'.[39]

The Emancipation Edict was the first act of Prussia's great social revolution. Other acts soon followed. The establishment of a citizens' conscript army was recommended by a Military Reform Commission. Self-government for municipalities was introduced. Piecemeal abolition of traditional guild monopolies was begun. Civil equality for Jews was promised. Permanent functional government ministries had been established the previous December to replace the provisional ones created after Tilsit. It was within the new Ministry of Interior that a Section for Worship and Public Instruction had been created, the Section that Humboldt now headed.

School reform, too, was well under way by the time of Humboldt's arrival. The groundwork had begun already during the summer of 1808 in a then provisional Department for Schools and Poor Relief, a body which Stein had placed under the jurisdiction of the temporary Ministry for Provincial Affairs. To head this Department Stein had named a well-connected member of the Königsberg bureaucratic patriciate, G. L. Nicolovius, whom he charged with drafting the preliminary plans that would school Prussia's lower orders. Working unofficially with Nicolovius was a young professor at the local university, the historian J. W. Süvern. Süvern was the man who would eventually become, in the judgement of Wilhelm Dilthey, the 'driving force' behind Prussia's school reform.[40]

Nicolovius' first proposal was submitted to Provincial Minister Leopold von Schrötter on 23 August 1808. Its title, 'Concerning the Introduction of a Better Method into Elementary and Rural Schools', signalled clearly where he thought school reform would have to begin: with the employment of an improved pedagogical method. No less than the 'moral regeneration of the lower orders' was at stake, he told Schrötter.[41] Citing the need for an 'instruction that cultivates the spirit' and allows 'the individual to develop according to his own inner essence', he urged that the drill and

39. For the Edict of Emancipation, see Ernst Rudolf Huber, *Dokumente zur deutschen Verfassungsgeschichte*, vol. I, pp. 38–40.
40. See Wilhelm Dilthey's excellent sketch, 'Johann Wilhelm Süvern', in *ADB*, vol. XXXVII, pp. 20–45; Alfred Rach, *Sachwörter zur deutschen Erziehungsgeschichte*, pp. 194–5. For background, see also Wilhelm Roessler, *Die Entstehung des modernen Erziehungswesens in Deutschland.*
41. Fritz Fischer, *Ludwig Nicolovius*, pp. 256–9.

memorisation associated with current rote teaching methods be dropped entirely. The immorality so prevalent among the lower orders could be traced directly to these methods, he believed. In their place he recommended introducing as quickly as possible the pedagogical method developed by J. H. Pestalozzi.

The most immediate practical need, he concluded, was to develop a large number of teachers trained in the Pestalozzian method. To expedite their training, he recommended the immediate dispatch of at least two students to study with the master at his school in Switzerland. In addition, he recommended the establishment in Königsberg of a demonstration institute in which regular teachers could be acquainted with the method. To head such an institute Nicolovius hoped that Prussia might be able to engage the services of K. A. Zeller, the Pestalozzi disciple celebrated for his courses in the master's method. Süvern supported Nicolovius' recommendation wholeheartedly, adding his view that for schooling to be effective it would have to be completely state-controlled. Private schools of every sort would have to be eliminated, said Süvern, if public education were to accomplish its 'most important' task of being 'an integrating force in the entire state organism'.[42]

Süvern endorsed Nicolovius' enthusiasm for Pestalozzi. Both he and Nicolovius were caught up in what is best described as the Pestalozzi craze sweeping across Prussia during the first years after Tilsit. The enthusiasm seemed well founded. Pestalozzi was then at the pinnacle of his international fame. Students from all over Europe were flocking to him at his school in Ifferton. He had recently turned down an offer from the Tsar of Russia to enter his employment as an educational adviser.[43] Pestalozzi's claim that his method was based upon pedagogical laws and, therefore, applicable 'even among the lowest classes',[44] could not help but appeal to those responsible for reviving a humiliated and moribund society. The same held true for his conviction that this method would not only treat the evils 'that are enervating the people of Europe, but cure them at their root'.[45] The Military Reform Commission, for one, was so impressed with

42. Süvern quoted in Gunnar Thiele, *Die Organisation des Volksschul- und Seminarwesens in Preussen, 1809–1819*, p. 20.
43. Max Liedtke, *Pestalozzi*, p. 144.
44. See 'The Method, a Report by Pestalozzi', in J. H. Pestalozzi, *How Gertrude Teaches Her Children*, p. 316.
45. Ibid., p. 315.

Pestalozzi's promise that it considered adapting his method to train army recruits.[46] Fichte had made Pestalozzi's methods the centrepiece of his 'Addresses to the German Nation', delivered in occupied Berlin during the winter of 1807–8. In the first of these addresses, Fichte told his audience that education would be the key to putting together a German nation and 'that a system of education such as we desire has actually been discovered . . . so that we have nothing to do but accept what is offered us'.[47] As a young man in the 1790s, during his grand tour, Nicolovius had stopped off in Switzerland to see Pestalozzi and the two were still in correspondence.[48]

Efforts to implement Nicolovius' proposals began immediately. Early in September Minister von Schrötter made his first enquiry of Pestalozzi, informing him of Prussia's desire to undertake 'a thorough reform of the school system' and of its intention of basing that reform on his method.[49] Would he accept two pupils? How long would it take to train them? How much would it cost? Pestalozzi was flattered. He thought two years would be needed for someone to master his method (a period he later extended to three) and that a fee per pupil of 360 thalers per year would be reasonable.[50] The first pupils left for Switzerland in February 1809, as soon as Frederick William III gave his approval. Another was sent later. Meanwhile, J. H. Plamann agreed to instruct two additional pupils in the method at his institute in Berlin.[51]

At the time of its enquiry to Pestalozzi, the Department also extended an invitation to Zeller to establish a demonstration institute in Königsberg. Zeller was reputed to be an educational *Wunderkind.* The much heralded successes of the numerous teacher-training institutes he had organised in South Germany made him one of the most sought-after educators in German-speaking Europe. Pestalozzi himself spoke of Zeller as 'an awakener of nations', which is exactly what Nicolovius had in mind in recommending him.

46. For Gneisenau's memorandum on Pestalozzi, see Karl-Ernst Jeismann, ed., *Staat und Erziehung in der preussischen Reform, 1807–1819*, p. 11; see also Heinz Stubig, *Armee und Nation; Die pädagogischpolitischen Motive der preussischen Heeresreform, 1807–1814*.
47. Johann Gottlieb Fichte, *Addresses to the German Nation*, p. 13.
48. See 'G. L. Nicolovius' in *ADB*, vol. XXIII, pp. 635–40.
49. Schrötter to Pestalozzi, 11 September 1808, in Bruno Gebhardt, *Die Einführung der Pestalozzischen Methode in Preussen*, p. 17.
50. Johann Heinrich Pestalozzi, *Sämtliche Briefe*, vol. VI, pp. 98–9; also Gebhardt, *Die Einführung*, p. 36.
51. Otto Wilhelm Beyer, *Deutsche Schulwelt des neunzehnten Jahrhunderts in Wort und Bild*, pp. 233–4.

The plans for Zeller were fully laid out. He was to begin by establishing a teacher-training institute in Königsberg and from there proceed to establish similar institutes in each of Prussia's five remaining provinces. In these institutes teachers, clergymen, and school inspectors were to be instructed in the master's method. Each institute, moreover, was to be connected with an orphanage, the plan being also to train male orphans as teachers. Thus, it was hoped that within two or three years a large body of teachers would at least have been made acquainted with the method and the foundation laid for the training of future teachers. It may have been a good plan, but nothing came of it. Zeller refused Prussia's offer. He had just accepted a similar post in his native Württemberg.

Zeller's refusal, which was followed in November 1808 by Stein's departure into exile, interrupted the momentum that had been gathering since August. The interruption was considered dangerous. At his departure Stein emphasised the need for haste in implementing schooling 'so that no generation will be lost'.[52] Increasing the danger was the fact that the Department did not yet have a permanent head. Nicolovius was serving only in an interim capacity. Stein had considered him insufficiently decisive to qualify for the permanent post.[53] Moreover, Stein's first choice for the position, A. H. Niemeyer, had turned the job down, preferring instead to accept Napoleon's offer to head the restored University of Halle.[54] Niemeyer had seemed the perfect choice. As the author of a widely known pedagogical text, *Foundations of Education*, and the rejuvenator of his great-grandfather's Francke Foundation in Halle, he was regarded by contemporaries as one of Germany's foremost practitioners of pedagogy.[55] Humboldt was only a second choice, and at Stein's departure it was not yet certain whether he would be willing to leave the comforts of his post in Rome for the rigours of Königsberg. Unlike Niemeyer, Humboldt had no reputation as an educator. Neither did he know anything about schools. Having been educated entirely by tutors, Humboldt had never attended an educational institution of any sort. He also had his doubts, which he confided to his wife, about being able to accomplish much of

52. Stein quoted in Gebhardt, *Die Einführung*, p. 21.
53. Fischer, *Nicolovius*, p. 6.
54. Richard Graf Du Moulin Eckart, *Geschichte der deutschen Universitäten*, p. 313.
55. Theodore Ballauf, 'Zur Entstehungsgeschichte der Pädagogik als Wissenschaft in der Neuzeit', p. 83. See A. H. Niemeyer, *Grundsätze der Erziehung*.

anything given Prussia's depressed situation.[56]

It was Humboldt's social and intellectual prestige that finally made him the effective spokesman for educational reform. He came to be associated most directly with the founding of the University of Berlin, and with the securing of the neo-humanistic curriculum of the classical Gymnasium. His thoughts on mass schooling, if he had any, were largely unformed. He was certainly no Pestalozzi enthusiast, although he was also clearly opposed to the utilitarian educational emphasis he had so recently seen in Bavaria. This latter approach to schooling he considered utterly soulless.[57] When in February 1809 he did, finally, accept the post as head of the Section for Worship and Public Instruction (as it was now called), he did so out of a sense of duty — and with the ambition of eventually being made a cabinet minister.

By the time of Humboldt's arrival in Königsberg in mid-April 1809, much of the momentum in school reform had been restored, largely because of the formal appointment to the Section in January of the energetic J. W. Süvern. Although formally in charge of Gymnasium affairs, Süvern was to have a profound effect upon the course of mass schooling as well. Süvern immediately arranged for a second offer to Zeller, promising him this time a salary of 1,200 thalers (the equivalent of a professor's salary in Königsberg) as well as 500 thalers in moving expenses, free housing, and several assistants. As a final inducement, he offered Zeller the flattering prospect of being 'a participant in the re-creation *(Mitschöpfer)* of Prussia'.[58] It was an offer Zeller could not refuse. 'Your numbers speak louder than all the pedagogical literature of the past decade', he informed the Section in his letter of acceptance.[59]

Süvern had in the meantime filled in the details of his ingenious plan for creating the large numbers of teachers that schooling would require. Zeller's assignment would be to convert Prussia's orphanages into teacher-training institutions. Here a generation of male orphans would be trained as teachers. The state would thus be

56. Humboldt to his wife Caroline, on 28 December 1808, in Wilhelm von Humboldt, *Briefe*, p. 290. Useful for the details it gives of Humboldt's work is Eduard Spranger, *Wilhelm von Humboldt und die Reform des Bildungswesens*.

57. Paul R. Sweet, *Wilhelm von Humboldt*, vol. II, pp. 58, 61.

58. Süvern quoted in Gebhardt, *Die Einführung*, p. 76. J. F. Herbart, who took Kant's chair in philosophy at the University of Königsberg in 1808, received an annual salary of 1,200 thalers; see Harold B. Dunkel, *Herbart and Herbartianism*, p. 44.

59. Zeller's acceptance letter quoted in Gebhardt, *Die Einführung*, p. 76.

spared not only the costs of erecting new teacher-training institutions, but the orphanages would become, Süvern believed, 'the foundations of education for Prussia's citizens'.[60] Thereby, in one bold stroke, a major social problem would be transformed into its own solution. Zeller was to begin this process by converting the orphanage in Königsberg into a *Normalinstitut* (demonstration school). Here orphans would be trained as teachers and courses organised to acquaint teachers, clergymen and school inspectors with the Pestalozzian method. Zeller's budget for the first year was to be 15,400 thalers.[61] The next part of Süvern's plan was to send additional students to Pestalozzi. By the end of the year there were fifteen Prussian students in Switzerland and Süvern was corresponding with every one of them. 'Warm yourselves at the holy fire, with the strength and love that glow in the heart of this man', he urged one of them in a letter.[62]

This basic schooling plan was firmly in place by the time Humboldt arrived to assume direction of educational affairs. Zeller was expected to arrive shortly. Humboldt was pleasantly surprised, he said, to learn how generous the King had suddenly become in his support of education.[63] In matters of schooling the Section now needed administration more than it needed ideas, leaving Humboldt free to concentrate upon his university project.[64] Fortunately, after sending his son off to Plamann's Institute in Berlin, he was also quickly reconciled to Pestalozzi and his pedagogical method.

Humboldt's greatest service to the cause of Prussian schooling, aside from lending his prestige to the enterprise, turned out to be almost accidental. It consisted of accepting the advice of an old friend, Baron von Vincke, to appoint Ludwig Natorp to a post in the school administration of the Province of Brandenburg. Natorp had been one of Vincke's protégés from their days in Westphalia, a region now controlled by Napoleon, where Natorp had established a considerable reputation as an educator. Natorp also happened to be a Pestalozzi enthusiast as well as being conversant with the pedagogical theories of the Englishman Joseph Lancaster, whose monitorial method was believed by many to rival that of Pestalozzi in its

60. Süvern's proposal of 20 February 1809 quoted in Fischer, *Nicolovius*, pp. 256–8.
61. Gebhardt, *Die Einführung*, p. 75.
62. Dilthey, 'Süvern', p. 224.
63. Humboldt to his wife Caroline, 19 May 1809, in Humboldt, *Briefe*, p. 297.
64. Sweet, *Humboldt*, vol. II, p. 65.

efficacy, and which had the seeming advantage of being much cheaper to implement. When Vincke became Governor of Brandenburg in February 1809, he urged that Natorp be given a post in its school administration.[65] Natorp was easily integrated into the larger schooling strategy then being developed in Königsberg. Until Zeller himself could come to Brandenburg, Natorp would be asked to uplift, as best he could, the province's lower schools.[66]

Natorp came to be what Joachim Schoeps has called 'the decisive figure in the reform of the Prussian system of *Volksschulen* and teacher training',[67] although no one had envisioned him in such a role. His first assignment was a modest one. In the autumn of 1809 he was sent on a tour of Brandenburg's schools to make an assessment of their condition. He came back appalled, convinced that school conditions had regressed, not advanced, since Frederick II's 1763 School Regulations. He found the teachers mostly to be ignorant and vulgar; the clergy little interested in the schools; the cultural level of the populace 'closer to that of animals than human beings'.[68] The only way out of this cycle in which the ignorant passed on their ignorance, Natorp believed, would be in a 'total and radical' reform of teacher-training, one that would break down the 'journeyman's mentality' (*Handwerkerburschengeist*)[69] so prevalent among even the best teachers. To accomplish this reform he urged that teachers be trained in academically-oriented boarding schools he called Seminars. Understandably Natorp's views were not well received. Such Seminars would be expensive, a vital consideration for a Prussia which was in dire financial straits. Moreover, he was intruding into a domain that had already been assigned to Zeller.

In Königsberg the Section's commitment to Zeller seemed to bear fruit quickly. Although he was several months late in arriving, he made up for the delay with a whirlwind of activity that seemed to transform overnight the local orphanage into the model of a *Normalinstitut.* All of Königsberg was watching. Even Frederick William III and Queen Louise visited periodically, only to marvel at the

65. On Vincke, see E. von Bodelschwingh, *Leben des Ober-Präsidenten Freiherrn von Vincke*, vol. I, p. 374; see also 'Vincke', in *ADB*, vol. XXXIX, pp. 736–43. See B. C. L. Natorp, *Andreas Bell und Joseph Lancaster.*

66. Humboldt to Natorp, 23 May 1809; see Ernst Lichtenstein, 'Aus dem Krisenjahr der Pestalozzischulreform in Preussen', p. 85.

67. Hans-Joachim Schoeps, 'Neues zur preussischen Kirchen- und Schulgeschichte des 19. Jahrhunderts', p. 38.

68. Natorp to Vincke, 3 December 1810; see Lichtenstein, 'Krisenjahr', p. 103.

69. Ibid., p. 94.

progress being made.[70] The king finally seemed to be comfortable, both with schooling and with Pestalozzi, and the queen instantly became one of Pestalozzi's great admirers. She had read his *Leonhard and Gertrude* and after the first visit to Zeller's institute confided her yearning to 'order my carriage and drive away along the road that leads to Switzerland and Pestalozzi'.[71] The contact between the royal couple and Zeller was to be brief, however. In December 1809 the king and queen were finally scheduled to return permanently to Berlin after a three-year absence. Shortly before his departure Frederick William III promoted Zeller to the rank of *Oberschulrat*, or High School Councillor.

Before leaving the king also received Humboldt's report on the work of his Section for 1809. It is the first comprehensive picture we have of the Section's schooling efforts. Humboldt focused his report upon the social and political objectives of schooling. Its primary purpose was to educate to nationhood 'the entire undifferentiated mass',[72] as he called it, that had been created by the other reforms. While each estate (Humboldt was now speaking in social, not legal, terms) was eventually to receive the measure of education appropriate to it, there were not to be, as was the case in Bavaria, separate schools for each estate.[73] First and foremost, schools had to engage in 'cultivating inherent human capacities' (*allgemeine Menschenbildung*).[74] The transmission of utilitarian, vocational skill was of secondary concern 'because even the coarsest day labourer and the most refined and educated gentlemen must first be brought to share in the common sentiment. . . .'[75] While no artisan needed to learn Greek and Latin, there did, at the beginning of the educational process, need to be 'unity and continuity in instruction', as well as an educational ladder available to those who were able to climb to higher levels. Although the ladder was to be accessible to everyone, Humboldt reminded his sovereign that individual inclination, ability, and limited resources would limit the accompanying social mobility to manageable proportions.[76] Humboldt also stated the Section's

70. Ruhlemann Eylert, *Charackter-Züge und historische Fragmente aus dem Leben des Königs von Preussen Friedrich Wilhelm III*, vol. II, pt. 2, p. 74.
71. Mary M. Moffat, *Queen Louisa of Prussia*, pp. 278–9.
72. For Humboldt's report of 1 December 1809 see Wilhelm von Humboldt, *Werke*, vol. IV, p. 213.
73. Ibid., p. 218.
74. See Humboldt's report of 27 September 1809, ibid., pp. 187–8.
75. Ibid., p. 189.
76. Ibid., p. 220.

position on the need for the state to control all educational institutions. For that reason he proposed the elimination of the private Knights' Academies, the municipal burgher schools, and the vocational industrial schools for the poverty-stricken.[77] He concluded his report with an enthusiastic endorsement of Zeller's work, remarking that it 'proved' the efficacy of Pestalozzi's method, and that he would soon be able to train some 600–1,000 teachers per year.[78]

Unfortunately, the confidence in Zeller proved to be misplaced. Trouble began almost as soon as the royal couple and the government left for Berlin. Rumours began to circulate about certain bizarre practices at the *Normalinstitut*; of Zeller trying to create, under the guise of religious discipline, a *Kinderrepublik* of terror; of Zeller taking children into the darkened chapel in the dead of night and frightening them into confessions of sin; of Zeller promising to absolve the sinner by taking these sins upon himself. Then began his demands for more money, with the suggestion that it be acquired by withdrawing financial support from the young men studying with Pestalozzi. None the less, there were still successes. During the early summer of 1810 some 400 clergymen, school inspectors, and school directors were brought to Königsberg for courses in the Pestalozzian method.[79] Zeller also managed that summer to establish institutes similar to the one in Königsberg in four other towns in East Prussia. In a lecture arranged by Scharnhorst he also talked to some seventy army officers on the 'Influence of the *Volksschule* on Military Preparedness.'[80]

Increasingly, however, these successes came to be overshadowed by the difficulties. Two investigations launched in 1810, the first secretly by the Section, the second openly by the Governor of East Prussia, left his position and his future seriously compromised. Had it not been for the crisis going on simultaneously within the top leadership of the Section, it seems likely that Zeller would have been dismissed rather than allowed to wither on the vine until his 'retire-

77. Eric Ashmore, 'Wilhelm von Humboldt's Ideas on the Formation of Character through Education', pp. 24–5; also Ludwig Kiehn, 'German Education and Economy in the Nineteenth Century', p. 486.
78. Humboldt, *Werke*, vol. IV, p. 226.
79. Emil Hollack and Friedrich Trommau, *Geschichte des Schulwesens der königlichen Haupt- und Residenzstadt Königsberg*, p. 471; Fischer, *Nicolovius*, p. 285; Dilthey, 'Süvern', p. 222.
80. Eduard Spranger, *Zur Geschichte der deutschen Volksschule*, p. 37.

ment' in 1812.[81] The crisis at the top was brought on by Humboldt's resignation in April 1810 over his failure to be made an independent minister. Once again Nicolovius was named interim head. A permanent replacement was not appointed until November.

Zeller's difficulties provided the perfect opening for Natorp. Zeller, as well as his *Normalinstitut* approach to teacher-training, was suddenly vulnerable. Natorp began by equating Zeller's methods with those of Joseph Lancaster whose monitorial system he now considered totally discredited.[82] Zeller's methods, he wrote to Vincke, were nothing more than a 'glorified Lancasterianism imposed upon a modified Pestalozzianism'. Teacher training 'à la Zeller requires no education, no knowledge, no insight, only drill and a little fanciness', he concluded.[83]

Natorp's attacks upon Zeller were not well received by superiors in the Section still smarting from embarrassment. Süvern took the occasion to point out to Natorp that he did not accept the view that it was pointless to attempt improvements in the schools until teacher education had been totally and radically reformed. Might not even minimal improvements in the schools — the task with which Natorp had been charged — provide more qualified candidates for teacher-training? While Süvern did not close the door entirely upon Natorp's Seminar idea, he did note that such a Seminar would serve only the best graduates of the *Normalinstitut*.[84] Prussia was very poor, Süvern pointed out, and could ill afford the expense of many such institutions. Friedrich Schleiermacher, who had joined the Section in 1809 to work on university affairs, and in 1811 took control of teacher-training for Brandenburg, also entered the lists against Natorp. He found Natorp's ideas 'at the least disrespectful' and altogether too expensive to implement.[85]

When it became clear that the Zeller experiment had failed, however, Schleiermacher asked Natorp for an elaboration of his Seminar plan. The result, which Natorp submitted to the Section in September 1812 under the title of 'An Outline for a School Teachers'

81. The crisis was exacerbated by the fact that Prussia had fallen behind in her payments to France, a situation that led the new Chancellor, Hardenberg, to agree to the levying of another tax.

82. G. Hausmann, 'A Century of Comparative Education, 1785–1885', p. 6.

83. Natorp to Vincke, 4 December 1810, in Lichtenstein, 'Krisenjahr', p. 101.

84. Süvern to Natorp, 4 June 1810; see Franz Kade, *Schleiermachers Anteil an der Entwicklung des preussischen Bildungswesens von 1808–1818*, pp. 18–19.

85. Ibid., pp. 18, 22, 136; see also R. C. Raack, 'Schleiermacher's Political Thought and Activity, 1806–1813', p. 382.

Seminar for the Electoral Mark',[86] although ludicrously ambitious at the time, did become the basis for the Seminar established in Potsdam in 1817 and, eventually, the model for the entire system of teacher-training in Prussia.

In his 'Outline' Natorp proposed the Seminar as a boarding school that would take in pupils for a two, possibly even three-year course in pedagogical training. Eligibility was to be limited to young men of high moral character between the ages of sixteen and thirty. They were to attend full-time classes and, except for holidays, all year round. The simultaneous practice of any trade was to be strictly prohibited. The curriculum was to be rigorous and included courses in mathematics, language, literature, music, history, geography, natural science, religion, and gymnastics, as well as extensive training in pedagogy, didactics, and the practical elements of teaching. Religious instruction was to be Christian, but non-confessional. The Seminar itself was to have no confessional identity. Finally, the Seminar's faculty was to be required to engage in pedagogical research and the Seminar's graduates required to purchase the publications of its results. Thus would they keep abreast of the latest pedagogical advances. The budget for the first year of such a Seminar, Natorp calculated, would be 5,000 thalers, not including the cost of acquiring a building.

Schleiermacher countered with a long list of objections.[87] The notion of Seminar teachers doing research struck him as pretentious, as did the curriculum, which he considered much too academic for teachers who were to be employed, mostly, in rural villages. Such teachers would need practical, not academic, courses. Moreover, the cost of the Seminar was too high. He did agree, however, with the importance Natorp attached to the teaching of German language and literature. In November 1812 Schleiermacher went so far as to enquire of Chancellor Hardenberg about the availability of funds for an institution of the type that Natorp had described. The time was obviously unpropitious. Hardenberg, more concerned with the fate of Prussia's forces involved since June in Napoleon's invasion of Russia, could respond only by saying that any such funds depended entirely upon the disposition of certain recently secularised church

86. For Natorp's full 'Outline', see Thiele, *Organisation des Volksschul- und Seminarwesens*, pp. 162–75.
87. For a discussion of Schleiermacher's response, see Kade, *Schleiermachers Anteil*, pp. 28–42.

properties.[88]

Süvern had in the meantime begun to draw together the various threads of educational reform for the purpose of drafting a comprehensive and coherent set of proposals for the king's consideration. In October 1812 Natorp received from Süvern the additional commission of making specific his suggestions for improving instruction in the elementary schools, the task for which he had been hired initially in 1809. Natorp's 'Outline for the Organisation of the Elementary Schools',[89] which he submitted in December 1812, served to specify a routine for the school day and the school year, the equipment each school would need, the disciplinary procedures to be used, and the content of the elementary school curriculum. Each school week was to have thirty hours of instruction, twelve of which were to be devoted to language and literature, six to arithmetic, three each to religion and music, and the remainder to science, history, and geography. Significantly, history was to be taught 'with emphasis upon the history of the Germans, not merely upon that of the Prussians'.[90] To facilitate this instruction, each school was to be provided with a handy reference work on general German history. Like the Seminars, the elementary schools were to be nonconfessional because, as Natorp explained, the elementary school was to be 'an establishment of the nation, and the teacher the educator and servant of the nation'.[91]

Süvern incorporated Natorp's outline almost word for word in the draft of a school bill, but for the time being his work was to be of little avail. War between 1812 and 1815 overwhelmed educational reform (and all others) in Prussia no less than it did in Bavaria. The war clouds had begun gathering already in 1811 when Russia withdrew from Napoleon's Continental System. Prussia's decision to side with Napoleon in his subsequent invasion of Russia committed it to providing him with 40,000 troops. The transformation of that invasion into the European-wide wars of liberation, which began with Prussia's decision in February 1813 to abandon Napoleon and to ally with Russia, absorbed Prussia's energy and resources for the next two and a half years.

88. Ibid., pp. 42–3.
89. For Natorp's complete proposal, see Thiele, *Organisation des Volksschul- und Seminarwesens*, pp. 145–61.
90. Ibid., p. 147.
91. Ibid., p. 161.

Although progress in Prussia's schooling was almost completely stopped by the wars of liberation, there was not, as was to be the case in Bavaria, any diminishment in the recognition of its importance. By 1813 the foundation for Prussia's schooling had been laid. Several Seminars, though not yet bearing Natorp's stamp, were in place. In practice they were likely to have resembled Zeller's pedagogical vision. School committees had been established in the towns newly empowered with self-administration, and in 1812 school boards, comprising the estate owner, the clergyman, and several of the more prominent heads of village households, were ordered for the rural villages. Direct supervision of the local school, however, was still expected to remain with the clergyman.[92] It was during 1812 also that many of the young men who had been studying with Pestalozzi began to return home. Some went to the so-called Seminars to begin teaching; others taught in various schools while awaiting assignments commensurate with their training. As far as actual schooling was concerned, very little, if anything, had changed. The foundation may have been laid, but on the superstructure itself there had been virtually no progress. In fact, conditions may have grown worse because of the numerous wars. A count of the schools in Brandenburg showed 200 fewer of them in 1811 than there had been in 1799. It also showed that at least one third of the children had never been in a school of any sort.[93]

Entirely new conditions were created by the wars of liberation. Victories at Leipzig and Waterloo restored to Prussia the honour lost at Jena-Auerstadt. The Congress of Vienna restored her territory. By 1815 Prussia once again ranked among Europe's major powers. Prussia's gains at Vienna were considerable. East of the Elbe it acquired part of Saxony and regained much of what it had taken in the second partition of Poland. This Polish territory was organised into a Grand Duchy of Posen, of which Frederick William III became Grand Duke. West of the Elbe Prussia found itself extended to the Dutch border and to the pre-revolutionary boundaries of France.

These new territories with their 5½ million people presented formidable problems of integration. The people in the West, while German, were overwhelmingly Catholic and had been under French

92. For the decrees of 26 June 1811 and 28 October 1812, see F. W. Niedergesäss, ed., *Das Elementarschulwesen in den Königlich Preussischen Staaten*, pp. 641–5.
93. Thiele, *Organisation des Volksschul- und Seminarwesens*, pp. 181–2, n. 70.

rule for two decades. Those in the East, except for the Saxons, were largely Polish as well as Catholic. There was reason to believe, however, that the population of Posen might present fewer problems than that of the Rhineland, for upon assuming control of Posen, Frederick William III had promised the Poles that they would be incorporated into his monarchy 'without having to deny your nationality. . . . Your religion will be preserved. . . . Your language shall be used, along with German, in all public business and transactions'.[94] There was to be no attempt to make Prussians or Germans of the Poles. In the West, however, the Rhineland territories would have to become part of the new Prussia. In the view of one provincial governor the greatest difficulty facing Prussia in the post-Napoleonic era was that it had 'the fewest instinctive bonds between its provinces of any state in Europe. . . . It can only be some spirit or intellectual bond that will hold it together'.[95] Prussian schooling, which had been inspired by defeat, suddenly found its task greatly enlarged by victory.

The impact of Napoleon's defeat on Bavarian schooling was less immediate than upon Prussia, partly because Bavaria's territorial integrity and continuity had been guaranteed by Austria in 1813 by the Treaty of Ried. In a subsequent agreement, however, Bavaria regained Würzburg and ceded to Austria the territories of Vorarlberg, Salzburg, and what it still held of the Tyrol. Montgelas' policy at the Congress of Vienna was to guard at all costs the independent identity of this new Bavaria. Whereas Prussia's delegates, Humboldt and Hardenberg, were proposing in great variety projects that could have led to a greater German unity, Montgelas' delegates were instructed to block anything that might contribute to the development of such a unity. An exasperated Stein, present as an adviser to Tsar Alexander, considered Montgelas' attitude as positively 'un-German'.[96] This is exactly what it was. Only with great difficulty was Bavaria pressured into accepting membership in the new German Confederation created at Vienna. The political task for Bavarian schooling was at least clear: to create a sense of Bavarian

94. Frederick William III quoted in Martin Broszat, *Zweihundert Jahre deutsche Polenpolitik*, p. 85.

95. Quoted in Reinhart Koselleck, 'Staat und Gesellschaft in Preussen, 1815–1848', p. 90.

96. Hannah Alice Straus, *The Attitude of the Congress of Vienna Toward Nationalism in Germany, Italy, and Poland*, p. 63.

identity in order to establish Bavaria as a base to stand independently between Austria and Prussia.

After 1815, however, the Bavarian reform movement quickly lost its remaining energies. Montgelas himself became ill. He also became vulnerable on several political counts. With Napoleon gone, his pro-French policies were easier to question. It was not a matter simply of a conservative political reaction gathering itself against enlightened absolutism. Personal animosities also played a role.[97] The Crown Prince Ludwig, long a foe of anything French, became the centre of an anti-Montgelas plot. It was a victory for these forces when on 2 February 1817 King Max. I Josef dismissed Montgelas, almost eighteen years to the day since the two of them had arrived in Munich to take control of Bavaria.

Two major questions regarding schooling were still unresolved at the time of Montgelas' departure: the nature of the relationship of the schools to the Church, and the means by which schools were to be financed. While the Section's commitment to absolute state control of education had greatly diminished under Niethammer's influence, the matter had never been settled. With the recent renewal of negotiations between Bavaria and the Roman Curia over a concordat, the question again became of critical importance. These negotiations over a concordat to settle the Church-state questions produced by the Imperial Resettlement of 1803 and the subsequent secularisation of ecclesiastic properties had been broken off in 1807 and then been renewed only shortly before Montgelas' fall. Rome's position, with Napoleon gone, had stiffened markedly; Bavaria's position, with Montgelas gone, had softened.

The final terms of a concordat were now agreed upon within a few months. Bavaria's division into two new archbishoprics, each with three suffragan bishops, presented no problem, but the basis for inevitable further state conflict with the Church seemed guaranteed when the negotiators agreed to recognise unspecified Church prerogatives as part of 'God's order'. On school questions the negotiators agreed that 'Because bishops are obliged to supervise the teaching of faith and morality, they are not to be hindered in any way in exercising this duty in connection with the public schools'.[98] One possible interpretation of this would have limited the Church to providing religious instruction in the schools. The Church shortly

97. Karl Otmar von Aretin, *Bayerns Weg zum souveränen Staat*, pp. 177–83.
98. Quoted in Held, *Altbayerische Volkserziehung und Volksschule*, p. 320.

came to insist upon a broader interpretation: that questions of faith and morality permeated every aspect of schooling, thereby consolidating the role of the Church in every aspect of its control. Rather than resolve the essential conflict over schooling, the Concordat of 1817 served to give it precise definition.

The question of school financing was also left unresolved. The hope that the required funds would flow from the secularisations had been dashed as soon as it became clear how expensive it was to throw in one's lot with Napoleon. Finally, in 1819, a Communal Tax Law stipulated what had long been practice: as much as possible schools were to be financed by private means (churches, charitable agencies, donations) and by the school fees required of each pupil in the 1802 compulsory school decree; only as a last resort was the local community to be called upon to tax itself.[99] The exception to this was the Rhineland Palatinate, which was returned to Bavaria in 1816 after twenty years of French rule and where school financing was firmly based upon local taxation.

An inside look into the state of Bavarian schooling is accorded by the statistics that were collected between 1815 and 1820 and published by Ignaz Rudhardt. At first glance the figures look impressive. Out of a total Bavarian population of roughly 3½ million people, 489,196 children were supposedly attending some 5,008 schools, and being taught by 6,384 teachers.[100] There were five Seminars for the training of teachers, four for men, and one for women. Yet the happy conclusions such statistics suggested evaporate quickly upon careful examination. The number of pupils counted were those eligible to attend school, not those actually attending. Despite the decree of 1802, attendance was probably no better in 1815 or 1820 than it had been in 1799 or 1800. Moreover, parents had learned the utility in sending their children to school on the official counting day. Until mid-century parents in the rural villages and smaller towns were reluctant to send their children to school except, perhaps, for a few weeks during the dead of winter.[101] Many of them were too poor to pay the prescribed school fees, needed the labour of their children at home, or saw little advantage

99. Seiler, ed., *Schulbedarfsgesetz*, p. 4.

100. Ignatz Rudhart, *Ueber den Zustand des Königreichs Baiern nach amtlichen Quellen*, p. 93.

101. Werner K. Blessing, 'Zur Analyze politischer Mentalität und Ideologie der Unterschichten in 19. Jahrhundert', p. 787.

either for themselves or their children in schooling. One school inspector–priest explained to school officials that even those peasants who did see utility in schooling 'were frightened off by the school fees alone'.[102]

Where children did attend school, neither the facilities nor the teachers had been much improved by reform. An 1802 order had prescribed a maximum salary of 300 gulden per year for teachers in the countryside and one of 400 gulden in the city; yet these limits were rarely reached in either place. Most teachers still had to supplement their income from other sources, perhaps by working as shepherds, as day labourers, or most often, as church sextons who played the organ for services, weddings, and funerals, rang the church bell, cleaned the church, dug the graves, waited on the priest, or attended to an endless list of other miscellaneous duties. Most of the teacher's income came from the school fees, which the pupils' parents might, or might not, choose to pay. Usually it was the teacher who had to enforce the payment of these fees, a task for which he had little authority and one which virtually ensured his unpopularity. Understandably, very few of these teachers had attended a Seminar. In fact, not until 1823 did Seminar attendance become compulsory for those henceforth aspiring to teach in the *Volksschule*.

Rudhardt's statistics are also instructive about disparities in schooling between various provinces. The Lower Main District, the former bishopric of Würzburg, where since the eighteenth century schooling had been most advanced, was on all counts far ahead of the Isar District, formerly known as Upper Bavaria, with Munich its capital. With populations of roughly the same size, the Lower Main District was outspending the Isar District by 384,488 gulden to 197,541 annually. The former had 958 schools and 1,054 teachers; the latter 609 schools and 760 teachers.[103] The Isar District, moreover, depended upon school fees to meet at least half of its annual schooling expenses. In these circumstances the recent estimate that forty to fifty per cent of the Bavarian peasants in the 1840s were still illiterate, i.e. unable to sign their names, becomes credible.[104]

A rare glimpse into the inside of a Bavarian school during this era

102. From an 1809 report from a village in Upper Bavaria; see Heinz Haushofer, 'Bauer und Schule in der Geschichte', p. 13.
103. Rudhart, *Ueber den Zustand*, p. 99.
104. Lee, *Social Change in Bavaria*, p. 346.

is to be found in the memoir of J. T. Petzet, a *Volksschule* teacher from 1819 to 1877 and a pupil from 1806 to 1812.[105] Born in the Principality of Bayreuth, which became part of Bavaria in 1810, Petzet in his memoir recounts his school experience. The village in which he was born did not then have a permanent school building. Classes were moved periodically from household to household in the fashion of a *Wanderschule*, and held usually in a room that had to be shared with the owner's pigs and chickens. Desks, books, and blackboards were unknown. Of his four teachers, Petzet recalled that one was a 77-year-old carpenter who slept most of the day; two of them were journeymen–masons, one with a dirty mind; and the fourth was a carpenter who had once made a living as a coach driver. The curriculum consisted mostly of memorising hymns, the Lutheran catechism, and assorted Bible verses, all of which had to be recited upon command. A lapse of memory inevitably invited a rap on the head from the teacher. Reading and arithmetic were not part of the regular curriculum, although the older pupils did occasionally receive instruction in these skills outside school hours. Once a year, on Shrove Tuesday, it was the custom for the teacher to whip all of his pupils with a fresh birch stick, the local belief being that such beatings had the effect of preventing the farm animals from contracting worms. This was exactly the kind of superstition that Wismayr's curriculum had been intended to combat. In 1814 or 1815, when Petzet himself decided to become a teacher, he apprenticed himself to a schoolmaster; it did not occur to him to attend one of the new Seminars. In 1819 he began teaching.

Unlike Bavaria, Prussia during the first years after Napoleon's fall experienced no discernible decline in the commitment to schooling. Many of the other reforms were indeed allowed to languish, but not those that had to do with education. Nowhere was this commitment more evident than in the decision to extend schooling to the newly-acquired territories along the Rhine, later divided into the provinces of the Rhine and Westphalia. No less a person than Frederick William III restated that commitment. In a proclamation directed to these new provinces he promised them, in addition to a bishop's seat and a university, the establishment of a system of *Volksschulen*

105. Johann Thomas Petzet, 'Meine Biographie', Bayerische Staatsbibliothek MS 30. 6. 78. Beilage I.

and of institutions in which to train teachers. Directors for public instruction were appointed immediately by the first provisional governors.[106]

The first such director for what would become the Rhine Province was Joseph Görres. A fervent liberal and ardent German patriot, Görres was also the editor of the *Rheinische Merkur*, a zealous proponent of schooling, and a vocal champion of the Pestalozzian method in pedagogy.[107] The first investigations of these directors into the schooling situation in these provinces revealed a picture no less dreary than had been found a decade earlier in the older provinces of the kingdom. At least forty, and perhaps as many as seventy, per cent of the children had never set foot inside a school. Teachers were few and lacking in training, and there existed no institution in which to train more of them.[108]

In Berlin Süvern was anxious about the difficulties the Section might have in subjecting the new territories to its schooling measures. Because the Prussian civil code did not apply in these regions, there was lacking the legal foundation upon which the educational reform in Prussia proper was based. As yet, schooling was not compulsory. Süvern was fearful also that in these provinces vocational objectives rather than ones of national integration might come to define the purpose of schooling. For that reason he warned the provisional governors of the importance of co-ordinating their schooling policies with Berlin. In the summer of 1815 he made a tour of the Rhineland region to see for himself what was being done.[109] A start was made in 1816 when Natorp left the employ of the Section in Berlin to return to his native region. That same year the region's first Seminar, albeit with provisional status only, was established in Trier.

In the older provinces of Prussia the implementation of school reform resumed in 1814 much where it left off in 1812. Between 1814 and 1817, eight new Seminars were created: three in West Prussia; two in Brandenburg, including the one in Potsdam patterned after Natorp's Seminar Plan; and one each in the provinces of Silesia,

106. Proclamation of 5 April 1814; see Wilhelm Zimmermann, *Die Anfänge und der Aufbau des Lehrerbildungs- und Volksschulwesens am Rhein, 1814–1840* (1946), p. 9.
107. Ibid., p. 11.
108. Ibid., p. 12.
109. Ibid., pp. 22, 26.

Pommerania, and East Prussia. Of the dozen or more of Pestalozzi's former students, many now headed these new Seminars or taught in them. As yet, however, there was no uniformity in their curricula, their procedures, or even in the prescribed length of study for their pupils. Some prescribed six months; others two years. These were matters that would have to be settled in the comprehensive plan for Prussian schooling.

The elevation of the Section in November 1817 to the status of a Ministry for Education and Public Worship gave promise that such a comprehensive plan would be soon in coming, as did the appointment of Karl von Altenstein as the first Education Minister. Altenstein's reform credentials were excellent. It had been his memorandum to Frederick William III in 1807 that had urged the 'use of force' if necessary to bring about mass schooling. It was to accomplish that end that Frederick William III appointed the commission in late 1817 to prepare the final version of a comprehensive schooling bill. His choice to head the commission naturally was Süvern. In appointing Süvern the king knew exactly what kind of bill to expect. Süvern had made public a few months before a statement of reform assumptions and principles upon which such a school bill would be based.

In large measure, the first years following the collapse of Napoleon witnessed not only the fulfilment in Prussia of many of its school reform plans, but also the gathering of a party that was to oppose those reforms and question the assumptions underlying them. It was around the fear of renewed revolution, and the hope of undoing some of the consequences of the one just past, that a new Prussian conservatism began to articulate itself. The refounding in 1816 of the Christian-German Roundtable Club marks the emergence of this new conservatism. In an earlier incarnation this body had been the voice of literary romanticism; now, under the intellectual influence of Karl Ludwig von Haller, it based itself on the proposition that reform was merely the forerunner of revolution.[110] In principle its members agreed with the Berlin Gymnasium director B. M. Snethlage, who in 1807 had diagnosed Prussia's defeat not as the failure of a political system, but as a judgement from God. Repentance, not

110. Sigmund Neumann, *Die Stufen des preussischen Konservatismus*, pp. 77–9; Mechthild Gleich, *Die Pädagogik des preussischen Konservatismus in der Epoche seiner Entstehung*, p. 51.

reform, had been the substance of his counsel ever since.[111]

On pedagogical matters these conservatives directed their first criticism at Pestalozzi and particularly at the social implications of his method. The method's promise to uplift the lower orders they equated with social levelling. Haller launched the attack upon Pestalozzi in 1811, when in the pages of the prestigious *Göttinger Anzeiger,* he charged Pestalozzi with calculating to instil in his pupils 'an aversion to Christianity, hatred of all natural authority, dissatisfaction with social conditions, and revolutionary conviction'.[112] He was soon joined by Goethe, who deplored the arrogance that Pestalozzi's method seemed to be breeding into the boys of Weimar. Goethe wondered how long it would be possible 'to resist the raving horde once it had mastered the elementary techniques of knowledge, which mastery (*sic*) has now been made infinitely easier through Pestalozzi'.[113] Although they seriously misread the social ideals of the reformers, both Haller and Goethe shared their basic assumptions about the powers of pedagogy. The only difference was that Stein believed it could awaken a morally powerful generation, whereas Goethe feared it would unleash a raving horde.

A party of conservatives soon began to collect at the court of Frederick William III. In 1816 Snethlage himself was appointed to the Berlin Consistory. In 1817 Ruhlemann Eylert, the king's confidant since the death of Queen Louise in 1810 and a prominent member of the Christian-German Roundtable, was made an Evangelical bishop. A year later he joined the powerful Council of State, a new body created to advise the king on legislation. The most powerful of this new circle, however, was Ludwig von Wittgenstein, since 1814 the Police Minister and after 1819 also the Minister of the Royal House. It was Wittgenstein who during the next years had daily access to Frederick William III and who would later become known as the 'Prime Minister behind the scenes'.[114] Wittgenstein immediately saw as his most important function the undermining of Hardenberg's influence upon the monarch.

Conservative fears had been stirred in 1816 with the appearance in Paris of an anonymously written pamphlet entitled: 'Will Ger-

111. See 'B. M. Snethlage' in *ADB*, vol. XXXIV, pp. 516–22.
112. See Dilthey, 'Süvern', p. 225.
113. Goethe quoted in Friedrich Heer, *The Intellectual History of Europe*, vol. II, p. 271; see also Ludwig Lewisohn, ed., *Goethe*, vol. II, pp. 238–9.
114. Heinrich von Srbik, *Metternich*, vol. I, p. 582.

many Have a Revolution?' The affirmative answer was based upon the author's conclusion that agricultural crisis would become the breeding ground of a German revolution.[115] The following year a student festival at the Wartburg, ostensibly called to commemorate the tercentenary of the Lutheran Reformation and the third anniversary of the Battle of Leipzig, ended in the burning of Haller's chief theoretical treatise and a copy of the Prussian police code prepared by Wittgenstein's ministry. A 'burning fever' seemed to be afflicting Germany's youth, Friedrich von Gentz informed Metternich in 1818. Then the ultimate happened: in March 1819 a radical university student, for political reasons, murdered the popular playwright August von Kotzebue. A few months later another student attempted to murder a government official in the Duchy of Nassau. With these incidents of violence, the revived university, itself the product of reform, fell under the dark cloud of suspicion, as did the whole system of educational reform.

This was the atmosphere into which Süvern introduced his completed school bill in June 1819. Süvern's bill represented the logical culmination of the educational reform era. Its principles were fully consonant with those that had animated the reformers in Memel and Königsberg during the bleak days of 1808. In the bill's introduction, which had been made public in August 1817, Süvern characterised the 'state as an educational institution writ large'. The task of schooling, he said, was 'to establish an *Organismus* in which each of society's components, be it province, nobleman, vassal, or region, is allowed to develop its life and activities and to take joy in its individuality [while] at the same time allowing these components to grow together into a unified whole (*Ganzen*)'.[116] Thus, he noted, would Prussia's schools become the signal to awaken a common spirit within Prussia and, by example, in all of Germany. There were no concessions here to those fretting about the possible adverse social effects of schooling.

The concessions, such as they were, Süvern made in the main body of his proposal. The universities he left out completely; they were to be treated later in a separate code. He also backed away from insistence upon a principle absolutely sacred to every one of the reformers, that of having only non-confessional schools. Süvern's bill

115. Karl-Georg Faber, 'Görres, Weitzel und die Revolution (1819)', p. 38.

116. *Die Gesetzgebung auf dem Gebiete des Unterrichtswesens in Preussen*, p. 10; see also Gerhardt Giese, *Quellen zur deutschen Schulgeschichte seit 1800*, p. 92.

allowed schools their confessional identities, but stressed that instruction in religion and history would have to emphasise that which bound the confessions together rather than that which separated them.[117] On the critical question of school supervision at the local level, Süvern was deliberately vague. He proposed that the pedagogical experts be involved, as well as those who paid for the schools, while at the same time maintaining the 'old and worthy relationship between school and Church'.[118] In other words, it was not made clear who was to provide local school supervision.

Most other essentials of the reform programme remained intact. The organic connection between educational levels Süvern reaffirmed, though more by implication than by explicit statement. From the ages of seven to fourteen, children from both countryside and towns were to attend the common elementary school. Beyond that there was the municipal school (*Bürgerschule*) for those entering business occupations, and the Gymnasium for those aspiring to a learned profession. To ensure the imparting of a common culture to children of all social classes, the Gymnasium was expressly forbidden to have its own elementary preparatory school.[119] Süvern was also insistent upon the need to maintain the lower school as an elementary school (*Elementarschule*). Any other designation, that of *Volksschule* for example, he feared would signal that the school was intended solely for the lower orders.

Süvern's curriculum proposal was modelled after the one recommended by Natorp in 1812.[120] German language and literature, along with history, geography, and gymnastics, were to be the core of the general, or 'national', education; arithmetic and natural science to be the elements of basic knowledge. This curriculum was not intended to serve any later vocational purpose. Vocational training was to begin only after the elementary school curriculum had been completed.[121] Girls as well as boys, non-Germans as well as Germans, Jews included, were to complete this curriculum. Parents who failed to comply with these schooling requirements, unless they had their children tutored privately, were subject to fines, a jail sentence, or even having their children taken away from them. In the case of Jews, there was the added threat of revoking

117. Ibid., p. 17.
118. Ibid., p. 60.
119. Ibid., p. 31.
120. Ibid., p. 21.
121. E. von Bremen, ed., *Die Preussische Volksschule; Gesetze und Verordnungen*, p. 5.

their recently-granted citizenship, although Jewish children were not to be proselytised, even in a confessional school.[122]

Teacher training, Süvern stipulated, was with rare exceptions to be within the purview of the state-funded Seminars, which, in turn, were to be located in each of the provinces in numbers sufficient to produce the required teachers.[123] Here again, Natorp's vision had carried the day. The Seminars were to be boarding schools, they were to have no more than seventy pupils, and they were to be non-confessional, unless the province could justify on the basis of need a Seminar for each confession.[124] The Seminar curriculum was to prepare the pupils to teach the courses required in the elementary schools. To prepare these pupils effectively, Süvern believed, would require a three-year course of study.[125]

Without specifying a figure, Süvern was very much concerned that teachers be accorded adequate salaries. 'It is our earnest desire that this be considered the first and foremost concern of school financing', he wrote.[126] The customs of paying the teacher in kind, of requiring him to move from family to family for his board, and of forcing him to collect the school fees he considered demeaning. Teaching was to become a profession worthy of respect, rather than remaining the lowest regarded of the trades.

The legal foundation for school financing was already provided in the civil code of 1794, but Süvern put its outline into his proposal none the less. Where private funds were available, schools were to be supported by them. Where they were not, a local school tax was to be levied. Should these sources prove insufficient, provision was to be made for a subsidy from a Provincial School Fund.[127] A local community could, where feasible, collect school fees, but Süvern did not want that to become regular practice.[128]

The political setting into which Süvern's Comprehensive School Bill was thrust in the summer of 1819 did not augur well for its approval. The shock waves created by Kotzebue's murder were felt everywhere. Frederick William III heard from Metternich that a German-wide radical conspiracy seemed to be centred in Prussia.[129]

122. *Die Gesetzgebung*, p. li.
123. Ibid., p. 47.
124. Ibid.
125. Ibid., p. 49.
126. Ibid., p. 38.
127. See ibid., pp. 37–46, for provisions on school financing.
128. Ibid., p. 44.
129. Peter Garrit Thielen, *Karl August von Hardenberg, 1750–1822*, p. 352.

Metternich was apparently serious. To his ambassador in London he wrote: 'Prussia has advanced so far onto the edge of the abyss that nothing in Europe is more problematical than the duration of her existence'.[130]

It was the king who would ultimately decide, with the aid of the State Council, whether or not Süvern's bill would become law. To bolster the bill's chances in this process, Education Minister Altenstein decided to submit it first to the various provincial governors,[131] who, because they were mostly reform-minded civil servants, were likely to give it a favourable hearing. Their endorsement, he believed, would be useful in the State Council. Having done that, however, Altenstein was unable to resist the pressure to submit the bill also to the Catholic bishops of Prussia. Thus did Süvern's bill become the subject of intense public debate.

Responses to the bill were predictable. The governors were mostly favourable to it; the bishops mostly hostile. Some of the governors were unhappy with the concessions Süvern had made to the Church. Theodor von Schön thought the concession to the confessional school idea a 'backward step'.[132] The main opposition, the governors all agreed, however, was likely to come from the rural areas where the possibility of a school tax would evoke stiff resistance. Some of the governors feared the tax would make the school a hated institution. A few of them suggested that the designation '*Volksschule*' would be more appropriate than *Elementarschule* because it would identify the school more closely with the lower classes.[133]

The Catholic bishops and most of the noble landowners were solid in their opposition. The landowners, most of whom had no intention of sending their children to an elementary school, resented particularly the provision that they would have to pay for the education of their farm labourers.[134] The bishops, on the other hand, opposed state control over the schools. They were not appeased in the least by Süvern's concessions to confessional schooling. To support their assertion that the school was necessarily a *causa ecclesiastica*, they cited the terms of the Imperial Settlement, the Treaties of Westphalia,

130. Paul W. Schroeder, *Metternich's Diplomacy at its Zenith, 1820–1823*, p. 46.
131. Altenstein to Hardenberg, 8 August 1819; see *Die Gesetzgebung*, p. 86.
132. Gottlieb Lüttgert, *Preussens Unterrichtskämpfe in der Bewegung von 1848*, p. 16.
133. *Die Gesetzgebung*, p. 90.
134. Hartmut Titze, *Die Politisierung der Erziehung*, p. 128; see also Reinhart Koselleck, *Preussen zwischen Reform und Revolution*, p. 68.

the Council of Trent, and appropriate provisions of canon law.[135] Their immediate demand was for direct control over the Catholic Seminars, including the power to appoint their faculties and directors.

Reactions from certain members of the Council of State were for Süvern even less promising, if only because they exercised such direct influence over the king. In August Bishop Eylert told Frederick William III that the revolutionary sentiment among the masses could be traced to academically-trained clergymen and bureaucrats. In October he submitted to the king a lengthy memorandum which served to set the theme for subsequent reactions to Süvern's bill. Calling his memorandum 'Candid Observations Concerning the Corruption of our Times',[136] Eylert used it to trace 'the source from which the evils of our time spring' to the 'one-sided, false direction taken by our *Volksschulen*, Gymnasien and universities', to the anarchy within the Protestant Church, and to the humanism of the state's bureaucrats.[137] The 'unending [pedagogical] experimentation for the past thirty years', he said, had led to the *Volk* being pumped full of 'a heterogeneous mass of undigested learning' and being thereby 'separated from its station in life'. His solution to the problem was to limit instruction in the lower schools to biblical history, hymn singing, and some writing and arithmetic. The Bible, the catechism, the hymnal, and one secular reader should be the only books allowed in the school. Instruction in the Seminar was to be stripped of 'all useless superfluities' and based upon a 'Christian piety in line with the unadulterated principles of biblical Christianity'.[138]

No less frightening to Eylert and his compatriots were the social-levelling implications they saw in Süvern's proposals. Such fears were occasionally nourished by the rhetoric Süvern's defenders used in his support. The most notable of these was Friedrich Schleiermacher. Although Schleiermacher had left the employ of the Section in 1815 and was now a professor at the University of Berlin, he had lost none of his ardour for reform. In a lecture to the Academy of Sciences, in which he defended Süvern's bill, he warned against attempts to maintain 'social conditions that history has passed by'.

135. *Die Gesetzgebung*, p. 94.
136. Reprinted in Max Lenz, *Geschichte der Königlichen Friedrich-Wilhelms-Universität zu Berlin*, vol. IV, pp. 380–90.
137. Ibid., p. 381.
138. Ibid., pp. 381–2.

Education would henceforth be 'an equalizing principle (*ein gleichmachendes Prinzip*)' which would work to 'counteract constantly re-emerging inequalities'. The bombshell, however, came when he argued that an increase in education would inevitably lead to the decline of authority; that 'the course of education is a gradual diminution of authority and gradual increase in common feeling'.[139] Authority would therefore wither away as education made it less and less necessary. To Schleiermacher this diminution of authority was the purpose of education; to others it was simply opening the gate to the raving horde. Edward Glanzow, the reactionary writer, immediately classified Schleiermacher among those 'pedagogical ultras' to be held responsible for the spread of revolutionary ideas.[140]

It was in the autumn of 1819 that the court party recruited into its circle Ludolf Beckedorff (1778–1858), the man who was to become the dominant figure in schooling during the 1820s and whose importance to the development of Prussian schooling ranks with that of Süvern and Natorp. A native Hanoverian who had studied theology and medicine, Beckedorff was in 1819 tutor to the Prince of Anhalt-Bernberg. He had come to the court party's attention early that year as the author of a pamphlet castigating the murderers of Kotzebue. Because his political views seemed to qualify him for a post on the government's High Censorship Board, a creation of the recent Carlsbad Decrees, he was invited to Berlin in November 1819. His arrival happened to coincide with the high-point of the debate over Süvern's bill.

Beckedorff's first assignment was to consider the merits of Süvern's bill. He could find none, a fact that endeared him greatly to his new friends.[141] His chief objection was that the type of schooling proposed by Süvern would promote the levelling of the social orders. To implement Süvern's plans, he noted, would be 'to establish general equality of all people', something both unnatural and dangerous. 'That differences of sex, age, strength, inclinations, talents, and, above all, unequally distributed wealth, are all rooted in nature simply cannot be denied', he said. Rather than as fissures, he saw these 'natural inequalities' as being 'actually the bonds of

139. Friedrich Schleiermacher, *Pädagogische Schriften*, p. 311; Ernst Hojer, 'Das Problem der demokratischen Erziehung bei Schleiermacher', p. 6; Koppel S. Pinson, *Pietism as a Factor in the Rise of German Nationalism*, p. 148.

140. Johannes Tews, *Ein Jahrhundert preussischer Schulgeschichte*, p. 100.

141. Beckedorff's assessment reprinted in Lothar Schweim, comp., *Schulreform in Preussen, 1809–1819*, pp. 222–44.

society'. To try to undo them would 'be an offense against nature's order' and yield nothing but 'envy, jealousy, enmity, strife and eternal struggle'.[142]

Wittgenstein was quick to take Beckedorff under his wing, and soon he was suggesting him for other more influential posts. Within a year Frederick William III had made him a councillor in the Education Ministry and by early 1821 he was in charge of its *Volksschule* division.[143] The circumstances of Beckedorff's rise involved considerable manoeuvring and, at one point, international politics at their highest level. In October 1820 Frederick William III and Wittgenstein attended the international conference at Troppau which had been convened by Metternich to consider the stance to be taken by Europe's conservative powers over the popular uprising that had recently occurred in Naples. During a lull in the proceedings, Metternich took Wittgenstein aside and complained to him about the policies of Prussia's Education Ministry, urging him to use his influence with the king to effect basic changes.[144]

Wittgenstein went to work immediately. While still at Troppau, he persuaded Frederick William III to promote Beckedorff to councillor and to launch an investigation of school policy. An investigative commission to be headed by Eylert (Wittgenstein narrowly averted the naïve Frederick William III from naming Altenstein) and including Snethlage and Beckedorff was to investigate the situation in the schools and propose improvements.[145]

The findings of this commission, submitted to Frederick William III in February 1821, were largely a rehearsal of positions long held by the court party, although the commission was more specific in assigning blame for what had gone wrong.[146] The 'growing moral corruption', the body concluded, grew out of 'the school and educational system of the Prussian state as it was introduced since 1809'. Responsibility for this corruption the commission placed squarely upon those 'persons in the Ministry of Education and Public Worship who since 1809 have been almost completely in control of schooling'.[147] Mentioned specifically in this context were the names of Fichte and Schleiermacher. These two the commission held

142. Ibid., pp. 224–5.
143. Hans Brunnengräber, *Ludolph von Beckedorff*, p. 33.
144. Fischer, *Nicolovius*, p. 422.
145. Ibid., pp. 422–3.
146. The commission's findings are reprinted in Lenz, *Geschichte*, pp. 390–401.
147. Ibid., pp. 390–7.

primarily responsible for promoting Pestalozzi's method and, thereby, opening the way for the events at the Wartburg and for the murder of Kotzebue. As a remedy for the ills created by Pestalozzi, the commission recommended reacquainting youth 'with the religious truths of positive Christianity'. Shortly thereafter Beckedorff was named head of the Education Ministry's *Volksschule* division.

The next years, until 1827 when Beckedorff was forced to resign, have recently been referred to as the 'Beckedorff Era'.[148] Presumably, reaction held full sway over the course of Prussian schooling. Beckedorff's presence did, in fact, dominate schooling during these years. By virtue of his political connections and his position, he had full jurisdiction over the *Volksschulen* and the Seminars. Whether his importance is fully captured within the meaning of the word 'reactionary', however, is another matter.

Beckedorff, as it turned out, was no less energetic than Süvern in his efforts to shape Prussian schooling. He began his tenure in 1821 with an inspection tour of Seminars in Brandenburg and Saxony. His report on their condition he made, significantly, not to his own minister, Altenstein, but to his mentor, Wittgenstein. In it he pointed to the dangers of over-educating teachers. Although he found little uniformity among the Seminars on curricular matters, or the length of study they required, or on much of anything else, he still noted that several of them aspired to providing an encyclopaedic curriculum. He was disturbed to learn that the Seminars were providing the same training for teachers whether they were destined for rural or urban schools.[149] He sensed potential social dangers in such a policy.

Beckedorff's efforts were quick to bear fruit. In October 1821 came the order disallowing non-confessional schools except in cases where the clergymen of both confessions agreed;[150] in July 1822 followed the order from Frederick William III restricting instruction in the Seminars to those things appropriate for the teacher to know, so as to prevent him from imparting 'half-truths and falsehoods to children of the common folks'.[151] Neither one of these orders changed much in the reality or practice of schooling, but they did mark a major shift in emphasis and ambition.

148. Flitner, *Politische Erziehung*, p. 95.
149. Brunnengräber, *Beckedorff*, p. 40.
150. See order of 4 October 1821, in Niedergesäss, ed., *Elementarschulwesen*, p. 62.
151. See Cabinet Order of 22 July 1822, ibid., pp. 107–8.

Both reality and ambition were seriously affected by the personnel changes of 1822, however. On 1 May, Nicolovius, still Beckedorff's nominal superior, was replaced as Director of the Instructional Division in the ministry. His successor was Heinrich von Kamptz, a high police official from the Interior Ministry. Kamptz, according to one observer, was the most important administrative figure of the reactionary party.[152] He had been the author of the Police Code that students had burned at the Wartburg in 1817, and he had been the one to lead the government's investigations into liberal-national movements after the murder of Kotzebue. Although now Nicolovius' successor, he also kept his old police post. Süvern managed to retain his position during these personnel shifts, but he had lost all influence.[153]

With the Wittgenstein-Beckedorff-Kamptz axis in place, the period from 1822 to 1827 is the pinnacle of what would come to be defined as the reaction. Local police officials were directed to keep watch on the behaviour and opinions of Seminar directors. In 1824 the regular bureaucratic practice of filing secret personnel reports, the hated *Conduitenliste*, was introduced into the Seminars and the schools.[154] Efforts to restrict the Seminar curriculum were undertaken. Language instruction was to be redesigned to teach logic and its rules; instruction in arithmetic restricted to the calculations required in everyday life. 'Natural history should be taught in just a few hours and in such a way that pupils will not become too interested', Beckedorff directed. 'It belongs with history, geography, and grammar to the non-essential elements of the curriculum'.[155]

Had Beckedorff been involved in efforts to undo the actual process of schooling, the label 'reactionary' might be more appropriate. In fact, he quickly came to accept the view held by the reformers, and largely shared by the court party, that the Prussian world had come apart and that schooling was necessary to put it back together. Eylert was fully persuaded that because of the French Revolution 'the holy bonds between legitimate rulers and the people who belong to them have been torn asunder'.[156] In his 1819 memorandum on

152. Ernst Rudolf Huber, *Deutsche Verfassungsgeschichte seit 1789*, vol. I, pp. 142–3.
153. Fischer, *Nicolovius*, p. 428.
154. Order of 20 June 1824; see Titze, *Politisierung*, p. 132.
155. Beckedorff quoted in *Die Brandenburgischen Lehrerseminare und die Ihnen Angegliederten Präparandenanstalten*, ed. Friedrich Buchholz and Gerhard Buchwald, pp. 34–5.
156. Eylert, *Charakter-Züge und historische Fragmente*, vol. I, p. 212.

Süvern's bill, which he attacked so caustically, he agreed, none the less, that schooling could 'create a unity of sentiment in the coming generation on the basis of uniform, time-honoured principles'.[157] Those principles were not those of Süvern, of course. He was later to reveal that they were to be found only in a 'positive Christianity'.

Beckedorff, too, recognised that the old world was gone. Henceforth, he said at one point, society 'will have to be moulded with forethought and purpose, like a work of art'.[158] Stein could not have said it better. Society was a human creation. Upon that they would both have agreed. The advances in Prussia's schooling during the Beckedorff era are not, therefore, surprising. Seven new Seminars were established between 1822 and 1825, all of them in the territories gained in 1814–15 and all of them with a confessional identity. By 1826 there were twenty-eight Seminars. No province had fewer than two Seminars, and three of them had four. Therewith, for the time being, the system was by 1825 considered completed. Pestalozzians, moreover, were still being appointed to direct and teach in these Seminars, although many of Prussia's Pestalozzians, even those who had been sent to Switzerland in 1809, were being caught up in the politically conservative neo-Pietist religious revival of the 1820s.[159]

By 1825 Beckedorff was ready to articulate a complete vision of what the *Volksschule* should be and how it should be fitted into the surrounding society. That year he published a long statement 'Concerning the Concept of the *Volksschule*',[160] which was the fullest elaboration to date of a conservative conceptualisation of schooling. It was in essence an anti-Süvern school bill. One by one Beckedorff took reform assumptions and turned them in upon themselves. Any effort to undo the 'natural differences' of sex, talent, social origin, or wealth, he warned, would sow the 'seeds of societal dissolution'. On this earth 'true equality' was not an 'equality of demands or unrestrained striving for fulfilment of selfish wishes and reckless caprice, but an equality of love, unselfishness, concern for others and an unselfish and unshakeable trust in the equalizing justice of God'.[161]

The implications for schooling Beckedorff thought clear. Its object

157. Eylert quoted in Lenz, *Geschichte*, p. 382.
158. Beckedorff quoted in Brunnengräber, *Beckedorff*, p. 28.
159. Franz Schnabel, *Deutsche Geschichte im neunzehnten Jahrhundert*, vol. I, p. 389.
160. Ludolf Beckedorff, 'Zur Geschichte des Preuss. Volks-Schul-Wesens', pp. 3–96.
161. Ibid., p. 31.

was not to be any longer the general *Nationalbildung* championed by the reformers, but the 'creation of orders and estates' (*Standesbildung*) to replace those that had been destroyed.[162] The estates necessary to the modern world were no longer the traditional *Nähr, Wehr-, und Lehrstand*, but ones that were responsible for the conduct of agriculture, manufacture, commerce, and learning. To promote the development of these estates was to be the primary objective of schooling. There needed to be *Landschulen* for the peasants; tuition-free *Armenschulen* for the urban lower classes; *Bürgerschulen* and *Hauptschulen* for the manufacturing and commercial estates. Together these were to be viewed as *Volksschulen.* There were to be no links between these schools, no passage from one to the next. Finally, beyond the reach of any of them were to be the schools for the learned estate, the Gymnasium and the university.

Beckedorff's proposals were enthusiastically received. Prussian schooling for the remainder of the century reflected his vision more closely than it did that of Süvern. Süvern's school bill was formally laid to rest in 1826 and sent off to the archives where it remained until 1869 when the Education Ministry published a collection of documents related to the development of schooling. None the less, for the rest of the century, it was Süvern's vision that inspired those who wanted to direct the course of schooling away from the path plotted by Beckedorff. Yet it was to Beckedorff's schools that the likes of Cousin, Stowe, and Mann were shortly to point in admiration, concluding that Prussia's schools were the most advanced in Europe and, therefore, in the world.

162. Ibid., p. 32.

4
Schooling and Social Crisis 1830–1848

Metternich's entreaties to Wittgenstein notwithstanding, they did not succeed in transforming Prussia's schools into the conservative bastions that he had in mind. Conservative dissatisfaction was not dispelled. In Bavaria, too, although Metternich's influence was minimal, the conservative King Ludwig was to become displeased with what he considered the continued untoward effects of schooling. Fears that schooling might contribute to social instability, it soon became clear, were not erased simply by declaring a change in direction. Reaction was no more easily effected than reform. Both Metternich and Ludwig lived to see the magnitude of their failures when it became apparent in 1848 that schoolteachers played a prominent role in driving the one from his office and the other from his throne.

An indication of the relationship between revolution and schooling came in the early 1830s during the first of the European-wide upheavals directed against the settlement of 1815. As in 1789, the upheavals began in Paris, but this time the German states were barely touched. Neither Frederick William III nor Ludwig were given cause to fear for their thrones, yet each of them was made exceedingly anxious. Their response was to effect major readjustments in their schooling policies.

It was the Prussian Grand Duchy of Posen that was most directly affected by the turmoil. An uprising that had begun early in 1830 in Russian Poland had spread by late November into the Grand Duchy. The insurrection in Posen was half-hearted and quickly spent, but not without bringing in its wake a major shift in Berlin's attitude toward its Polish subjects. In 1815 Frederick William III had promised Posen the preservation of its language, religion, and nationality. That promise was withdrawn in December 1830 by the dispatch to Posen of Eduard von Flottwell as its new governor. Flottwell's task was to connect this Polish province to Prussia once and for all. This he was expected to accomplish by means of a gradual elimination in 'its Polish inhabitants of their characteristic customs, habits, and inclinations'.[1] For the first time, says Martin Broszat, Posen came to be administered 'like an occupied province'.[2] Polish was replaced by German as the language of public administration; Poles were excluded from high level administrative posts; the estates of Poles who had fled in 1830 were seized and, whenever possible, sold to Germans. In support of these measures, the schools were to be engaged in 'Germanising' the lower classes. Here the Polish language was to be disadvantaged in such a way that German would gradually replace it as the language of instruction.[3] Thus German customs, habits, and inclinations would replace those of the Poles.

The Flottwell era, which lasted only until 1841, was not yet marked by the harsher Germanising measures introduced into Posen's schools during the 1870s. The backward state of schooling in Posen was alone sufficient to undermine its effectiveness as an instrument of Germanisation. Despite annual grants of 21,000 thalers from Berlin[4] to improve Posen's schools, attendance at them was much lower than in any of the other provinces. The rate of illiteracy in Posen was therefore much higher than elsewhere. As late as 1841, forty per cent of the army recruits from Posen had never attended a school.[5] Ironically Beckedorff's insistence upon confessional schools served to strengthen the hand of the Polish clergy in their administration. It was in reaction to Flottwell's Germanising efforts, moreover, that the Polish clergy began its so-called 'organic work', i.e. the cultivation within the lower classes of a consciousness of Polish culture and nationality.[6]

1. Order to Flottwell quoted in Theodor Schieder, *Vom Deutschen Bund zum Deutschen Reich, 1815–1871*, p. 46.
2. Martin Broszat, *Zweihundert Jahre deutsche Polenpolitik*, p. 102.
3. Otto Hintze, *Die Hohenzollern und Ihr Werk*, p. 520.
4. Wilhelm Harnisch, *Der jetzige Standpunkt des gesammten Preussischen Volksschulwesens*, p. 263.
5. Heinrich Busshoff, 'Die preussische Volksschule als sozialer Gebilde und politischer Bildungsfaktor in der ersten Hälfte des 19. Jahrhunderts', p. 390.
6. Piotr S. Wandycz, *The Lands of Partitioned Poland, 1795–1918*, p. 121.

Flottwell's campaign ended in June 1840 with the accession to the throne of Frederick William IV. The new king, a romantic whose conservatism was shaped more by idealisations of the mediaeval world than by modern realities, had little sympathy with Flottwell's policies because they presumed the validity of the modern and liberal notions of nationality. Flottwell was replaced in 1841 and his Germanisation policies rescinded. To assuage Polish sentiment there was created with the Education Ministry a separate section for Catholic schools and in 1842 Polish was restored as the language of instruction in the Polish areas of the Grand Duchy.[7]

In Bavaria the turmoil of the early 1830s was more shadow than substance. There was less real revolutionary activity than there had been in Prussia. Not until the summer of 1832 when a series of popular national festivals were held in several of the newly-acquired territories was it possible to see a revolutionary danger. Mild as the danger may have been, the reaction to it was for that reason no less harsh, and Ludwig saw cause to focus most of it upon the kingdom's schoolteachers.

Ludwig from the beginning of his reign had been suspicious of the schools. He was also eager to end Bavaria's long flirtation with the rationalism of the Enlightenment and to anchor its future in the Catholic conservatism that developed in the post-Napoleonic era. He began by creating within the Interior Ministry a new Division for Church and School Questions and appointing as its head Eduard von Schenk (1788–1841).[8] Schenk was the protégé of Ludwig's one-time tutor, J. M. Sailer, the current Bishop of Regensburg and long a foe of the Enlightenment. Schenk's assignment was to strengthen the position of the Church in school matters, something he set out to accomplish by disbanding the Provincial School Councils (*Kreisschulräte*) that had been established in 1808 to make more effective the will of the state in school affairs. Then, in 1828, when he also became Interior Minister, Schenk saw to it that the terms of the Concordat were more rigidly enforced, one of the effects of which was to encourage the Church to reassert its traditional prerogatives in education.[9] Soon monasteries were being restored, clerical seminaries erected, and long-forbidden religious processions again per-

7. Hans-Joachim Schoeps, *Preussen: Geschichte eines Staates*, p. 185.

8. On Schenk, see Ernst Rudolf Huber, *Deutsche Verfassungsgeschichte seit 1789*, vol. I, p. 371; on Sailer, see Alfred Rach, *Biographien zur deutschen Erziehungsgeschichte*, pp. 204–6.

9. Huber, *Deutsche Verfassungsgeschichte*, vol. I, p. 371.

mitted. Piece by piece, parts of the old world were being restored.

Into this setting in late 1830 came the shadow of revolution. In December came student demonstrations in Munich and almost simultaneously the successes of liberal candidates in the elections to the lower chamber of the *Landtag*. Both were seen as dangerous signs of popular disaffection. When the Chamber's liberals in 1831 took the offensive in school questions by asking for a comprehensive school bill, and also a change in the school curriculum, and then for a revision of the monarchy's censorship laws,[10] the nervous Ludwig, rather than yielding, gave them Schenk's resignation instead. The sacrifice of Schenk, it soon became apparent, served to enliven the hopes of the liberals.

The half dozen or so national festivals sponsored by liberals in the spring of 1832 in such scattered places as Regensburg, Augsburg, Dinkelsbühl, and Gaibach were seen by Ludwig and his circle as the harbingers of revolution itself.[11] The largest of these festivals was held at Hambach in the Rhineland Palatinate in May when some 20,000 to 30,000 demonstrators came to hear speeches and to sing songs in celebration of the hope for German national unity. So frightened was Ludwig by this prospect that he dispatched 8,000 of his troops to disperse the demonstration.

At first glance, Hambach seems to have had little, if anything, to do with the schools. But then the police reported that two pupils from the nearby Seminar at Kaiserslauten had attended the festival in Hambach and that they were believed to have participated in the singing.[12] Whether for that reason or not, Ludwig's wrath was for the next years to be directed against the *Volksschule* and especially against its teachers. Neither was it lost upon him that the Kaiserslauten Seminar was non-confessional. These institutions were to bear the brunt of his resentments.

Soon after Hambach, Ludwig's government began an enquiry into the political activities of teachers, looking specifically for evidence of their membership in teachers' associations. In August 1832 each of the provincial governors was warned by Ludwig's new Interior Minister, Ludwig Prince von Oettingen-Wallerstein, that teachers, particularly those from the bigger cities, were tainted with liberal

10. Paul Schramm, *Hundert Jahre bayerische Schulgeschichte*, p. 48; Josef Neukum, *Schule und Politik; Politische Geschichte der bayerischen Volksschule*, pp. 67–8; Rainer Roth, *Politische Bildung in Bayern*, p. 72.

11. George Heer, *Geschichte der Deutschen Burschenschaft*, vol. II, p. 246.

12. Albert Fritz, *Geschichte der Lehrerbildungsanstalt Kaiserslauten von 1818–1918*, p. 60.

ideas. 'A large number of *Volksschule* teachers have made common cause with the revolutionaries', Oettingen-Wallerstein told the governors.[13] Moreover, much of the money being designated for the schools, he feared, was being funnelled by teachers into revolutionary causes. From each of the governors he wanted a report on the situation in his province.

In November 1832 Oettingen-Wallerstein began a tour of the Seminars in Franconia and those of the other northern provinces. The Würzburg Seminar in particular was under suspicion. Critics spoke of it as being the 'nursery of revolution',[14] perhaps because the city itself was emerging as the centre of Franconian opposition to Munich, or perhaps because a national festival similar to the one at Hambach had taken place outside Würzburg at Gaibach. Oettingen-Wallerstein, after talking to the pupils at the Würzburg Seminar, felt the situation to be under control and so reported to Ludwig.

Ludwig remained unappeased, his rage at the *Volksschule* teachers still unspent. In August 1833 he announced his intention to turn the entire *Volksschule* system around so that it could be used 'to eradicate the evil spirit of our times and to steer future generations toward that spirit of patriotism, contentment, and loyalty upon which a people's happiness can depend'. [15] To accomplish this turnabout he demanded a circumscribed *Volksschule* curriculum and the complete reshaping of teacher-training. Seminars were to be disbanded. They had done nothing, he said, but create an over-educated, arrogant, and sensuous generation of teachers. Henceforth teachers were to be trained by clergymen, and were to be called schoolmasters once again, so as to underline their non-professional, dependent status.

Ludwig's blueprint for reaction was never fully carried out. He began gradually to regain his political composure. Then, too, the considerably more liberal Oettingen-Wallerstein acted as a brake upon the mercurial monarch. Ultimately, of course, the whole matter was little more than a tempest in a teapot. The simple fact was that there was very little schooling about which to be reactionary. Still, Ludwig's ravings were not entirely without effect. Johann Petzet, who was a *Volksschule* teacher in Upper Franconia during the

13. Neukum, *Schule und Politik*, p. 106.
14. Ibid., p. 107.
15. Ludwig quoted in Michael Doeberl, *Entwicklungsgeschichte Bayerns*, vol. II, p. 220.

1830s, recalled that 'Always more catechism verses, always more songs from the hymnal had to be memorised; this became the main job of the *Volksschule* teacher and the most effective means of winning the approval of the inspectors and supervisors'.[16] The renewed emphasis upon religion did come, as Ludwig had demanded, at the expense of the rudiments of other knowledge; only the history of the Bavarian Fatherland was not sacrificed. Perhaps the most significant of Ludwig's actions was symbolic: his order of October 1835 renaming the *Volksschule* the 'German Work-Day School' (*teutsche Werktagschule*).[17] The new name represented a demotion in status no less important than when Niethammer changed Wismayr's *Elementarschule* into the *Volksschule*.

It was Oettingen-Wallerstein, apparently, who dissuaded Ludwig from carrying out his plan to disband the Seminars. However, in January 1836 a new set of Teacher-Training Regulations was issued to replace those which Niethammer had formulated back in 1811. Although teachers were henceforth to receive two years of Seminar instruction, their preparatory training was to come from private tutors, most likely a local clergyman.[18] Ludwig's proposed schoolmaster designation was never systematically implemented, but when Eduard von Schenk was invited to speak at the opening of a new Seminar in Eichstätt in 1836, he reminded those assembled that their task was to prepare a teacher who would be satisfied to be the 'first and most important assistant to the clergyman'.

Ludwig's conservatism was considerably reinforced in late 1837 when he named Carl von Abel to replace Oettingen-Wallerstein. Abel, who was to become the symbol of the Bavarian reaction during the *Vormärz*, had views on schooling that were entirely consonant with those of Ludwig. Like Ludwig, he feared that the schools were being used to promote dangerous social and political ideas, and he fully shared the monarch's determination to prevent the schools from being used for such purposes. Abel's appointment also happened to coincide with another of Ludwig's periodic conflicts with the *Landtag* over school matters. This time liberal delegates in the lower chamber were calling for a seventh year of

16. Johann Thomas Petzet, 'Meine Biographie', Bayerische Staatsbibliothek MS 30. 6. 78. Beilage I.

17. Neukum, *Schule und Politik*, pp. 110–11.

18. Heinrich Held, *Altbayerische Volkserziehung und Volksschule*, p. 327; Joseph Heigenmooser, 'Aus der bayerischen Volksschulgeschichte des 19. Jahrhunderts', p. 408; Neukum, *Schule und Politik*, pp. 110–11.

compulsory schooling, as well as for the government to present a school bill for their consideration.[19] The very idea of *Landtag* interference was too much for Ludwig. School and educational matters, he told the deputies, did not fall within their competence; these were matters he reserved entirely for himself.[20]

The 'Abel era', as it came to be called, lasted until 1847 when a new Ministry of Church and School Affairs was created to assume jurisdiction over schooling. The Abel era began when an old problem with one of the Seminars crossed Abel's desk. The precise connection between the Kaiserslauten Seminar and the Hambach Festival of 1832 had never been ascertained. Although the Seminar's director had been dismissed in 1832 for allowing his students to participate in the festival, the Seminar had, none the less, remained under suspicion. The fact that it was still non-confessional bothered many of its critics, the most clamorous of which came from the Catholic Church. One of its periodicals called confessional mixing of any sort 'corrupting and perverting',[21] and took particular objection when it had the effect of corrupting future teachers. Twice, once in 1835 and again in 1836, Oettingen-Wallerstein had sent investigators to Kaiserslauten to look into the matter. On both occasions their recommendations had been to separate the confessions, a measure which would have required the creation, and the expense, of a second Seminar. Liberal protests against such separation came from as far away as Berlin and its Seminar director Adolf Diesterweg.[22] Both times, Oettingen-Wallerstein refused to act on the recommendations. Abel was of a different mind. The situation in Kaiserslauten, he warned Ludwig, 'was nurturing religious indifference, and then spreading that indifference, which the spirit of our times tries to disguise, by calling it tolerance'.[23] Ludwig immediately ordered the confessional separation. Shortly thereafter a new Seminar to train Catholic teachers was established in Speyer.

Not one of the hopes that Ludwig or Abel had ever placed in the powers of schooling to arrest declining social conditions, or to prevent revolution, was ever realised. Instead, the decade of the

19. Neukum, *Schule und Politik*, p. 69.
20. Roth, *Politische Bildung in Bayern*, p. 78.
21. Fritz, *Lehrerbildungsanstalt Kaiserslauten*, p. 65.
22. Neukum, *Schule und Politik*, pp. 114–15.
23. Abel quoted in Werner K. Blessing, 'Allgemeine Volksbildung und Indoktrination im bayerischen Vormärz. Das Leitbild des Volksschullehrers als mentales Herrschaftsinstrument', p. 525; Fritz, *Lehrerbildungsanstalt Kaiserslauten*, pp. 79–80.

1840s came to be marked by a growing crisis that, with hindsight, seems to make the upheavals of 1848 nearly inevitable. Little, if any, progress was made during the decade in the incorporation of Bavaria's large underclass into the society. Despite the lack of an overall population growth, that underclass continued to grow. Bavaria's illegitimacy rate was still rising during the 1840s: roughly one birth in four was illegitimate.[24] The problem was understandably concentrated in the poorest classes, among the daughters of cotters and day labourers.[25] Restrictions on who could marry and under what circumstances, although designed to ameliorate the problem, merely served to exacerbate it.[26] There were other dislocations as well. Sexual licence, disrespect for authority and public drunkenness seemed everywhere on the increase. The arrests of beggars and vagrants doubled between 1840 and 1847.[27] Large numbers of those arrested were women and children, children who should, by law at least, have been in school. Rapidly rising grain prices also took their toll. By 1844 there were popular disturbances in Munich and other cities in protest against the high cost of bread.[28] Then came the crop failures during the summers of 1845 and 1846. The products of these, one observer notes, were 'little domestic civil wars'[29] in the rural villages throughout the countryside.

Abel's Interior Ministry had reason to keep an eye upon these developments, fearful that they might render the simple folk susceptible to the preachment of radical ideas. Reports of a dangerous religious mysticism, some of it being propagated within the schools themselves, flowed into the ministry.[30] In 1847 Crown Prince Maximilian, fearful that pauperism could lead to revolution, requested for his own edification a report on Bavaria's social problems and on their possible solution.[31] The report concluded with the advice that

24. *Die Bewegung der Bevölkerung im Königreich Bayern in der fünf Jahren 1857/58 bis 1861/62 mit Rückblicken auf die 22 Jahre 1835/36 bis 1856/57*, p. 90.

25. J. Michael Phayer, 'Lower-Class Morality: The Case of Bavaria', p. 83.

26. Edward Shorter, 'Sexual Change and Illegitimacy: The European Experience', pp. 248–9; also John Knodel, 'Law, Marriage and Illegitimacy in Nineteenth-Century Germany', p. 281.

27. F. B. W. von Hermann, ed., *Beiträge zur Statistik des Königreichs Bayerns; Leistungen der Sicherheitspolizei und Strafrechtspflege*, vol. II, pp. 31, 55.

28. Artur Müller, *Die Deutschen; Ihre Klassenkämpfe, Aufstände, Staatsstreiche, und Revolutionen*, p. 119.

29. Pankraz Fried, 'Bauerntum und Landvolk (1800–1945)', p. 780, n. 2.

30. Reports of this nature are to be found in the Bayerisches Hauptstaatsarchiv (BHStA), MK716 and MK718.

31. Günther Müller, *König Max II und die soziale Frage*, p. 7; Leonhard Lenk, 'Revolutionär-kommunistische Umtriebe im Königreich Bayern'.

'effective schools must finally be established'.[32]

Whether the crisis was primarily social or moral, it was unclear what schooling could do to alleviate it. The schooling statistics collected for Bavaria in 1846 looked impressive, but they were no less misleading than those collected by Rudhardt after 1815. The figures for 1846 showed that 556,239 pupils were being taught by 8,797 teachers in some 7,353 schools.[33] But attendance was still erratic, often limited to counting days. Even in the best of cases, children from the rural villages rarely attended school except in winter when they were not needed in the fields, or to tend the sheep or cows. Peasants who were relatively well-off saw little advantage in having their children attend school; those who were less so had their doubts reinforced by the school fees they could ill-afford.[34] These fees were still the single most important source of money for the schools. Thus teachers were paid poorly — and often irregularly. For their room and board, many of them were still shunted from family to family in the village. Their maximum pay of 400 gulden a year, a figure few of them reached, had been set as long ago as 1802. There was no extra pay for longevity; neither was there the prospect of a pension on retirement.

In the rural district of Freising, the average teacher in 1833 (at least on counting day) had 103 pupils; by 1852 the average had risen to 136.[35] Whether social problems could be addressed by an institution so poorly staffed was questionable. Although Bavarian-wide literacy statistics for this period do not exist, recent local studies suggest that they may have seen very little improvement during the first half of the century. There were still districts in the 1840s in which sixty per cent of the populace was illiterate.[36] In places like this schooling had barely gained a foothold.

Most of Bavaria's Work-Day school teachers lived as teachers had always lived, close to the edge of poverty. Rapidly rising food prices brought on by the crop failures of 1845 pushed most of them over

32. Leonhard Lenk, 'Revolutionär-kommunistische Umtriebe im Königreich Bayern'.
33. The statistics for 1846 were published in the *American Journal of Education*, 6 (1859), p. 282.
34. Werner K. Blessing, 'Zur Analyze politischer Mentalität und Ideologie der Unterschichten im 19. Jh.', p. 786.
35. W. R. Lee, *Population Growth, Economic Development and Social Change in Bavaria, 1750–1850*, p. 347.
36. W. R. Lee, 'Tax Structure and Economic Growth in Germany (1750–1850)', p. 155.

that edge. Their only cushion heretofore had been eligibility for poor relief in the communities in which they taught. They had not been subject to the 1834 regulation that empowered the village community to reduce its poor relief costs by refusing the right of domicile to newcomers. That changed suddenly when in January 1846 Abel brought an end to the practice of granting the rights associated with domicile to teachers and to their families.[37] Without such rights teachers were rendered immediately ineligible for poor relief. Communities eager to lighten their financial burdens hastened to use their new powers. Neither the teacher nor his family could now hope for relief of any sort. Of this new situation the first chronicler of Bavaria's teaching profession wrote, 'The poor schoolteacher in Bavaria has no right to a home until he reaches the grave'.[38]

On the one hand, Abel's decree merely underlined the low status of teachers in their communities. On the other hand, it also helped to politicise them. Teachers' associations sprang up in nearly every one of Bavaria's cities and towns, the new domicile regulations being their inspiration.[39] Meeting after meeting produced petition after petition of protest. To Abel most of these petitions were fruitless, but by early 1847 they had received sufficient public notice to come to the attention of one of his most influential enemies, the king's new mistress, Lola Montez. She, who was having domicile problems of her own and rightly saw Abel as the source of many of her problems, undertook to persuade Ludwig to approve a small pay supplement for school teachers.[40] Abel, who was rapidly falling in the king's favour, was soon to be dismissed and Lola thereupon received her right of domicile. The school teachers were not similarly favoured and remained unmollified.

An English writer travelling through Europe in the early 1840s took note of educational advances in Germany, and explained that just 'As George III wished that every man in his dominions might never want a Sunday dinner and a Bible to read after it, so the Germans have wished that every man, woman, and child have an education; and they have not only wished it, but decreed it'. 'This glorious advance in the true science of government', he told his readers, 'has

37. For a discussion of Abel's decree of 27 January 1846, see Neukum, *Schule und Politik*, pp. 112–13.
38. Christian Weinlein, *Der Bayerische Volksschullehrer-Verein*, p. 2.
39. Ibid., p. 12.
40. Veit Valentin, *Geschichte der deutschen Revolution von 1848–49*, vol. II, p. 117.

raised no little sensation throughout Europe'.[41] He was not talking about the Bavarians. His was another voice in the long line of those singing the praises of Prussian education. All of these glowing reports seemed supported by a contemporary statistical compilation of Prussian education.

These statistics, gathered during 1837, showed that 2,171,745 children, or eighty per cent, were attending a school.[42] In 1822 that figure had barely reached fifty per cent. King Frederick William III, upon hearing these latest figures, was once again pleased with schooling. 'I was very happy to learn', he told friends, 'that compared with other countries, in mine more children were receiving instruction'.[43] Even if the eighty per cent figure represents a considerable exaggeration, which it no doubt does, in relative terms the king's understanding was unquestionably correct. Measured in percentages, more children were attending school in Prussia than in any other country, and educational reformers the world over knew it.

There were other reasons during these years for Prussians to be pleased. Their Seminar system, declared complete in 1825 when there were twenty-eight of them, had grown to thirty-eight by 1840, leading Horace Mann to note, after his tour of Prussia in 1843, that 'there are now seminaries sufficient to supply the wants of the whole country'.[44] Moreover, nearly 3,700 new school buildings were built, purchased, or renovated between 1816 and 1846, eliminating thereby the most obviously inadequate structures as well as the old institution of the *Wanderschule*.[45] The first product of these advances seems to have been an increased literacy rate. Statistics for this period are still scattered and unreliable, but Peter Flora has estimated that by 1850 some eighty per cent of Prussia's adults could read and write. His estimates for England and France are twenty-five to thirty per cent lower.[46] In 1841 it was only one recruit in ten who entered the Prussian army without ever having attended a school.

41. William Howitt, *The Rural and Domestic Life of Germany*, p. 485.
42. Johannes Tews, *Ein Jahrhundert preussischer Schulgeschichte*, p. 107.
43. Ruhlemann Eylert, *Charakter-Züge und historische Fragmente aus dem Leben des Königs von Preussen Friedrich Wilhelm III*, vol. I, pp. 372–3.
44. Horace Mann, *Annual Reports of the Secretary of the Board of Education of Massachusetts for the Years 1839–1844*, p. 348.
45. Reinhart Koselleck, *Preussen zwischen Reform und Revolution*, p. 442, n. 177; also Harnisch, *Der jetzige Standpunkt*, p. 262.
46. Peter Flora, 'Die Bildungsentwicklung im Prozess der Staaten- und Nationalbildung', p. 432; Busshoff, 'Die preussische Volksschule', p. 390; Harnisch, *Der jetzige Standpunkt*, p. 261.

In large part these advances were made possible by the fact that school financing in Prussia was on a more solid footing than it was in Bavaria. In the old provinces of Prussia the provisions of the 1794 civil code applied. A local community was clearly obliged by the code to establish and maintain a school and to supply it with a teacher. The code left open whether this was to be done by private philanthropy (religious or lay), through community taxes, or at the expense of the noble landowners as was the case in East Elbia. There were also the school fees, although in Prussia they provided for only twenty per cent of the cost of schooling, whereas in Bavaria it was approximately fifty per cent. None the less, ambiguities in financing were to plague Prussian schooling until uniform provisions for all the provinces could be established in a comprehensive school law. Meanwhile, state subsidies to local communities were considerably larger in Prussia than in Bavaria. The 7,200,000 thalers that came from Berlin in 1830 represented nearly five per cent of the total Prussian expenditure for schooling.[47] There was no Bavarian subsidy whatsoever.

Even on the question of having a sufficient number of teachers, Prussia's successes seemed noteworthy. Süvern had been the first to recognise the magnitude of the problem and had urged that it be addressed by training male orphans to become teachers. In 1831 Victor Cousin remarked that Prussia was still expecting orphans to enter teaching.[48] When in 1817 Prussia's pastors and school officials were asked to recommend pupils for the new Potsdam Seminar, they were instructed to 'look for the sons of poor parents, preferably the sons of teachers . . . boys, who because of their good and simple rearing, because of their moral character, their religious beliefs, because of their natural talents seem most suited to fill conscientiously the profession of teacher in the rural villages'.[49]

The number of teachers in Prussia grew by forty per cent between 1816 and 1846, the overwhelming majority of them coming from the peasant and artisan classes. That pattern continued to apply for most of the century. The case of the Neuzelle Seminar in Brandenburg is in this respect typical. From the time of its founding in 1819 until 1849, eighty-three per cent of Neuzelle's pupils were the sons of

47. Albert Lotz, 'Die Kosten der Volksschule in Preussen', p. 257.
48. Victor Cousin, 'Report on the State of Public Instruction in Prussia', p. 169.
49. Quotation in *Die Brandenburgischen Lehrerseminare und die Ihnen Angegliederten Präparandenanstalten*, ed. Friedrich Buchholz and Gerhard Buchwald, p. 23.

artisans (thirty per cent), peasants (twenty-three per cent), or teachers (thirty-two per cent). Most of the remaining fifteen per cent came from the lower classes as well, being the sons of factory workers, agricultural labourers, or church sextons. Only five per cent were the sons of lower or middle-level government officials.[50] An exception to this pattern was the experience of the Berlin Seminar which had been established in 1831 to specialise in training teachers for urban schools. Here the middle classes played a much larger role. Of the 958 pupils who attended the Berlin Seminar during its first two decades, 803, or eighty-five per cent, were the sons either of businessmen (420), teachers (245), lower level officials (114), or clergymen (16).[51] Elsewhere the Neuzelle pattern predominated.[52]

Despite Prussia's apparent success in recruiting teachers, shortages became apparent by the 1840s. While the number of teachers grew by forty per cent during the *Vormärz*, the number of pupils during that same period grew by 108 per cent.[53] Schooling was still unable to keep pace with the growth of the Prussian population. Thus the number of pupils per teacher grew steadily during these years. In 1844 Wilhelm Harnisch calculated that it would take 35,379 teachers to bring the ratio down to eighty pupils per teacher.[54] That alone would have required over 8,000 additional teachers. To recruit that number of new teachers in a short time was impossible. The pay was still very low. In 1820 it had been roughly at the level of the day labourer and there had been little improvement since. Most teachers earned fewer than 100 thalers a year, and thus lived, says Tony LaVopa, 'on the edge of real poverty'.[55] They were still heavily dependent upon the regular collection of school fees, upon free board, free firewood, and even simple charity. Those with a family to support often left teaching if an opportunity presented itself. In 1836 Carl Schurz's father was earning ninety thalers a year as a *Volksschule* teacher in the Rhineland when he quit to open a hardware store.[56] To encourage teachers, the government

50. Busshoff, 'Die preussische Volksschule', p. 389.
51. Douglas R. Skopp, 'Auf der untersten Sprosse: Der Volksschullehrer als "Semi-Professional" im Deutschland des 19. Jahrhunderts', p. 391.
52. Buchholz and Buchwald, eds, *Die Brandenburgischen Lehrerseminare*, p. 151; see also Josef Mooser, 'Sozial Mobilität und familiale Plazierung bei Bauern und Unterschichten', p. 187.
53. Koselleck, *Preussen zwischen Reform und Revolution*, p. 441.
54. Harnisch, *Der jetzige Standpunkt*, p. 269; also Tews, *Ein Jahrhundert*, p. 106.
55. Anthony LaVopa, *Prussian Schoolteachers*, p. 84.
56. Carl Schurz, *Reminiscences*, vol. I, p. 21.

during the 1840s cut their term of obligatory military service from three years to six weeks.[57]

The social status of the schoolteacher was correspondingly low, not in keeping with his growing self-image of entering into the circles, even if it were the outer ones, of the educated classes. For his livelihood he still depended heavily upon additional jobs, often as the church sexton, a position that merely underlined his subservience to the parish clergyman. Large-scale recruitment in such circumstances was difficult at best. By the 1840s Education Ministry officials were once again considering the possibility of recruiting into teaching the large number of non-commissioned officers retired from the army.[58]

In 1844 Wilhelm Harnisch pointed to another possibility: women. Among the advantages he saw was that their introduction into the schools could be accomplished 'without significant costs'.[59] Pedagogical theory, at least on the surface, seemed open to the idea of women teachers. Pestalozzi's main theoretical work was called *How Gertrude Teaches Her Children*. His famous method he had devised by drawing heavily upon the example of the mother as teacher. Moreover, Friedrich Froebel, the inventor of the *Kindergarten*, was saying during the late 1830s that women, because of their inherent sensitivity, were the natural teachers for his schools. There was precedent also in Bavaria. In 1799 a commission had recommended to Montgelas that the coarse behaviour so prevalent in the young might be countered most effectively by having women teach the small children. The Seminar for women established in Munich in 1814 was an attempt to implement the commission's proposal.[60]

Some early effort to recruit women had been made in Prussia as well. Two Seminars for Catholic laywomen had been established in the Rhine Province in 1832, and that same year a course for women was attached to the new men's Seminar in Berlin.[61] Private girls' schools (*höhere Töchterschulen*) occasionally offered pedagogical courses as part of their own curriculum. In 1837 the Province of Brandenburg defined the route by which women could qualify for

57. See the order of 16 May 1844 in Fr. Nüchter, 'Die geschichtliche Entwicklung der Lehrerbildung', p. 47.

58. Ibid.

59. Harnisch, *Der jetzige Standpunkt*, p. 272.

60. Berta Sachs, *Pläne und Massnahmen der Regierung des Königs Max I. Joseph im Mädchenschulwesen Altbayerns*, pp. 67–8.

61. Wilhelm Zimmermann, *Die Anfänge und der Aufbau des Lehrbildungs-und-Volksschulwesens am Rhein*, vol. III, p. 276.

teaching positions in the lower schools and in 1845 those legal guidelines were extended to all of the provinces.[62] Not many women were brought into teaching, however. In 1843 fewer than seven per cent (1,801) of Prussia's 29,631 teachers were women. During the next three years only fifty-five more were recruited, although the number of newly recruited men approached one thousand.[63]

Neither in Prussia nor in Bavaria (or in any other German state) did school-teaching ever become the female profession that it did in the United States. At the end of the century only fifteen per cent of Germany's *Volksschule* teachers were women. The figure for the United States was seventy per cent.[64] None the less, school teaching became during the 1840s the first, and for a long time the only, respectable profession open to girls from the middle classes.[65] Therefore, the Seminars for women, few as they were, consistently drew their pupils from these classes. As a Bavarian official of the time explained: in school-teaching 'daughters of respected families find an opportunity to add to the support of themselves and their families in an acceptable manner. . . .'[66] Not surprisingly, when the first stirrings of a German women's movement emerged in the 1850s, it was organised largely by women who had been trained as teachers. Women teachers also came to provide, as we shall see later, the first generation of that movement's leaders.

Efforts to recruit women into teaching remained half-hearted at best. The continuing economic stagnation of the *Vormärz*, together with the rapidly growing population, continued to supply young men in large numbers for the teaching force. During these years, teaching was at least a means to keep from sinking lower on the social scale. As we have seen, male Seminar pupils were regularly drawn from the social groups whose economic security and social status were being rendered most vulnerable to the pressures of population growth and economic stagnation — the peasants and the artisans. In Westphalia, for instance, officials noted that Seminar pupils were being recruited from the poorer elements of the

62. Pauline Herber, *Das Lehrerinnenwesen in Deutschland*, p. 29.
63. W. Dieterici, ed., *Die statistischen Tabellen des preussischen Staates nach der amtlichen Aufnahme des Jahres 1843*, p. 111.
64. Herber, *Das Lehrerinnenwesen*, pp. 115–25; David B. Tyack, *The One Best System; A History of American Urban Education*, p. 61.
65. Quoted in Barbara Greven-Aschoff, 'Sozialer Wandel und Frauenbewegung', p. 335.
66. Quoted in Joanne F. Schneider, *An Historical Examination of Women's Education in Bavaria*, pp. 156–7, n. 19.

peasantry, not from those more well-to-do. The same held true for recruitment among the artisans, not only in Prussia, but all over Germany.[67] Rather than an avenue of upward mobility, it would seem that teaching during the first half of the nineteenth century had become a means of hanging on to a social position.

Horace Mann, after his visit to Prussia in 1843, noted of women teachers that 'No necessity for them could be perceived'.[68] Neither was German pedagogical theory as kindly disposed toward women teachers as it appeared at first glance. Pestalozzi's model teacher may have been a woman, but it was men whom he trained to teach. Süvern, when he recommended the training of orphans as teachers, was referring to male orphans. Female orphans, he said, were ideally suited to become the wives of such teachers.[69] Also, Protestant areas were not favourably inclined towards hiring women as teachers. Catholic areas, with their tradition of female teaching orders, were much more open to the idea. Thus, when officials in Westphalia urged the establishment of Seminars for women, the Ministry located them in the Catholic cities of Münster and Paderborn. The pattern held for the rest of the century. As late as 1880 when Prussia had 6,848 women teachers, two-thirds of them were from Catholic Westphalia and the Rhine Province.[70]

Bavarian Catholics and Protestants responded to the idea of women teachers exactly as did their Prussian counterparts. Of the 313 women *Volksschule* teachers in Bavaria during the early 1850s only eight were Protestant.[71] Bavaria was seventy-per-cent Catholic, however, and so the relative figures are not surprising. In theory, at least, Bavaria had long been more disposed to the recruiting of women into teaching, as was witnessed in 1814 when a Seminar for women was established in Munich. But when the Bavarian school system did not expand rapidly enough to absorb the new women teachers, the Seminar was closed in 1826.[72] Not until 1872 was it re-established.

The most remarkable of the statistics gathered during the *Vormärz*, however, were those suggesting that eighty per cent of Prussia's

67. See Mooser, 'Soziale Mobilität und familiale Plazierung', p. 187; also Karl Bungardt, *Die Odyssee der Lehrerschaft*, pp. 91–2.
68. Mann, *Annual Reports*, p. 356.
69. Bruno Gebhardt, *Die Einführung der Pestalozzischen Methode in Preussen*, p. 68.
70. Ilse Gahlings and Elle Moering, *Die Volksschullehrerin*, p. 31, n. 3.
71. See statistics published in the *American Journal of Education*, 6 (1859), p. 292; see also Schneider, *An Historical Examination of Women's Education in Bavaria*, p. 147.
72. Sachs, *Pläne und Massnahmen*, p. 70.

children were attending school. Unquestionably, these figures are exaggerated. Nevertheless, they do reveal interesting variations in rural–urban and regional attendance patterns. School attendance was highest in the provinces of Saxony (ninety-three per cent), Brandenburg (eighty-seven per cent without Berlin), and Silesia (eighty-six per cent), and lowest in those of Prussia (seventy-two per cent), Pomerania (sixty-seven per cent), and Posen (fifty-nine per cent).[73]

Beckedorff long before had noted the difficulty of enforcing school attendance in the cities. Here the poorer classes were simply that much more concentrated, and that much more difficult to control. Berlin in particular was a magnet for Prussia's poor during the *Vormärz*. Its population of 180,000 in 1819 had grown to well over 400,000 by 1846. School attendance, to say nothing of the collection of school fees, became increasingly difficult to enforce as the numbers of day labourers, servants, and under-employed, or unemployed, craftsmen grew.[74] The greater proclivity toward 'moral degeneracy in these classes', had also been noted by Beckedorff.[75]

The annual expenditures of the Berlin government for its charity or free *Volksschulen* during the 1820s was about 3,000 thalers; by 1837 it was 35,783 thalers; ten years later, 88,300 thalers.[76] Still, thousands of children remained outside the system completely.[77] The situation was hardly better in other growing industrial cities where, according to Reinhart Koselleck, the 'demands of the state for general schooling actually stopped at the factory gate and at the domestic worker's front door'.[78] Although there were exceptions, few factory owners saw the need for an educated, or even literate, labouring force. The child labour laws of the 1820s and 30s, though they paid lip-service to school attendance, always qualified themselves by pointing out that their enforcement was intended to serve the interests of parents as well as those of factory owners.[79] It was to this reality that Frederick William III bowed in 1835 when he

73. See Harnisch, *Der jetzige Standpunkt*, p. 269.
74. Hermann Zwick, 'History and Development of the Common-School System of Berlin', pp. 245–6.
75. Ludolph Beckedorff, 'Einzelne vorläufige Notiz über das Berliner Schulwesen', p. 290.
76. Tews, *Ein Jahrhundert*, p. 107.
77. Benjamin M. Smith, 'Reverend Benjamin M. Smith's Report on Education in Prussia' (1839), p. 452.
78. Reinhart Koselleck, 'Staat und Gesellschaft in Preussen, 1815–1848', p. 107.
79. For the laws of 1827 and 1839, see *Das Elementarschulwesen in den Königlich Preussischen Staaten*, ed. F. W. Niedergesäss, pp. 197–8 and 200–1.

removed the police of the Rhine Province from direct enforcement of school attendance laws; henceforth their enforcement was to be left to the discretion of local administrative authority.[80]

Although the statistics suggest it to be so, it is unlikely that the attendance picture was much brighter in the countryside. There were still areas where outright resistance to schooling manifested itself, as was the case in several communities near Magdeburg where local officials absolutely refused to hire a teacher. The regularity with which some local governments restated attendance regulations suggests that these were often honoured only in the breach. As late as the 1870s ministerial officials in Berlin were still appalled at the numbers of rural clergymen school inspectors who failed to enforce school attendance.[81]

The recent claim that between 1815 and 1860 neither 'agricultural workers nor their children ever received, even briefly, systematic instruction'[82] may be extreme, but it is not without some substance. East Elbian estate owners, who had been among the most stubborn opponents of Süvern in 1819, continued to drag their feet on schooling throughout the *Vormärz*. Their patrimonial powers, even after emancipation, left the local church, police, court, and school largely dependent upon them. Although the civil code clearly made estate owners responsible for the schooling of peasants within their jurisdiction, the growing poverty of the 1830s and 40s increased the burden substantially. Evidence of collusion between lords and peasants to circumvent school attendance laws is not uncommon. Thereby the lord saved the cost of school fees and the peasant the labour of his children. At best the schooling of these children was regular only during a few of the winter months. Theodor von Schön, the governor of the Province of Prussia and a holdover from the Stein era, recalled spending a great deal of his time trying to force his noble compatriots into supporting the schooling of their peasants.[83]

Complicating the situation in both Prussia and Bavaria were the accumulating social tensions of the 1840s, which the crops failures of

80. For the Cabinet Order of 20 June 1835, see *Die Preussische Volksschule*, ed. E. von Bremen, p. 606.
81. Christa Berg, *Die Okkupation der Schule*, p. 50.
82. Hansjoachim Henning, *Sozialgeschichtliche Entwicklungen in Deutschland von 1815 bis 1860*, p. 192.
83. See 'Theodor von Schön' in *Allgemeine Deutsche Biographie* (*ADB*), vol. XXXII, pp. 781–92.

1845 and 1846 quickly transformed into a social crisis. Two cardinal factors shaped this crisis in Prussia: population growth and economic stagnation. Prussia's population grew from 10.5 million in 1817 to 16.1 million in 1847, nearly twice as fast as the rest of Germany and three times faster than the population in Bavaria. In the face of economic stagnation, the situation was becoming classically Malthusian, a fact noted by Malthus himself when he looked at Prussian census returns for 1817.[84]

Population problems and economic pressures were everywhere evident. The rural peasant villages, the leading feature of agricultural life, were 'plagued with excess labour, with large numbers of landless peasants or those with holdings too small to support themselves'.[85] Crime statistics for these rural areas, though unreliable, do show a steep increase in the number of crimes reported to have been committed by the pauperised masses. Thefts of wood, transgressions of forest and hunting regulations, and commissions of arson constituted eighty-five per cent of all crimes reported in 1835.[86] In the Province of Prussia the number of these crimes grew dramatically between 1836 and 1850. Having no industry to speak of, over a third of the population of this eastern province was living on potatoes by the early 1840s. Then came the crop failures of 1845 and 1846. Within three years the price of potatoes was to triple.[87] So was the crime rate. Statisticians noted the correlation.[88]

Most observers related these problems to schooling. Some saw schooling as the solution; others as the cause. Beckedorff had already seen a connection between the acts of youthful criminals and their lack of schooling. It was the neglect of schooling, particularly of religious instruction, that he cited as the cause of the rising crime rates. His ministry traced this neglect to the many children either being sent to work in the factories or being kept at home to do agricultural work.[89] As a partial remedy the Education Ministry reminded provincial governors in 1827 of the need to enforce school

84. Thomas R. Malthus, *An Essay on the Principle of Population*, pp. 162–3.

85. P. H. Noyes, *Organization and Revolution; Working-Class Associations in the German Revolutions of 1848–1849*, pp. 18–19. See also Werner Conze, 'Vom "Pöbel" zum "Proletariat", Sozialgeschichtliche Voraussetzungen für den Sozialismus in Deutschland'.

86. Dirk Blasius, *Bürgerliche Gesellschaft und Kriminalität*, p. 31.

87. Wilhelm Abel, *Agrarkrisen und Agrarkonjunktur*, p. 227.

88. Blasius, *Bürgerliche Gesellschaft und Kriminalität*, p. 30.

89. See its announcement of 2 October 1826 in *Elementarschulwesen*, ed. F. W. Niedergesäss, pp. 175–6.

attendance laws, although with the qualification that the interests of neither parent nor factory owner could be ignored.[90] Ultimately, the Child Labour Law of 1839 stipulated that no child under the age of nine was to work in a factory full-time, and that a child under the age of sixteen was to work no longer than ten hours a day. Although the law provided that school attendance laws were to be enforced, a special three-year attendance minimum was to be allowed for working children. The factory owner was to provide the school.[91] Not subject to the law were children from the rural villages, who were often hired out to herd sheep or cattle, or to be servants in the households or barns of the estate owner.

There were also those who saw schooling as the cause, not the cure, of social dislocation, and many of them had a direct line to Frederick William III. In 1837 the king was informed by one of his provincial officials that the present decline in religious and moral sensibilities was being produced by the schools, because it was there that 'the powers of reasoning' were being developed among the lower orders. That same year the Silesian provincial assembly advised the king that 'the growing immorality of the lower classes' was to be traced not to their economic needs, but to the 'educational system which is serving to deepen social cleavages that would otherwise heal over'.[92] Frederick William III, who so recently had expressed his pride in the advanced state of Prussian schooling, began to worry, as he had so long ago, about the dangers inherent in 'the simultaneous growth of intelligence and pauperism'. To Eylert he admitted that 'The experts have said and written so much pro and con that I have become quite confused'.[93]

Neither Frederick William III's confusion, nor the anger of those who rejected schooling, seem to have had much practical effect upon its actual course. Not until the deaths of Frederick William III and Education Minister Altenstein in the summer of 1840 did a full-scale reaction appear to have set in. Until then 'the reaction stood outside the school door . . . and attempted to get in at every crack. But to no avail',[94] said Johannes Tews, a leading liberal educational reformer

90. See the announcement of 27 April 1827, ibid., pp. 197–8.

91. For the law of 9 March 1839, see *Das Unterrichts-Wesen des Preussischen Staates*, ed. Ludwig von Rönne, vol. I, pp. 618–21.

92. For quotations, see Blasius, *Bürgerliche Gesellschaft und Kriminalität*, pp. 60–1.

93. Eylert, *Charakter-Züge und historische Fragmente*, vol. I, pp. 372–3.

94. Tews, *Ein Jahrhundert*, p. 113; see also Robert Rissmann, *Geschichte des Deutschen Lehrervereins*, pp. 7–8.

in late nineteenth- and early twentieth-century Germany as well as a historian of lower education in Prussia. The response in Prussia to the revolutionary wave of the early 1830s serves to illustrate his point. In contrast to Bavaria where King Ludwig used the disturbances to launch his campaign against school teachers, Prussian officials responded by attempts to strengthen schooling, particularly in Posen where improved schools were to enhance Flottwell's efforts at Germanisation. Moreover, the Education Ministry seemed satisfied to request of local authorities that they prevent teachers from making reference to political events in their classrooms.[95]

The relative mildness of this reaction can be explained in part by the fact that Friedrich von Altenstein was still the Education Minister. Altenstein represented a continuity with the reform era that had in most other areas of public policy been broken by the reaction of the 1820s. Thus, when Heinrich von Kamptz resigned in 1830 as Director of the Ministry's Instructional Division, Altenstein put Nicolovius back into that post, one that Nicolovius then held until his retirement in 1839. Throughout the 1830s, therefore, Pestalozzians continued to play a leading role in the Seminars and even in the Education Ministry. Beckedorff's successor in 1827 was K. A. Dreist, one of the fifteen students whose study with Pestalozzi during the reform era had been sponsored by Süvern. Dreist's successor in 1832 was J. W. Kortüm who had been a member of that same group. Although both Dreist and Kortüm, like Nicolovius, had become considerably more conservative, particularly on religious questions, they continued to resist attacks that focused upon Pestalozzi or the employment of his method.[96]

The action that more than any other attests the continuation of reform influence is the appointment in 1832 of Wilhelm Diesterweg to head the new Seminar established the year before in Berlin. Diesterweg, then forty-two years old, was well known as an outspoken opponent of the 'positive Christian' attitudes around which so much of Prussian conservatism was organising itself. As director of the Seminar at Mörs in the Rhine Province since 1822, and as editor of the pedagogical *Rheinische Blätter* since 1827, he had established himself as an impassioned nationalist and progressive in politics and as an outspoken champion of Pestalozzi in pedagogy.

95. For the announcement of 2 May 1831, see Hartmut Titze, *Die Politisierung der Erziehung*, pp. 133–4.
96. Harnisch, *Der jetzige Standpunkt*, pp. 77, 86.

He was to become known eventually as the 'Prussian Pestalozzi', and, according to Eduard Spranger, was 'a figure of pure enlightenment'.[97] The Berlin Seminar, which had been designed to meet the special needs of teachers in the cities, was expected also to become the model Seminar for the entire kingdom.[98] Under Diesterweg it was to become the best-known Seminar in Germany, as well as a mecca for foreign visitors.

The deaths in 1840 of Frederick William III and Altenstein, coming as they did shortly after Nicolovius' retirement, brought the formal end to an era that had begun with Tilsit in 1807. King Frederick William IV, much more intelligent and imaginative than his father, and much less capable of governing, appointed as his Education Minister Friedrich Eichhorn, the man who would come to exemplify the cultural reaction in Prussia in much the way that his contemporary Abel did in Bavaria. Ironically, Eichhorn's appointment was welcomed by Prussia's liberals. Eichhorn was considered a reformer. He had until recently worked in the Foreign Ministry on the creation of the *Zollverein*, a product of German economic liberalism, and was well known also as the advocate of reform in matters of Church governance.[99] Wittgenstein, who had exercised such great influence upon Frederick William IV's father, was in despair.

Of education and schooling Eichhorn knew very little, although he seems to have harboured some reservations about the social ambitions of school teachers. At least, such suspicions were harboured by those whom he appointed to critical posts in his ministry. His most trusted official in educational affairs was to be the arch-conservative Gerd Eilers whom he brought into the ministry in 1841. Eilers had been a school councillor in the government of the Rhine Province at Koblenz since 1833, and was a prime example of the kind of social mobility afforded by the emergence of the new educational bureaucracy.[100] His father had been a peasant in the Grand Duchy of Oldenburg where young Eilers had attended a *Volksschule*. With additional instruction from the pastor in his village, he qualified for theological studies which he pursued at Heidelberg and

97. Eduard Spranger, *Zur Geschichte der deutschen Volksschule*, p. 40.
98. For background, see Buchholz and Buchwald, eds, *Die Brandenburgischen Lehrerseminare*, pp. 168–72.
99. Gwendolyn Evans Jensen, 'Official Reform in *Vormärz* Prussia: The Ecclesiastical Dimension', p. 146.
100. See 'Gerd Eilers' in *ADB*, vol. V, pp. 756–8.

Göttingen. Upon completing these studies he became a Gymnasium director and, after 1833, a school councillor with responsibility for supervising teachers. It was because of this experience that Eichhorn brought him to Berlin in 1841.

Eilers was extremely critical of the Altenstein ministry. Its policies, he believed, had been predicated on the assumption that Christianity was something the modern, educated classes had managed to transcend and would now, through schooling, be transcended by the lower classes as well.[101] This assumption, Eilers believed, had determined appointments to the Seminars and to key posts in the upper levels of the educational bureaucracy. Efforts to separate the school from the Church he saw as the product of the same assumption. Thus the common people were being alienated from their religion. His immediate suspicions he directed at the Seminars, particularly the one in Berlin headed by Diesterweg. Here was being trained, he believed, a dangerous class of teachers, much over-educated for the modest station of the country's lower schools.[102]

Eiler's worst fears seemed substantiated when in 1842 he received a petition signed by dozens of teachers from Westphalia asking, on the one hand, to be freed from all their Church custodial duties, and on the other hand, to be given higher pay, representation on local school boards, and professional pre-Seminar training for future teachers.[103] The petition represented the kind of professional consciousness and status ambitions that Eilers disapproved of most. Even worse, it had been inspired by the leading Rhineland liberal and industrialist, Friedrich Harkort. Harkort was emerging during the early 1840s as a prominent spokesman for school improvement and for the professional independence of teachers. As such, he was to become a thorn in the flesh of Eilers and Eichhorn. In scores of pamphlets he publicised his view that schooling was the only possible solution to the growing social crisis, the only sure prophylaxis against revolution. 'In every newly born pauper who remains uneducated, society nurtures a new enemy', he wrote. 'The material goods of this world are divided; open the infinite domain of knowledge so that these citizens [paupers] can acquire a property. The study of language, literature, law, and morality will tie those so

101. Gerd Eilers, *Meine Wanderung durchs Leben*, vol. V, pp. 195–6.
102. Tews, *Ein Jahrhundert*, p. 116.
103. Bungardt, *Die Odyssee der Lehrerschaft*, p. 40.

instructed more securely to the Fatherland than several acres of land'.[104] To promote the cause, Harkort organised in 1843 an 'Association for the German *Volksschule* and for the Dissemination of Knowledge for the Common Good'. Although few industrialists shared his views, Harkort's association did acquire some 2,500 members and supported a 'Weekly Journal of the German *Volksschule*'.[105] Eichhorn, fearful of associations through which teachers would attempt to promote their status, forbade all such organisations.[106]

It was also in the summer of 1842 that the young director of the Neuwied Seminar in the Rhine Province, Ferdinand Stiehl, sent to Eilers a pamphlet he had published that was critical of any teacher-training that emphasised the imparting of knowledge at the expense of character-building.[107] Eilers was much impressed. Stiehl's background happened to be much like his own. Stiehl, too, had come from peasant stock, had been recognised as being very able, had been sent off to a Gymnasium, and finally to the university to study theology. In 1836, at the age of twenty-three, he had begun teaching religion at the Neuwied Seminar and a year later became its director.[108] In 1844 Eilers called him to the ministry in Berlin to take charge of school and Seminar affairs. Stiehl's hand became evident in March 1844 soon after his arrival in Berlin.

During the next months there began that long series of sporadic social eruptions that was to culminate four years later in the German-wide revolutions of 1848. In June 1844 some 5,000 weavers and peasants in Silesia rose in protest against the machines and factories that were reducing them to near-starvation. The revolt spread quickly to other artisans in the region, and then to Breslau, the provincial capital. From Breslau the revolt reached to Berlin where it set off strikes in the textile and locomotive factories.[109] Then, in July, a disgruntled provincial official, recently censured for misconduct, attempted to assassinate Frederick William IV.[110]

This was the setting in 1844 in which Eichhorn proposed the recruitment of non-commissioned officers into school-teaching.[111]

104. Friedrich Harkort, *Schriften und Reden*, ed. Karl-Ernst Jeismann, p. 417.
105 Bungardt, *Die Odyssee der Lehrerschaft*, p. 41.
106. Ibid., p. 38.
107. Zimmermann, *Die Anfänge und der Aufbau*, pp. 196–7.
108. Reinhard Lüdicke, *Die Preussischen Kultusminister und ihre Beamten*, p. 60.
109. Noyes, *Organization and Revolution*, p. 34.
110. *The Annual Register* (1844), pp. 276–7.
111. For the order of 16 May 1844, see Nüchter, 'Die geschichtliche Entwicklung

Presumably the loyalty and discipline represented by a corps of 'sergeant-teachers' would restore the *Volksschule* as a bulwark against a rising tide of social disorder. Ministry officials empowered to do the recruiting were able to promise those interested that they needed only two months of Seminar training to qualify for a teaching position. The recruitment drive was eventually carried over into 1845,[112] but it produced only meagre results. In the meantime, Harnisch's proposal that women be recruited into teaching was completely ignored.

Stiehl was at the same time turning his attention to the *Volksschule* curriculum and to the reading habits of the teachers. Once again the *Volksschule* curriculum came to be circumscribed, and by an order of June 1844 the list of books approved for use in the *Volksschule* was restricted to the Bible, a catechism, a hymnal, a reading primer, and a book for instruction in arithmetic.[113] As for the private reading of the teachers, school inspectors and supervisors were asked to look into what books teachers were reading and to enquire into their membership in reading clubs or circles. The purpose was to ensure that 'planless and corrupting reading and the inevitably accompanying intellectual shallowness (*Vielwisserei*) is avoided'.[114] Inspectors who encountered teachers with promiscuous reading habits were instructed to steer the offender away from them. Above all, care was to be taken to steer teachers away from readings in the natural sciences.[115]

That the attention directed at teachers was not misplaced seemed confirmed by several incidents of insubordination at the Seminars, the suspected source of many of the problems associated with schooling. On 13 October 1845 an incident occurred at the Protestant Seminar in Breslau that within three months led to its being closed down completely. The problem began harmlessly enough when Seminar Director Gerlach became angry with several of his pupils for causing a disturbance at a birthday celebration for Frederick William IV. When shortly thereafter two pupils were insolent to a teacher, Gerlach expelled them both summarily. The crisis began when the classmates of those expelled petitioned Gerlach to

der Lehrerbildung', p. 47.

112. Tews, *Ein Jahrhundert*, p. 116.
113. Theodore Ballauff and Klaus Schaller, *Pädagogik*, vol. III, p. 361.
114. Tews, *Ein Jahrhundert*, p. 118.
115. Rudolf Engelsing, *Analphabetentum und Lektüre*, p. 67.

reconsider his decision and he refused. Thereupon the whole class sent a petition to the Silesian Provincial School Commission demanding either the reinstatement of their friends or the expulsion of the entire class. Gerlach decided to set an example. With the approval of the provincial governor he expelled the whole class, an action that sent the entire Seminar into an uproar. Soon all of Breslau was caught up in it. Berlin authorities were exceedingly upset at this further evidence of insubordination in Silesia, coming as it did on the heels of the weavers' uprising of the year before. Frederick William IV was eager to condemn such behaviour. In December Stiehl came from Berlin to investigate. He visited classes, interrogated pupils and teachers, and looked carefully at the books that were being read.

On the basis of Stiehl's report Frederick William IV ordered the Seminar to be closed. At 10:30 on the morning of 29 January 1846, an official from the Silesian governor's office assembled the remaining pupils and their teachers into the Seminar's conference room to make the announcement. His Majesty has ordered, he said, 'the immediate closing of this Evangelical Teachers' Seminar because there has been found here in the recent disciplinary proceedings, and in the wake of the investigation that followed, a spirit of insubordination that does not conform with the purpose of teacher training'.[116]

Silesia during these years was believed to be rife with radical conspiracies. In one case suspicion came to be focused upon Wilhelm Wander, a *Volksschule* teacher in the town of Hirschberg in the Silesian Mountains, ominously close to the centre of the 1844 weavers' revolt.[117] Authorities were eventually to place Wander in a number of radical conspiracies. Wander was a graduate of Silesia's Bunzlau Seminar where both his political and pedagogical views had been stamped by the influence of Rousseau and Pestalozzi. Since coming to Hirschberg in 1827 he had been active in liberal political movements. He had begun by organising district festivals for teachers and local reading circles for his colleagues.[118] His objective, he said, was the 'emancipation of the teacher', a condition

116. Order of 29 January 1846 quoted in Christian Gottlieb Scholz, *Meine Erlebnisse als Schulmann*, pp. 243–7; for a summary of the incident, see LaVopa, *Prussian Schoolteachers*, pp. 127–30.
117. See 'Wilhelm Wander' in *ADB*, vol. XLI, pp. 139–43.
118. Scholz, *Meine Erlebnisse*, pp. 232–5.

he believed possible only if the *Volksschule* teacher were to be allowed to take his training at a university. This position he spelled out in detail in a pamphlet on 'The *Volksschule*' which, in order to escape the Prussian censors, he published under an assumed name in the Kingdom of Saxony.[119] It was in Leipzig that he also became acquainted with Robert Blum, a self-made radical journalist and democrat who was soon to emerge as a leader in the German radical left. None of these activities were a secret to authorities in Berlin. Most recently Wander had incurred Berlin's disfavour by his call for the creation of a German-wide association of teachers, a proposal to which Robert Blum had given his public support.[120]

In the spring of 1845 Berlin sent to Silesia secret police agent Wilhelm Stieber, disguised as an itinerant landscape painter, to investigate Wander's role in what was believed to be the Hirschberg conspiracy.[121] Stieber, who under Bismarck was to be the founder of a centralised German intelligence service, found evidence to implicate a Hirschberg industrialist in illegal political activities, but could find nothing to implicate Wander. Police then tried to link Wander to the nearby 'Warmbrunn Conspiracy' reputed to be dedicated to overthrowing the existing social order and replacing it with one based upon total social equality.[122] In March 1845 Wander's house was searched. Although evidence linking him to this newest conspiracy was also lacking, he was, none the less, suspended from his teaching position until 1855.[123]

In the meantime, a circumstance had developed in Berlin that finally allowed Eilers to undermine the position of Wilhelm Diesterweg, the man he believed most responsible for the many ills besetting German education. Eilers confided later on that he had been determined all along to get rid of Diesterweg because it was in his Seminar that were being produced those 'pretentious, arrogant, mis-educated teachers, completely alienated from Christianity'.[124] Eilers had repeatedly warned Diesterweg against his taking of positions contrary to official policy on Church–state

119. Bungardt, *Die Odyssee der Lehrerschaft*, p. 35.
120. Gottlieb Lüttgert, *Preussens Unterrichtskämpfe in der Bewegung von 1848*, pp. 74–5.
121. Wilhelm Stieber, *Spion der Kanzlers*, pp. 5–7 and 19–23; see also Walter Obenaus, *Die Entwicklung der preussischen Sicherheitspolizei*, pp. 132–3, and Scholz, *Meine Erlebnisse*, p. 263.
122. Noyes, *Organization and Revolution*, p. 43.
123. Franz Hofmann, *Karl Friedrich Wilhelm Wander*, p. 49.
124. Eilers, *Meine Wanderung durchs Leben*, vol. IV, p. 89.

matters, or encouraging the formation of teachers' associations.[125] In recent years, particularly, Diesterweg had been promoting the creation of Pestalozzi Associations to commemorate the 1846 centennial of the great pedagogue's birth. Eiler's chance to get even with Diesterweg came in 1846 when the name of Eduard Hintze, one of the instructors in his Seminar, appeared on a police list of radical leaders in Berlin. According to the police, Hintze was the leader of an organisation ostensibly dedicated to helping unemployed artisans, but one which in fact was corrupted, they said, 'by a leaning toward communism and atheism'.[126] Hintze managed to keep his position at the Seminar, but in late April 1847, in the midst of a major food riot in Berlin, Diesterweg was suspended. Soon thereafter two cabinet orders directed school officials to be sure that only teachers belonging to established Churches and with orthodox religious views be considered for employment, and that those who did not were to be dismissed from their posts.[127]

Thomas Nipperdey argues that the policies of Eichhorn, Eilers, and Stiehl contributed substantially to the radicalisation of Prussia's teachers during the 1840s, particularly because their policies evoked so much administrative resistance that they produced only what he calls a 'half-reaction'.[128] The government's closing of the Breslau Seminar, for instance, 'caused great dissatisfaction among teachers and schoolmen of the country', said the director of another Seminar.[129] At the very least, it is fair to speak of the increased politicisation of the teachers during the 1840s, as manifested in the spread of teachers' movements, associations, festivals, and reading circles. All of these activities were aimed at improving the income, the social status, and the professional identity of the teacher and to loosen his connection with the Church;[130] these were the very same objectives the government hoped to suppress.

The same pattern holds true for Bavaria. There the politicisation

125. Buchholz and Buchwald, eds, *Die Brandenburgischen Lehrerseminare*, p. 173.
126. Karl Haenchen, 'Zur revolutionären Unterwühlung Berlins vor den Märztagen des Jahres 1848', pp. 105–6.
127. Bungardt, *Die Odyssee der Lehrerschaft*, p. 39.
128. Thomas Nipperdey, 'Volksschule und Revolution im Vormärz', p. 132.
129. Dr Thilo, head of the Berlin Seminar, quoted in the *American Journal of Education*, 20 (1870), p. 415.
130. Douglas Skopp, 'The Elementary School Teachers in "Revolt"; Reform Proposals for Germany's Volksschulen in 1848 and 1849', and Anthony LaVopa, 'Status and Ideology: Rural Schoolteachers in Pre-March and Revolutionary Prussia'.

of teachers followed hard on the heels of Abel's efforts to strengthen the connection between the Work-Day Schools and the Church and, particularly, upon the domicile restrictions he placed upon teachers in 1846. To be sure, the concerns of most teachers, whether in Prussia or Bavaria, were likely to be more mundane than the political ones articulated by Diesterweg or Wander. Nevertheless, the events of 1848 were to demonstrate that teachers could be mobilised in large numbers for political ends.

5
Schooling and Revolution 1848–1866

The revolutions that swept through the German states in March 1848 drove from office most of those who had placed their stamp upon the decade. Abel was the first to go. He had become the object of Ludwig's displeasure in early 1847 for having objected to the growing influence of Lola Montez. A year later Ludwig himself was forced to abdicate. Lola once again was the immediate cause. In Prussia Eichhorn and Eilers were dismissed on 19 March when a frightened Frederick William IV barely managed to save himself by abandoning the conservative–monarchical principles for which he stood. He began by promising Berlin's revolutionaries a liberal ministry, a constitution, and a policy that would merge Prussia into a larger German unity.

The upheavals of 1848 were revolutions from below, the variety that had so frightened reformers early in the century. The same spectre had haunted the imaginations of Abel and Eichhorn, both of whom directed their policies at its excision. Not since the Reformation had an uprising in German lands been as widespread or as violent. In Bavaria the violence was centred in the regions of Franconia, Swabia, and the Rhine Palatinate, evidence that the integration policies pursued after 1815 had failed. In Prussia, the troubles outside Berlin were concentrated in the western provinces and in Silesia. So serious did the problem become in Silesia that in early April Bismarck expressed the fear that the province might be 'close to dissolution.'[1] The uprisings in the cities were led most often

1. Theodore S. Hamerow, *Restoration, Revolution, Reaction*, p. 110.

by the unemployed and underemployed artisans and journeymen whose livelihood and social status were being undermined by economic stagnation and by the early stages of machine production.

By June of 1848 the violence had largely spent itself, although by then nearly every prince in Germany had promised his subjects large measures of political participation and social change. By June of the following year, however, most of these same princes had regained sufficient political composure to begin rescinding piecemeal what the year before they had surrendered wholesale. They were also beginning to ask themselves what had gone wrong. Why had so many of their subjects engaged so wantonly in disobedience and rebellion?

The first extensive and widely-circulated answer appeared in 1851 with the publication of Wilhelm Riehl's *The Civil Revolution.* Riehl was a journalist of profoundly conservative convictions who had watched the revolutions from Baden and concluded that the blame for them lay squarely upon the village schoolteachers. How else could be explained the revolutionary behaviour of what was so widely believed to be an innately conservative and loyal peasantry? The 'perverse schoolmaster was in fact the evil demon', wrote Riehl, 'the Mephisto who led the peasant astray'.[2] But did not the schoolmaster come from this same conservative and loyal peasantry? If so, whence his perversity? From 'mis-education', charged Riehl. 'Only recently have governments . . . come to realize that through the mis-education of teachers they have created a whole army of rootless proletarians; the very spectre they fear so much among the literati and the intellectuals they have created in the schoolmaster'.[3]

Never again during the remainder of the century was the image of the revolutionary schoolteacher completely expunged from the German political imagination. The political reaction of the 1850s focused as clearly upon him as did the reaction of the 1820s upon the university student. The situation sent King Maximilian II of Bavaria, Ludwig's son, into panic. 'Help me against these radical schoolteachers', he appealed to the bishop of Würzburg.[4] An angry Frederick William IV was by the early 1850s being quoted as telling his Seminar faculties that they bore the responsibility for 'all the misery that visited itself upon Prussia during the year now past'.

2. W. H. Riehl, *Die bürgerliche Gesellschaft*, p. 133.
3. Ibid., p. 102.
4. Christian Weinlein, *Der Bayerische Volksschullehrer-Verein*, p. 9.

Although he did not actually say this, given Prussia's policies toward teachers during the 1850s, he might as well have done so. In literature, too, the radical schoolteacher became an important figure. The most revolutionary schoolteacher in German fiction, Konrad Tusky, was the creation of the novelist Friedrich Spielhagen, himself a former schoolteacher and a political liberal who aspired to literary realism. It is in Spielhagen's *Reih' und Glied* (1867), set in the German *Vormärz*, that Tusky comes to teach in the *Volksschule* in the village of Tuchheim, only to end up leading the peasants into revolt against noble landowners and the clergy.[5] Konrad Tusky was in fiction what authorities feared Wilhelm Wander might be in fact.

Wilhelm Riehl and Friedrich Spielhagen notwithstanding, there were very few Wilhelm Wanders in 1848, and almost certainly no Konrad Tuskys. Yet the image of the radical schoolteacher is not entirely unwarranted. There may not have been much fire, but there was a great deal of smoke. It was a Berlin Seminar student, Theodor Hielscher, who on 19 March 1848, shouted at Frederick William IV to remove his hat in respect for those who had died in the previous night's violence on the barricades.[6] It was the village schoolhouse that time after time during 1848 had served as a political assembly hall. Schoolteachers by the score stood for election in the wave of voting that came in April and May, and seven of them were ultimately elected to the Prussian constituent assembly. Even if Riehl's charge about 'mis-education' was accurate, the schoolteacher, next to the clergyman, would have been the best-educated man in most villages. It was from the clergyman, of course, and his authority as school inspector, that the *Volksschule* teacher was trying to break loose. That alone, Thomas Nipperdey suggests, was sufficient to connect him closely to the revolution.[7] Heinrich Busshoff goes so far as to claim that teachers in 1848 were the 'most dynamic and excitable element from within the lower classes'.[8]

There is more evidence of teacher radicalism for Prussia than for Bavaria. But then it must be remembered that Bavaria had had a

5. Friedrich Spielhagen, *In Reih' und Glied*; see also Kurt Böttscher, 'Das Bild des deutschen Lehrers in Literatur und Wirklichkeit'.
6. Veit Valentin, *Geschichte der deutschen Revolution von 1848–49*, vol. II, p. 578.
7. Thomas Nipperdey, 'Volksschule und Revolution im Vormärz', p. 140, n. 38; also G. Lüttgert, *Preussens Unterrichtskämpfe von 1848*, p. 57.
8. Heinrich Busshoff, 'Die preussische Volksschule als sozialer Gebilde und politischer Bildungsfaktor in der ersten Hälfte des 19. Jahrhunderts', p. 396.

constitution since 1818 and that the *Landtag* elected in 1845 stayed on through 1848. Thus there were fewer opportunities to stand for election. None the less, one of the leading agitators in Nuremberg was the Work-Day schoolteacher Wilhelm Diezel. In mid-March of 1848, at a meeting of teachers from Nuremberg and Fürth, he called for the abolition of the Bavarian monarchy a week before Ludwig abdicated. Under Diezel's leadership that same meeting produced a radical nine-point programme for political and educational reform. The large number of teachers arrested or punished in the reaction of 1849 is another indication, says W. K. Blessing, that by 1848 a liberal–national ideology had taken root in the Bavarian teacher corps and that teachers had often played significant roles in the year's revolutionary proceedings.[9] Douglas Skopp is also correct in cautioning that no more than one per cent of the teachers in Germany ever took part in any direct revolutionary action.[10] However, given the 9,000 teachers in Bavaria, and the 30,000 in Prussia, that percentage is large enough to count. Riehl was certainly wrong about teachers being the source of revolutionary sentiment among the peasants, but he was quite right in placing teachers among those whom he considered to be the 'forces favouring change'.

The teacher's circumstances necessarily placed him among those seeking change. A growing professional consciousness, rooted in the common Seminar experience, was evidence that the 'marginal journeyman's mentality', so decried by Natorp, was being transcended. Nowhere was this new consciousness awarded its due. In the village community the teacher was still clearly subservient to the clerical school inspector, who belonged, in Riehl's approving phrase, to the 'forces favouring stability'. For the teacher, emancipation could come only at the expense of these forces. Neither his income nor his status in the village met his growing sense of self-esteem. And at the highest political levels, the policies of neither Abel nor Eichhorn were calculated to elevate his status, his self-esteem, or his income. Rather than being the fomenter of discontent among the lower classes, the teacher, who himself came from these classes, shared their discontent and thus associated himself with it.

If evidence ever did exist of teachers being significantly involved

9. W. K. Blessing, 'Zur Analyze politischer Mentalität und Ideologie der Unterschichten im 19. Jahrhundert', p. 791.

10. Douglas R. Skopp, 'Auf der untersten Sprosse: Der Volksschullehrer als "Semi-Professional" im Deutschland des 19. Jahrhunderts', pp. 399–400.

in the violent outbreaks of 1848, it is likely to be lost for ever. They may have been quite active at the village level — Riehl certainly thought they were — but there were no *Volksschule* teachers among the notables who made decisions of import about German-wide, or even state-wide, political significance. Neither were any of them elected to the national assembly that was to meet in Frankfurt. This was an honour reserved for men of *Bildung*. None the less, seven *Volksschule* teachers were elected to the constituent assembly for Prussia.[11] With its sixty-eight peasant delegates, some of them illiterate, and twenty-eight artisans, the Prussian assembly was considerably more radical and representative of the lower classes than that in Frankfurt. The seven teacher–delegates consistently supported the liberal–radical faction in the assembly's proceedings, but they did not play much of a role in directing the course of those proceedings, even on matters related to schooling. Although we know their names, we know little else about them.

For Prussia's teachers the revolution began formally on 19 March when a frightened Frederick William IV dismissed his entire ministry, including Eichhorn and his aide, Eilers. Eichhorn's replacement was Maximilian Count von Schwerin-Putzar, the scion of one of Prussia's oldest families, whose moderate liberal credentials were enhanced by his being married to the daughter of Friedrich Schleiermacher. The head of the new ministry, Adolf Count von Arnim-Boitzenberg, also had connections with the tradition of Prussian reform; he was Stein's nephew. Teachers reacted quickly to the change. Berlin was soon inundated with petitions from newly constituted teachers' associations that were proposing, or demanding, reform. One of the first of these petitions came from a teachers' group in Westphalia, asking that Diesterweg be made an official in the Education Ministry. The request was immediately supported by teachers from Berlin. Schwerin turned down the request, but he did dispatch Ferdinand Stiehl to sound out Diesterweg on his ideas

11. From information provided by roll-call votes in *Stenographische Berichte über die Verhandlungen der zur Vereinbarung der preussischen Staats-Verfassung berufenen Versammlung*. The teachers, for whom only family names are given, were Gladbach, Schulze, Schönborn, Igel, Moldenhauer, Appelt, and Feldhaus. See also Donald J. Mattheisen, 'Voters and Parliaments in the German Revolution of 1848: An Analysis of the Prussian Constituent Assembly'; Valentin, *Geschichte der deutschen Revolution*, vol. II, p. 43; and Ernst Rudolf Huber, *Deutsche Verfassungsgeschichte seit 1789*, vol. II, p. 584; L. Rosenbaum, *Beruf und Herkunft der Abgeordneten zu den Deutschen und Preussischen Parlamenten, 1847 bis 1919*; Wilhelm Appens, *Die pädagogischen Bewegungen des Jahres 1848*; Adolf Matthias, 'Die Pädagogischen Bewegungen des Jahres 1848'.

about how to improve the Prussian *Volksschule*. It was an odd encounter. Diesterweg's response was entirely in character: discard the 'enslaving orthodoxy of Eichhorn', and replace the confessional schools with non-denominational ones so as to promote a 'unity of spirit' among all Germans.[12]

Diesterweg's views came to be widely publicised during this year of revolution. In April he joined the editorial board of the liberal *Nationalzeitung*. In his own *Rheinische Blätter* he urged newly-formed teachers' associations to demand the passage of a comprehensive school bill that would define schools as institutions of the state. Such a legal designation, he argued, would remove the influence of both the Church and the local community over the schools. He wanted financing, too, to come from the state.[13] Diesterweg's programme was soon to be elaborated upon by his one-time subordinate at the Berlin Seminar, Eduard Hintze. In mid-April Hintze offered a school reform programme that called for the creation of comprehensive and non-denominational schools and an end to all school fees, to clergymen school inspectors, and to the hated conduct lists. The final provision was that all school councillors in the Education Ministry be professional educators.[14]

The teachers' assemblies that were held in April all over Prussia found themselves in essential agreement with Diesterweg and Hintze. In Breslau teachers resolved that the *Volksschule* be elevated to an 'independent national institution'. In Berlin teachers adopted Hintze's programme in its entirety and added a demand that in the cities they be paid a minimum salary of 400 thalers.[15] In Halle, they made similar demands and in addition took an expressly anti-clerical stance. A Magdeburg newspaper reported of the Halle meeting that the 'presence of a clergyman seemed to poison the air'. At a second Halle meeting in June, teachers produced at least one demand[16] for the creation of a liberal political catechism and for a ceremony of political 'confirmation' to certify political maturity. At Preussisch-Eylau in the Province of Prussia, an assembly of several hundred teachers voted to have the county or *Kreis* school inspectors

12. Lüttgert, *Preussens Unterrichtskämpfe*, p. 61.
13. Ibid., pp. 55, 60.
14. Ibid., p. 62.
15. Ibid., p. 68; see also Konrad Fischer, *Geschichte des deutschen Volksschullehrerstandes*, vol. II, p. 253; Karl Bungardt, *Die Odyssee der Lehrerschaft*, pp. 47–8; and Valentin, *Geschichte der deutschen Revolution*, vol. II, p. 578.
16. Lüttgert, *Preussens Unterrichtskämpfe*, p. 68.

chosen by election and to restrict eligibility for the office to professional schoolmen. Similar sentiments were articulated by the teachers from Prenzlau who pointed to the 'disgrace of an entire estate of *Volksschule* teachers being supervised by members of an entirely different estate — the clergy'.[17]

Much of this activity was intended to influence the constituent assembly whose meetings began in Berlin on 22 May. The task of this assembly was, as the royal government phrased it, to 'come to an agreement [with the Crown] upon a state constitution'. When the delegates assembled for their opening session in the Great White Hall of the Royal Palace, they were presented with a draft constitution already prepared by the government. Articles 12 and 13 of this draft dealt with school matters. These were sufficiently vague, however, to allow the assembly to do almost anything it liked. 'Freedom of instruction is to be subjected to limitations only by legislation', said Article 13, although Article 12 also promised churches that their educational functions would not be tampered with.[18] Still unspecified was whether those functions included anything other than providing instruction in religion.

Questions about the *Volksschule* came before the assembly for the first time on 3 June when Education Minister Schwerin was asked whether the government actually intended to redefine schools as agencies of the state and whether it proposed finally to abolish all school fees. Schwerin was prepared with a long answer. No, the schools were to remain agencies of the local community. As such they could provide the ties that held the community together. He agreed that local laws might require modifications to strengthen the position of the schools. The question of school fees he avoided altogether, turning instead to the grievances of the teachers. At least one million thalers would be required to bring their salaries up to a minimally acceptable level, he explained. No such funds were now available, but he had recently asked the king and finance minister to see if some state money could not be provided for those teachers in most desperate need.

To deal with what he called the 'general agitation' so prevalent among teachers, reflected in the thousands of petitions pouring into his offices and those of the assembly, Schwerin announced a policy designed to channel this agitation into more orderly paths. A new set

17. Ibid.
18. *Stenographische Berichte*, vol. I, p. 2.

of county school conferences for teachers was to be held shortly. Here, under the leadership of school inspectors (he did not point out that these were usually clergymen), teachers were to deliberate on school questions and to elect deputies to higher-level conferences scheduled to be held later at the provincial level. At these conferences the teacher-delegates were to confer with Seminar directors and officials from the Education Ministry.[19]

Late in June Schwerin, along with the rest of the ministry, fell victim to the political crisis that followed the storming of the Berlin Armoury by radicals. His successor in the new government was the moderately liberal bureaucrat, Adalbert von Ladenberg, long an official in the ministry he now came to head.[20] Since 1839 Ladenberg had been head of the ministry's Protestant educational division, although differences with Eichhorn and Eilers served to limit his influence.[21] Upon Stiehl's arrival in 1844 his influence was even further reduced.

Ladenberg carried out most of Schwerin's plans for holding a two-tiered set of school conferences. Objections from the liberal left were no less vigorous for that reason. Diesterweg used his *Nationalzeitung* to denounce the conferences as government-supervised meetings. Others objected to their being dominated by clerical school inspectors.[22] In Berlin, however, the objections as well as the results of the conferences were simply ignored.

On July 11 the assembly received from its major committee a draft constitution. Its three school articles had been prepared by a sub-committee, which did not, incidentally, include any one of the assembly's school teacher delegates. The draft articles proposed that the *Volksschule* remain a community institution financed primarily by the community. There were to be no school fees, however, and the possibility of state subsidies was broached. Clerical supervision in all of its forms was to be ended. Ultimately a comprehensive school law was to be drawn up within this constitutional framework.[23]

Liberals inside and outside the assembly found the draft's school

19. *Die Gesetzgebung auf dem Gebiete des Unterrichtswesens in Preussen*, p. 126.
20. Reinhard Lüdicke, *Die Preussischen Kultusminister und ihre Beamten im ersten Jahrhundert des Ministeriums, 1817–1917*, p. 607.
21. Gerd Eilers, *Meine Wanderung durchs Leben*, vol. IV, p. 65.
22. Hugo Gotthard Bloth, *Adolph Diesterweg*, p. 162; see also *Stenographische Berichte*, vol. I, p. 345.
23. *Stenographische Berichte*, vol. I, p. 631.

articles inadequate. Twenty-one of the assembly's delegates immediately formed a sub-committee to propose an alternative set of school articles. Co-opting to themselves Diesterweg and a prominent Gymnasium teacher, this committee produced a school programme that managed to distil into its seven points the essence of nineteenth-century pedagogical liberalism: (1) the school was to be a state institution, (2) instruction was to be based on general human, civic, and national ideals, (3) religious instruction in the schools was to be non-confessional, (4) anyone who qualified was to be allowed to teach, (5) instruction was to be without fee, (6) schools at all levels were to be supervised by the state, and (7) a comprehensive school law was to be the means by which the principles were to be implemented.[24] Thus matters stood in late July.

In Bavaria the great symbolic event of the revolution was the abdication on 20 March of King Ludwig. His successor was the thirty-seven-year-old Crown Prince who became Maximilian II. Two days later the *Landtag* went into session to consider reform legislation. These events had been preceded by widespread unrest in areas of Franconia and the Rhine Palatinate. Evidence of teacher involvement in this unrest, though less immediate than in Prussia, is clear. Abel's policies during the decade had politicised many teachers and rendered most of the rest susceptible to political mobilisation.

Bamberg and Nuremberg were the major radical centres in 1848; the Rhine Palatinate became so in 1849. In Nuremberg a huge demonstration had taken place on 2 March, shortly after the arrival of news from Paris of the abdication of Louis Philippe. Among the leaders of the demonstration was the teacher Wilhelm Diezel, the democratic agitator who wanted the monarchy overthrown and who urged Franconians to fight against 'Bavarianism' with a larger 'Germanism'.[25] On 12 March the teachers of Nuremberg and Fürth produced an 'Appeal to All the Teachers in Bavaria' asking them to demand the restoration of their domicile rights, schools free of Church influence, legal status as state servants, training in univer-

24. Deutsches Zentral Archiv (DZA) II Merseburg, Rep. 92, Mühler, IV, 1; see also Lüttgert, *Preussens Unterrichtskämpfe*, p. 72; and Bungardt, *Die Odyssee der Lehrerschaft*, p. 52.

25. Heinz Gollwitzer, 'Die politische Landschaft in der deutschen Geschichte des 19./20. Jahrhunderts', p. 535.

sities, representation in the *Landtag*, a role in curriculum formulation, an end to school fees, higher salaries, and a comprehensive school law.[26] A week later, on the day of Ludwig's abdication, these same teachers submitted to the *Landtag* a lengthy address pointing out that the uplifting of schools and their teachers was 'the sacred duty of governments'. The address went on to claim that a 'state that has good schools requires fewer soldiers, fewer prisons and poor houses, less expenditure for judicial systems, and, that in times of social unrest, the education of the many is the sole guarantee of law and order'. The document ended by condemning the last two decades of school policy. Though Abel was not mentioned by name, there could be no question that references to 'backward steps taken', and 'one-sided religious instruction', were directed at him.[27]

Bavaria's teachers, like their colleagues in Prussia, spent much of the spring and summer of 1848 producing petitions for the *Landtag* in Munich and the Parliament in Frankfurt, and drafting appeals to each other for unity. Meeting after meeting repeated the pattern set by the Nuremberg petition.[28] One of the few original demands came from the teachers of Kulmbach in Upper Franconia who added the call for the creation of a German-wide association for teachers.[29]

Ripples of unrest spread into the Seminars.[30] Again the centres were in Franconia. None of the unrest was serious, although in the instance of the Schwabach Seminar near Nuremberg it could easily have become so. The problem began, one of the Seminar's pupils recalled, when he and his peers were urged by a fervently nationalistic teacher to form a volunteer free corps. Soon the boys were drilling daily in the Seminar's courtyard. Their ambition was to receive weapons from a nearby armoury. The unit's first mission came when the boys, though without weapons, took it upon themselves to march upon the local jail to free a newspaper editor who had been imprisoned for unknown political reasons. Soldiers were called in to disperse the Seminar's unit. Though no shots had been

26. Hans Rall, 'Die politische Entwicklung von 1848 bis zur Reichsgründung 1871', p. 233. See also Josef Neukum, *Schule und Politik*, pp. 154–5; Weinlein, *Der Bayerische Volksschullehrer-Verein*, p. 3; and Rainer Roth, *Politische Bildung in Bayern*, p. 157.

27. Bayerisches Hauptstaatsarchiv (BHStA), MK 22994 (Verhältnisse der Schullehrer).

28. Weinlein, *Der Bayerische Volksschullehrer-Verein*, p. 5.

29. J. F. Ludwig, *Ein Lehrerleben*, p. 54.

30. Joseph Heigenmooser, 'Aus der bayerischen Volksschulgeschichte des 19. Jahrhunderts', p. 409.

fired, the unit's organiser suddenly realised how dangerous a game was being played. To cover himself, he ordered all of the pupils in the unit to write to their parents for permission to take the risk of being killed. 'Thus did our military activities come to an end', recalls the participant, who went on to become a teacher and then a county school inspector for more than half a century.[31]

Teachers' hopes were buoyed in early August when news reached them from Dresden of Wilhelm Wander's dramatic appeal at the Saxon Teachers' Congress for the formation of a German-wide teachers' association. 'At St. Paul's Cathedral in Frankfurt is being constructed the edifice of German unity and freedom', Wander had told the assembly of 800 Saxon teachers. 'But what good will this wonderful edifice be, if it is not inhabited by the right spirit. . . . Let us work together as brothers on the great task entrusted to us: the creation of the German *Volk*'.[32] An All-German Teachers' Association was created in late September 1848 in Eisenach in the Grand Duchy of Saxe-Weimar, where some 300 *Volksschule* teachers had gathered to accomplish this most grandiose of their organisational ambitions. At the conclusion of their conference they joined in a festive march to the nearby Wartburg to pay homage to Martin Luther's contributions to German cultural unity. Along the route they cheered the exiled republican leader Friedrich Hecker, who had been in Switzerland since the collapse of the German republic he had proclaimed earlier that year.[33]

The Frankfurt Parliament, in the meantime, had passed a set of resolutions regarding schooling that augured well for teacher interests. Schools, the Parliament had declared, should be independent of the Church and be supervised by officials of the state. Before deciding upon how to implement these principles, the Parliament's school committee intended to await the results of a nationwide *Volksschule* Teachers' Congress scheduled to be held in Frankfurt in mid-October. Ten teachers from Bavaria attended this conference, and most of the other delegates came from the south German states. Teachers from Prussia, where the reaction had begun to settle in, were forbidden by the government to attend. The Congress in Frankfurt adopted what had by now become the standard educa-

31. Joh. Friedr. Methseider, *Erinnerungen aus meinem Leben nach einem 53-jährigen Dienste in der Schule*, pp. 6–7.
32. Wander quoted in Bungardt, *Die Odyssee der Lehrerschaft*, pp. 49–50.
33. Lüttgert, *Preussens Unterrichtskämpfe*, p. 75.

tional resolutions: schools were to be state institutions and teachers were to be state servants paid from the state treasury; clergymen were to be excluded from school supervision which was to be reserved for professional and experienced personnel.[34] Although the Parliament generally ignored these resolutions,[35] liberals remained hopeful when its Declaration of the Fundamental Rights of the German People called for state control of education.

The rumour that the government was preparing a school law consistent with the Declaration of Fundamental Rights led several hundred teachers, mostly from southern Bavaria, to convene hastily in Munich shortly after Christmas. Their purpose was to add to the pressures they saw building for a liberal school law. The petition they addressed to the government stressed their belief that schools be state, not community, institutions. Only as state institutions, they argued, could the schools have a civilising effect upon the local community. Their status ambitions were manifested in their request that the Seminars be replaced by three-year pedagogical courses conducted at the universities. They requested also a minimum annual salary of 300 gulden (roughly 200 thalers) and free living quarters.[36]

The seemingly bright prospects for liberal school reform were quickly transformed into portents of disaster by the exigencies of Bavarian politics. A storm of protest had been let loose when the lower house of the new *Landtag*, elected in January 1849 on the basis of a reformed suffrage law, voted without reservation to accept the fundamental rights enumerated in Frankfurt. Too much was being surrendered to Frankfurt, and therefore Prussia, said many of its critics, some of whom still favoured German unity in different form. When the *Landtag*'s upper house voted to reject the Frankfurt declaration, Maximilian II, who also opposed it, used the occasion to dissolve the lower house. Maximilian II's objective was to retreat as quickly as possible from any further commitment to participating in a German unity. On 23 April 1849 he informed the Frankfurt Parliament that Bavaria rejected both its declaration of rights and its constitution.

34. K. Fischer, *Geschichte des deutschen Volksschullehrerstandes*, vol. II, pp. 255–7; Weinlein, *Der Bayerische Volksschullehrer-Verein*, p. 5.

35. Rudolf Murtfeld, *Der Weg der preussischen Volksschullehrerschaft zum Dienst am deutschen Volke, 1815–1871*, pp. 104–5.

36. Weinlein, *Der Bayerische Volksschullehrer-Verein*, pp. 6–7; Paul Schramm, *Hundert Jahre bayerische Schulgeschichte*, p. 33.

Within a week Bavaria was on the verge of civil war. Its centres were again in Franconia, and this time also in the Rhine Palatinate. Huge protests were mounted in Bamberg and Nuremberg with the radical democrats providing much of the leadership. The threat of peasant unrest in the Franconian countryside frightened Munich into sending troops.[37] More serious troubles were brewing in the Rhine districts, however. On 2 May, in Kaiserslauten, a demonstration of some 12,000 to 13,000 people called for total disobedience to the Bavarian government until it had accepted the Frankfurt constitution. That same day there was created in the Palatinate a provisional revolutionary government which committed itself to continuing the revolution begun the year before. With his troops committed in Franconia, Maximilian II had no choice but to call upon Prussia to put down the rebellion, a task that took the Prussian army until the end of June.

Volksschule teachers, the Munich government soon discovered, had played a disproportionately large role in the Palatinate uprising. Although unrest had been most prevalent in regions with economic difficulties, government investigators discovered that sympathy for the Frankfurt constitution was evident in all classes, and particularly among *Volksschule* teachers.[38] More than any other social group, they were found to be solidly aligned in its support. Two *Volksschule* teachers were also found among the thirty-nine leaders of the revolutionary government; a sizeable number of teachers were among the 333 revolutionaries who were charged with political crimes, and 208 teachers were among those eventually punished for having participated in the uprising.[39]

In Prussia the reaction had begun to set in in the autumn of 1848, much earlier than in Bavaria. A great symbolic turning point had come in October when the constituent assembly voted to remove the phrase 'by the grace of God' from the royal title. Frederick William IV became furious at this attack upon what he considered the divine origin of his authority. When news reached him shortly thereafter that the Austrian emperor's troops had retaken Vienna, he was sufficiently emboldened to bring his own soldiers back into Berlin.

37. Rudolph Stadelmann, *Social and Political History of the German 1848 Revolution*, pp. 180–1.

38. Christoph Klessmann, 'Zur Sozialgeschichte der Reichsverfassungskampagne von 1849', p. 309.

39. Ibid., pp. 311–12; see also Heigenmooser, 'Aus der bayerischen Volksschulgeschichte', p. 409.

On 10 November he used these soldiers to force the constituent assembly to leave Berlin and to continue its deliberations in the much smaller city of Brandenburg. In Brandenburg the assembly would be out of touch with its supporters in the capital. Finally, on 5 December 1848, the king dissolved the assembly completely, and promulgated his own constitution.

For a document produced by counter-revolution, Frederick William IV's constitution was surprisingly liberal, a fact for which one of its principal authors, Education Minister Ladenberg, bears considerable responsibility.[40] Most important for liberals was the constitution's provision for a two-house legislature, with the lower house to be elected by universal and equal male suffrage. The constitution's school articles (18–23) were equally liberal. Even Diesterweg was willing to admit that 'the [school] articles of the imposed constitution do represent a big step forward; who can deny it?'[41] The teachers of Breslau immediately made plans to send a delegation to the king thanking him for his service to the schools.[42]

The constitution stipulated that the state would guarantee teachers an adequate salary and provide financial subsidies to communities too poor to support their schools adequately. The *Volksschulen* were to be tuition-free. Only professionally qualified persons were to be eligible to teach in them. Moreover, teachers were to have the same rights as state servants, although not their formal status. Article 20 provided that school supervision was to be carried out by 'state appointees'.[43] Ladenberg later explained that some of these provisions had been left deliberately vague. There was no reason, for example, why clergymen could not be state appointees. He explained also that controversial and 'inappropriate definitions' of the schools as agencies of the state, the community, or the Church had been avoided altogether.[44]

A signal of things to come was evident when Ladenberg warned teachers in late December to refrain from letting political events interfere with their school duties. Apparently schoolchildren in Berlin had spent as much of the year in the streets as they had in the

40. Hans-Joachim Schoeps, *Preussen*, p. 201.
41. Diesterweg to Langenberg, 20 December 1848, in Bloth, *Adolph Diesterweg*, p. 255.
42. Christian Gottlieb Scholz, *Meine Erlebnisse als Schulmann*, p. 271.
43. Ernst Rudolf Huber, *Dokumente zur deutschen Verfassungsgeschichte*, vol. I, p. 387.
44. See Ladenberg's 'Erläuterungen', in Gerhardt Giese, *Quellen zur deutschen Schulgeschichte seit 1800*, pp. 140–4.

classrooms. At the same time he ordered all the provincial governors to make certain that schoolhouses were no longer used for political meetings.[45] Signals came from other sources as well. On 14 November the German bishops meeting in Würzburg issued a statement reiterating their stand on educational questions. 'Among the prerogatives of the Church, the God-given right to teach and educate stands at the top',[46] the bishops proclaimed. Obviously the Bavarian bishops had no intention of following in the direction that Prussia, and Bavaria, seemed to be taking.

The full reaction in Prussia did not take hold until after Prussia's diplomatic defeat at Olmütz in November 1850. The Frankfurt Parliament was still in session in early 1849; the elections to the first Prussian *Landtag* produced no conservative majority, and Ladenberg was hard at work drafting a school bill to present to the *Landtag*.

To advise him on this bill, particularly in regard to its teacher-training provision, Ladenberg scheduled a conference of Seminar personnel to be held in January 1849.[47] Liberal teachers had hoped that delegates to this conference would be elected, an idea Ladenberg rejected out of hand with the argument that such elections would 'take too much time'.[48] Instead, he picked the delegates himself, nine of them Seminar directors and four Seminar teachers. Each of the provinces was represented, but the only delegate solidly associated with liberalism was Hintze of the Berlin Seminar.[49] To chair the conference Ladenberg picked Ferdinand Stiehl, recently promoted to the rank of Privy Councillor for *Volksschule* and Seminar Affairs.

Legend has long maintained this to be the conference at which Frederick William IV blamed the Seminars for 'all the misery that has been visited upon Prussia during the year now past. . . .' He did nothing of the sort.[50] Stiehl opened the conference undramatically on 15 January by presenting the delegates with a set of twenty-two proposals that became the basis for the two-week-long discussions.[51]

45. Lüttgert, *Preussens Unterrichtskämpfe*, pp. 77, 59.
46. *Volksschulwesen und Kirche in Bayern*, p. 2.
47. For Ladenberg's order of 13 December 1848, see *Die Gesetzgebung*, p. 136.
48. Ibid.; see also Johannes Tews, *Ein Jahrhundert preussischer Schulgeschichte*, p. 125.
49. Friedrich Adolph Wilhelm Diesterweg, *Sämtliche Werke*, vol. VIII, p. 203.
50. See Bernhard Krueger, 'Die Rede Friedrich Wilhelms IV. vor den Teilnehmern der Seminarlehrerkonferenz 1849'. Krueger concludes that the Camarilla is likely to have invented the speech and given it to the press, from where it entered into collections of Frederick William IV's speeches and writings.
51. F. W. Dörpfeld, 'Die Schulkonferenz im preuss. Unterrichtsministerium', p.

Essentially his proposals called for the strengthening of the Seminar, albeit along confessional lines, and for the possibility of Seminar graduates becoming eligible for special one-year courses to be established at the universities. The atmosphere at the conference evidently remained cordial. Diesterweg attended several of the evening social gatherings, and one witness, at least, found these occasions to be lively and friendly.

Two days into the conference, on 17 January, the teachers' delegation from Breslau arrived in Berlin for its audience with Frederick William IV. In the delegation was Christian Scholz, a teacher in the Breslau Seminar until its closing in early 1846 and since then the head of a private Seminar for girls. During 1848 Scholz had become active in Breslau's moderate constitutional party. He recalls being anxious about the reception the king would give to a delegation of teachers. The audience certainly would have given him the perfect occasion to say whatever was on his mind. Rather than castigating teachers, as legend has it, Frederick William IV delivered no more than a mild rebuke. 'By and large, during the recent excitement against my government, teachers did not conduct themselves in such a way that I would be able to express my satisfaction', he told the delegation. 'I do not want to place upon your shoulders the blame that belongs to your colleagues, but it is my expressed will that the Seminars produce teachers who respect my government'.[52] Scholz was relieved. Though teachers were not being absolved entirely of responsibility for the recent troubles, neither were they being held totally responsible.

The outcome of the Seminar conference was in some respects a relief to liberals. Stiehl's proposals were changed very little. The liberals had expected that the Seminars were to remain confessional. What pleased them most was that the Seminars were also to be maintained as boarding schools and to remain in medium-sized cities. Thus the pupils would not be completely isolated from modern reality. The prospect of additional study being allowed at the universities did not displease them either.[53] It was conservatives who were the most bitter. From retirement Eilers wrote of his 'deep sadness' at the outcome of the conference. Its decisions seemed to

---

298; for a list of Stiehl's proposals, see *Die Gesetzgebung*, pp. 137–43.

52. Scholz, *Meine Erlebnisse*, p. 270.

53. K. Fischer, *Geschichte des Deutschen Volksschullehrerstandes*, vol. II, pp. 275–6; Giese, *Quellen*, pp. 135–6.

him calculated to produce teachers who would 'make of the revolution something permanent'.[54] Moreover, rumours he was hearing about Ladenberg's school bill filled him with dread.[55]

The truly reactionary proposals during this period came not from the government, but from the Churches. Understandably, they saw the events of 1848 as constituting one long attack upon their prerogatives, and much of their bitterness was directed at the teachers who had been so vocal in their resentment of the Church's role in school supervision. These resentments were vented at the numerous bishops' conferences and synodal meetings of 1849 and 1850. The 1851 meeting in Breslau of the Evangelical Church of Silesia is typical in this respect. The Seminars were blamed for 1848, particularly for having failed to produce 'a teachers corps that is pious and loyal'.[56] As remedies the Evangelical delegates proposed strengthening the traditional ties between the *Volksschule* and the Church and granting a greater role to the clergy in preparing pupils for entry into the Seminars. Other Church meetings produced other suggestions, including ones to eliminate the Seminars entirely, or for placing them under direct Church control.

The government at first seemed little inclined to heed such advice. Even the appearance of doing so was likely to stir up some resistance. In one case, when Frederick William IV ordered local officials to report on the activities of teachers outside the schoolrooms, the authorities in Berlin and Breslau simply refused to comply, saying that the revolution had ended the need for such conduct reports.[57] For two years the arch-conservative newspaper, the *Berliner Zuschauer*, published denunciations of teachers it suspected of revolutionary or liberal sentiment, but the government took little notice and even less action.[58]

When in January 1850 the government issued a more conservative version of its December 1848 constitution, the articles that referred to schooling were left basically unchanged. The only difference was that the new constitution stipulated that, whenever possible, the *Volksschule* was to have a confessional identity.[59] As yet there was no reason to expect Ladenberg's comprehensive school bill to sac-

54. Gerd Eilers, *Zur Beurtheilung des Ministerium Eichhorn*, p. 114.
55. Anita Mächler, 'Aspekte der Volksschulpolitik im 19. Jahrhundert', p. 237.
56. DZA II, Merseburg, Rep. 76 VII, neu Sekt 1C, Gen Teil I, Nr. 1, vol. V, p. 334.
57. Lüttgert, *Preussens Unterrichtskämpfe*, pp. 77–8.
58. Karl Müller, 'Lehrer in der Revolutionsbewegung des Jahres 1848'.
59. Huber, *Dokumente*, vol. I, pp. 386–7 and 403.

rifice the apparent gains of 1848. Nothing was to come of his bill, however.[60] Although a draft version was completed by October 1850, Ladenberg, along with the entire ministry of Count Brandenburg, resigned in December in the face of the diplomatic humiliation visited upon it by the Austrians at Olmütz. To replace Ladenberg, the new Manteuffel government named an extreme reactionary who had no intention of drafting a school bill of any sort. With Olmütz the final seal was placed upon the revolutionary epoch begun in March 1848.

In Bavaria Olmütz was celebrated for reducing Prussia's influence in German affairs, and thereby enhancing the prospects for Bavaria to establish herself as the political base for a third Germany. No less essential than this political base was the creation of a strong sense of Bavarian identity. The assignment to create that identity was very consciously given to the schools. It is not surprising, therefore, that during the decade following the revolution, Bavaria produced the most significant advances in schooling since the days of Montgelas. The initiative the state had lost to the Church under Ludwig was regained. The school attendance law of 1802 was for the first time vigorously enforced; a seventh year of schooling was required of Catholic children, and teacher-training regulations were redesigned to improve the teachers' effectiveness in the classrooms. It is fair to say that the reaction of the 1850s completed what the reformers of the first decade had left incomplete.

Maximilian II's panic of early 1849, during which he appealed to the Church for help against the schoolteachers, proved to be short-lived. After regaining his composure, he was to emerge as an intelligent and perceptive statesman. Although the competition was not notably stiff, he may have been the most able German monarch of the century. In Bavarian history he had the misfortune of being sandwiched between a father notorious for his philandering and a son famous for his madness. Conservative, flexible, realistic, Maximilian II demonstrated that he was eager to learn and capable of doing so.

Before Olmütz allowed him to breathe more easily, Maximilian II had come to see Bavaria's basic problem in much the same way that his grandfather had seen it: that of preserving Bavaria's exist-

60. See *Die Gesetzgebung*, pp. 162–87, for the full text of the bill. Paras 1–95 deal with the *Volksschule*.

ence. To the outside world that existence had to be maintained against the pressures of the German national idea; to the inside, against the pressures of Franconian and Palatine regionalism, and against the continuing dangers generated by widespread poverty. It was to this understanding of Bavaria's situation that Maximilian II's policies came to be geared.

As head of his first government, Maximilian II named the politically conservative Ludwig von der Pfordten, a Franconian Protestant, and an advocate of the Trias policy. In June 1849, even before the dust had settled after the Palatine revolt, Pfordten's government began seeking advice on how to bring the regions of Bavaria back together. Dignitaries and notables, clerical and lay, were asked to submit proposals on 'the most appropriate means and methods of awakening a Bavarian national consciousness'.[61] For the next few years, this request yielded countless suggestions: for the reform of education, the sponsoring of popular festivals, the erection of public monuments and the commemoration of important persons.

On the social question, too, Maximilian solicited advice. Already in November 1848 his government had announced an essay competition on the question: 'By what means can the material misery of Germany's lower classes, and in particular those of Bavaria, be most expeditiously and permanently relieved?'[62] Six hundred and fifty-six essays were submitted. The prize was awarded to an Augsburg civil servant who had argued that the point of departure for any solution had to be the recognition that the old world of feudal social divisions was 'irretrievably gone'. In their place, he said, the state must establish 'new and organic divisions that are more than reflections of the rule of money'.[63] Religion, he suggested, could be used 'to refasten the loosening bonds between the various social classes';[64] certainly the 'moral improvement of the lower classes was a precondition to improving their material circumstances'. Such moral improvement could only be accomplished by improvements in schooling, he concluded. Maximilian II read with special interest the recommendations for the improvement of schooling, underlining in pencil those which urged strict enforcement of attendance laws,

61. BHStA, MInn 45987.
62. Günther Müller, *König Max II und die soziale Frage*, p. 32.
63. Quoted in Wolfgang Zorn, 'Gesellschaft und Staat im Bayern des Vormärz', p. 139.
64. G. Müller, *Konig Max II*, p.43

better preparation of teachers, and the adoption of a curriculum that taught useful skills as well as religion, and by means more advanced than those of rote memorisation.[65]

Maximilian had long been concerned with these kinds of questions. As a young man he had surrounded himself with intellectual counsellors, remarking that had he not been born to be king, he would have liked to be a professor.[66] His chief adviser since their student days together at the University of Berlin was Wilhelm von Doenniges who still arranged during the 1850s to have the lectures of their old teacher, Leopold von Ranke, transcribed and sent to Munich. Maximilian was also one of the first in 1851 to read W. H. Riehl's analysis of the 1848 revolution. Riehl was immediately invited to Munich to lecture at the university on the subject of politics and to take charge of government relations with the press. He was to spend the rest of his career in the service of Bavaria. Riehl also became one of the experts invited regularly to the royal residence for evening seminars that Doenniges organised for the king's benefit and instruction. The topics of these seminars ranged from the nature of the *Zeitgeist*, to possible solutions for the social question, and to the prospects for preserving a conservative social order. From these discussions Maximilian II came to the conclusion that the most serious threats to Bavaria were the German national idea and war, neither of which he expected the conservative social order of Bavaria would be likely to survive.[67]

These conclusions Maximilian and his advisers attempted to translate into policy. That meant the immediate rejection of the renewed claims by the Church for control over education. In part, at least, these claims were a response to Maximilian's appeal for help against radical schoolteachers, but they were also early sallies in the great counter-offensive against modernity that was being launched by the Church during the 1850s. The Church's claim was firmly restated at an October 1850 conference of Bavarian bishops chaired by the Archbishop of Munich-Freising, Count K. A. von Reisach. 'The best remedy for the failures of the *Volksschulen*', the bishops said, would be to return them to Church control.[68] School inspec-

65. Ibid., p. 45.
66. See 'Maximilian II., K. v. Baiern', in *ADB*, vol. XXI, pp. 39–53.
67. Hans Rall, 'Ausblicke auf Weltentwicklung und Religion im Kreise Max' II und Ludwigs II', p. 490.
68. Schramm, *Bayerische Schulgeschichte*, p. 40; Rall, 'Die politische Entwicklung von 1848', p. 236; Michael Doeberl, *Entwicklungsgeschichte Bayerns*, vol. III, p. 544.

tors, they proposed, were to be directly responsible to a bishop, thereby giving him also the virtual powers of appointment over teachers. Seminars, too, were to come directly under a bishop's supervision.

Suspicious as he was of teachers and their role in the recent upheavals, Maximilian had no intention of turning them over to the Church. His intention was to strengthen the state, not weaken it. The bishops' appeal was for the time being ignored. At the same time, the teachers' associations of 1848 were ordered to disband, and restrictions were placed upon teachers who could qualify to train *Präparanden*, the *Volksschule* graduates apprenticed to teachers for several years in order to qualify for entry into a Seminar.[69] Likewise school inspectors were sent out to check libraries of teachers and of Seminars for seditious literature. The writings of Diesterweg were considered especially dangerous.[70] During the course of the 1850s the works of any writer deemed to be democratic, republican, irreligious, or immoral were ordered purged from Seminar libraries. Eventually the Education Ministry drew up its own list of approved books and journals. This list of 335 titles, which was sent out in late 1852 after having been approved by Maximilian II himself, consisted of books on religion and morals, but also included thirty-two books on history, mainly on that of Bavaria.[71] Significantly, these measures were counterbalanced in late 1849 by the revocation of Abel's restrictions upon the domicile rights of teachers. At the same time the official designation of *Volksschule* was restored to the lower schools,[72] replacing the name of German Work-Day School that Ludwig had imposed upon them in 1836.

The government's formal rejection of the bishops' proposals did not come until April 1852. A concession to the Church was made soon thereafter, however, when Interior Minister Zwehl replaced Friedrich Ringelmann as Education Minister. Zwehl was considered by the bishops to be more trustworthy than Ringelmann, a belief buttressed when he entered office with the promise to interpret the Concordat of 1817 in a manner more favourable to the Church. Yet school policy, which by 1851 had been firmly set under Ringelmann, changed not at all.[73]

69. Schramm, *Bayerische Schulgeschichte*, p. 36.
70. Weinlein, *Der Bayerische Volksschullehrer-Verein*, p. 10
71. BHStA, MK 22900 (Nr. 6050).
72. Neukum, *Schule und Politik*, p. 112.
73. Dieter Albrecht, 'Von der Reichsgründung bis zum Ende des Ersten Weltkrieges', p. 326.

The first significant step in that policy had been taken in January 1851 when, under Maximilian II's guidance, the Council of State ordered the schools to promote the development of a Bavarian national consciousness.[74] This promotion of 'national feeling', the Council advised, could best be accomplished by emphasising Bavarian history, a history that could also be used to demonstrate how the common people of Bavaria had been traditionally loyal to the ruling Wittelsbach house. Thus a sense of Bavarian nationhood was to be established as one of the pillars of Maximilian's conservative order. Care was to be taken in these history courses that teachers did not praise the idea of revolution.

A recent study of school books in nineteenth-century Bavaria shows a pronounced emphasis upon Bavarian particularism in those published during the 1850s.[75] Maximilian's policy was obviously being carried out. It was also during these years that the Education Ministry distributed to the schools some 25,000 copies of a booklet entitled *Sketches of Bavarian Princes*.[76] That these efforts had a positive effect has been noted by Karl Bosl in his analysis of the Bavarian national identity of the nineteenth century.[77]

The reinforcement of the conservative order was the object also of Ringelmann's decree in December 1851 regarding the training of teachers. Teacher-training was henceforth to be rooted, read the decree, in 'a positive Christian belief and the pious and morally sensitive character that it generates'. Ringelmann ordered the provincial governors to make such changes in their own Seminars as would promote the creation of 'a satisfactory and sound Christian school teacher'.[78]

The full institutionalisation of 'positive Christianity' came in May 1857 with the promulgation of a new set of Teacher Education Regulations to replace those of 1836. The new regulations were needed, Ringelmann said, because in teacher-training lay the basis for the 'moral corruption which has become so widespread'. The 'main source' of this corruption, he said, lay in 'the previous teacher training', and he cited the Prussian Seminars as examples of what could go wrong.[79] The declared purpose of the regulations was

74. BHStA, MInn 45787.
75. Gudrun Heller, *Geschichtsschulbücher im 19. Jahrhundert in Bayern*, pp. 112–15.
76. Blessing, 'Zur Analyze politischer Mentalität', p. 788.
77. Karl Bosl, 'Die historische Staatlichkeit der bayerischen Lande', pp. 3–19.
78. *Volksschulwesen und Kirche in Bayern*, pp. 27–8, 30.
79. Badisches Generallandesarchiv, 235/19229, pp. 1–2.

probably more significant than their effect. The curriculum in the Seminars was changed only slightly, but again with the purpose of 'cultivating a positive Christian belief'.[80] To demonstrate the Seminars' ties to the Church, every one of their inspectors was to be a clergyman, albeit a clergyman named by the king.[81] As in Prussia, 'positive Christianity' was too important to be left to the Church.

The Teacher Education Regulations of 1857 had been preceded by an increased emphasis upon the enforcement of school attendance and by the addition of a seventh year of compulsory schooling for Catholic children, a provision in force for Protestants since 1838.[82] Short-term improvements in the effectiveness of schooling are extremely difficult, if not impossible, to measure. By the mid-1860s, when improvements might have begun to show, the War Ministry found them noticeable among army recruits. Military officials regularly collected data on the number of recruits who had 'inadequate schooling', something they defined as being unable to read, write, or do simple calculation. By 1866 the ministry reported the numbers with such inadequate schooling to be 11 per cent; by 1871 it had been reduced to 8.6 per cent. The improvement was found to be most dramatic in the province of Lower Bavaria where the 1866 percentage of 23.6 was reduced to 11.7 in 1871, and to 1.3 by 1879. These figures the Education Ministry published prominently in its regular bulletins.[83]

No similar advance in schooling can be attributed to the Prussian reaction of the 1850s. The ministerial change-over that followed the resignation of the Brandenburg government moved Prussia's centre of political gravity far to the right. At the forefront in this movement were Kurt von Raumer, Ladenberg's successor as Education Minister, and Ferdinand Westphalen, the Interior Minister. It was 'in such men [that] the efficient bureaucrat had completely repressed the constructive statesman', says Theodore Hamerow.[84] It was in

80. Quoted in Weinlein, *Der Bayerische Volksschullehrer-Verein*, p. 10; see also Heinrich Held, *Altbayerische Volkserziehung und Volksschule*, p. 327.

81. Michael Geistbeck, *Geschichte des Oberbayerischen K. Schullehrerseminars von 1814–1904*, p. 35.

82. Neukum, *Schule und Politik*, p. 118; see also Albert Reble, 'Das Schulwesen', p. 965.

83. *Ministerialblatt für Kirchen- und Schul-Angelegenheiten im Königreich Bayern*, vol. II (1866), p. 39; vol. VII (1871), p. 22, and vol. XVI (1880), p. 169.

84. Hamerow, *Restoration*, p. 212.

such men, also, that the reactionary clique, or camarilla, led by the Gerlach brothers and Julius Stahl, found its allies within Frederick William IV's ministry. As Ludwig von Gerlach formulated it, the task of statesmanship in a world after 1848 must be to divide the masses in order to prevent them from acquiring a single shared consciousness.[85] The group's leading theorist, Julius Stahl, proposed that the state would be secure only if it came to be formally rooted in Protestantism. For this purpose he initiated a movement to undo the constitutional provisions guaranteeing religious freedom.[86] This group saw even the highly conservative Minister President Otto von Manteuffel as too willing to accept constitutional restrictions upon the royal prerogative.[87]

When Christian Scholz in Breslau learned that Raumer had replaced Ladenberg, he counted it a complete victory for reaction. Raumer's appointment was 'a blow for teachers that destroyed all hopes', he wrote.[88] Under Raumer, the hunt for teachers who had been involved in 1848 began in full force. They were watched to see how they voted, what groups they belonged to and what religious views they held, Scholz recalls.

Raumer acted quickly to rein in Prussia's presumably revolutionary schoolteachers. In May 1851 an earlier law, which had forbidden women, apprentices, and school pupils membership in political societies, was extended to teachers, who were, for good measure, also prohibited from attending political gatherings of any sort.[89] At the same time he withdrew from the *Landtag* the school bill he had inherited from Ladenberg. A school bill had become unnecessary, he told the *Landtag*, although he did admit what he called 'a pressing need to address the matter of teachers' salaries'.[90]

The most bizarre of Raumer's measures came in August 1851 when he banned from Prussia the *Kindergarten* schools of Friedrich Froebel. His decree explained: 'Whereas it appears by a pamphlet written by Carl Froebel that *Kindergartens* form a part of the Froebelian socialistic system which is calculated to train the youth of the country to atheism, such schools and *Kindergartens* cannot be suffered

85. Schoeps, *Preussen*, pp. 223–4.
86. Huber, *Deutsche Verfassungsgeschichte*, vol. III, p. 115.
87. Walter Bussmann, 'Das Zeitalter Bismarcks', p. 19.
88. Scholz, *Meine Erlebnisse*, p. 282.
89. Huber, *Deutsche Verfassungsgeschichte*, vol. III, p. 1018, n. 30.
90. Quoted in *Das Unterrichts-Wesen des Preussischen Staates*, ed. Ludwig von Rönne, p. 234.

to exist'.[91] It is difficult to follow Raumer's thinking. Friedrich Froebel, the movement's founder, did happen to be Carl's uncle; however, Friedrich despised his nephew and his revolutionary views. Friedrich Froebel protested the injustice to Raumer, but to no avail. Even an audience with Frederick William IV proved fruitless. The ban stayed in effect until 1862.

The centrepiece of the Prussian reaction, however, was put into place with the promulgation in October 1854 of the so-called 'Stiehl Regulations'. These three regulations concerning Seminar training, training preparatory to the Seminar, and instruction in the one-room rural schools have symbolised the educational reaction in Prussia ever since. For the remainder of the century their author, Wilhelm Stiehl, was to be the whipping boy of liberal reformers. Stiehl, however, had proved himself to be a survivor. He had already managed to weather the storms of 1848 by bending with the political wind. He had also survived Ladenberg, an old rival, and then proceeded to thrive during the 1850s, only to bend again when the winds became more liberal late in the decade.

The Stiehl Regulations are a wordy pronouncement of the social and political attitudes governing the Prussian reaction. The first of Stiehl's regulations concerned training in the Protestant Seminars. It imposed upon them a curriculum designed to dampen the educational and social ambitions of aspiring teachers. So that these teachers would be less likely to consider themselves educated, there were to be no more readings in the curriculum from either the German or Greek classics;[92] no more from Goethe, Schiller, or Sophocles. Also removed from the curriculum was pedagogical theory, presumably because it was thought to stimulate anti-social sentiments. It was replaced by the more practical *Schulkunde*, or school practice. At another level Raumer made clear his negative view of the schoolteachers by withdrawing his earlier support for raising their salaries. He thought a low income appropriate for a teacher's modest social position. 'It would be doing the elementary teachers the worst disservice', he said, 'if one were to change their living situation or income in such a way as to enable them to make greater material demands on life'.[93] Stiehl's further concern was that

91. Raumer quoted in H. Courthope Bowen, *Froebel*, pp. 40–1.
92. Giese, *Quellen*, p. 149; also Karl-Ernst Jeismann, 'Die "Stiehlschen Regulative"', p. 144.
93. Quoted in Folkert Meyer, *Schule der Untertanen*, p. 143.

their intellectual demands be no higher than their material ones.

Stiehl's second regulation concerned training in preparation for the Seminar, the so-called *Präparandenbildung* that took place after an aspiring teacher left the *Volksschule* at the age of fourteen and before he was old enough for the Seminar. Such training, the regulation stipulated, was to be in the hands either of clergymen or of especially qualified teachers. Under their guidance the aspirant was to be given a long list of tasks to master. He would have to be able to recite from memory, clearly and with expression, the Heidelberg Catechism in its entirety, to have memorised the Bible verses that conveyed the Protestant view on salvation, to be able to comprehend sermons, and to know the pericope of the Evangelical Church year, the messianic prophecies in Scripture and eighteen of the Psalms, as well as the outline of biblical history from both the Old and New Testaments before he could be admitted to the Seminar.[94] Knowledge of the more practical studies Stiehl consciously de-emphasised. All of this represented a considerable departure for Stiehl from the position he had taken at the 1849 Seminar conference in Berlin. Then he had viewed as outdated such pedagogical practices as having pupils copy dictation or being forced into rote memorisation of things they would find meaningless.[95]

Stiehl's third regulation was formally an 'Outline for Instruction in the One-Room Rural School', which was the standard school in the overwhelming majority of communities in Prussia. Religion was to be the centre of their curriculum. Of the twenty-nine hours of instruction each week, twenty-six were to be devoted to religion. Even reading, writing, and arithmetic were to be integrated into religious instruction. The three remaining hours were to be given to such subjects as history and nature study.[96] Stiehl warned against the 'cultivation of the intellect through the use of abstractions'. Rather, the *Volk* required an education rooted in the 'Christianity upon which rest the justifications for the shape of life in the family, occupation, community, and state'.[97] Thus was to be rebuilt

94. DZA II Merseberg, Rep. 76 VII neu Sekt 7C Gen Teil I, Nr. 1, vol. VI, pp. 115–20.

95. *Die Gesetzgebung*, p. 140. Stiehl had objected at the 1849 Seminar teachers' conference to 'Diktiren, Abschreiben, und Auswendiglernen'.

96. DZA II Merseburg, Rep. 76 VII neu Sekt 1B Gen Teil I, Nr. 35, vol. VI, pp. 373–8.

97. Stiehl quoted in Jeismann, 'Die "Stiehlschen Regulative"', pp. 42–3.

the conservative social base of rural Prussia. Riehl's influence was obviously as strong in Prussia as it was in Bavaria.

Stiehl would eventually claim that his regulations were less reactionary than critics interpreted them to be and that they had been designed to prevent worse things from happening.[98] There were, he declared with some justice, powerful forces that wanted to do away with the Seminars entirely. If there is substance to Stiehl's claim of having been a moderate, it must also be noted that his Regulations seemed to appease entirely his potential reactionary critics. Criticism of Stiehl consistently came from those who held more liberal views, and his response to it was always drawn from the spirit of the Regulations. His severest critic in the *Landtag*, until the election of Diesterweg in 1858, was the liberal industrialist Friedrich Harkort, long a champion of the *Volksschule* and its teachers. Responding to Harkort, Stiehl at one point accused him of wanting to have the *Volksschule* based in industry rather than in Christianity.[99] Actually, Stiehl had few critics as vocal as Harkort or Diesterweg.[100] Liberals, although they objected to what they thought to be a one-sided emphasis upon religion, were not social egalitarians either. In principle, if not in degree, they shared Stiehl's belief that the lower classes did not need to know the same things as their social betters.

The Regulations were enforced with remarkable energy. Stiehl himself travelled around to the various provinces consulting with authorities on how best to implement them.[101] Pupils studying at the Seminars during these years recalled the suddenness with which their courses in history, geography, and pedagogy were de-emphasised,[102] although certain Seminar directors did continue to allow the study of a few German and ancient classical writers.[103] That the Regulations did actually reach down into the *Volksschule* is attested by the experience of Johannes Tews, who was a pupil in a village school in Pomerania during the 1860s. Tews recalls being required to memorise some eighty Bible stories, 120 hymns, and 300 Bible

98. Karl Schneider, *Ein halbes Jahrhundert im Dienste von Kirche und Schule*, pp. 288–9.
99. Karl-Ernst Jeismann, 'Volksbildung und Industrialisierung als Faktoren des sozialen Wandels im Vormärz', pp. 322–4; see also Jeismann, 'Die "Stiehlschen Regulative"', p. 157.
100. Peter Martin Roeder, 'Gemeindeschule in Staatshand, Zur Schulpolitik des Preussischen Abgeordnetenhauses', p. 214.
101. Dörpfeld, 'Die Schulkonferenz im preuss. Unterrichtsministerium', pp. 299–300.
102. Adam Langer, *Erinnerungen aus dem Leben eines Dorfschullehrers*, p. 88.
103. Karl Schultze, *Aus acht Jahrzehnten: Lebenserinnerungen*, pp. 69–70.

verses.[104] An important perspective is gained from the fact that the most common complaint about the Regulations was that they set unattainable standards of achievement.[105] The memorisation of 300 Bible verses was no easy task for the average pupil.

An unintended effect of the Regulations was their role in strengthening the hand of the Berlin bureaucracy in determining the course of schooling. Not since Süvern's day had there been such a conscious attempt to centralise and regularise requirements in the *Volksschule* and Seminar. Equally unintended was the role the Regulations may have played in dissuading young men from entering teaching. Stiehl's successors in the early 1870s blamed him for at least part of the teacher shortage that was becoming critical during the 1860s.[106]

It was during the late 1850s that the reaction began to break apart in both Bavaria and Prussia. In Bavaria's *Landtag* elections of 1858 liberals gained a majority, beginning their decade-long control of its lower house. During the first *Landtag* session this liberal majority came into conflict with the conservative Pfordten over military expenditures, shortly after which he resigned. His replacement as Maximilian II's chief minister was Karl von Schrenk, a proponent of the Trias idea in German affairs, but considerably more liberal in his domestic outlook. Schools and teachers were soon to experience a number of welcome changes.

In Prussia the reaction collapsed quickly in October 1858 when Crown Prince William established a regency in place of the totally incapacitated Frederick William IV. Manteuffel resigned soon after, as did the architects of Prussia's reaction, Raumer and Westphalen. In their place William appointed what came to be called the 'New Era Ministry' led by Rudolf von Auerswald, a government head in 1848. Other moderate liberals were given posts as well, among them Eduard von Flottwell, the former 'Germanising' governor of Posen, who became Interior Minister. Within a year he was replaced by Count von Schwerin, the Education Minister during much of 1848. To replace Raumer as Education Minister, William named Moritz von Bethmann-Hollweg, a leader of Berlin's moderately liberal '*Wochenblatt*' party. The augury was for a more liberal course in domestic policy and for a more assertive one in German affairs. Those who wanted Olmütz undone were now in power.

104. Tews, *Ein Jahrhundert*, p. 30.
105. Meyer, *Schule der Untertanen*, p. 38.
106. Schneider, *Ein halbes Jahrhundert*, p. 290.

In Bavaria the shift toward liberalism after 1858 was more gradual. Maximilian was still concerned with his conservative social order. However, a more liberal commercial code came to be introduced, and a greater measure of civil equality came to be accorded to Jews. Eventually the government also approved the founding of a Bavarian Teachers' Association. The new association, created at a meeting in Regensburg in December 1861, was much more restrained than its forerunners of 1848 or 1849. There was to be no call this time for the emancipation of the school from the Church; indeed, the association had promised to stay away from such questions in order to gain government sanction. The association promised to restrict itself to activities that would serve only the material and intellectual position of its members. Because these touched directly upon teacher incomes and status, however, the organisation proved to be of immediate consequence.[107]

In May 1861 the liberals in the *Landtag* asked the government to prepare legislation that would put the Bavarian *Volksschule* on a more stable financial foundation. The basis of school financing was still the inadequate Communal Tax Law of 1819 which allowed school support by taxation only as a last resort. In asking for a new law, the *Landtag*'s intentions were to reduce the dependence upon school fees and also to make possible an increase in teachers' salaries, both of which were fully consonant with Maximilian II's own desire to improve schooling. The School Financing Law prepared by the government passed the *Landtag* with overwhelming support in October 1861. For the first time, local communities were required to levy taxes to support their schools. They were also empowered to abolish school fees if they wished, and thereby to make the *Volksschule* free of charge. In addition, the law provided teachers with a new minimum salary schedule: 500 gulden in cities with a population over 10,000; 400 gulden in cities of 2,500–10,000; and 300 gulden in communities under 2,500.[108] Moreover, no teacher was to be responsible for more than 100 pupils for longer than five years. After that, a second teacher would have to be hired. The law did allow communities to turn their schools over to female teaching orders if they wished to spare themselves the costs of these higher

107. Josef Nissl, *Die Schulpolitik in Bayern von 1850–1914 im Volksschulwesen*, pp. 11–12; see also Matthias Simon, *Evangelische Kirchengeschichte Bayerns*, pp. 633–40.
108. Schramm, *Bayerische Schulgeschichte*, p. 42.

teacher salaries.[109] Bavaria's school financing was to be governed by this legislation until 1902.

The tentativeness of Bavaria's shift toward liberalism is illustrated by the government's failure, in this setting, to consider a comprehensive school law, despite the fact that such a measure remained a clear constitutional requirement. Although Bavarian officials studied with interest the progress being made on such a bill by the New Era government in Prussia, they were not tempted to imitate its example. The former Education Minister Ringelmann, now an elder statesman, explained to the State Council why such a bill would be problematic: 'It touches on a problem in which the boundaries between law and the public good (*salus publica*), and between legislation and administration, overlap; also because no one quite realizes the difficulties of enforcing a strict principle.'[110] Ringelmann's caution did not inspire daring.

Not until the late 1860s, during the great wave of legislative reform under Hohenlohe, would a school bill come to be drafted, and that came in a setting radically transformed by the war of 1866. In the German civil war of that year, Bavaria sided with Austria against Prussia. Prussia's victory in this war was quick and overwhelming, and therewith power relationships in Central Europe were immediately turned upside down. The new leader in German affairs was Prussia. For Bavaria the Trias idea was finally dead. By year's end it found itself forced into an alliance with this new German power.

In Prussia no less than in Bavaria, matters of schooling were overwhelmed by the effects of the victory over Austria. The New Era of 1858 was by then long forgotten, its promises and policies ground up by the constitutional crisis of the early 1860s. An era that began so hopefully managed to produce in the end little more than a change of intentions. Prince William had told his ministers in 1858 that Prussia's cultural policy needed to undergo drastic changes. The use of 'religion as a cloak for political actions' would have to cease, he said. Evangelical orthodoxy would no longer be an official state doctrine. Catholics, he implied, could again expect equal treatment. As for educational matters, William wanted to guarantee an 'education appropriate to the various social classes, without

109. Helmut Beilner, *Die Emanzipation der bayerischen Lehrerin*, p. 30.
110. BHStA, Staatsrat 1083, Protokol des Sitzung des kgl. Staatsrathes, vom 8ten Juli 1861, no. VIII, p. 29.

any one of these being lifted beyond its station'.[111] Not exactly radical in its promise, William, none the less, wanted it known that 'Great resources will be needed to accomplish this' advance in education.

Prospects for the New Era had appeared to be buttressed by the substantial liberal victory in the *Landtag* elections of 1858. When the *Landtag* turned out to be more liberal than the government, however, the stalemate set in. Diesterweg had been among those elected in 1858, and his immediate target was Stiehl, whose Regulations became the regular target of his *Landtag* speeches. Stiehl would occasionally appear in the *Landtag* to defend himself. On one occasion, after Diesterweg had called for the complete dissociation of Church and school, Stiehl offered the proposition that 'The school is the daughter of the Church and the handmaiden of the family'.[112] Stiehl again survived these attacks, although his Regulations were somewhat tempered. In 1861, for example, Education Minister Bethmann ordered that Seminar pupils become acquainted once again with German classical writers such as Schiller and Goethe. However, the ancient classical writers remained proscribed.[113]

At the heart of Bethmann's activities were his efforts to produce a school bill, a constitutional mandate the New Era had taken seriously.[114] The draft of his bill was completed in July 1861, and his intention was to submit it to the coming *Landtag* session. The bill was cautious in its liberalism, promising little more than to fit existing school conditions into a legal framework. Schools were to remain confessional; attendance from the age of six to fourteen was to remain compulsory. Only in the section dealing with the sensitive question of school inspection was there any cause for conservative objection. During the course of the century school inspection had become, in practice, the nearly exclusive prerogative of the Church, and during the 1850s the reaction had even provided new ideological underpinnings for that prerogative. In Bethmann's school bill the clergy's role was to be considerably diluted. School inspection, the bill proposed, was to be exercised collegially by a directorate composed of the local magistrate, local council representatives, and a

111. Huber, *Dokumente*, vol. II, pp. 32–3.
112. Roeder, 'Gemeindeschule in Staatshand', p. 542.
113. Tews, *Ein Jahrhundert*, p. 147.
114. Preussisches Geheimes Staatsarchiv (PGStA), Rep. 90, Staatsministerium, Nr. 2397, Protokol des Staatsministeriums, 11 December 1858, p. 89.

clergyman.[115] Nothing was to come of Bethmann's bill; it was never submitted to the *Landtag*. The *Landtag* elections in December 1861, which returned 243 liberals and only fourteen conservatives, would have made it pointless to do so. Such a majority, already locked in conflict with the government over questions of army reform, would not have taken Bethmann's cautious school proposals seriously.[116]

School questions were soon overshadowed by the constitutional deadlock that developed over army reform. In March 1862, William, king in his own right since 1861, tried to break through the impasse by dissolving the *Landtag* and dismissing his New Era ministers. Their successors, however, formed a government nearly as conservative as that of the 1850s. Heinrich von Mühler, the new Education Minister, was an extreme conservative who proved to be mainly interested in Church affairs.[117] School matters he left largely to Stiehl. When the new minister president proved no more successful than his predecessor in bringing the liberals in the *Landtag* to heel, William in September 1862 turned in desperation to Otto von Bismarck. Bismarck, who had no intrinsic interest in schooling, saw no need to replace Mühler at the Education Ministry, and so the turbulent years of the Prussian constitutional struggle from 1862 to 1866 brought no surprises in educational policy. The school bill that Mühler produced in 1865 was drafted largely by Stiehl and was little more than the Stiehl Regulations writ large.[118] It placed religion squarely in the centre of the *Volksschule* curriculum and provided a legal foundation for the clergy's monopoly over school inspection. There was no reason for the anti-government majority in the *Landtag* to take it seriously.

The conservatism of this school policy was not matched in other areas. Bismarck's economic policy was liberal and his foreign policy radical. It was his success in the latter that would shortly produce for schooling an entirely new set of problems. It would also spark Bismarck's interest in what schooling might be able to accomplish in domestic political affairs.

115. For Bethmann's bill see PGStA Rep. 90, Staatsministerium, Nr. 2398, vol. II, 1862–1872, pp. 210-38; also *Die Gesetzgebung*, pp. 201–274. Paras 63–69 deal with school inspection.

116. Bungardt, *Die Odyssee der Lehrerschaft*, p. 81.

117. Huber, *Deutsche Verfassungsgeschichte*, vol. III, pp. 294–5, 376–7.

118. For the draft of Mühler's bill, see DZA II Merseburg, Rep. 92, Mühler IV, 3.

6
Schooling and Nationhood 1866–1880

The extraordinary revolution in German affairs produced by Prussia's victory over Austria in 1866 was matched on the larger European stage in 1870–1 by the Prussian-German victory over France. More dramatic reversals in the traditional political relationships between the states of Germany, or of Europe, are difficult to imagine. The victory over Austria made Prussia the dominant force in Germany; the victory over France, the dominant power on the continent.

For Prussia's *Volksschule* teachers the events of these years brought their own dramatic reversal of fortune. They entered these years as the scapegoats for 1848; they emerged from them as the heroes credited with having made Königgrätz and Sedan possible. Every one of Prussia's soldiers, after all, had gone through the *Volksschule*. War Minister von Roon and Education Minister von Mühler were convinced that 'the Prussian *Volksschule* teacher was the victor at Königgrätz', a conviction of which they promptly informed William I in 1866.[1] In 1871 Bismarck sent greetings to a nation-wide teachers' meeting being held in Hamburg, according the teachers the gratitude of the Fatherland for their 'outstanding contributions' to recent national successes[2] and charging them with the task of building a sense of German nationhood.

Only a larger sentiment of nationhood could elevate Prussia's military successes out of the realm of force into the legitimising

1. Robert Rissmann, *Deutsche Pädagogen des 19. Jahrhunderts*, p. 219.
2. Friedrich Kreppel, 'Der Lehrer in der Zeitgeschichte', pp. 205–6.

realm of idea. Germany was still, in the words of the poet Georg Herwegh, 'an empty shell'.[3] A unifying national consciousness was lacking especially among the lower classes, the peasants and workers who had yet to be tied to the new German nationhood.[4] Until such a national consciousness was developed, complained the patriotic publicist Georg Hirth, the new Germany would be little more than 'a conglomeration' of separate regions, communities, and individuals.[5]

The fact that German unification was largely a story of Prussian successes gave a peculiar twist to the problem of constructing a German consciousness. In Prussia the view was held that with the events of 1866 to 1871, the consciousness of Prussian statehood and the wider German consciousness had been merged into one. The Prussian historian, Heinrich von Treitschke, spoke of a 'Holy Prussian Empire of the German Nation'.[6] The stamp of Prussia's Protestantism was undeniable. Her success had clearly come at the expense of Catholic Austria, Catholic Bavaria, and Catholic France. In 1871 William I became the world's first Protestant emperor, a fact not lost upon his military chaplain Adolf Stoecker who,during the same year at Metz, delivered a sermon in which he gloried in the establishment of the 'Holy Evangelical Empire of the German Nation'.[7] There were those who saw in this establishment evidence of divine wisdom. Prussia's *Neue Evangelische Kirchenzeitung* advised Catholics everywhere to repent. Had God not used Prussia's armies to punish France for its crimes against Protestantism? Was France's defeat not proof that 'All nations that reject the Gospel must die?'[8]

In Bavaria, these circumstances were understood somewhat differently. That a Catholic Bavaria might have difficulty fitting into a 'Holy Prussian Empire of the German Nation' was self-evident. There had been reports, for example, of Bavarian priests in 1870 praying publicly for the defeat of Protestant Prussia.[9] Moreover, for Bavaria the events of 1866 had represented defeat, not victory. The last hopes for establishing a Bavarian-led third Germany had been

3. Georg Herwegh, 'Dem Siegestrunken', *Werke*, pt. 3, p. 1333.
4. Otto Pflanze, *Bismarck and the Development of Germany*, p. 13.
5. Georg Hirth, 'Über Culturpolizei and Rechtsgleichheit zur Lösung der socialen Frage', pp. 828–9.
6. Treitschke quoted in Hans-Joachim Schoeps, *Preussen*, p. 269.
7. Stoecker quoted in Thomas Buske, *Thron und Altar*, pp. 58–9.
8. Quoted in Karl Heinrich Höfele, 'Sendungsglaube und Epochenbewusstsein in Deutschland 1870/71', pp. 270–1.
9. Ibid.

crushed by Prussian troops on 29 June at the Battle of Langensalza. The great reversal for Bavaria was that suddenly she found herself playing mouse to a Prussian rather than an Austrian cat, a circumstance made abundantly clear when Bavaria found herself forced into a military alliance with the victorious Prussia.

Not all of Bavaria was averse to German unification. At the official level Bavaria's adjustment to the circumstances created in 1866 was fairly smooth. Public policy during these years was defined largely by a liberal state bureaucracy, which generally was supported by liberal majorities in the lower house of the *Landtag*. The young King Ludwig II, on the throne since his father Maximilian II's death in 1864, was usually content to allow his ministers to do the governing. Thus it was that the years following Langensalza witnessed concerted efforts by the government to adjust to the new reality by modernising Bavaria. The result was a wave of liberal social legislation. The legislative successes were considerable. By 1869 this effort had produced a new poor law and an army law, a law de-regulating the trades, and new laws regulating marriage, residence, and domestic rights. Critical to the modernisation effort also was the drafting of a comprehensive school bill.

The request for a school bill had come from the *Landtag* on 30 August 1866, before the full meaning of Königgrätz was clear. The request stipulated that such a school bill be based upon 'progressive foundations'.[10] Pressure for such a school bill had been mounting since 1858 when liberals first gained control of the lower chamber of the *Landtag*. In 1864 the Bavarian Teachers' Association added its voice by petitioning the Education Ministry for greater state control over the *Volksschulen*. The association's aim was to reduce the authority of the Church. In place of the current designation of the schools as 'local institutions' (*Gemeindeanstalten*), the teachers wanted them designated as 'public institutions' (*öffentliche Anstalten*), the disingenuous calculation being that as local institutions the schools were being dragged down by the low educational levels of local communities. As 'public institutions', they presumably would be better positioned to carry out the more elevated intentions of the state. As for teacher-training, the association's petition gave expression to the social and intellectual ambitions of its members. They wanted the Seminar transformed into a 'university for teach-

10. Quoted in Christian Weinlein, *Der Bayerische Volksschullehrer-Verein*, p. 43.

ers', with Latin, French, and German classical literature as essential parts of the curriculum. Thus, the *Volksschule* teacher, they hoped, might find greater social acceptance from the educated classes.[11]

The impetus for liberal reform was substantially enhanced in December 1866 with the appointment, at Bismarck's behest, of Chlodwig, Prince Hohenlohe-Schillingsfürst (1819–1901) as the head of Ludwig II's ministerial council.[12] As a progressive of practical bent, Hohenlohe favoured Bavaria's ties with Prussia and brought with him an extensive programme for reshaping the army, the economy, the civil code, Church–state relations, and education.[13] However, the outline of a school bill was in place when Hohenlohe took office. In the wake of the *Landtag*'s instruction of 30 August, Education Minister Franz Gresser and his staff had set to work drafting a bill that was laid before Hohenlohe in December.

Gresser's school bill was the first of the pieces of reform legislation the Hohenlohe government submitted to the *Landtag*. The intent of Gresser's bill was to secularise the *Volksschule*. As the Teachers' Association had requested, the bill proposed that the *Volksschule* be designated a 'public institution'.[14] With the exception of religious instruction, school supervision was to be taken out of the hands of the clergy and placed in those of Local School Commissions to be comprised of representatives from the community, the Church, the heads of households, and also of teachers.[15] To allow for the creation of non-confessional schools, Gresser envisioned the creation of special school districts separate from parish and community boundaries. Financing was to be the responsibility of the local community, although the prospect was held out for occasional state or district subsidies to help communities with unusual financial problems. Teachers themselves were to be designated 'public servants' rather than community ones, and therefore no longer subject to demeaning janitorial services in the local church. Salary increases for longevity

11. Ibid.; for petition, see pp. 31–40.
12. Karl Bosl, *Bayerische Geschichte*, p. 231.
13. For the programme, see Chlodwig Hohenlohe-Schillingsfürst, *Memoirs*, vol. I, pp. 172–4.
14. For the full text of Gresser's bill, see Bayerisches Hauptstaatsarchiv (BHStA), MF68456, 'Entwurf eines Gesetzes über das Volksschulwesen im Königreich Bayern'.
15. Joseph Heigenmooser, 'Aus der bayerischen Volksschulgeschichte des 19. Jahrhunderts', p. 410; see also Josef Nissl, *Die Schulpolitik in Bayern von 1850–1914 im Volksschulwesen*, pp. 305–9.

were also envisioned. The larger purpose of the bill, as Gresser explained it to his ministerial colleagues, was to construct a *Volksschule* that had as its primary purpose the formation of a 'cultural and moral civil society' (*Staatsgesellschaft*).[16]

When Gresser's bill was made public in October 1867, it generated a storm that marked the opening, in all but name, of the Bavarian *Kulturkampf*. Bavaria's Catholic bishops were the first to enter the fray.[17] They had long feared efforts to reduce the role of the Church in education. Their new fear was that Bavaria might go the way of Baden where the legislature in 1864 had adopted a law excluding the Church from school inspection. Since 1864, moreover, bishops everywhere had been emboldened by the Church's offensive against modernity that had taken the form of Pius IX's 'Syllabus of Errors'. The 'Syllabus' specifically cited as erroneous the modern notion that 'popular schools open to children of all the classes . . . should be subject to the civil and political power. . . . '[18] This same argument the bishops now adduced in their petition to Ludwig II requesting the withdrawal of Gresser's bill from the *Landtag*. Ludwig's refusal of the bishops' request set off a debate that escalated into a newspaper and pamphlet war credited, in large measure, with the politicisation of Bavaria's Catholic peasantry. Bavaria's Protestants also became involved. Adolf von Harless,[19] the President of the Evangelical High Consistory since 1852, objected particularly to the bill's proposal for collegial school inspection and, more generally, to its 'progressive foundations'.[20]

The government was stunned by the fury of the opposition. For more than a year it retreated into taking periodic soundings of public opinion. Only when there were indications that opposition was dying down did it submit the bill to the *Landtag*.[21] When the vote finally came in February 1869, the lower house, with its liberal majority, approved the bill by a margin of five to one. However, in

16. BHStA, Staatsrat, Protokoll der Sitzung des Kgl. Staatsraths vom 17 Oktober 1867, No. XI.
17. For their address to the king, see *Volksschulwesen und Kirche in Bayern*, pp. 118–30.
18. Eugene C. Black, ed., *Posture of Europe; 1815–1940: Readings in European Intellectual History*, p. 394.
19. See 'Adolf von Harless' in *Allgemeine Deutsche Biographie* (*ADB*), vol. X, pp. 763–6; also Friedrich Wilhelm Kantzenbach, 'Adolf Stählin und das Landeskirchentum', p. 211.
20. Harless to a representative of the Bavarian Teachers' Association. See Weinlein, *Der Bayerische Volksschullehrer-Verein*, pp. 43, 327.
21. BHStA, MInn, 66318 (Nr. 66 BJ).

the upper house, the *Reichsrat*, controlled by conservatives, the bill failed 28 to 13. Leading opponents were Bishop Dinkel and Adolf von Harless. With its failure in the *Reichsrat* Gresser's school bill was dead.

It was now Hohenlohe's turn to be furious. He blamed Pius IX and his 1864 encyclical for the failure of the bill. To the *Reichsrat* he delivered a scathing rebuke, pointing out the dangers for modern civilisation in an encyclical that 'reckons religious toleration among the damnable heresies',[22] and that justified papal interference in affairs of state. None the less, the first round of this *Kulturkampf* was won by the Church. Gresser resigned in late 1869. In March 1870 Hohenlohe joined him.

By the time of these resignations, the second round of the *Kulturkampf* was well under way. Pius IX had given the signal in June 1868 by announcing the summoning of a Church council, the first since the sixteenth century, to consider the question of papal infallibility and to ratify his 1864 'Syllabus of Errors'.[23] Bavaria's liberals were horrified at what they considered the political implications to the infallibility doctrine and determined to fight this challenge from Rome. Their powers were seriously weakened in the elections of November 1869, however, when the recently formed Patriot party, the voice of the newly-politicised Catholic peasantry, unexpectedly won a majority in the lower house of the *Landtag*.

Compared to the domestic turmoil in Bavaria, the situation in Prussia during the years between Königgrätz and Sedan seem positively tranquil. It was as if Prussia were being compensated for the upheavals that marked Bismarck's early years in office. School politics were unusually quiet, unrelated it seemed to the new position in German affairs being occupied by Prussia. In large measure this new quiet can be traced to the easing during the 1850s of the social crisis that for a century had shaped political developments and social perceptions in Prussia and elsewhere in Germany. The decade following the revolutions of 1848 witnessed for the first time since the 1750s a decline in the rate of population growth as well as the most massive emigration ever of the poor to the new world. At the same time industrial expansion began to provide work for large

22. Hohenlohe, *Memoirs*, vol. I, p. 331.
23. Lillian Parker Wallace, *The Papacy and European Diplomacy, 1869–1878*, p. 67.

numbers of people who until recently had been without it. Thus it was that for the next several decades the social question came to be replaced by the national question as the shaping force in the politics of schooling. Not until the emergence of a large socialist movement during the 1880s did the perception of social crisis again establish itself as a central concern of schooling.

Not even the introduction in 1868 of a school bill, although it stirred some controversy, served to create more than a temporary ripple on the Prussian political waters. Education Minister von Mühler, described by the visiting English school inspector and poet, Matthew Arnold, as 'a strong Tory and strong Evangelical',[24] remained in his post after 1866 and Ferdinand Stiehl remained as one of his chief aides. Mühler was a personal friend of William I, making his position all the more secure. It was also made more comfortable when the death of Adolf Diesterweg in 1866 removed from the *Landtag* his most outspoken critic.

Mühler had been asked by the *Landtag* in 1865 to draft a school bill, thereby fulfilling a constitutional mandate, but the proposal that he finally presented in 1868 had to be withdrawn almost immediately. The bill was in every sense traditional and conservative, its assumptions rooted in Mühler's Protestant world view.[25] The *Landtag*'s Progressives and National Liberals, the latter being an important support for Bismarck's government, were incensed. On the critical question of school inspection, Mühler's concessions to liberals were not even symbolic. The *Landtag*'s liberal majority simply ordered the bill reworked, a job that took Mühler's ministry until late 1871, by which time he had also fallen into official disfavour. This last of his drafts was not even accorded preliminary consideration in the council of ministers.

Political leaders in Prussia studiously avoided the question of papal infallibility, the specific issue that most stirred the passions of Bavarian politics in the late 1860s. Liberals everywhere were appalled at the papal claim to infallibility, and Prussia was shortly to provide the most bitter of the battlefields for the German *Kulturkampf*. None the less, Bismarck at first thought the whole question a concern solely for Catholics. He had no preference, he told a friend,

24. Matthew Arnold, 'The Prussian Schoolmasters, their Training, Examination, Appointment and Payment', p. 228.

25. For Mühler's 1865 draft, see Deutsches Zentral Archiv (DZA) II Merseburg, Rep. 92, Mühler IV, 3.

whether Catholics received their truths from councils or popes. Neither was he eager to stir up unnecessarily Prussia's eight million Catholics, many of them in territories annexed in 1866.

Yet it was these annexations that kept the infallibility question simmering in Prussian politics, and that eventually led to its boiling over in the early 1870s. This occurred not because the annexed territories were overwhelmingly Catholic, but because the annexations could be justified only on the principle of nationality, that is of Germans being joined together with other Germans.[26] The application of that principle raised immediate questions among the leaders of the Polish minorities in the eastern provinces. If Prussia were putting together a Germany on the basis of nationality, it 'can no longer avoid facing up to the Polish question', a Polish *Landtag* delegate told William I.[27] The Polish delegation, he warned, would protest the incorporation of its territory into a 'national' Germany, a situation it would regard as quite different from being part of a dynastic Prussian state. Because the new Germany promised to be dominated by Protestants, and because the Poles were overwhelmingly Catholic, the national question was inseparably linked to the religious one. Inevitably, schools would become the battlefield.

It was not until the formation of the German Empire in 1871 that the conflict came to be fully joined. The circumstances were these. On 18 June 1870, the Vatican Council in Rome voted in favour of the doctrine of papal infallibility,[28] a vote that was temporarily overshadowed when on the following day war broke out between France and Prussia. The war ended in May 1871. Shortly thereafter the *Kulturkampf* was fully launched.

Little noticed in the turmoil of the war was the formation in October 1870 of a Centre, or Catholic, political party. The Centre's avowed purpose was to preserve the independence of the Catholic Church in a Protestant Prussia. Confessional schools were among the things the Centre considered vital to its interests.[29] When the new party won forty-eight seats in the *Landtag* elections that same autumn, and three-quarters of a million votes in elections to the new imperial *Reichstag* the following March, Bismarck took notice. For

26. Oswald Hauser, 'Zum Problem der Nationalisierung Preussens', p. 531.
27. Quoted in Martin Broszat, *Zweihundert Jahre deutsche Polenpolitik*, p. 125.
28. The final vote was 533 to 2, with many of the bishops who were opposed absenting themselves from the vote.
29. Koppel S. Pinson, *Modern Germany*, p. 185.

one thing, he was irritated that a Centre candidate had managed to defeat a friend of his for a *Landtag* seat,[30] and he could not disregard the fact that in the *Reichstag* the Centre had become an immediate political force, second only to the National Liberals in the number of seats. At the same time provincial governors in the eastern provinces were reporting an upsurge in the activities of anti-Prussian and pro-Polish clerical agitators. From Posen came word of the Polish language spreading at the expense of German. There was talk even of the 'Polonisation of Germans'.[31] Prussia's 'mistaken school policy', as one governor called it, came under immediate fire, especially the continuing appointment of clergymen as school councillors and as county school inspectors. Was not the anti-German, 'organic work' of the Polish clergy thereby guaranteed success by Germany's own hands? Critics pointed out that all eighty-six of the county school inspectors in the provinces of Posen and Prussia, and in the district of Upper Silesia, were Polish clergymen.[32]

The policies under attack were those of Education Minister von Mühler, although he was doing no more than following long established practice. The turning point for Mühler came in May 1871 when he appointed a vocal supporter of the infallibility doctrine to head a new Catholic teachers' Seminar in Habelschwert, Silesia.[33] Critics took their case to King William I and to Bismarck, some of them going so far as to accuse even Bismarck of fostering the spread of the Polish language on German soil. By mid-July William I was complaining about the Habelschwert appointment and asking his ministers whether they thought it advisable for his government to go on the offensive against the infallibility doctrine.[34] Bismarck urged that Mühler be ordered to remove quietly from their school positions such clergymen as were likely to use their powers to undermine the authority of the state.[35] When William gave such an order in early August, Mühler proved reluctant to carry it out, arguing that it struck him as a general attack upon the Church. It also ran contrary to provisions that were included in his latest draft of a school bill. Mühler's reluctance had immediate consequences: it put at risk his

30. Walter Bussmann, 'Das Zeitalter Bismarcks', p. 161.
31. Rudolf Korth, *Die preussische Schulpolitik und die polnischen Schulstreiks*, p. 38.
32. Erich Schmidt-Volkmar, *Der Kulturkampf in Deutschland, 1871–1890*, pp. 73–4.
33. Ibid., p. 74.
34. William I in a ministerial council meeting of 17 July 1871; see *Die Vorgeschichte des Kulturkampfes*, ed. Adelheid Constabel, pp. 115–16.
35. Bismarck to William I, 18 July 1871; ibid., p. 119.

friendship with a powerful ally, and it created a new and powerful enemy.

By autumn Bismarck himself was ready to seize the initiative. At a meeting of Prussia's cabinet ministers on 13 October, he warned of the dangerous effects the infallibility doctrine was having in the schools. His view, he said, was that 'the rights of the state must be protected above all and that too much consideration seems to have been given in this area to the ultramontane, anti-Prussian efforts in West Prussia, Posen and Upper Silesia'.[36] He wanted the schools engaged in combating the ultramontanes, and for that reason, he believed, it might be necessary to employ non-clerical school inspectors and to adjust the law in such a way as to make this possible. Again Mühler demurred. Non-clerical inspectors would have to be paid, he noted, whereas most clergymen were not. His first concern was the expense. In addition, he said, qualified laymen would be difficult to find. But, above all, he disapproved in principle of the removal of clergymen from such posts unless it could be demonstrated that their belief in papal infallibility was having an inadmissible effect upon their work.[37] Bismarck insisted, however, and Mühler finally agreed to adjust the provisions of his school bill draft in such a way as to make the change legally possible. To save time, Bismarck ordered him to rework only those sections that affected clergymen. The product of Mühler's labour was an elaborate 'Program for Legislative and Administrative Measures in the Area of Educational and Church Administration' that Bismarck rejected as too cumbersome.[38]

A few days later, on 18 October, Bismarck simply instructed Mühler to draft a separate school inspection law that would address the problem directly. A simple law was all he wanted, he said, one that would make possible, with a minimum of commotion, the removal of some, not necessarily all, clerical school inspectors. Only thus could the schools be engaged effectively in combating the influence of Catholics and Poles, both of whom he was prepared to label as *Reichsfeinde*, enemies of the empire. Such a law, Bismarck pointed out, could be applied selectively.

36. DZA II Merseburg, Staatsministerium Sitzung, 13 October 1871, Rep 90a, BIII 2b Nr. 6, vol. LXXXIII, pp. 226–39.
37. Staatsministerium Sitzung of 18 October 1871, ibid., p. 229; see also *Die Vorgeschichte des Kulturkampfes*, ed. Constabel, pp. 126–7.
38. Constabel, ed., *Die Vorgeschichte des Kulturkampfes*, pp. 131–2.

When Mühler again failed to produce a satisfactory proposal, Bismarck lost all patience. At a long, tense session of the cabinet on 1 November, he catalogued Mühler's many policy failures, the foremost of which he counted to be his reluctance to oppose the influence of the Polish clergy upon the schools. Why had the eighty-six Polish priests not been removed from their posts as county school inspectors? What was needed was a law, said Bismarck, to empower the state to remove clergymen as school inspectors, at the county as well as at the village level. Only then could the school be effective in checking the spread of the Polish language and culture.[39] Although Mühler's stock was low, he managed, at Bismarck's insistence, to produce an appropriate bill.

The proposed law, which was submitted to William I on 27 November, ended the right, held exclusively by clergymen, to be named 'school inspectors'. In future the powers of appointment to such posts were to be placed in the hands of the state.[40] The need for such a law, William I was told, lay in the 'recognition that in Polish-Catholic parts of the kingdom, the Germanising task of the elementary schools has been pushed into the background'.[41] The bill was sent to the *Landtag* in early December 1871.

The School Inspection Law did for Prussian politics what Gresser's school bill had done for those of Bavaria in 1867: it launched in earnest the *Kulturkampf*. The reaction of the bill's opponents was furious. By February 1872 they had managed to get nearly 300,000 signatures on more than 2,300 protest petitions, the largest number of people to sign a petition in Prussia's history.[42]

In the meantime, Bismarck, eager to have a committed spokesman defend the bill's merits before the *Landtag*, had arranged for the resignation of Mühler as Education Minister.[43] As his successor he chose Adalbert Falk, an official from the Justice Ministry and a former National Liberal *Landtag* delegate who during the 1860s had

39. DZA II Merseburg, Staatsministerium Sitzung, 1 November 1871, Rep. 90, BIII 2b Nr. 6, vol. LXXXIII, pp. 244–9; see also Werner Frauendienst, 'Preussisches Staatsbewusstsein und polnischer Nationalismus', p. 343.

40. For the law, see Gerhardt Giese, *Quellen zur deutschen Schulgeschichte seit 1800*, pp. 167–8, or *Centralblatt für die gesammte Unterrichts-Verwaltung*, (*Centralblatt*), no. 3, 30 March 1872, pp. 129–30.

41. DZA II Merseburg, 27 November 1871, 2.2.1. Nr. 22129, pp. 1–2.

42. DZA II Merseburg, Rep. 77, Tit 123 No. 10, vol. V, p. 393; see also Christa Berg, *Die Okkupation der Schule*, p. 29.

43. Mühler resigned ostensibly because he had lost favour with the Crown Prince over a personnel appointment in the Education Ministry.

supported Bismarck in his fight with the Progressives over military policy.[44] Falk's task in the upcoming *Landtag* debate, Bismarck told him, would be to 'restore the rights of the state over against those of the Church, and to do so with as little fuss as possible'.[45] It was an impossible request. The most tactful of spokesmen would have had difficulty carrying it out, and Falk was anything but tactful. On the contrary, he was inclined by temperament to bring matters to a boil, not to cool them off.

The formal debate began in the lower house in early February 1872. The National Liberals and Progressives were naturally in favour of the bill, and the Conservative and Centre parties as naturally opposed. Because the two factions were of roughly equal strength, the vote of the fifty Free Conservatives, usually Bismarck's supporters, would be decisive. It was for their benefit that he entered the debate, warning ominously 'that in our Polish provinces the ground beneath us . . . is so undermined that it could collapse as soon as pressure is placed upon it by an Austrian policy that is pro-Polish and pro-Catholic'.[46] The debate raged for a week, exploring every nuance of the conflict between Church and state, scraping every nerve raw twice-over. The Free Conservatives were the deciding factor. When the vote came on 13 February, the School Inspection Law passed 207 to 155.

In the House of Lords, the bastion of Prussia's old conservatism, resistance was to be much stiffer. Passage of the bill, one of its committees warned, would open the gates through which 'the wild waters of unbelief will flow from the de-Christianized state and flood into the schools'.[47] Twice Bismarck addressed the Lords, beseeching them to see the schools as essential elements of Germanisation. They failed to be persuaded by Bismarck's arguments. Only his threat to create new peers finally brought the Lords around. On 8 March 1872, they voted 125 to 75 to accept the law.

Three days later the School Inspection Law went into effect, therewith drawing Prussia into the vortex of the *Kulturkampf*. Falk and his fellow liberals saw the law as absolutely crucial to the task of fashioning a German national sentiment. To fellow Education Min-

44. See 'Adalbert Falk' in *Neue Deutsche Biographie* (*NDB*), vol. V, pp. 6–7.
45. Bismarck quoted in Schmidt-Volkmar, *Der Kulturkampf*, p. 79.
46. Bismarck quoted in Frauendienst, 'Preussiches Staatsbewusstsein und polnischer Nationalismus', p. 343.
47. Quoted in Johannes Tews, *Ein Jahrhundert preussischer Schulgeschichte*, p. 163.

isters in the *Reich* he wrote that schools everywhere were being called upon 'to strengthen and enliven the German national consciousness'.[48] This could be accomplished, he suggested, through the study of German history, language, and literature, and by promoting 'special celebrations' to commemorate important events in German history. This was the theme Falk was to stress continuously during his years in office. At a Federal School conference in Dresden later in 1872, Falk's representative, Ludwig Wiese, took occasion to note that developments in 'German history have reached such a major turning point, that it will be one of peacetime's most pleasant tasks to awaken and strengthen a German national consciousness'. At a conference held in Berlin a year later, Falk asked Oskar Jäger, the ardent National Liberal Gymnasium director from Cologne, to address the assembly of schoolmen on the 'Promotion of a German National Consciousness'.[49]

Falk's most enthusiastic supporters in this endeavour came from the ranks of Prussia's teachers. 'We schoolmasters', one of them wrote later, 'helped lay the foundation stones for that magnificent structure we call the German *Reich*'.[50] It was within this new structure that teachers hoped to see fulfilled the state's promise to free them from their subordinate role to the Church. They saw the School Inspection Law as a sign that this promise would soon be realised.

The glories of the German victory over France had etched themselves indelibly into the consciousness of Prussia's teachers. Even among Seminar pupils this was the case. Immediately upon the outbreak of war in July 1870 the Education Ministry had been besieged by petitions from Seminar pupils requesting permission to volunteer for military service.[51] Permission was usually granted. When on 3 September the Director of the Berlin Seminar, Karl Schneider, received news of the great victory the day before at Sedan, he called together his faculty and pupils for a prayer of thanksgiving and then dismissed them for the remainder of the

48. Falk to the Education Minister of Baden, 30 December 1872, Badisches Generallandesarchiv, Karlsruhe, 235/199959.

49. Niedersächsisches Staatsarchiv, Bückeburg. For Protokol, see Acta Ecclesiastica, Schulen und Schullehrer, in. sp. Rep. II Ec. Nr. 42. L3 Ec Nr. 42.

50. Friedrich Marcks, *Oskar Jäger, Das Leben eines deutschen Schulmannes*, pp. 109–10; see also K. O. Beetz, *Die Lehrerbildung, eine soziale Frage*, p. 19.

51. Preussisches Geheimes Staatsarchiv (PGStA), Thiele Nachlass, Rep. 92, Nr. 87 'Generalia' 1870-Juni-November 1872, p. 3.

day.[52] During the next years a national liturgy began to establish itself in the Seminars. On 18 June 1871, the six-month anniversary of the proclamation of the *Reich* was celebrated at the Drossen Seminar in Brandenburg with the planting of an oak tree dedicated to the Kaiser. Director Schultze explained in his speech to the Seminar's pupils that the oak was the symbol of the powerful longing for unity within the German people, and that it represented the steadfast dedication of the Drossen Seminar to 'remain for all time a source of Christian and German education. And when you enter your own classrooms later on', he said, 'your main task will be to cultivate a Christian and national (*vaterländisch*) education'.[53]

It was from sentiments such as these that there arose also the idea of establishing a German-wide *Volksschule* system. The hope was thereby to transcend the particularist traditions of the old Germany. Such hopes had to ignore the federal nature of the new Germany, but their bearers often believed that enthusiasm alone could overcome such a mundane obstacles. 'Fatherland must remain an empty word' as long as the states control the schools, argued a Breslau school official.[54] There were Bavarian voices raised in support of the idea as well. M. G. Conrad, a *Volksschule* teacher from Bavaria, wrote in 1871 that Bismarck's 'blood and iron pedagogy' had finally made it possible to end the 'particularist swindle' that had heretofore concerned itself with educating Jews, Catholics, Evangelicals, Prussians, and Bavarians, but not Germans. Should a national school system be established, he said, 'The teachers in the various German states may again cultivate German sentiments (*Deutschtum*) without fear of punishment or reprimand'.[55]

It was the Bavarian publicist Georg Hirth who took matters into his own hands by trying to persuade the *Reichstag* to create a nationwide school system. A reformer by nature, Hirth was a former member of the German *Nationalverein* and also the former editor of Augsburg's *Allgemeine Zeitung*. He was currently the editor of the *Annalen des Deutschen Reiches*, a serial publication purporting to provide technical solutions to the problems of new nationhood. Among the solutions it purveyed was the one calling for wholesale educa-

52. Karl Schneider, *Ein halbes Jahrhundert im Dienste von Kirche und Schule*, p. 275.
53. Karl Schultze, *Aus acht Jahrzehnten, Lebenserinnerungen*, pp. 104–5.
54. Rector Bock of Breslau quoted in Robert Rissmann, *Geschichte des Deutschen Lehrervereins*, p. 94.
55. M. G. Conrad, 'Die Erziehung', p. 129.

tional reform. This reform was to include the creation of a national school system and bring about the complete exclusion of the Church from education.[56] Early in 1874 Hirth began collecting signatures on a petition designed to force the *Reichstag* into considering the creation of a national school system. Hirth's movement was bound to fail. In returning his petition, *Reichstag* officials explained to him that they did not have the competence to consider questions of education. By then, however, he had found important allies. The General German Teachers' Association, founded in late 1871, had endorsed Hirth's petition by asking at its first national congress for a *Reichs* school law.[57]

Although nothing was to come of the *Reichs* school law, the idea was kept alive in educational reform circles by its regular appearance on the agenda of teachers' associations' conferences. In the 1880s the idea was brought back into the general public's eye through Hugo Göring's 'New German School' movement. In 1906 the Social Democrats became the first political party to endorse the idea of a nationwide school law.[58] Only such a law, the drafters of the resolution argued, would make possible a victory in the fight against confessional control of schools.

Falk was far too realistic to become involved in the *Reichs* school idea, but he was not for that reason any less concerned with the promotion of national sentiments. It was obvious to him that such a task would require more than just a School Inspection Law. Schooling itself would need to be modernised. To begin with, the Stiehl Regulations needed to be replaced, despite the fact that their author was still a high level official in the ministry. Then there remained the unfulfilled constitutional requirements that called for the regulation of education within the framework of a comprehensive school law.

To advise him on these matters, Falk arranged for a conference of educators, legislators, and Education Ministry officials to be held in Berlin in June 1872. Invitations to the conference were eagerly sought, especially by the numerous teachers' associations which hoped to use it as a forum for promoting their own programmes.[59] Falk ultimately selected twenty-one people to receive invitations.

56. Franz Carl Endres, *Georg Hirth*, p. 35.
57. 'Reichsgesetzgebung', p. 101.
58. Otto Schmidt, *Die Frage der Reichsschulgesetzgebung*, pp. 55–6.
59. DZA II Merseburg; for examples of solicitations see Rep 76 III neu Sekt. 1B Generalia, Teil I Nr. 1, pp. 42–76.

Only thirteen of them were educators; of these, six were district school councillors, five were Seminar directors, and two were *Volksschule* teachers. The others were communal or *Landtag* delegates and ministerial officials. No delegate was politically to the left of Falk, and only four of them were Catholic, one of them an 'old Catholic' who rejected papal infallibility.[60] Two Jews were invited for a single session only.

The conference began on 11 June and ran for ten days. Falk himself presided over the sessions, although the agenda had been left to Stiehl. The main items on this agenda concerned the *Volksschule* curriculum, school inspection, a school law, and the problem of what to do about the odd assortment of schools that had emerged during the past decades to serve the needs of the lower middle classes.[61] But Falk also had an agenda of his own, one item of which was to undermine Stiehl's position. To the Seminar director from Bromberg, Falk confided his plan soon to have Stiehl replaced. Thus, when Stiehl made the unusual argument that Prussia's constitution actually required confessional schools, Falk took the occasion to contradict him, arguing instead that the constitutional requirement was only that confessional interests be given consideration in religious instruction.[62]

The most important question before the conference was addressed on its fifth day when the *Volksschule* curriculum was discussed. Falk wanted advice, he said, on how to overcome the curriculum limitations of the Regulations established in 1854. The Conservative *Landtag* delegate Kleist-Retzow immediately warned against reintroducing the indiscriminate dissemination of useless knowledge. The liberal *Volksschule* teacher F. W. Dörpfeld, on the other hand, proposed a curriculum that would be based almost entirely on the *Realien*, such modern and useful subjects as arithmetic, history, language, drawing, and natural science.[63] Dörpfeld was particularly concerned that there be sufficient emphasis upon history, for 'experience shows', he said, 'that the child must be made acquainted with

60. For names of the delegates, see *Centralblatt*, July 1872, pp. 385–6; also Berg, *Die Okkupation der Schule*, pp. 214–15, n. 3.

61. DZA II Merseburg, Rep 76 VII neu Sekt 1B, Generalia, Teil I Nr. 1, pp. 13–16; also PGStA, Thiele Nachlass, Rep. 92, Nr. 87 'Generalia' 1870-Juni-November 1872, pp. 27–8.

62. *Centralblatt*, 1872, pp. 400–1.

63. Ibid., pp. 411–12. Also Alfred Rach, *Sachwörterbuch zur deutschen Erziehungsgeschichte*, pp. 228–9.

the history of his Fatherland and with the lives of men known to the *Volk*. . . .'[64]

The final sessions of the conference were devoted to the problems connected with creating a level of schools for the children of the lower middle classes. Their educational requirements were more sophisticated than those which the *Volksschule* curriculum could provide, but less so than would be provided for in the higher schools.[65] The eventual product of these deliberations was the *Mittelschule*. But on this question, as on all others, the conference reached no final decisions. Falk had made it clear to the delegates at the beginning that their role was purely advisory, a cause for frustration among some of them; Dörpfeld, for example, left unhappy about the lack of attention that had been given to preparatory training (*Präparandenbildung*) for Seminar candidates and dubious about the prospects for what he believed to be the need for wholesale school reform.[66]

Reforms were soon to come, however. The conference was hardly over when Falk asked Karl Schneider, the director of the Berlin Seminar, to draft a set of regulations governing the *Volksschule* and teacher-training that would replace those of Stiehl. Falk and Schneider had been boyhood friends in Silesia; during the 1840s they had been students together at the University of Breslau, Falk in law and Schneider in theology. Falk had then entered the bureaucratic service, and Schneider had taken a position as pastor and school inspector in Posen. From there he had gone on to become the Seminar director at Bromberg in Posen (1863–7) and at Bunzlau in Silesia (1867–70). In April 1870 he had been called to Berlin to take Diesterweg's old post.[67] Schneider admitted to feeling slighted when he did not receive an invitation to the 1872 school conference. Therefore he was surprised when Falk commissioned him to draft new school regulations.[68] Falk told him that Stiehl had decided to retire and that he, Schneider, was to be his replacement, but that for the time being all of this was to be kept secret. So secret was this arrangement, it appears, that Stiehl himself did not yet know of his

64. Dörpfeld quoted in ibid., p. 412.
65. Ibid., pp. 424–7.
66. See his report in F. W. Dörpfeld, 'Die Schulkonferenz in preuss. (sic) Unterrichtsministerium'.
67. On Schneider, see Reinhard Lüdicke, *Die Preussichen Kultusminister und ihre Beamten*, p. 73.
68. Schneider, *Ein halbes Jahrhundert*, p. 295.

impending retirement. When the word did reach him he was not pleased.

Schneider went to work immediately, using his summer holiday, and by late July 1872 had a long first draft ready for Falk's consideration. To each of his specific proposals Schneider attached lengthy reflections and justifications, just as Süvern, Beckedorff, and Stiehl had done before him. Falk liked the specific recommendations, but he urged that the reflections and justifications be dropped as excess verbiage.[69] It was Schneider's second draft, bereft of the verbiage, that became the basis for the ministerial conference at which Stiehl learned formally that his own regulations of 1854 were to be replaced. Stiehl and several of his supporters put up a serious resistance to the proposed changes, Schneider recalled later, but to no avail.[70] On 15 October 1872, only six months after the passage of the School Inspection Law, Falk officially promulgated Schneider's 'General Regulations Concerning the *Volksschule* and Teacher Training in Preparatory Schools and Seminars'. Stiehl resigned immediately, twenty-eight years after entering the Education Ministry. Schneider, who succeeded him, was to remain until his own retirement in 1898.

For the *Volksschulen*, Schneider's General Regulations prescribed new minimum standards to be met by rural and urban schools alike.[71] Standards for equipment and supplies were set, as were limits on class size and the number of pupils per teacher. No class was to have more than seventy, and no teacher be responsible for more than eighty pupils. The most important changes were reserved for the curriculum, where, in contrast to Stiehl, the emphasis was to be upon modernity. History and the German language and its literature were to replace religion as the core of the curriculum, thereby reflecting Falk's concern with promoting a national consciousness. The reduced emphasis upon religion was reflected in the number of hymns pupils were to memorise; Stiehl had set the number at 120; Schneider reduced it to twenty. More important, the emphasis in religious instruction was to be placed upon its nonconfessional and morally edifying aspects. Ultimately, the Regula-

69. Ibid., pp. 296–7.
70. In 1872 Stiehl published a defence of his regulations entitled *Meine Stellung zu den Regulativen* in which he argued that their pious rhetoric had been designed to win over the clerical school inspectors.
71. Reported in *Centralblatt*, 1872, pp. 585–646.

tions were designed to encourage the creation of non-confessional schools. Wherever a village had schools of differing confessions, local authorities were encouraged to convert them into a single school that was non-confessional.[72]

The major changes in the Seminars, aside from requiring a full three-year course of study, were also curricular. As in the *Volksschule*, the new emphasis was to be on German history, language, and literature. Reintroduced also was the formal study of pedagogical theory, a subject Stiehl had forbidden. Insofar as it allowed a return to the classical authors, the new Seminar curriculum resembled that of the more prestigious higher schools.[73] To enhance the state's control over teacher education, the formal supervision of training preparatory to the Seminar was taken from the clergy and given to the Seminar directors.

Teachers felt their self-esteem greatly enhanced by both the new Seminar curriculum and by the new provisions for preparatory training. The same was true of the new opportunities opened to them to become school rectors and, under special circumstances, Seminar teachers.[74] Traditionally these positions had been reserved for theologians and the less qualified graduates in philology.[75] Schneider's Regulations now included *Volksschule* teachers among those eligible to take the examinations to qualify for these posts. Left untouched was the educational caste-line that prevented Seminar graduates from continuing their studies at a higher school or a university.

Teachers rightly saw the General Regulations as a significant break with the past. Years later one of them recalled 'the jubilation caused by the appearance of this little brown volume'[76] in which the Regulations were bound. Johannes Tews wrote that these Regulations 'were born of the efforts to give the *Volk* its share of the intellectual treasures of the nation. . . .'[77] Despite the bitterness of his conflict with the Church, Falk was supremely confident about the prospects for continued school reform. At the height of this conflict, in early 1873, he informed William I that a comprehensive school bill would not be long in coming.

72. Schneider, *Ein halbes Jahrhundert*, pp. 366–8.
73. Folkert Meyer, *Schule der Untertanen*, p. 69.
74. Rissmann, *Deutsche Pädagogen*, pp. 133–4.
75. Meyer, *Schule der Untertanen*, p. 70.
76. Rissmann, *Deutsche Pädagogen*, p. 131.
77. Tews, *Ein Jahrhundert*, p. 171.

The prospects for the passage of a school bill were certainly better in Prussia than they were in Bavaria where the shockwaves generated by Gresser's proposal of 1867 were still reverberating. Falk enjoyed the solid support of a Progressive–National Liberal majority in the Prussian *Landtag*, whereas his Bavarian counterpart, Johann Lutz, Gresser's successor as Education Minister, was just as solidly opposed by a Patriot majority in the Bavarian *Landtag*.

Johann Lutz was in many ways a Bavarian version of Adalbert Falk. Like Falk, he was National Liberal and pro-German in his social and political outlook. The Prussian diplomat Philipp Eulenberg spoke of him as 'the German sentiment of Bavaria incarnate'.[78] Like Falk, Lutz was the initiator and carrier of *Kulturkampf* policies for his government. Unlike Falk, however, Lutz was to become for two decades the dominant figure in the political life of his state, as Education Minister from 1869 to 1890, and also from 1880 to 1890 as head of the monarchy's ministerial council. In this latter sense he resembled Bismarck more closely than Falk. Lutz was certainly the most forceful figure in Bavarian political life since Montgelas.

Johann Lutz was born in 1826 in Lower Franconia, the son of a Catholic *Volksschule* teacher.[79] After studying law at Würzburg in the 1840s, young Lutz entered the Bavarian civil service in 1851. For the son of a lowly teacher, his rise in the bureaucratic hierarchy was remarkably rapid, although not as unusually so as it would have been in Prussia. Of Bavaria's high-level bureaucrats after 1850, one in five was the son of a *Volksschule* teacher.[80] By 1857 Lutz was negotiating a new commercial code for the German *Zollverein*; by 1863 he was on the king's cabinet secretariat, and by 1867 its head. It was in 1867 also that he became Justice Minister. In December 1869, shortly before Hohenlohe's resignation as head of the ministerial council, he was named Education Minister.

Lutz's appointment, which came as the Vatican Council in Rome was beginning its deliberations on the question of papal infallibility, was a clear signal that the Bavarian government had no intention of backing away from conflict with the papacy in Rome, or with the Patriot majority in the *Landtag*. Although nominally Catholic, Lutz was a religious sceptic who fully intended to continue the modernising policies associated with Gresser and Hohenlohe. If, in educa-

78. Johannes Haller, *Philipp Eulenburg*, p. 53.
79. See 'Johann von Lutz' in *ADB*, vol. LV, pp. 555–8.
80. Hartmut Kaelble, 'Sozialer Aufstieg in Deutschland, 1850–1914', p. 55.

tional affairs, this could not be accomplished by means of a school bill, then piecemeal administrative measures would have to be employed. By whatever means, Lutz was determined to break the hold of the Church over the schools.

Following Hohenlohe's resignation in March 1870, Lutz emerged quickly as the informal leader of the Bavarian ministerial council. The first major question he faced was the Vatican Council's impending vote on papal infallibility. How would Bavaria's bishops vote? Lutz knew that they were fully aware of the government's position on papal infallibility, but he also knew that the government could not afford to risk telling them how to vote. The vote finally came on 18 July, with five of the Bavarian bishops voting in favour of the new doctrine and one bishop, and both archbishops, abstaining by absenting themselves from the proceedings. The doctrine was approved by a vote of 547 to 2.

As everywhere else in Europe, in Bavaria, too, the vote in Rome was overshadowed by the diplomatic conflict that had erupted the week before between Prussia and France over the question of Spanish succession. Suddenly war between the continent's two main powers seemed imminent, with Bavaria committed by treaty to fight on Prussia's side. How would Bavaria respond to this latest crisis? Lutz and most of the government were pro-Prussian, or at least pro-German. The Patriot majority, on the other hand, was overwhelmingly anti-Prussian. Thus it was that on the same day that the infallibility vote was being taken in Rome, the Bavarian *Landtag* was confronted with the question of voting war credits. It was Lutz who steered the war credit bill through to a favourable vote. The following day, 19 July, France and Prussia declared war upon each other.

By early August 55,000 Bavarian troops were fighting in France under Prussia's command. The participation of those troops in the great Sedan victory over the French in September contributed greatly to the war's popularity in Bavaria. Nevertheless, pockets of unhappiness continued to manifest themselves. Soundings of public opinion being taken by the Interior Ministry showed indications of resistance coming from the Catholic clergy. In Lower Franconia large numbers of priests were found praying publicly for a French victory.[81] Despite such signs of potential trouble, in November the

81. BHStA, MInn 66319 (8957/ZO).

government signed a series of treaties committing Bavaria to joining a Prussian-led German unity. Again it was Lutz who steered these treaties through the *Landtag*, making Bavaria part of the German Empire proclaimed in January 1871.[82]

Probably the most vocal of Lutz's supporters in endorsing the new empire were Bavaria's *Volksschule* teachers. As early as 1869 the *Bayerische Lehrerzeitung* had argued that because 'Bavarian history is part of German history and not the other way around', the study of 'German history is more important for Bavaria's pupils than that of Bavaria'.[83] And it was the *Volksschule* teacher M. G. Conrad who celebrated the 'blood and iron pedagogy' of Bismarck that had put an end to what he called the 'particularist swindle' in German national affairs. Similar to their counterparts in Prussia, Bavaria's teachers saw the German Empire as strengthening the state in its struggles against the Church. Thus Bavaria's teachers were among the most enthusiastic supporters of the *Reich*'s school idea and of the principle of confessional mixing in the schools.[84] Certainly not all of these teachers were ardent German nationalists, yet as a group they were clearly in the forefront of those Bavarians eager to promote a German national consciousness.

The development of such a consciousness was enormously complicated by the sharpening of the *Kulturkampf* that followed the Vatican Council vote on infallibility. Lutz's immediate reaction had been to forbid Bavaria's bishops from announcing the doctrine without royal permission. As a counter move, the Church in April 1871 excommunicated Bavaria's leading Catholic opponent of papal infallibility, the theologian–historian Ignaz von Döllinger. Thus the situation escalated until December 1871 when Lutz guided through the *Reichstag* a so-called 'Pulpit Paragraph' which made illegal the use of the pulpit for political announcements. Presumably the Catholic clergy would thereby be constrained from broadcasting its growing opposition to government policies.[85] Unlike Falk in Prussia, Lutz was unable to use the *Landtag* as an ally in his struggle with the

82. Walter Grasser, *Johann Freiherr von Lutz*, pp. 50–4; see also Michael Doeberl, *Entwicklungsgeschichte Bayerns*, vol. III, pp. 535–7.

83. Quoted in Sigrid Ullwer, *Der Geschichtsunterricht in der Volksschule nach den Vorstellungen der bayerischen Regierung und der bayerischen Lehrervereine*, p. 21.

84. Weinlein, *Der Bayerische Volksschullehrer-Verein*, p. 92, and Grasser, *Lutz*, pp. 102–3.

85. Doeberl, *Entwicklungsgeschichte Bayerns*, vol. III, p. 546; Hans Liermann, 'Staatsgedanke und Kirchenpolitik in Bayern seit der Reichsgründung 1871', p. 132; Hans Rall, 'Die politische Entwicklung von 1848 bis zur Reichsgründung 1871', p. 269.

Church. Patriot majorities continued to grow during the 1870s, fuelled by Lutz's actions and by rhetoric from the north that celebrated the Protestant nature of the new German Empire.

As in Prussia, the great battles of the *Kulturkampf* in Bavaria were to be fought in the schools. Unlike the case in Prussia, Lutz had no hopes of getting a school bill passed by his *Landtag*. He had to rely entirely upon his powers as Education Minister to issue orders, decrees, and directives that would circumvent parliamentary opposition. These powers were substantial, however, and allowed Lutz to remain on the offensive during a twelve-year-long campaign to break what he considered the clerical hold on schooling.

In Bavaria, as in Prussia, it was conflict over school inspection that brought the full joining of battle between Church and state. The inspection question had been vitally alive in Bavarian politics since Gresser's efforts in 1867 to replace clergyman school inspectors with a collegial body of local school commissioners. Gresser had failed, but unless the clerical monopoly could be broken by other means, Lutz knew that the larger objective of establishing non-confessional schools would remain illusory. The first initiatives in school inspection came to be taken not by Lutz, but by local authorities in the larger cities who were themselves eager to end the clergy's role in school inspection. Munich was the first to act in 1871 when it replaced its clerical school council with a secular one. When the Archbishop of Munich-Freising protested, Lutz let it be known that the measure had his full approval.[86] During the next years most of Bavaria's larger cities — Nuremberg, Augsburg, Würzburg, Ansbach, and Bayreuth — followed Munich's example.[87] Although accepted in practice in the cities, the principle of secular control in the villages was never established either in law or in practice.

More directly, Lutz was also urging the provincial governments to establish at the county level 'professionally trained supervisory commissions' that would serve as full-time technical advisers to the schools and, by their frequent visits to the *Volksschulen*, act as quasi-supervisors in practice.[88] Upper Bavaria was the first to respond to Lutz's suggestion. By October 1874 the other provinces

86. Wolfgang Zorn, 'Die Sozialentwicklung der nichtagrarischen Welt (1806–1970)', p. 856.
87. Paul Schramm, *Hundert Jahre bayerische Schulgeschichte*, pp. 55, 114.
88. *Ministerialblatt für Kirchen- und Schul-Angelegenheiten im Königreich Bayern*, (*Ministerialblatt*), IX (1873), pp. 20–1.

had also created County School Inspectorates (*Kreisscholarchen*) of their own.[89] Lutz himself appointed the heads of these inspectorates, choosing in each instance a secularly-trained, professional schoolman. To attract capable people, salaries of 1,800 gulden a year were offered. These inspectors were to advise the government on school questions, and spend at least three months of every year visiting local schools. Here they were to concern themselves with the physical condition of the school building and the quality and methods of instruction, and ensure that teachers were holding to the prescribed curriculum. Special care was to be taken also that the local community was enforcing the school attendance law.[90] For the first time, the Bavarian educational bureaucracy was reaching down into the local *Volksschule*.

It was by instalments, also, that the *Volksschule* curriculum came to be modernised. In many areas that curriculum was still essentially the one that Niethammer had devised a half-century before. The process of revision had begun in 1862 when Upper Bavaria introduced basic curriculum changes, followed in 1869 by the Upper Palatinate and in 1870 by Lower Franconia and the Rhine Palatinate. The remaining four provinces completed their own revisions during the course of the 1870s.[91]

By far the most ambitious and controversial of Lutz's attacks on Church prerogatives was his order of August 1873 calling for the creation of school districts separate from the parish boundaries of the Church. Such secularly defined school districts, Lutz recognised, were an absolute prerequisite to his objective of replacing confessional schools with non-confessional ones. Gresser had tried a few years before to create such districts and failed. Before that, in 1810, Zentner had tried, only to have Niethammer reverse his order in 1815.

By virtue of Lutz's order, school districts were to coincide with communal, not parish boundaries.[92] To avoid any misunderstanding, the order spelled out that school districts were to include children of both confessions. Financial reasons were pointed to as an additional inducement for a community to combine its several confessional schools into a single non-confessional one. Lutz's order

89. Grasser, *Lutz*, p. 111.
90. Lutz's instruction to County School Inspectors in *Ministerialblatt*, IX (1873), pp. 225–7.
91. BHStA, MK 22821, 'Lehrplan für die Volksschulen Niederbayerns'.
92. For Lutz's order, see *Ministerialblatt*, IX (1873), pp. 235–330.

also addressed the sensitive question of school inspection, proposing that it eventually be placed in the hands of professionally-trained educators and laymen. As if to dramatise the seriousness of his intent, Lutz ordered that the Catholic Seminar in Bamberg become non-confessional: this after the opening in 1871 in Munich of a non-confessional Seminar for women.[93]

Lutz's school district order opened the Bavarian *Kulturkampf*'s most bitter round. Extraordinary passions were raised in opposition. One Patriot *Landtag* delegate called Lutz's order 'the hardest blow to have hit the Church in Bavaria in this century'.[94] Others equated Lutz with the devil. His relations with the Patriots in the *Landtag*, long strained, were virtually broken. Their powers to oppose him were formidable. They controlled the government's pursestrings and were, therefore, in a position to oppose him at every turn. From 1873 onwards, the fierce annual budget battles in the *Landtag* became forums for castigating Lutz and his policies.

Budget cuts were the usual outcome of these parliamentary battles, although occasionally they degenerated into attacks on the idea of schooling itself. Early in 1876, when Lutz recommended the elimination of all school fees, a Patriot delegate was moved to argue that 'I know what the demands of these modern pedagogues are about. Their axiom is free schools, non-religious schools, and forced schooling, a monopoly over the schools by the state for the sake of the state'.[95] Later in that same session the *Landtag* refused to approve any of the funds that Lutz had requested to establish a Seminar at Regensburg in the Upper Palatinate, despite the fact that the province had a severe teachers' shortage and no Seminar at all.[96] A few years later the house voted to reduce from seven to six the number of years of compulsory schooling, a measure Lutz bitterly opposed. Only its rejection by the upper house, the *Reichsrat*, kept the bill from becoming law.[97] In 1882 the *Landtag* cut in half the amount Lutz requested for state subsidies to needy Seminar pupils. At the same time his request for funds to help support needy pupils in the preparatory schools was cut by more than 80 per cent.[98]

93. Helmut Beilner, *Die Emanzipation der bayerischen Lehrerin*, p. 243.
94. *Verhandlungen der Abgeordneten, Stenographische Berichte* (*VdAbg. St. Ber.*) 1879/80, vol. IV, Session 131, 9 January 1880, p. 476.
95. *VdAbg. St. Ber.*, 1875/76, vol. I, Session 18, 24 March 1876, p. 222.
96. *VdAbg. St. Ber.*, 1875/76, vol. II, Session 65, 15 July 1876, p. 634.
97. Schramm, *Bayerische Schulgeschichte*, p. 75.
98. *VdAbg. St. Ber.*, 1871/72, vol. III, Session 64, 3 April 1872, pp. 121–2.

Meanwhile, the lower house voted to restore the Catholic confessional identity to the Seminar in Bamberg. Only the continued support from the *Reichsrat* during these years kept the Patriot majority in the lower house from undoing most of Lutz's work.

Catholics were not alone in their resistance to Lutz. Among the things his policies evoked was a strong Protestant opposition, one that was eventually to form itself into a Bavarian Conservative Party, a Protestant version of the Patriots. Protestants no less than Catholics had objected to the school district order of 1873. The non-confessional schools it was supposed to produce were seen as a danger also to Protestant education. A resolution to that effect was passed by the Evangelical Synod of Bavaria at its 1873 meeting in Bayreuth.[99] For most of the decade the leader of the Protestant opposition was the same Adolf von Harless who had led its campaign against Gresser's school bill. Though ill and growing blind, Harless was known to grow livid at the mere mention of Lutz's name,[100] promising that he would never retire as long as Lutz remained in office. Only the death of Harless in 1879 relieved him of his commitment.

Harless' successor as Lutz's chief Protestant nemesis was to be August Emil Luthardt, one of the founders of the Bavarian Conservative Party.[101] A jurist and a lay member of Bavaria's Evangelical Synod, Luthardt was elected to the *Landtag* in 1881, the same year in which the Patriots scored the most spectacular of their electoral successes. It was Luthardt's initiative that eventually forced Lutz into retreat. On 5 November 1881, Luthardt introduced into the lower house a resolution to reverse Lutz's school district order of 1873.[102] Such a resolution was by now routine, as was its passage in the *Landtag*. As usual, when the resolution was sent up to be voted on in the *Reichsrat*, it was defeated, and once again Lutz was saved.

But in January 1882 the situation in the *Reichsrat* suddenly changed when Harless' successor in the Evangelical High Consistory, Dr von Mayer, proposed a vote on the principle that non-confessional schools should be allowed only in absolutely unavoid-

99. August Emil Luthardt, *Mein Werden und Wirken im öffentlichen Leben*, p. 218.
100. See 'Harless' in *NDB*, vol. VII, pp. 680–1.
101. On Luthardt, see Remigius Stölzle, 'Ein bayerischer conservativer Politiker, sein Werden und Wirken'.
102. Luthardt, *Mein Werden und Wirken*, p. 237.

able circumstances.[103] Although Lutz was present for the debate and vigorously opposed the resolution, the *Reichsrat* for the first time voted in its favour by a 30 to 24 margin.[104] The vote was a mortal blow to Lutz's school district policy. With both chambers in opposition he had no choice but to back down. None the less, he waited to do so until August 1883, just before the lower chamber, which would inevitably force his hand, was scheduled to reconvene. Ten years after its issue, Lutz rescinded his order calling for independent school districts.[105]

The major battle of the Bavarian *Kulturkampf* was over. Lutz had lost. Once again confessional considerations were to be paramount in the drawing of school district boundaries. Once again Church authorities had the power to veto confessionally-mixed schools. By 1884 fewer than two per cent (129 in total) of Bavaria's *Volksschulen* remained non-confessional.[106]

Whatever setbacks Lutz was forced to endure, he had, by the time of his retirement in 1890, managed to outlast his Prussian counterpart, Adalbert Falk, by more than a decade. Falk ran into difficulty immediately after his successes of 1872. Even his success with the School Inspection Law was not untainted. He had not succeeded as Bismarck had asked in delivering it with 'as little fuss as possible'. The growth of the Centre Party was checked neither by the policy nor by the laws that came to be associated with Falk's name. In the *Landtag* elections of 1873, the first since the School Inspection Law, the Centre captured eighty-eight seats, thirty more than in 1870, and in the *Reichstag* elections of 1874 it doubled its support of 1871, capturing nearly 1.5 million votes. Although the National Liberals continued to dominate both legislative bodies, there was no overlooking the fact that the Centre was establishing itself in a strong second position. Obviously the anti-Catholic measures, including the 1873 May Laws, were not having their intended effect. Indeed, when the Prussian Bishops' Conference later in the year rejected the May Laws, declaring its refusal to abide by them, the *Kulturkampf*

103. Grasser, *Lutz*, p. 114.

104. Michael Doeberl, 'Zur Geschichte der bayerischen Schulpolitik im 19. Jahrhundert', p. 22.

105. For the full text of the 1883 order, see *Schulbedarfsgesetz vom 28. Juli 1902*, ed. Gustav Seiler, pp. 465–70.

106. *Die Ergebnisse der Unterrichts-Statistik im Königreich Bayern für das Schuljahr 1884/85*, p. 17.

was just reaching its peak. Soon the Bishop of Fulda was arrested; then the Archbishop of Cologne; and, in February 1874, Archbishop Ledochowski of Gnesen–Posen.[107] By 1876 all of Prussia's bishops were under arrest or had fled abroad, and one in every five Catholic parishes was without a priest. Yet, neither the Catholic Church nor the Centre Party seemed daunted.

Equally unsuccessful were those measures Falk directed toward 'Germanising' the Poles in the eastern provinces. The legal foundations for these measures lay in the School Inspection Law which allowed for the removal of Polish-Catholic priests from their positions as school inspectors. Within a few days of the passage of the School Inspection Law, Falk's ministry decreed that teachers in Posen be forbidden membership in any type of Polish cultural association. The decree was later extended to teachers in West Prussia and Upper Silesia.[108] In April 1872, the Cabinet also decided on a policy of paying bonuses to teachers in Polish districts who would encourage their pupils to learn German.[109] Falk established special review commissions to visit the schools and to test the success of these programmes. During the next months a series of language decrees ordered that German be made the sole language of instruction for Polish children. At first religious instruction was excepted, but for Posen even that exception was lifted in 1874.[110] With the arrest in February of Archbishop Ledochowski, the *Kulturkampf* reached its high-point. Two years later a law went into effect in the Polish regions prohibiting the use of Polish in the conduct of any official business.[111]

None of these measures proved to be effective, as Falk was soon to learn. Reports from Upper Silesia indicated that many school inspectors were not enforcing the official Germanisation measures. Resistance to these measures from the clergy was nearly unanimous. One report told of a Polish priest warning his parishioners that

107. Lech Trzeciakowski, 'The Prussian State and the Catholic Church in Prussian Poland, 1871–1914', p. 262.

108. PGStA, Thiele Nachlass, Nr. 134, Posen 1870–1887, p. 150.

109. DZA II Merseburg, Staatsministerium Sitzung, 13 April 1872, Rep 90a BIII 2b vol. LXXXIV, pp. 86–7.

110. The decree went into effect for Upper Silesia on 20 September 1872; for the Province of Prussia on 24 July 1873; for the Province of Posen on 27 October 1873. See PGStA, Thiele Nachlass, Nr. 131, Ostpreussen, 1892–1924, p. 72; also Bruno Schumacher, *Geschichte Ost- und Westpreussens*, p. 284, and Korth, *Die preussische Schulpolitik*, pp. 41–3.

111. Frauendienst, 'Preussisches Staatsbewusstsein und polnischer Nationalismus', p. 315; Broszat, *Zweihundert Jahre deutsche Polenpolitik*, p. 139.

learning German 'is the greatest enemy of genuine Christian belief and peace in the family'. To use the 'German language in religious instruction', he said, 'is to misuse the word of God'.[112] The bonus plan for teachers did not work either. Schneider was soon to discover that teachers, in order to impress the review commissions and to qualify for the bonus, would lend their best bilingual pupils to each other.[113] But resistance from the Poles was not the only reason for the failure of Germanisation. The growing teacher shortage of the 1870s was particularly visible in the Polish-speaking regions. Posen alone had 273 vacant teaching positions in 1877.[114] Moreover, the greatest shortage was of those teachers who could teach the German language to Polish-speaking pupils. Eventually, a realistic Provincial Governor of Posen explained to Berlin that 'Teachers who could barely express themselves in German were now supposed to use it in their teaching, and at that, to children who had only a few German words in their vocabulary. Small wonder, therefore, that Polish-speaking teachers were helpless in the face of the task assigned them'.[115]

In the long run, Germanisation did more than fail; it backfired. Foreign pressure proved to be the most effective instrument that Falk could have handed to the Polish nationalists. Unwittingly, Falk had eased their principal task; that of awakening in the masses of the peasantry a political consciousness. How else would the clergy have been able to convince their parishioners that outsiders were trying to destroy their religion? The extent of the reaction in Polish regions became evident as early as 1873 when nationalist leaders enjoyed a surge of success in organising Polish peasant associations.[116] The arrest in 1874 of Archbishop Ledochowski, known, ironically, as a pro-Prussian moderate, merely served to strengthen the nationalist cause.

Falk's original intention, and Bismarck's too, had been to apply the School Inspection Law only in the eastern Polish regions. During 1873, however, circumstances required that the law be applied in the Catholic Rhineland as well. Falk explained to William

112. DZA II Merseburg, Rep 92, Falk 3b, pp. 14–20.
113. Schneider, *Ein halbes Jahrhundert*, pp. 287–8.
114. PGStA, Thiele Nachlass, Nr. 134, Posen 1870–1887, p. 57.
115. Zedlitz-Trützschler to Gossler, 3 March 1888, PGStA, Thiele Nachlass, Nr. 135, Posen, 1888–1902, pp. 3–29.
116. Frauendienst, 'Preussiches Staatsbewusstsein und polnischer Nationalismus', p. 345; Broszat, *Zweihundert Jahre deutsche Polenpolitik*, p. 141.

I that it was the 'growing opposition and agitation from ultramontane circles' that forced him to impose the law here.[117] Falk was disturbed, he said, by the failure of clerical school inspectors in these western provinces to encourage the schools to celebrate the great Prussian victory at Sedan. Sedan-Day celebrations had by 1873 come to enjoy a certain popularity, at least in Protestant circles.[118] Catholic resistance to this emerging national liturgy Falk saw as a sign of anti-German sentiment, and sufficient justification for dismissing large numbers of Catholic school inspectors.[119] By 1875 at least 770 such inspectors had lost their positions in the Rhine Province alone, more than half the total of those dismissed elsewhere in the kingdom. At the same time Falk ordered the last members of the Catholic teaching orders removed from the classroom, a measure also felt most immediately in the Rhineland.[120]

Not all of the measures associated with Falk created as much controversy or produced such mixed results as did those concerning Germanisation or the *Kulturkampf*. On numerous other schooling fronts unquestionable progress was being made. Schneider's General Regulations, for example, managed to produce a degree of uniformity in schooling that had never before been achieved. Attendance became more regular; inspection more systematic; standards more effectively enforced.

Falk's efforts to use the schools to construct a national consciousness scored some successes. Textbook uniformity became a high priority. Textbook revision was carefully supervised by Karl Schneider. Schneider had discovered when he took office in 1872 that there were 165 different readers (*Lesebücher*) in use, some of them going back to editions published in 1802. Understandably, very few of these readers did justice to the political events of 1866–71. Most of them still showed Austria to be in control of a German Confederation and Alsace-Lorraine as belonging to France. In Catholic Westphalia readers that were openly anti-Protestant and anti-Prussian were still in use.[121] In Silesia Schneider found a reader that blamed Frederick II for the war of 1740 against Maria Theresa and closed with a prayer for the Austro-Hungarian Emperor Francis Joseph

117. Falk to William I on 17 August 1875, DZA II Merseburg, 2.2.1. Geheimes Zivilkabinett, Nr. 22129, pp. 65–70.
118. George L. Mosse, *The Nationalization of the Masses*, pp. 90–1.
119. Berg, *Die Okkupation der Schule*, p. 56.
120. Meyer, *Schule der Untertanen*, p. 241, n. 65.
121. Schneider, *Ein halbes Jahrhundert*, pp. 350–4.

II.[122] Obviously, more appropriate versions of modern events had to be published if their study was to promote the development of a German national consciousness. Eventually, a new version approved by Schneider referred to the recent war with France in these terms: 'The only cause was France's envy and jealousy of Prussia's growing greatness and Napoleon's desire to stabilize his quaking throne by a war of conquest'.[123] Thus was laid into place one of the cornerstones of the new national consciousness.

The most measurable of the advances during Falk's tenure was the extraordinary growth in the expenditures that Prussia committed annually to its *Volksschule* system. That total made up of local, provincial, and state funds, doubled between 1871 and 1878, as did the portion of the total that was provided by the state. In 1871 Prussia spent 55,648,398 marks on its *Volksschulen.* Of that amount, 2,890,156 marks, or 5.2 per cent, came from state appropriations. By 1878 total school expenditures had grown to 100,750,000 marks, 12.3 per cent of which came from the state.[124] Translated into per pupil expenditures, the increase was from fourteen marks in 1871 to twenty-four marks in 1878.[125]

These growing expenditures were reflected also in the establishment during the 1870s of twenty-nine new Seminars, bringing their number to 105 in 1879.[126] Four of these new Seminars were established in Brandenburg in response to the growth of Berlin, but special emphasis was also placed upon the Rhineland where the teacher shortage had been exacerbated by Falk's dismissal of the teaching orders.[127] In 1870 there were 4,786 Seminar pupils in Prussia's Seminars; by 1879 that number had risen to 9,404.[128]

Neither the new Seminars nor the increased number of pupils addressed the teacher shortage fully. Although the number of teachers grew from 52,000 to 59,000 between 1871 and 1879,[129] the shortage was in fact worsening. In 1872 the ministry calculated the

122. Ibid., pp. 353–4.
123. Friedrich Götze, *Geographie und Geschichte* (1874), quoted in DZA II Merseburg, Rep 76 neu, Sekt 1B, Generalia, Teil I, Nr. 1, vol. III, p. 268.
124. For the 1871 figure, see *Das Volksschulwesen und das Lehrerbildungswesen im Deutschen Reich*, ed. W. Lexis, pp. 11–12; for the 1878 figure, see Albert Lotz, 'Die Kosten der Volksschule in Preussen', p. 257.
125. *Statistisches Handbuch für den Preussischen Staat*, (1888), vol. I, p. 425.
126. Tews, *Ein Jahrhundert*, p. 223.
127. Schneider, *Ein halbes Jahrhundert*, pp. 343–5.
128. DZA II Merseburg, Rep 76 VII neu, Sekt 1c, Gen. Teil I, vol. X, pp. 3–24.
129. *Statistisches Handbuch für den Preussischen Staat*, (1888), vol. I, p. 414.

shortage at 2,780; in 1877 at 4,581.[130] Part of the shortage can be explained by the continuing growth of the population, although the extraordinary growth rates of the early part of the century had begun to level off in the 1850s, and part resulted from the economic expansion of the 1850s and 1860s. Earlier in the century young men might have been attracted to teaching through the lack of other possibilities. Now there was also the attraction of new industries. The rapidly expanding railway and telegraph industries in particular had positions for which men with Seminar training were qualified. It was during the 1860s that Seminar classes became harder to fill,[131] and when graduates were beginning to reject teaching positions to accept jobs with the railway.[132] Understandably, shortages were worst in the booming industrial areas, not merely because of teachers who had left the profession, but also because enrolments increased as large numbers of people streamed into them. In these areas the limitations on class size stipulated in the 1872 Regulations were impossible to maintain. In the industrial districts around Düsseldorf, for example, there were hundreds of classes with over a hundred pupils.[133] Adding to the teacher shortage were the additional problems of attracting teachers to the eastern Polish districts where conditions were primitive, the pay poor, and the level of tension high. Moreover, there was the added problem presented by Austrian recruiters. An Austrian school law of 1869 enabled recruiters to offer teachers higher salaries as well as pensions after forty years of teaching.[134] The temptation to leave Prussia was in these circumstances often irresistible.

The two means Falk devised to alleviate the teacher shortage were to raise salaries and to recruit more women into teaching. Salaries had stagnated even during the boom years of the 1850s and 1860s, a fact fully consonant with the modest status accorded to teachers by people like Raumer and Stiehl. Thus the average salary for a teacher in a rural *Volksschule* in 1871 was 797 marks and 1,042 marks for his counterpart in the city.[135] In the meantime the teacher had been transformed from the villain of 1848 into the hero of Königgrätz and Sedan. As an emergency measure in 1872 Falk ordered local govern-

130. DZA II Merseburg, Rep 76 VII neu, Sekt 1c, Gen. Teil, Nr. 1, vol. X, p. 31.
131. Meyer, *Schule der Untertanen*, p. 42.
132. Kreppel, 'Der Lehrer in der Zeitgeschichte', p. 217, n. 8.
133. Meyer, *Schule der Untertanen*, p. 44
134. Adam Langer, *Erinnerungen aus dem Leben eines Dorfschullehrers*, p. 283.
135. Tews, *Ein Jahrhundert*, p. 177.

ments to pay out the last of their financial reserves as salary increases to their teachers. Then, in his school budget of 1873 Falk included a subsidy of 7.5 million marks, most of it designated for teacher salaries. By the end of the decade salaries had risen by more than thirty per cent. The average for a rural teacher in 1878 was 1,102 marks and for a city teacher 1,414, providing them with an income well above that being earned by a fully employed factory worker.[136] The social implications of this differential were not lost upon the teachers. Schneider hoped that this elevation in status would make it possible to recruit into the Seminars more young men from higher social levels, or possibly the less talented graduates of the Gymnasium.[137] His hopes were largely in vain. For the middle classes, *Volksschule* teaching still held few attractions.

The exceptions were middle-class women who for the first time during the 1870s entered teaching in large numbers. In 1871 only 3,848, or seven per cent, of Prussia's 52,059 teachers were women, and many of these belonged to the teaching orders that Falk was to disband in 1872. By 1886 the number of women *Volksschule* teachers had doubled to 6,721, and by 1901 their number had doubled again to 13,866.[138] Teaching during these years was still one of the few respectable occupational outlets for girls from middle-class families.[139] Of the 24,000 young women from Prussia's middle classes who were employed in 1865, nearly all were engaged in some form of either teaching or nursing.[140] Eight out of ten women teachers in Prussia during the 1860s came from families headed by businessmen, civil servants, medical doctors, clergymen, or military officers. For male *Volksschule* teachers that figure was only one out of ten.[141]

The pressures during these years upon middle-class girls to find employment have been traced by Barbara Greven-Aschoff to the changing nature of the middle-class family in nineteenth-century Germany.[142] As the average age for marriage for these girls rose to twenty-five during the latter half of the century, the need developed

136. Gerhard Bry, *Wages in Germany, 1871–1945*, p. 51.
137. Meyer, *Schule der Untertanen*, p. 73.
138. *Statistisches Handbuch für den Preussischen Staat*, (1888), vol. I, p. 414; also Lexis, *Das Volksschulwesen*, pp. 11, 13.
139. George Bernstein and Lottelore Bernstein, 'Attitudes Toward Women's Education in Germany, 1870–1914'.
140. See Rolf Engelsing, *Sozial- und Wirtschaftsgeschichte Deutschlands*, p. 150.
141. *Centralblatt*, no. 12, 20 December 1860, pp. 723–4.
142. Barbara Greven-Aschoff, 'Sozialer Wandel und Frauenbewegung', p. 335.

in many families for the daughter to have at least a transitional income.[143] Teaching, or nursing, offered such a possibility. It was also these middle-class teachers who were to become the carriers of the German feminist movement of the late nineteenth century.[144] Luise Otto-Peters and Auguste Schmidt, the founders in 1865 of the General German Women's Association (*Allgemeine deutsche Frauenverein*), were both teachers.[145] Otto-Peters had been associated in the 1840s with Froebel's *Kindergarten* movement; Schmidt had been a teacher in the 1850s in a *Volksschule* in Posen. At its second general meeting in 1868 their new association addressed a petition to the North German Confederation requesting that its member states open more positions in the *Volksschulen* to women. The same petition was addressed to the new German *Reichstag* in 1872, with the added appeal that more Seminars be created to train women.[146]

Whatever Falk's successes, they did not prevent him from being sacrificed when Bismarck decided that socialists rather than Catholics presented the more immediate danger to the *Reich.* As Bismarck began to back away from the *Kulturkampf* during the course of 1878, Falk found himself increasingly exposed. He had failed not only to Germanise Prussia's Poles, but also his efforts to create non-confessional schools, called 'Falk Schools' by his enemies, had served to politicise a large Catholic electorate outside the Polish provinces.[147]

Early signs of trouble had come in 1877 when he delivered a draft of a comprehensive school bill, promised since 1873, to Bismarck. The bill provided that 'the entire system of education, as well as the supervision over all public and private instruction, is, in accordance with this law, in the hands of the state'.[148] It seemed entirely

143. Pauline Herber, *Das Lehrerinnenwesen in Deutschland*, p. 34. Herber contends that it was a rise in the cost of living that made this necessary.

144. Richard J. Evans, 'Liberalism and Society; The Feminist Movement and Social Change'.

145. See 'Luise Otto-Peters' in *ADB*, vol. LII, pp. 737–42; see also 'Auguste Schmidt' in *Lexikon der deutschen Geschichte*, p. 1085.

146. Helene Lange and Gertrud Baumer, eds, *Handbuch der Frauenbewegung*, pt. 1, p. 55.

147. Only 500 of the some 32,000 schools had become 'Falk Schools'. Meyer, *Schule der Untertanen*, p. 54.

148. This began para. one of the bill. For the full text, see PGStA, Rep 90, Staatsministerium, Nr. 2398 a ('Die gesetzliche Regelung des Schul- und Unterrichtswesens im Allgemeinen'), vol. III, 1873–1904. See also Manfred Heinemann, '"Bildung" in Staatshand; Zur Zielsetzung und Legitimationsproblematik der "niederen" Schulen in Preussen, unter Berücksichtigung des Unterrichtgesetzentwurfs des Ministerium Falk (1877)'.

consistent with the aims Bismarck had once espoused. Yet Falk found his bill virtually ignored by the chancellor.

Bismarck, it seems, had finally seen through to the dilemma at the heart of Prussian schooling. On the one hand, Falk's national focus was obviously failing to address effectively the social dissatisfactions that were fuelling socialist sentiments among the labouring classes. At the same time his focus was serving to increase the anti-German sentiments of Catholics both in Germany proper and in the Polish territories. Yet to yield on the confessional school principle, although confessional schools might conceivably employ religion more effectively to inculcate social deference and obedience, would also encourage the Catholic and Polish enemies within the new German nation–state.

How Bismarck would attempt to extricate himself from this dilemma became clear shortly after Pius IX died in early 1878. When the new pope proved to be as eager as Bismarck to back away from the decade-long conflict, the first steps toward reconciliation between the Church and the German state soon followed. In these circumstances, on 14 July 1879, Falk resigned. His replacement was a man known for his arch-conservative, pro-Church attitudes, the Governor of Silesia, Robert von Puttkamer. Puttkamer's appointment caused great apprehension in the Education Ministry, Karl Schneider recalled.[149] It was a clear signal from Bismarck of an entirely new direction in domestic affairs.

At the time of Falk's resignation, Lutz in Bavaria was approaching the most bitter stage of his battle with the Patriots over the school district question. Although he harboured no illusions about the passage of a school bill, Lutz faced many problems similar to those confronting Falk in Prussia. The teacher shortage in Bavaria, for example, was proportionately as severe as in Prussia, a fact that reflected not merely a growing population, but the effective enforcement of school attendance laws. Moreover, economic expansion in Bavaria, no less than in Prussia, was creating jobs that attracted teachers and Seminar graduates. Munich alone lost forty teachers to the telegraph service in 1870–1, while the Rhineland Palatinate lost another forty to the railways.[150] Numerous others entered the postal service or took jobs in the new factories. In 1882 Lutz's ministry

149. Schneider, *Ein halbes Jahrhundert*, p. 379.
150. J. Böhm, ed., *Statistisches Handbuch des bayerischen Volksschulwesens*, I, p. 177.

calculated the shortage at 1,000 teachers, this at a time when Bavaria had only about 10,000 teachers in all.[151]

Unlike Falk, Lutz had a *Landtag* majority against him, and so was not able to address the shortage by bringing about significant salary increases. Even the new minimum salary schedules set in 1875, which ranged from 857 marks annually for a teacher in towns of 10,000 or more to 600 marks in towns of 2,500 or fewer,[152] although an improvement on the schedule of 1861, were still 400 to 600 marks lower than in Prussia. In many places, moreover, salaries remained below the new schedules. Most communities were still requiring teachers to perform sexton services; many still paid them in kind. Often teachers had to collect the school fees themselves. When in 1877 the lower chamber voted against a salary increase for teachers, one Patriot delegate admonished teachers to learn to live more frugally, and to drink only five beers if they could not afford six. He also used the occasion to attack teachers for their membership in what he called the anti-Christian Bavarian Teachers' Association.[153]

Lutz was never able to persuade the *Landtag* to appropriate the sums required for Seminar expansion or for the support of needy Seminar pupils. Funds for the new Seminar he proposed be erected in the Upper Palatinate were turned down completely and the appropriations for scholarships and other subsidies cut drastically by the *Landtag*. Thus the number of Seminar pupils grew only from 716 to 948 between 1873 and 1879.[154] In Prussia during these same years their numbers had nearly doubled. Other solutions for solving the teacher shortage came to be suggested. It was in this setting that the old idea of recruiting discharged soldiers into teaching was revived.[155] The mayor of Nuremberg had a different solution: allow law students who failed their state law-board examinations to become eligible automatically for a *Volksschule* teaching position.[156]

Lutz was more interested in recruiting women into teaching, not merely to address the general shortage of teachers, but to allow him to replace the teaching nuns whom he was eager to be rid of.[157] In

151. *VdAbg. St. Ber.*, 1881/82, vol. III, Session 64, 3 April 1882, p. 109.
152. Heigenmooser, 'Aus der bayerischen Volksschulgeschichte', p. 414.
153. *VdAbg. St. Ber.*, 1877/78, vol. I, Session 21, 5 December 1877, p. 297.
154. *Ministerialblatt*, XII (1876), p. 14.
155. Ibid., (1879), p. 92.
156. Konrad Fischer, *Geschichte des Deutschen Volksschullehrerstandes*, vol. II, p. 381.
157. Grasser, *Lutz*, p. 243.

theory Bavaria had long been receptive to women teaching in the *Volksschule*. In practice, however, very few lay women had entered teaching. Of the 776 women *Volksschule* teachers in 1869, only seventy-five were lay women.[158] To remedy this, Lutz established in 1871 a women's Seminar in Munich. He also began using certain discretionary funds to subsidise the private women's Seminars in Memmingen and Aschaffenburg.[159] By 1877 there were 316 lay women teachers and another 385 who were pupils in the various Seminars.[160] Although Lutz worked hard to get women accepted as teachers in the rural villages,[161] most of them ended up teaching in the larger cities. By 1889 nearly forty per cent of the *Volksschule* teachers in Munich were women. Among the advantages of women that Lutz touted was the fact that they were less expensive to employ than men. Their salary schedules were set permanently one level below that of male teachers. The minimum salary of 608 marks per year set in 1888 was effective into the next century and was considerably below that earned by a janitor in the Education Ministry.

During the school year 1884–5 there were 1,748 women *Volksschule* teachers in Bavaria, compared to 10,748 men. Of these women, 913 were from the laity and 835 from the Church.[162] The total of men and women teachers together gave Bavaria a teacher-pupil ratio of 1:65, better than was the ratio in Prussia. As usual, caution must be used in interpreting the figures. School inspectors were still reporting 'often running into more than a hundred children in a low, narrow schoolroom, penned in like sheep and packed like herrings'.[163] Also, the per pupil expenditure of 16 marks was only two-thirds that of Prussia.[164] In contrast to Prussia, school fees, despite Lutz's efforts to end their collection, still played an important role in financing Bavaria's schools. Such fees in 1884–5 provided 1,815,394 marks, nearly fifteen per cent, out of a total Bavarian expenditure on its *Volksschulen* of 13,781,341 marks.[165] Teachers still depended upon these fees for ten per cent of their salaries.

158. *Ministerialblatt*, XIII (1877), p. 382.
159. Ibid., XV (1879), p. 89.
160. Ibid., XII (1876), p. 15; also XIII (1877), p. 382.
161. See Lutz's order of 7 January 1876 in *Schulbedarfsgesetz*, ed. Seiler, pp. 451–2.
162. *Ergebnisse der Unterrichts-Statistik* (1884/85), p. 21.
163. Eugen Leipold, *Erinnerungen aus meinem Leben*, p. 77.
164. *Ergebnisse der Unterrichts-Statistik* (1884/85), p. 178.
165. Ibid., p. 16.

Whatever their weaknesses, the statistics collected for 1884–5 do provide a basis for assessing the state of Bavaria's schools in the late nineteenth century. Eighty-seven per cent, or 842,628 of Bavaria's school-age children were attending 7,075 *Volksschulen*, where they were being taught by 12,296 teachers. Of the *Volksschulen*, seventy per cent were Catholic, twenty-six per cent Protestant, and one per cent Jewish; fewer than two per cent were non-confessional.[166] It should be noted that during the latter half of the nineteenth century the Bavarian War Ministry continued to observe a steady decline in the number of recruits who were unable to read, write, or do simple calculations.[167] Such a measure of success, though a rough one, indicates that schooling, after nearly a century, had finally taken firm hold in Bavaria.

By the mid-1880s, moreover, the problems of school financing began gradually to abate. Not only did Lutz's relations with the *Landtag* improve after he withdrew his school district order, but Bavaria's portion of the income from Bismarck's agriculture tariffs of 1879 was beginning to relieve the financial pressures on the government. A rider to the tariff law stipulated that a portion of the income going to the federal states was to be used for social purposes. Thus was made possible the increase in expenditures upon schools, universities, academies, libraries, art collections, and monuments that characterised public spending in late nineteenth-century Bavaria.[168]

Schools alone do not a nation make. That conclusion, whether applied to Prussia or Bavaria, seemed inescapable in the early 1880s. Prussia's schools had not Germanised the Poles, and questions would soon be raised about whether Bavarian schools were any more successful in making Germans out of their own pupils. Neither did schools win a *Kulturkampf*. To that both Falk and Lutz could attest. A new question that was to emerge in the next few years was how effective the schools could be in harnessing the lower classes to the social order. In essence, this was a revival of the question that had been raised a century earlier about a rootless peasant underclass. This time it was raised by the sudden appearance and extraordinary growth of an industrial labouring class.

166. Ibid.

167. Compare the figures for 1860, 1871, and 1879, in *Ministerialblatt*, I (1860); VII (1871), and XVI (1880).

168. Agatha Ramm, *Germany, 1789–1919*, p. 347; also Dieter Albrecht, 'Von der Reichsgründung bis zum Ende des Ersten Weltkrieges (1871–1918)', pp. 288, 350.

7
Schooling and Modernity 1880–1900

When Bismarck dismissed Falk in 1879, it brought to an end the second great era of educational reform in nineteenth-century Prussia; much the same held true for Bavaria in 1883 when Lutz withdrew his school district order. In Prussia, particularly, Falk's dismissal was followed by a political reaction. Once again the critics of schooling held sway, pointing to schools and teachers as the source of social ills rather than their solution. As if to dramatise these ills, there were two attempts in 1878 upon the life of William I. Bismarck immediately blamed the growing socialist movement and proposed legislation for its suppression. Others blamed the assassination attempts directly upon the non-confessional 'Falk Schools' which they believed encouraged radical behaviour.[1]

Falk's replacement as Education Minister was Robert von Puttkamer, most often remembered for his next post as Prussia's arch-conservative Interior Minister during most of the 1880s. Eckart Kehr has characterised Puttkamer as the central figure in the political and social reaction of that decade.[2] The scion of an East Elbian Junker family, Puttkamer has been compared to the reactionary Education Minister of the 1850s, Kurt von Raumer.[3] Puttkamer's tenure as Education Minister lasted only until May 1881 when he moved to the Interior Ministry. His chief aim during that short time was to restore the bonds between school and Church, bonds that

1. Konrad Fischer, *Geschichte des Deutschen Volksschullehrerstandes*, vol. II, p. 376.
2. Eckart Kehr, 'The Social System of Reaction in Prussia under the Puttkamer Ministry'.
3. Johannes Tews, *Ein Jahrhundert preussischer Schulgeschichte*, p. 184.

Falk had fought so hard to remove.

Once again the teacher became the whipping boy. Puttkamer began by reactivating the compulsory teachers' conferences that Raumer had instituted in the 1850s to eradicate the 'agitational efforts' of the teachers' associations.[4] Themes for Puttkamer's conferences were chosen by the Education Ministry and clergymen school inspectors who conducted them. The younger teachers particularly came to resent these conferences. Johannes Tews recalled years later that any discussion of pedagogical theory was declared out of bounds by the clergymen co-ordinators. Tews had wanted to discuss Herbart at one of these conferences, but his first question was immediately shut off.[5] Puttkamer also brought to an end Falk's policy of granting teachers days off to attend meetings of their associations.[6]

In one sense at least Puttkamer's efforts bore fruit. Membership in the Prussian Teachers' Association declined during the next years by more than 2,000, from 16,107 to 14,072.[7] His ministry also refused permission to communities that asked to be allowed to combine their several confessional schools into a single non-confessional one.[8] Thus the creation of new 'Falk Schools' was stopped in its tracks. Although these had never numbered more than 500, even that figure came to be reduced during the next years. As was to be expected, many of the secular school inspectors that Falk had appointed were dismissed. Clergymen, the 'natural authorities', were returned to their traditional places.

Puttkamer gave the clearest exposition of his views about teachers in his so-called Ash Wednesday speech to the *Landtag* on 11 February 1880. He claimed to have found among many teachers a 'deep-seated ethical and moral depravity', especially among those in the large cities where their 'moral conduct has suffered a most flagrant decline'.[9] He warned the political parties against any efforts to gain the support of teachers. The *Volksschule* teacher, he said, 'would do much better to leave to his superiors those important matters he mistakenly believes he must concern himself with, and to use his

4. Folkert Meyer, *Schule der Untertanen*, p. 156; PGStA, Thiele Nachlass, Nr. 130, Ostpreussen, 1870–1891, p. 97.
5. Tews, *Ein Jahrhundert*, pp. 85–6.
6. Meyer, *Schule der Untertanen*, p. 157.
7. Tews, *Ein Jahrhundert*, p. 187.
8. Karl Schneider, *Ein halbes Jahrhundert im Dienste von Kirche und Schule; Lebenserinnerungen*, pp. 382–3.
9. Quoted in Meyer, *Schule der Untertanen*, p. 155.

energies in that narrow sphere to which his calling assigns him'.[10]

Puttkamer's speech represented the low point of his relations with Prussia's teachers, but it did not signal the start of a full-scale reaction.[11] There were no major purges in the Education Ministry. Schneider stayed on as the top official in *Volksschule* administration. Though associated closely with Falk, he was given no hint that he was in trouble. No new regulations were promulgated, and no new school bill was proposed. In fact, there was less of an effort during the 1880s to undo what had been done, than there was simply to draw back from using the schools to address Prussia's principal problems. Measures other than schooling came to be emphasised in dealing with the Poles and Prussia's social question. Not until a decade later, at the instigation of William II, was the emphasis upon schooling reestablished.

The decreased emphasis upon schooling during the 1880s is best illustrated by cuts in funding. One of Puttkamer's first orders to school authorities was that they exercise restraint in the financial demands they were placing upon local communities.[12] A decade earlier Falk had urged these same authorities to increase their demands. Bismarck had begun to fear that Falk's demands were affecting his own political standing. The financial burden appeared to be especially heavy upon the indebted noble landowners who were still required by law to provide for the schooling of their peasant labourers. 'Some owners of heavily mortgaged estates', a Bismarck aide noted, were being forced to 'pay out nearly half of their net incomes for schools'.[13] Much of the effort that would be devoted to schooling in the 1880s was expended in trying to relieve the local tax burden.

In the face of this de-emphasis, the government came to address major social problems by measures more direct than schooling. In the eastern provinces expulsions and colonisation came to take priority over efforts to Germanise the Poles through schooling. As for the growth of a socialist movement, Bismarck added to the stick of his anti-socialist law of 1878 the carrot of welfare legislation during

10. Quoted in Tews, *Ein Jahrhundert*, p. 187.

11. Lavinia M. Anderson and Kenneth Barkin, 'The Myth of the Puttkamer Purge and the Reality of the Kulturkampf: Some Reflections on the Historiography of Imperial Germany'.

12. For Puttkamer's order of 28 May 1881, see Meyer, *Schule der Untertanen*, p. 161.

13. Quoted in Norman Rich, *Friedrich von Holstein*, vol. I, pp. 109–10.

the 1880s. The schools were not enlisted in the campaign against socialism until late in the decade.

It was during the 1880s that the Bavarian experience in schooling became that of Prussia writ small. Lutz's retreat on the school district question ushered in an era of compromise between the ministerial oligarchy on the one hand, and the Patriot majority and the Church on the other. Schooling was the heart of this compromise. The compromise was affected neither by the death of Ludwig II in 1886, nor by the uniting of the Patriots with the German Centre Party in 1887. It outlasted Lutz himself, whose failing health forced him to retire in 1890. His successors in the Education Ministry, August von Müller from 1890 to 1895, and Robert von Landmann from 1895 to 1902, were both more conciliatory than he in recognising the role of the Church in schooling.[14] Both were so conciliatory toward the Church, particularly Landmann, that they alienated the Bavarian Teachers' Association and raised doubts in the minds of some Prussians about Bavaria's loyalty to the larger German Empire.

The era of compromise that followed 1883 resolved no basic educational questions. No school bill was presented to the *Landtag* or even drafted. Not even the collection of school fees was brought to an end. The only thing resolved at all was the question of school financing in the form of a School Financing Law in 1902.[15] The law became the chief monument to Landmann's tenure as Education Minister. His critics called it a law that 'wore ultramontane colors'.[16] On the one hand it improved teachers' salaries by establishing a 1,200 mark minimum; on the other it solidified the role of the clergy in school supervision.[17] Although communities were empowered to eliminate school fees if they wished, very few of them did so. At the time of the law's passage such fees were still being collected in over seventy per cent of Bavaria's schools.[18] So embittered were *Landtag* liberals by Landmann's bill that they worked to undermine his political base, and eventually they did

14. See Walter Schärl, *Die Zusammensetzung der bayerischen Beamtenschaft von 1806 bis 1918*, p. 98, and Otto Wilhelm Beyer, *Deutsche Schulwelt des neunzehnten Jahrhunderts in Wort und Bild*, pp. 171–2.

15. For the details of the Schulbedarfsgesetz of 28 July 1902, see *Schulbedarfsgesetz vom 28. Juli 1902*, ed. Gustav Seiler.

16. Paul Schramm, *Hundert Jahre bayerische Schulgeschichte*, p. 106.

17. Karl Möckl, *Die Prinzregentenzeit; Gesellschaft und Politik während der Aera des Prinzregenten Luitpold in Bayern*, p. 522.

18. Seiler, ed., *Schulbedarfsbesetz*, pp. 21, 277.

force his resignation.[19] The Centre majority retaliated by cutting 100,000 marks from the budget of the new Education Minister.[20]

In Prussia the political direction for the 1880s was determined by Bismarck's fear that school costs were eating away at his conservative political support. It was in June 1881, from his Varzin estate, that he instructed his new Education Minister Gustav von Gossler to take measures that would reduce the tax burden of local communities.[21] The income gained from the new agricultural tariffs would make additional state subsidies possible, he thought.[22] He also let it be known that he wanted the burdensome school fees abolished,[23] though they were still being collected in many parts of the kingdom. Gossler appears to have felt himself more constrained by existing legislation than Bismarck thought necessary. The two had quarrelled over the slowness with which Bismarck's wishes were being carried out.[24] That Gossler was merely following the dictates of the 1794 civil code failed to impress the Chancellor. When the two finally did reach agreement on a new school financing measure, its primary effect was to limit the authority of Falk's county school inspectors to make spending demands upon the local community. Gossler still saw potential danger in the measure. Would some schools thereby be rendered incapable of carrying out the basic educational tasks? It was a concern that Bismarck dismissed out of hand. He had been worried for a long time, he said, about the social dangers represented by an over-educated rural population, especially of girls who might want to run off to cities and there fall into an immoral life.[25]

The situation was not resolved until March 1886 when a secret ministerial order absolved estate owners from making additional contributions to the maintenance of the schools.[26] Secrecy was necessary for political as well as legal reasons: the order contravened the school financing provisions of the civil code. The government also devised a scheme by which state money that had been budgeted

19. Karl, Möckl, 'Gesellschaft und Politik während der Aera des Prinzregenten Luitpold; Ein Beitrag zur Vorgeschichte der Revolution in Bayern', p. 17.
20. Dieter Albrecht, 'Von der Reichsgründung bis zum Ende des Ersten Weltkrieges (1871–1918)', p. 356.
21. Schneider, *Ein halbes Jahrhundert*, pp. 393–4.
22. Michael Tracey, *Agriculture in Western Europe*, pp. 87–8.
23. Meyer, *Schule der Untertanen*, p. 160.
24. Friedrich von Holstein, *The Holstein Papers*, vol. II, pp. 109–10.
25. Meyer, *Schule der Untertanen*, p. 163.
26. Tews, *Ein Jahrhundert*, p. 160.

for teacher salary supplements could be routed through them directly into the local school coffers.[27] Thus teachers came to bear the burden of bringing financial relief to the local community. Their incomes suffered accordingly.

The average salary for a teacher dropped from 1,122 to 1,067 marks between 1878 and 1886,[28] this at a time when the shortage of teachers was growing especially acute in the new industrialised areas. Numerous Westphalian communities, for example, could not keep up with their growing school needs. In town after town, the need for schools and teachers doubled every few years.[29] Only in one respect did the teachers' situation improve in the 1880s, and that was because of the provisions of the Teachers' Pension Law of 1885. Until then it had been the custom in many areas for teachers to pay a so-called *Emeritendrittel*, one-third of their salaries, to their retired or incapacitated predecessors.[30] Under the new law a teacher, at the age of sixty-five, became eligible for a pension that was funded largely by state contributions. No longer was it necessary to prove disability in order to be allowed to retire. The effect of the law was felt almost immediately. By 1891 nearly 6,000 teachers had chosen to take their annual pensions of 980 marks rather than to continue teaching.[31]

It was in the late 1880s that school financing finally came to be regulated by new legislation. A May 1887 'Law Regulating Financial Requirements for *Volksschulen*' placed strict limits upon the demands that could be placed upon the local community.[32] These communities found their powers to resist the demands of the county school councils considerably enhanced. Understandably the law was unpopular with teachers who saw it as a barrier either to higher salaries or to improved conditions in the schools. Many of them referred to it as the 'Handcuff Law', or, in parody of the formal name of Bismarck's anti-socialist law, the 'Law Against the Publically Dangerous Endeavors of the County School Councillors'.[33]

A second law, one 'Regarding the Easing of the *Volksschule* Finan-

27. Johannes Tews, *Aus Arbeit und Leben; Erinnerungen und Rückblicke*, p. 131.
28. *Statistisches Handbuch für den Preussichen Staat*, (1888), vol. I, p. 427.
29. Albert Lotz, 'Die Kosten der Volksschule in Preussen', p. 255.
30. Ernst Cloer, 'Sozialgeschichtliche Aspekte der Solidarisierung der preussischen Volksschullehrerschaft im Kaiserreich und in der Weimarer Republik', p. 61.
31. Meyer, *Schule der Untertanen*, p. 105.
32. For the 26 May 1887 law, see *Preussisches Schulrecht*, ed. Walter Landé, vol. I, pp. 361–6.
33. Tews, *Aus Arbeit und Leben*, pp. 155–6; Landé, ed., *Schulrecht*, pp. 359–60.

cial Burden', was effected in June 1888, just as William II was ascending the throne. This law ended once and for all the collection of school fees.[34] For the first time in its history the entire Prussian *Volksschule* was free of charge to all of its pupils. The law also laid the foundation for greatly expanded subsidies to the local communities. In 1886 that subsidy had been 14,000,000 marks, or twelve per cent of the 112,500,000 marks expended upon the *Volksschulen*. By 1891 the subsidy was up to 46,500,000 marks, or thirty-two per cent of 146,225,000 total.[35] The agricultural tariff increase of 1887 helped to finance these subsidies,[36] which now also came to include direct contributions to teachers' salaries.[37]

Salaries had not been the only aspect of schooling to decline during the 1880s. Pupil–teacher ratios had grown steadily worse during the course of the decade in all but seven of Prussia's thirty-five governing districts.[38] Schools were still so crowded that one out of every four classes in Prussia had to share its room with another class, meaning that each class went to school only half-time,[39] a fact that one observer noted helped to make the idea of schooling more palatable in certain rural areas.[40] By the standards of Schneider's 1872 Regulations, moreover, nearly half of the classrooms in Prussia were overcrowded; more than 86,000 pupils were in classes of over 120 children. The worst situation applied in Posen where the average for the whole province was 110 children to each teacher. Still, in spite of their shortcomings, Matthew Arnold noted during an inspection tour of Prussia's schools in 1886 that school attendance in Prussia was being taken for granted by both pupils and parents, something he could not say for France or England.[41]

It was the school situation in Posen that made Gossler most unhappy. An ardent Germaniser who considered himself a hardliner on the Polish question, he was stung by the criticism of his cabinet colleague, Finance Minister Scholz, that efforts to improve the *Volksschulen* of Posen served mainly to help the Poles solidify their

34. Berlin had ceased to collect school fees in 1870. See Lotz, 'Kosten', p. 259.
35. Ibid., p. 257; W. Lexis, *Das Volksschulwesen und das Lehrerbildungswesen im Deutschen Reich*, pp. 11–12.
36. Wolfgang Zorn, 'Staatliche Wirtschafts- und Sozialpolitik und öffentliche Finanzen, 1800–1970', p. 155.
37. Meyer, *Schule der Untertanen*, p. 276, n. 100.
38. Tews, *Aus Arbeit und Leben*, pp. 131–2.
39. 20,818 of the 75,097 school classes had to share their rooms with another class.
40. Matthew Arnold, 'Special Report on Certain Points Connected with Elementary Education in Germany, Switzerland, and France', p. 50.
41. Ibid., pp. 47–8.

national identity.[42] Certainly, by mid-decade, the problems in Posen seemed to be worsening. Interior Minister Puttkamer pointed out that the Polish population was growing twice as fast as that of the German one.[43] He made this point in defence of Bismarck who in February 1885 had ordered the expulsion from Prussia's eastern provinces of recent Polish and Jewish immigrants from Russian Poland or Galicia. The order led in July 1885 to the expulsion of some 30,000 Poles and Jews from Prussian territory.[44]

It was in 1885 as well that Gossler became involved in a Germanisation measure that had nothing to do with schools or teachers. He had been aware for some time, he told the Cabinet, that large numbers of Polish-owned estates were for sale. If these estates could be purchased by Germans, their element in the eastern provinces would be greatly strengthened.[45] It was in September 1885 that he informed the Cabinet that the Education Ministry itself had purchased several of these estates, and had offers out on twelve more. The estates the ministry owned, he said, were being rented out profitably to German tenants.[46] Bismarck was delighted at the success of this latest venture in Germanisation.

Bismarck, none the less, was concerned with effecting a more comprehensive strategy for Germanisation. He selected his protégé Heinrich von Tiedemann, the former head of the chancellery office and the current administrator for the governing district of Posen,[47] to formulate this strategy. Tiedemann submitted his recommendations in January 1886. In the main, his recommendations enlarged upon what was currently being done. To promote Germanisation, he urged the creation of a special fund to be used for the purchase of Polish-owned land. As for schooling measures, he recommended re-examination of the language laws and, particularly, that the appointment of teachers be taken away from local officials and given to the state.[48] It was Tiedemann's recommendation also that led in

42. Deutsches Zentralarchiv (DZA) II Merseburg, Staatsministerium Sitzung of 24 January 1886, Rep 90a BIII, 2b Nr. 6, vol. XCVIII, pp. 27–37.
43. Reported in *Annual Register* (1885), p. 234.
44. Helmut Neubach, *Die Ausweisungen von Polen und Juden aus Preussen, 1885–86*, p. 35.
45. DZA II Merseburg, Staatsministerium Sitzung of 16 December 1884, Rep 90a BIII, 2b Nr. 6, vol. XCVII, p. 179.
46. DZA II Merseburg, Staatsministerium Sitzung of 24 September 1885, Rep 90a BIII, 2b Nr. 6, vol. XCVIII, pp. 14–16.
47. See 'Heinrich von Tiedemann', in *Lexikon der deutschen Geschichte*, p. 1201.
48. For Tiedemann's recommendations, see DZA II Merseburg, Staatsministerium Sitzung of 24 September 1885, Rep. 90a BIII, 2b Nr. 6, Vol. XCVIII, pp. 14–16.

April 1886 to the *Landtag*'s passage of a 'Law Concerning the Promotion of German Settlement in the Provinces of West Prussia and Posen', and to the creation of a Colonisation Commission that was given a fund of 100,000,000 marks.[49]

Tiedemann's suggestions for the schools were acted upon immediately by Gossler. By July he had manoeuvred through the *Landtag* a bill that made teachers in the eastern provinces appointees of the state.[50] At the same time he issued guidelines that only those 'who give a guarantee of complete trustworthiness and will offer the children a German-monarchical education' could receive appointment as teachers.[51] To prevent the spread of Polish culture into German areas, he ordered that Polish-speaking teachers be excluded from schools serving mixed German-Polish populations. Even where Germans were a minority, great effort was to be made to find German-speaking teachers. For a teacher to know Polish was in this market a disadvantage. Polish applicants to the Seminars, moreover, were to be turned down whenever possible, said Gossler, in order to build up a 'reliable body of German teachers'.

Puttkamer pointed out the obvious fact that there were simply too few German-speaking teachers to accomplish Gossler's goal.[52] The shortage of teachers was greatest among those who were most needed — German-speaking Catholic teachers. Traditional proponents of confessional schooling suddenly found themselves confronted with the realisation that confessional schools were emerging as a powerful block against the policies of Germanisation.[53] None the less, Gossler established 350 new teaching positions in the eastern provinces.[54] Who would fill them was a question left unanswered. The high-point of this latest schooling offensive came in October 1887 when Gossler ordered an end to the 'teaching of the Polish language in all elementary schools in [the Province of] Posen'.[55] The hours gained thereby were to be devoted to providing Polish pupils with instruction in German. Massive protest demon-

49. Martin Broszat, *Zweihundert Jahre deutsche Polenpolitik*, pp. 148–50; see also Robert Lewis Koehl, 'Colonialism Inside Germany: 1886–1918', pp. 255–72.

50. DZA II Merseburg, Rep 90a BIII, 2b Nr. 6, Vol. XCVIII, pp. 38–42.

51. Gossler quoted in Rudolf Korth, *Die preussische Schulpolitik und die polnischen Schulstreiks*, p. 20.

52. PGStA, Thiele Nachlass, Nr. 134, Posen 1870–1887, pp. 132–3.

53. Korth, *Die preussische Schulpolitik*, p. 21.

54. PGStA, Thiele Nachlass, Nr. 134, Posen 1870–1887, p. 153.

55. For the order of 10 October 1887, see *Akten zur preussischen Kirchenpolitik in den Bistümern Gnesen-Posen, Kulm und Ermland, 1885–1914*, ed. Erwin Gatz, p. xli.

strations greeted Gossler's order.[56] Ministry officials in Berlin were kept busy for weeks making inspection trips and delivering situation reports. It was during this turmoil that Gossler extended Falk's 1872 order prohibiting Polish teachers from belonging to Polish cultural associations to include a prohibition upon their depositing money in a Polish-owned *Volksbank*.[57]

The tensions produced by these Germanisation measures would probably have reached their explosive potential very quickly had it not been for the redirecting of schooling efforts that followed the accession of William II as the new Prussian king and German emperor in June 1888. William II was more immediately concerned with what he saw to be the growing alienation of the German working classes than he was with the problem of the Poles. Young, naîve, undisciplined, supremely self-confident, the new monarch decided to be, for all practical purposes, his own education minister. The result was a momentary lull in the Germanisation of the Poles while energies were directed toward harnessing the German working classes to the national idea.

Wherever William II looked in 1888, he saw the signs of threatening social crisis, something that had seemed to recede after the 1850s. Electoral support for the outlawed socialist party had doubled during the course of the 1880s. Since 1885, moreover, the number of industrial strikes had grown at an alarming rate.[58] Then, in 1889, came the greatest strike wave of the century. The strikes began in January with weavers and dyers in the textile industries of western Prussia.[59] In May they had spread to coalminers in the Ruhr and from there to the miners of Silesia where the problem was exacerbated by the fact that the mine-owners were usually German and the workers Polish.[60] Ultimately, during the course of 1889, nearly half a million workers were involved in over 1,100 strikes. Panic was not William's alone. Albert Schäffle, the Tübingen econ-

56. Korth, *Die preussische Schulpolitik*, p. 47; Manfred Radtke, *Der schulpolitische Kampf in Preussen-Deutschland*, p. 224.

57. PGStA, Thiele Nachlass, Nr. 134, Posen 1870–1887, p. 153.

58. Hans-Dieter Gimbel, 'Sozialistengesetz und "grosse Depression": Die deutsche Gewerkschaftsbewegung von der Wirtschaftskrise 1873 bis zum Kölner Parteitag der deutschen Sozialdemokratie 1893', p. 51.

59. Max Jürgen Koch, *Die Bergarbeiterbewegung im Ruhrgebiet zur Zeit Wilhelms II (1889–1914)*, p. 33; see also Vernon Lidtke, *The Outlawed Party; Social Democracy in Germany, 1878–1890*, p. 293.

60. Lawrence Schofer, 'Patterns of Worker Protest: Upper Silesia, 1865–1914', p. 449

omist, declared the situation to be of 'immediate danger to state and nation'.[61] Could revolution be far behind?

For both Schäffle and William II, however, the perception of crisis differed markedly from those which had excited German thinking during the first half of the century. Earlier in the century specific social ills such as beggary, banditry, vagrancy, or infanticide had been taken into account. Now it was an ideology, itself a set of social perceptions, that was defined as the problem, not industrialisation, not urbanisation, not the trade unions. Socialism was being defined as the cause of dislocations rather than as their product. The specific problems, therefore, remained unaddressed.

Bismarck and William II could not agree on how to deal with the strikers. Bismarck at first favoured non-intervention, believing that to give the strikers free reign would be the most effective way to demonstrate to liberals the dangers emanating from the lower classes. William II, on the other hand, wishing to be the 'social Kaiser', wanted to intervene in order to gain some symbolic concessions for the workers. Accordingly, in May, he met with a delegation of strikers, but solely to warn them against succumbing to the dangerous ideas of socialism.[62] In the meantime, Bismarck changed his mind. The growing number of strikes persuaded him that only the declaration of a state of siege and the call-up of troops could remedy the situation.[63] Therewith was defined the disagreement that would lead to Bismarck's dismissal.

This was the setting in late July 1889 when the news arrived from Paris of the founding of an international league of socialist parties from twenty different countries. It was evident that the German socialist party was the back-bone of this so-called Second International. Moreover, representatives of the striking Ruhr miners had gone to Paris to present their case and the socialist delegates had passed a resolution endorsing all of the strikers' demands.[64] German socialists were not, in fact, involved with the strikes, but to the nervous Bismarck and William II the connection seemed perfectly clear. On top of this came the February 1890 *Reichstag* elections in

61. Quoted in Dieter Fricke, *Bismarcks Prätorianer: Die Berliner politische Polizei im Kampf gegen die deutsche Arbeiterbewegung (1871–1898)*, p. 272.
62. Walter Bussmann, 'Das Zeitalter Bismarcks', pp. 237–8.
63. DZA II Merseburg, Staatsministerium Sitzung of 12 May 1889, Rep 90a BII, 2b Nr. 6, vol. CI, pp. 192–202.
64. Fricke, *Bismarcks Prätorianer*, p. 276; Lidtke, *The Outlawed Party*, p. 295; James Joll, *The Second International 1889–1914*, pp. 44–6.

which the socialist vote once again doubled. Nearly a million and a half people (twenty per cent of those voting) voted for the socialists, more than for any other single party. The greatest gains for the socialists came, significantly, in the strike-plagued Ruhr where in some districts their vote grew as much as eight-fold.[65] In the face of these election results Bismarck came to believe that the only rescue from social revolution would be a *Putsch* that would extract from the constitution its provision for universal male suffrage. William II still hoped that the situation could be alleviated by more peaceful means, perhaps by the international labour conference that he was sponsoring in Berlin in March 1890. When Bismarck continued to resist the convening of this conference, as well as certain proposals for changes in Russian policy, William II ordered him to ask permission to resign. It had been a crisis in Prussian military policy in 1862 that had brought Bismarck to power; it was a crisis in social policy nearly three decades later that was to bring his power to an end.

William II, determined to be a 'social Kaiser', had by now also become determined to be a 'school Kaiser'. The idea of addressing the social question 'through reform and proper organization of the *Volksschule*', as he put it, had come to him even before the 1889 strike wave began.[66] It was at a royal hunt in December 1888 that he told Lucius von Ballhausen, his Minister of Agriculture, of his belief that a teacher, if he had no more than forty pupils, could easily make them immune to the erroneous notions of social democracy. Ballhausen, although sympathetic to William II's intent, pointed out the enormous cost of implementing such a proposal. He also asked William whether he was certain that teachers would be an entirely reliable element in the fight against socialist ideas.

William II was not to be dissuaded, especially in the face of the strikes that began early the following year. The result was one of his frequent interventions in the making of policy. On 30 April 1889, he summoned his ministers to the palace for the purpose 'of discussing an effective battle plan against social democratic tendencies'. Laws, decrees, all such things tried in the past, had failed, he said. 'The main battlefield, therefore, lies in the schools'. Only in the schools could the masses be 'shown through appropriate instruction that social democratic teachings are impractical and ruinous for all alike'.[67]

65. Gimbel, 'Sozialistengesetz und "grosse Depression"', pp. 51–2.
66. Lucius von Ballhausen, *Bismarck Erinnerungen*, p. 485.
67. PGStA, Rep 90a (Staatsministerium), Nr. 2400, pp. 44–5.

The ministers apparently were taken by complete surprise. Bismarck said something incoherent about the need for a new school curriculum and possibly a 'political-monarchical catechism' that might be designed to inculcate the proper social and political principles in children.[68] It was Gossler who felt himself most directly under attack, however. He defended himself by pointing out that more than half of Prussia's children were attending inadequate rural schools and that, in fact, the most dangerous time for young males came after they had left the *Volksschule* and before they were eligible for induction into the military service. For these years the *Volksschule* bore no responsibility.

On the following day, 1 May, without so much as consulting Gossler, William II issued his famous order that read: 'For some time now I have been thinking that the schools at all levels should be employed in combatting the spread of socialistic and communistic ideas'.[69] Schools, he continued, 'must be concerned with securing in young people the conviction that the teachings of social democracy are not merely contradictory to God's commandments and Christian morality, but are in reality impractical and destructive of the individual and the whole of society'. So that the schools might cultivate 'a fear of God and a love for the Fatherland', William requested that they emphasise the teaching of recent history to show how 'Prussian kings have consistently worked to improve the living conditions of workers from the time of Frederick the Great and the abolition of serfdom, down to today'. To use the schools in this way, he acknowledged, would require more teachers. Consequently he proposed also the expansion of teacher-training institutions. Such confidence in the powers of pedagogy had not been heard for a long time. It should be pointed out also that William II did not hold teachers responsible for the social crisis he was analysing, but saw them as its solution.

The Kaiser's order sent Education Ministry officials scurrying. Gossler promised to have ready within a month a set of proposals for implementing the Kaiser's edict. The job of preparing them he turned over to Schneider.[70] It took Schneider six weeks to produce a specific set of proposals, which on 14 June Gossler submitted to the

68. Ibid.
69. For William II's order, see PGStA, Rep 90 (Staatsministerium) Nr. 2400, pp. 50–3; see also Gerhardt Giese, *Quellen zur deutscher Schulgeschichte seit 1800*, pp. 194–5.
70. Schneider, *Ein halbes Jahrhundert*, pp. 426–7.

Cabinet in the form of a 'Memorandum Concerning Implementation of His Majesty's Order of 1 May 1889'. The document was a twenty-eight-page printed pamphlet marked 'secret'.[71] The proposals were remarkable for their lack of subtlety. To begin with, Schneider proposed that the schools celebrate a series of patriotic days 'so that the eyes of children will be directed to the good deeds' of the ruling house. At the top of his list was the date of 27 January, William II's birthday. The second date to be designated for celebration was 15 June, to commemorate William II's accession to the throne. Then came 2 September, Sedan Day; 18 October, the surrender of Metz; 9 March, the death of William I; and 22 March, the birthday of Frederick III. Next Schneider recommended the convening of teachers' conferences at which could be disseminated the most effective techniques for combating social democratic ideas.

The most substantive of the proposals were for the reform of the *Volksschule* and Seminar curricula. The mainstays of the *Volksschule* curriculum were to be religion, language, history, and arithmetic, and each of these was to be engaged in the struggle against socialistic ideas. Arithmetic, for example, could be used to teach the moral value of interest. Religious instruction utilised the Ten Commandments; language instruction would consist of the moral lessons drawn from literature. History lessons were to be used to teach the utility of private property, as well as to convey stories of poor boys who had become wealthy, and of the wealthy who, in the past, had helped the workers, the poor, and the lame. The curriculum as a whole was to be used to show that the 'existing, natural inequalities, be they of ability, health, strength, etc., cannot be undone in this world by artificial equalizing'.[72]

For the Seminars, Schneider stressed the inadvisability of trying to refute directly the theories of social democracy. The theorising he thought beyond the capacity of most Seminar pupils. Instead, he recommended the elucidation of the basic laws by which a state and society functioned. These he took to be monarchy, marriage, family, property, the unequal distribution of goods, and the right to inheritance.[73] History instruction was to cite examples of men who through their own efforts had risen high, men like the Fuggers,

71. For Gossler's pamphlet, see DZA II Merseburg, Rep 77, Tit 123, Nr. 10, vol. VII, pp. 230–45.
72. Ibid., p. 10 of the pamphlet.
73. Ibid.

Borsig, Krupp, Scharnhorst, as well as those who had used their wealth to aid the poor, A. H. Francke, for example, or Johann Wichern. Of course, it was the great deeds of the Hohenzollerns that were to be central to the history lessons. Special instructions were included also for the study of the French Revolution. 'Because one should not enliven the phantasies of the young by describing crimes', no mention was to be made to the Seminar pupils of the storming of the Bastille, the September Massacres, or the execution of Louis XVI.[74] Instead, the emphasis was to be on the misery and hunger that the revolution had produced.

Schneider's recommendations were approved quickly at a Cabinet session on 17 July. Only Bismarck had a few additional thoughts. To William II he communicated privately his belief that religious instruction would do well to ignore dogmatic confessional differences, and that perhaps even the number of hours devoted to religion in general should be reduced. Perhaps the choice in favour of confessional schooling in 1879 had been a mistake after all. Bismarck also expressed doubts that a greatly increased emphasis upon the Fatherland would necessarily serve to combat socialism. The simple cultivation of common sense, he thought, could accomplish that more effectively.[75] His reservations were not serious, however, and on 30 August 1889 William II empowered Gossler to implement the plans.

The first report on the effect of these measures Gossler made to the Kaiser a year later, in April 1890. In the meantime, momentous events had taken place. In February, *Reichstag* elections had brought the socialists their spectacular success. In March Bismarck had been dismissed. None the less, Gossler could report that most of the measures that the Kaiser had approved were in effect, and that a commission of popular writers had been assembled to produce histories of Brandenburg–Prussia that would illustrate how industrious individuals had risen and how social democratic ideas were hopelessly utopian.[76]

Karl Schneider was also at work preparing textbook supplements that would show how Prussia's rulers had always had the welfare of their people, especially that of the workers, foremost in their

74. Ibid., p. 18.
75. Bismarck to William II, 16 August 1889, PGStA Rep 90 (Staatsministerium) Nr. 2400, pp. 90–95.
76. Ibid., pp. 109–113.

minds.[77] Schoolchildren would soon read about a Kaiser who had himself been a model child, the embodiment of virtue who, according to one textbook author, was 'accustomed since early childhood to obedience, order, and punctuality', and who always had 'played nicely with children of the burgher class'. Thus, German children learned, they were fortunate to have as their Kaiser a man of 'true piety, fear, and with an unshakeable belief in God'.[78] Another writer stressed the Kaiser's sympathy for workers: 'He is especially concerned about the workers . . . and is often called the 'Workers' Kaiser,' . . . the best friend and protector of workers, who have every cause to thank him with their love and trust'.[79] Other writers stressed the long German tradition of loyalty to princes. Never had a German throne been sullied by the execution or assassination of a ruler.[80]

To William II, these were the sort of attitudes worth anchoring in a school bill. Gossler was instructed to prepare one immediately. Gossler's was the sixth attempt of the century to produce a comprehensive school law, each of the previous ones having gone down in defeat. This time prospects seemed to be much better. The bill had the Kaiser's full backing; the *Landtag* cartel parties in support of the government were securely in place, and the new Minister–President, Leo von Caprivi, favoured such a bill. Gossler's bill was ready by the early autumn of 1890. When William II opened the *Landtag* in November he pointed out that the assembly would be asked to consider a school bill that promised to distribute the costs of schooling fairly and that would secure for teachers a fair income, while at the same time give 'the *Volksschule* a secure foundation in local government'.[81] When Caprivi introduced the bill formally a few days later, he said very candidly that the bill's main purpose was to strengthen the state in its battle against the forces of revolution. For that reason alone, he expected most of the political parties, as well as religious groups, to give it their support.[82]

Neither the Kaiser's nor Caprivi's blandishments sufficed to stifle the inevitable controversy. Catholic protest to the bill was immedi-

77. Schneider, *Ein halbes Jahrhundert*, pp. 426–7.
78. H. Dettmer and G. Baarke, *Lehr- und Lernbüchlein für den ersten Geschichtsunterricht*, pp. 31, 32.
79. Quoted in Helmut König, 'Der Kaiser-Erlass vom 1. Mai 1889', p. 53.
80. K. Keck and Chr. Johannsen, eds, *Vaterländisches Lesebuch für die mehrklassige evangelische Volksschule Norddeutschlands*, p. 370.
81. *Schulthess' europäischer Geschichtskalendar*, 11 November 1890, p. 162.
82. Ibid., p. 164.

ate and mighty. Although it left untouched such controversial questions as curriculum and internal school structure, two of the bill's features did directly violate Catholic interests. The Church found unacceptable the provision that removed the powers of teacher appointment from the local community, as well as the one that increased the powers of the state in school inspection.[83] Both provisions were central to Gossler's bill and both the Catholic bishops and the Centre party were quick to oppose. Within a week the bishops were petitioning the *Landtag* to reject the bill. Their complaints included the fact that they had not been consulted on it, that it included no promise that pupils would receive religious instruction from teachers of their own confession, and that religious instruction would be seriously neglected. In the *Landtag* the leader of the attack was Bismarck's old nemesis, the Centre party leader, Ludwig Windhorst. In one of his last great speeches the ageing Windhorst charged that Gossler's bill, because it would weaken the Church, would promote rather than retard the growth of social democracy.[84]

Teachers, too, were unhappy with the bill, but for very different reasons. It left intact the traditional obligation in rural areas that they perform custodial duties in the church, it did not grant them the role on local school boards that they had wanted, and it made no mention of the non-confessional school idea that they had long promoted.[85] Their unhappiness came to a head at the German Teachers' Congress (*Lehrertag*) held in Berlin in December 1890 at which Prussia's school policy was the focus of attention. The conference was opened by Friedrich Dittes, a prominent liberal educator from Austria, who used his speech to criticise Prussia's school leadership. The speech, ostensibly in commemoration of Adolf Diesterweg, became an encomium for non-confessional schooling. Karl Schneider, who was at the conference representing the Education Ministry, was scandalised. The Catholic press was shocked. The *Aachener Zeitung* called Dittes a 'nihilist and anarchist and a prophet of Beelzebub'.[86] The uproar continued when a socialist teacher urged the conference to consider the doctrines of social democracy as an answer to the social question. Centre and Con-

83. For final draft, see DZA II Merseburg, Rep 77, Tit 123, Nr. 10, vol. VIII, pp. 115–33. See especially sections 4 and 7.

84. Werner Frauendienst, 'Das Deutsche Reich von 1890 bis 1914', p. 37; Meyer, *Schule der Untertanen*, p. 167.

85. Tews, *Ein Jahrhundert*, pp. 189–90.

86. Quoted in Radtke, *Der schulpolitische Kampf*, p. 57.

servative delegates in the *Landtag* were furious, blaming Gossler for the meeting and for allowing un-Christian tendencies to develop among teachers. Conservative newspapers attacked teachers and their associations for being 'pitchmen of Social Democracy' (*Handlanger der Sozialdemokratie*).[87]

Whatever the opposition, Gossler remained confident that the support of the cartel majority in the *Landtag* would secure passage of his bill. At a 7 December meeting of the Cabinet he recommended that the government simply ignore the opposition. Caprivi, however, seems to have been taken aback by the vehemence of the opposition. The protocol records that he broached the idea of a compromise.[88] In doing so, Caprivi had a larger political goal in mind; he would soon need Centre party support to pass his proposed tariff reductions.[89] For both Gossler and for his bill, Caprivi's wavering was the beginning of the end. Then, when the Kaiser also criticised Gossler's policies at a School Conference later in December, Gossler saw the handwriting on the wall. Early in 1891 he resigned.

Upon Gossler's resignation, the Caprivi government, without missing a step, reversed itself completely in matters of cultural policy. Gossler's successor, Robert von Zedlitz-Trützschler, was in effect the candidate of the Centre party. Zedlitz-Trützschler was called to his new position from Posen where he had been the provincial governor since 1886. Before that he had served in the administration of Polish Silesia.[90] His appointment in March 1891 as Education Minister finally closed the book on the Prussian *Kulturkampf*. In addition to withdrawing Gossler's school bill from the *Landtag*, Zedlitz-Trützschler restored to the Church some of the monies confiscated during the 1870s, and allowed the return to Prussia of some minor monastic orders.[91] It was on the Polish question, however, that Zedlitz-Trützschler proved most conciliatory. He blunted Gossler's energetic Germanisation efforts by ordering that the Polish language be restored to the schools of Posen and West Prussia. Gossler's opposition to the appointment of a Pole, Florian Stablewski, as the new Archbishop of Gnesen-Posen, he also dropped.

87. Ibid.; see also Johannes Tews, *Der achte deutsche Lehrertag und seine Gegner*.
88. DZA II Merseburg, Rep 90a BIII 2b, Nr. 6, vol. CIV, pp. 158–62.
89. J. C. G. Röhl, *Germany without Bismarck*, pp. 75–6.
90. Reinhard Lüdicke, *Die Preussischen Kultusminister und ihre Beamten*, pp. 10–11.
91. Röhl, *Germany without Bismarck*, p. 78.

By December 1891 Zedlitz-Trützschler had his own school bill ready for the *Landtag*. Most of the bill he had written himself.[92] He merely took Gossler's outline and turned its major provisions upside down, thereby meeting the objection of those who had protested its anti-Church provisions. Confessional schools found solid footing in this latest proposal. All newly-established schools would have to be confessional and any community that had sixty or more children of one confession would be required to erect a confessional school for them. Teacher training was likewise to be totally confessional, with supervisors from the Church overseeing all religious instruction. In the *Volksschule*, religious instruction, which would be required of all pupils, was to be imparted by a teacher of the child's own confession. The Church was also guaranteed a larger role in the appointment of teachers. For good measure, the powers of the county school councils — Falk's creation — were to be reduced.[93]

This latest, and also the last, of Prussia's nineteenth-century school bills was introduced into the *Landtag* on 15 January 1892. The Centre was understandably very pleased. The protests came from the liberals. Their opposition was, if anything, more fierce than had been that of the Centre to Gossler's bill. An exasperated Caprivi was at one point moved to tell them that 'it is a question . . . not of Protestant and Catholic, but of Christian and atheist',[94] an unfortunate formulation that brought down upon him the full wrath of Prussia's liberals. The intensity of the public reaction to Zedlitz-Trützschler's bill has been likened to that of the *Konfliktzeit* of the early 1860s,[95] when tensions between the government and liberals had reached their height over army reform. Everyone seemed to enter the lists, from the German and Prussian teachers' associations, to the Berlin historian, Heinrich von Treitschke, to the retired Chancellor, Bismarck.

Bismarck objected, he said, to the idea of the debate itself. Such politically-sensitive questions should not be discussed so openly. He feared the effect of such a discussion upon domestic social tranquility.[96] William II, too, was reported to be unhappy with the

92. Schneider, *Ein halbes Jahrhundert*, p. 428; L. Clausnitzer, *Geschichte des Preussischen Unterrichtsgesetzes*, vol. I.
93. Meyer, *Schule der Untertanen*, pp. 174–7; J. Alden Nichols, *Germany After Bismarck*, pp. 160–1; Ellen Lovell Evans, *The German Center Party, 1870–1933*, pp. 121–2.
94. Quoted in Nichols, *Germany After Bismarck*, pp. 173–4.
95. Meyer, *Schule der Untertanen*, p. 179; see also Kurt Richter, *Der Kampf um den Schulgesetzentwurf des Grafen Zedlitz-Trützschler vom Jahre 1892*.
96. Ibid., p. 175.

debate, principally because of the vehemence of the opposition from the liberals. Their leader, the National Liberal *Landtag* delegate, von Eynern, organised petition drives among university faculties, elicited protest resolutions from local government councils, and sponsored protest publications of all sorts.[97] The most prominent of the bill's intellectual opponents was Heinrich von Treitschke. It was Treitschke who circulated a protest petition among his colleagues at the University of Berlin and who wrote a series of newspaper articles in opposition to the Zedlitz-Trützschler bill. These articles he then published as a pamphlet under the title 'The Proposal for a Prussian *Volksschule* Law'. His chief objection, Treitschke wrote, was that the bill surrendered to the Church certain 'inalienable rights of the state and endangers the future of German culture in the eastern [Polish] regions'.[98] In the Polish areas only the non-confessional school would protect German culture, he argued, because 'a Catholic school in Posen or West Prussia can in reality be only a Polish school'.[99] He objected also to the bill's provision for de-regulating private instruction. The result, he said, would be unhappy educational 'Manchesterism'.[100]

Teachers' associations were no less opposed to the bill than was Treitschke, and for many of the same reasons. Teachers objected vigorously to the prospect of continued subordination to the Church, a position they had sought to escape since the beginning of the century. The Berlin Teachers' Association took the lead in opposing the bill, trying to persuade the public of its fundamentally reactionary nature. Its effect would set back the Prussian educational clock for a century, they argued.[101]

Behind the scenes it was political intrigue, however, and not public opposition that doomed Zedlitz-Trützschler's school bill. The central figures in this intrigue were Friedrich von Holstein, once a protégé of Bismarck and currently Privy Councillor in the Foreign Office, and Philipp von Eulenburg, friend and confidant of the Kaiser and Prussia's ambassador to Bavaria. The two of them were crucial figures in that group of twenty or so notables who actually governed in Berlin during the Wilhelmian era.[102] It was a remark-

97. Radtke, *Der schulpolitische Kampf*, p. 61.
98. Heinrich von Treitschke, *Der Entwurf des Preussischen Volksschulgesetzes*, p. 3.
99. Ibid., p. 6.
100. Ibid., p. 18.
101. Tews, *Aus Arbeit und Leben*, pp. 140–1.
102. Röhl, *Germany without Bismarck*, p. 271.

able pair: Holstein, the devious figure in the Foreign Office, who, with Bismarck gone, became the most influential figure in foreign policy; Eulenburg, the Kaiser's close friend and probably the most influential figure in his entourage during the early 1890s.

Holstein thought Zedlitz-Trützschler's bill dangerous because it courted the Centre and Conservative parties, neither of which he believed was committed to the idea of a united German *Reich*. The courting of these parties necessarily entailed alienating those that were faithful to the *Reich*. Therein lay the danger. Holstein first took these views to Caprivi, urging that he withdraw his support for the Zedlitz-Trützschler bill. When Caprivi refused, Holstein turned to Eulenburg, with the prospect of influencing the Kaiser directly.[103] Eulenburg, although he happened to agree with much of Zedlitz-Trützschler's bill, was receptive to Holstein's point about the risks involved in constructing a policy that depended upon the unreliable Centre and Conservative parties. Urged on by Holstein, Eulenburg informed the Kaiser in late January 1892 of his own opposition to an alliance with the Centre, warning also that it could have the effect in South Germany, and particularly in Bavaria, of weakening the liberal and moderate forces that supported the *Reich*.[104] Stimulated by repeated hints from Holstein, Eulenburg let his imagination run away with him. He began to see signs of separatist sentiment in Bavaria where he had not seen them before: officers of the Munich garrison failing to celebrate the Kaiser's birthday; the Bavarian Education Minister reprimanding a Munich teacher for sending a poem of German patriotism to the Kaiser; shamelessly anti-Prussian articles being published in that most pernicious of Bavarian gutter-rags, the *Bayrischer Vaterland*.[105] These signs were all inventions of Eulenburg's imagination, although the head of the Bavarian government, Count von Crailsheim, did express reservations to him about the disquieting effect Prussia's school bill was having on the political situation in Bavaria.[106]

Finally, on 10 March, Eulenburg wrote to William II, warning him that in South Germany the bill was 'undermining the *Reich* idea

103. Rich, *Holstein*, vol. I, pp. 380–1.

104. Eulenburg to William II, 28 January 1892, in Johannes Haller, *Philipp Eulenburg; The Kaiser's Friend*, vol. I, pp. 110–11.

105. Ibid., p. 104.

106. Möckl, *Die Prinzregentenzeit*, p. 63, n. 102 and p. 357; see also Haller, *Eulenburg*, vol. I, pp. 109–11.

and the authority of the imperial crown'.[107] He called into question Caprivi's judgement in allowing Zedlitz-Trützschler to lead German policy into such a morass. It was the kind of argument to which the Kaiser was unusually susceptible.

It was a week later, at a Crown Council meeting, that William II dropped his bombshell, announcing that he no longer supported the school bill.[108] Criticisms of the bill had come to him from all sides, he explained. Trusted advisers were urging him to take a more moderate path. Caprivi was outraged. Until now, he said, he believed he had been backing a bill that the Kaiser supported. If he no longer enjoyed His Majesty's confidence he would have to resign. William II thought such drastic action unnecessary; it was merely that he did not want to see the National Liberals permanently antagonised, he explained. Perhaps, with appropriate revisions, the bill could be reintroduced some other time. With that observation the meeting was closed, and William II set off for a week of hunting at his lodge north of Berlin. Zedlitz-Trützschler went home to draft his letter of resignation. The next day Caprivi resigned as well, both as Prussia's Minister–President and as Germany's Chancellor. Only with great difficulty was he persuaded to stay on as Chancellor and as Foreign Minister of Prussia. His successor to the minister–presidency was Count Botho Eulenburg, Philipp's cousin, a former Minister of the Interior and an opponent of Caprivi's tariff policy.[109]

Zedlitz-Trützschler's replacement was Robert Bosse, a career official from the *Reich*'s Interior Ministry, who during the 1880s had worked on the preparations for Bismarck's social legislation.[110] Bosse's first act as Education Minister was to withdraw his predecessor's school bill from the *Landtag*, a measure that earned him the immediate good will of the liberals and of the various teachers' associations. Bosse was to become extremely popular with Prussia's teachers during his seven-year tenure as Education Minister. The measures he took on their behalf were to earn him the sobriquet 'Social Minister'.[111]

It was a question of policy toward the Poles in the eastern

107. Philipp Eulenburg, *Politische Korrespondenz*, vol. II, pp. 796–8.
108. DZA II Merseburg, Rep 90a BIII 2c, Nr. 3, vol. V, pp. 16–26.
109. Nichols, *Germany After Bismarck*, pp. 181–2; Frauendienst, 'Das Deutsche Reich von 1890 bis 1914', p. 42.
110. See 'Robert Bosse' in *Neue Deutsche Biographie*, vol. II, p. 484; see also Lüdicke, *Die Preussischen Kultusminister und ihre Beamten*, p. 11.
111. Tews, *Ein Jahrhundert*, pp. 210–226.

provinces that presented itself to Bosse most immediately. Would he continue the conciliatory policies of his predecessor? Zedlitz-Trützschler had very consciously backed away from the aggressive Germanisation policies of his own predecessor, Gossler. Zedlitz-Trützschler, in an order of 11 April 1891, had allowed private instruction in the Polish language to take place in Posen's *Volksschulen*,[112] a reversal of Gossler's earlier order outlawing all such instruction. Likewise, Zedlitz-Trützschler had approved Rome's appointment of Florian Stablewski as Archbishop of Gnesen-Posen.[113] Gossler had continually insisted that the archbishop be German. Stablewski had been a delegate in the *Landtag* and an energetic defender of Polish interests, but he was also politically loyal to Prussia and the idea of monarchy. He saw himself, he said, as politically Prussian and culturally Polish.[114] The combination was perfectly acceptable to Zedlitz-Trützschler.

For Bosse the Polish question was raised in May 1892 by a Polish *Landtag* delegate who asked why Zedlitz-Trützschler's order of April 1891 had been limited to private language instruction, and why only to Posen.[115] Other Polish delegates had in the meantime demanded that Posen's relationship to Prussia be restored to the status of 1815. To get an understanding of the problem, Bosse undertook during his first summer as Education Minister an inspection tour of Posen and Polish Silesia. At each of his stops he was greeted with requests and petitions asking for greater freedom in language instruction.

Not until the autumn of 1893 did Bosse formulate a response to these petitions. By then he had come to believe that public language instruction might actually be more in line with Prussia's interests than was the private instruction allowed by Zedlitz-Trützschler. Public instruction would be easier to keep track of and to regulate. In November 1893 he proposed to the Cabinet that two hours each week of Polish language instruction be made optional at the beginning levels of the *Volksschule*, and that pupils at the higher levels be allowed to have Polish as the language of instruction in religion. As a counterbalance he suggested the simultaneous upgrading of instruc-

112. Harry Kenneth Rosenthal, 'Poles, Prussians, and Elementary Education in Nineteenth-Century Posen', p. 210.

113. Gatz, ed., *Akten zur preussischen Kirchenpolitik*, p. lviii, n. 299.

114. Nichols, *Germany After Bismarck*, p. 128; see also Harry Kenneth Rosenthal, 'The Election of Archbishop Stablewski'.

115. Rosenthal, 'Poles, Prussians, and Elementary Education', pp. 210–11.

tion in the German language.[116] Caprivi, as Foreign Minister, responded favourably to Bosse's proposals. Private instruction, he agreed, had its dangers. He, too, favoured the idea of conciliating the Poles. In the event of a two-front war Germany would badly need the support of its Polish population. Certainly that support, he said, 'is worth a couple of hours a week of Polish language instruction'.[117] The order allowing the two hours of instruction in the Polish language was promulgated in December. Attached to it was the gratuitous declaration that this was as far as the Prussian government was prepared to go.

Bosse's order elicited an unexpectedly bitter reaction from the Poles. Archbishop Stablewski assailed the limitation of two hours it placed on language instruction, as well as its restriction to the beginning level in the *Volksschule*. He addressed to Caprivi his request for a full eight years of such instruction without an hourly limitation of any sort.[118] Rather than soothing the passions, Bosse's order was having the effect of exciting them. There matters stood until October 1894 when the controversy over a proposal for constitutional revision, the so-called 'revolution bill' or *Umsturzvorlage*, led to the resignation of both Caprivi and Minister–President Eulenburg.[119] To their successors, these efforts to conciliate the Poles were seen as being totally bankrupt.

From October 1894 onwards, the initiative in Polish policy passed back into the hands of the more extreme Germanisers. Their ascendancy was marked by the founding in late 1894 of the Eastern Marches Association, often called the HKT Society after the initial letters of the names of its three founders, Hansemann, Kennermann and Tiedemann. The HKT's objective was the thoroughgoing Germanisation of the eastern marches.[120] Anything less, it believed, would be a German capitulation to an inferior culture. The society's early efforts were geared to pressuring the Prussian government into a more assertive policy of Germanisation. Its first concern was to bring about an increase in the funding for the Colonisation Commission that had been established in 1886. The first success came in 1898 when the government doubled to 200,000,000 marks its annual

116. Ibid., pp. 214–15.
117. Quoted ibid., p. 216.
118. Ibid.
119. Nichols, *Germany After Bismarck*, pp. 340–2; Röhl, *Germany without Bismarck*, pp. 116–18.
120. Piotr S. Wandycz, *The Lands of Partitioned Poland, 1795–1918*, pp. 284–5.

appropriation to the commission.[121]

Not until late in the decade did HKT leaders take a direct interest in schooling. They had long considered Bosse too indulgent of Polish cultural pretensions. The same they believed to be true of the elderly Minister–President and Chancellor Hohenlohe. Although Bosse continued to reject major Germanisation initiatives in the east, he was disappointed by the failure of the Poles to appreciate his moderation. The Poles, in turn, were disappointed in Bosse, so Archbishop Stablewski informed William II .[122] When Bosse was replaced in September 1899, the HKT society welcomed the appointment of Konrad Studt, a loyal bureaucrat, as his replacement.[123] Expecting support from Studt, the society immediately proposed the total elimination of the Polish language as a subject in any school at any level.[124] When Bernhard von Bülow replaced Hohenlohe a year later, the HKT also had a supporter in the new head of the Prussian government and German Chancellor.

Bülow would later blame his predecessors for Prussia's failure to Germanise the Poles. Caprivi he marked with particular opprobrium for having failed to buy up Polish estates during the agricultural crisis of the early 1890s. 'Nothing has harmed us more than our vacillations and constant return to old mistakes', Bülow was to write of Polish policy in his memoirs.[125] It was an attitude that greatly encouraged the most ardent Germanisers.

Although Studt was much more kindly disposed toward the HKT position than was Bosse, pressures for initiatives in the Polish question had been mounting for some time before Bosse was replaced.[126] Huge protest demonstrations during the summer of 1899 had greeted Bosse's efforts to suppress private instruction in the Polish language. Twenty thousand demonstrators had gathered in Posen's Zoological Park to demand the complete restoration of the Polish language in the schools.[127] Shortly after taking office in September, Studt sent a subordinate, Dr Peische, to make an inspection tour of all the schools in the eastern provinces. Peische returned pessimistic particularly about the situation in Posen.

121. Bruno Schumacher, *Geschichte Ost- und Westpreussens*, pp. 284–5.
122. Korth, *Die Preussische Schulpolitik*, p. 58.
123. Lüdicke, *Die Preussischen Kultusminister und ihre Beamten*, p. 12.
124. Richard Wonser Tims, *Germanizing Prussian Poland, 1894–1919*, p. 81.
125. Bernhard von Bülow, *Memoirs*, vol. I, p. 647.
126. Gatz, ed., *Akten zur preussischen Kirchenpolitik*, p. lxiv.
127. Korth, *Die preussische Schulpolitik*, pp. 60–1.

Throughout the province, he noted, German seemed to be losing ground to Polish. His recommendation was for a vigorous promotion of German in all schools that had Polish-speaking pupils.[128] By early 1900, the battle lines were being drawn for what would become the German-Polish cultural wars of the early twentieth century.

The Prussian government began its offensive on 18 August 1900, the day Studt ordered that German be the language for religious instruction in the middle and upper levels of the *Volksschulen*.[129] Therewith was reversed the Zedlitz-Trützschler order of 1891. Studt's order was for the moment limited to the southern governing district of the Province of Posen, but the extension of the order through the rest of the province was the key element to the government's strategy. When Studt's order was implemented the following spring in Wreschen, a Polish city of 5,000 inhabitants to the east of Posen, it met stiff resistance. Schoolchildren by the hundreds refused to buy the required German texts or to answer questions that had been asked in German. Each day the situation grew more serious. Pupils were being browbeaten by their teachers, and the teachers, in turn, were being harassed and threatened by parents. By early summer, twenty-five parents had been arrested, and prison sentences of nine to twelve months meted out to each of them.[130]

The difficulties in Wreschen were greater than the government had anticipated, but Studt made use of them to argue for greater expenditures for Germanisation policies. To the Cabinet he spoke of the need for millions of marks to build new schools and to hire more teachers. There were schools in the Province of Posen that had more than 200 pupils to a teacher. Teachers were still hard to recruit. Over 700 teaching posts were vacant. New Seminars would have to be established. He explained also that he was in touch with Stablewski about reining in the 'polonising' efforts of his clergy.[131]

Studt pushed relentlessly during the next years for the implementation of his language order, especially in the critical province of Posen. By Easter of 1906 it had been introduced into 301 of the 1,100 schools in the province's southern governing district; in the northern

128. Ibid., p. 62.

129. Ibid., p. 64; see also Broszat, *Zweihundert Jahre deutsche Polenpolitik*, p. 161, and Tims, *Germanizing Prussian Poland*, p. 82.

130. Korth, *Die preussische Schulpolitik*, pp. 89–100.

131. DZA II Merseburg, Staatsministerium Sitzung of 21 November 1901, Rep 90a BIII 2b Nr. 6, vol. CXLIII, pp. 79–127.

district it had been introduced into nearly all of the 1,098 schools.[132]

It was during the Easter holiday of 1906 that Studt, with the full backing of Bülow, took the fateful step of reiterating his order of 1900 regarding the removal of all Polish-language instruction from the schools. The reaction this time went far beyond the petitions and protest demonstrations that had greeted the order originally. By October 1906 75,000 of Posen's schoolchildren were involved in a general boycott of the schools, marking the beginning of the great Polish school strikes of 1906–7. As usual, the protests began in Posen and from there spread into West Prussia and the Polish districts of Silesia. Priests were commonly leaders of the protest meetings at which petitions by the hundreds to Studt and Stablewski were produced. The first actual school strikes came in June 1906 in the area surrounding Wreschen.[133] The ensuing summer holidays did nothing to ease the tensions. The signal for a larger strike was given by Archbishop Stablewski in his pastoral letter of October in which he insisted that religious instruction be in the child's mother-tongue. On 17 October an anonymous leaflet distributed surreptitiously in Posen called for a general strike against the schools.[134] Within a month over half the schools in Posen were being boycotted. In addition to the 75,000 children in Posen being kept at home by their parents, another 70,000 joined them in Silesia and West Prussia.[135] Although some parents gradually relented during the next months, there were still 30,000 children out of school in March 1907.[136] But when Pope Pius X refused to give his blessing to the strike, even its most ardent supporters lost heart. Those less ardent had been discouraged earlier by threats from the government that parents who supported the strike could lose their jobs — or even custody of their children.[137]

Studt could not count the collapse of the school strikes as a victory. He had expended most of his political capital during their course. His Cabinet colleagues had feared the strikes would spread outward from Posen and had been proved right. The Minister of Interior, Bethmann-Hollweg, went so far as to express sympathy for

132. Korth, *Die preussische Schulpolitik*, p. 120.
133. Broszat, *Zweihundert Jahre deutsche Polenpolitik*, p. 161; Gatz, ed., *Akten zur preussischen Kirchenpolitik*, pp. lxviii–lxix.
134. Korth, *Die preussische Schulpolitik*, p. 142.
135. Ibid., p. 134.
136. Ibid., pp. 133–4.
137. PGStA, Thiele Nachlass, Nr. 136, Posen 1903–1910, p. 136.

the Poles. He found quite natural their desire to use the Polish language.[138] Only Bülow's support was unqualified, and even that evaporated when he saw that Studt's catering to Centre party interests was hindering the government's search for a new coalition.[139]

Studt's association with the Centre was the result of his one great success as Education Minister, that of steering through the *Landtag* in 1906 a major School Financing Law. After more than a century of confusion growing out of the hodge-podge of financing arrangements in the various provinces, the law of 1906 finally made school financing the uniform obligation of the local civic community (*bürgerliche Gemeinde*), or, in East Elbia, of the estate owner's patrimonial district (*Gutsbezirke*).[140] Progressive and National Liberals viewed the first part of the bill favourably, but had to concede to Conservatives the principle that the 15,000 estate owners would serve as their own school administrators.[141] To the Centre was conceded the principle long enshrined in practice, that of confessional schools. Studt's School Financing Law was called the 'Jena of the Prussian *Volksschule*' by liberal critics.[142] Studt was ennobled by the Kaiser for engineering the compromise that made the bill possible, and then dismissed by Bülow for becoming too closely associated with the Centre Party.

Teachers felt betrayed by Studt. The legal recognition his financing law accorded the confessional school was contrary to their century-long ambition to free themselves from Church influence. They deserved better, they thought, particularly for the enthusiasm with which they had answered William II's earlier call to engage themselves in the combating of social democracy. The social question had quickly become a major topic at teachers' conferences and conventions. The Teachers' Congress of 1891, held in Halle, had been devoted entirely to the theme of 'School Reform and Social Life'. The tone for the congress was set by K. O. Beetz, a teacher from Nordhausen, who opened the proceedings by calling for a 'social Kaiser', and a 'social school', so as to make possible the creation of a 'social kingdom'.[143] From a teacher in West Prussia

138. Konrad H. Jarausch, *The Enigmatic Chancellor; Bethmann Hollweg and the Hubris of Imperial Germany*, pp. 48–9.
139. Evans, *The German Center Party*, p. 160.
140. For the bill, see *Schulrecht*, vol. I, ed. Landé, pp. 294–7.
141. Tews, *Ein Jahrhundert*, p. 237.
142. Ibid., p. 228.
143. K. O. Beetz, *Die Lehrerbildung, eine soziale Frage*, p. 60.

came the appeal for 'the bridging of differences of class, estate, religion, and party. . . . We have one Kaiser, one army, one navy, one postal service, but we do not have one school. . . . Perhaps the idea of unity for all of Germany would be nurtured more effectively if all of Germany had one school'.[144] Thus might the lower classes be transformed into Germans, he said. The same, he thought, might also be accomplished for Bavarians.

Thus was renewed Süvern's vision that a common school experience would become the basis for a common national consciousness, and Hirth's notion that a national school system would solve the German social problem. Speculation that schools could bridge class differences was common currency. Gustav Schmoller of the *Verein für Sozialpolitik* argued that the basic differences between social groups were no longer rooted in property, but in education. A movement calling itself 'social pedagogy' (*Sozialpädagogik*) was developed in response to this view, its primary objective being to heal class antagonisms.[145] The advocates of social pedagogy promoted the idea of a comprehensive elementary school, an *Einheitsschule*, that would be the bottom rung in an educational ladder leading upwards to the higher school levels. The 1891 Teachers' Congress in Halle was quick to endorse a resolution calling for the establishment of a comprehensive elementary school.[146]

Teachers during the 1890s seemed eager to assist in imparting an anti-socialist citizenship education (*staatsbürgerliche Erziehung*).[147] The social healing, everyone from the Kaiser down to the *Volksschule* teacher seemed to agree, was to have its moral base in an enhanced German nationalism, rather than in the positive Christianity that had served the 1820s or the 1850s. The study of history alone could inspirit this kind of nationalism. At a conference of Seminar teachers in 1891 the connection between the study of history and the solution of the social question was spelled out more clearly. 'Its [history's] power to develop the spirit (*gemütsbildende Kraft*) places it on a level

144. *Die Deutschen Lehrerkonferenzen* (1891), p. 37.

145. Robert Rissmann, *Deutsche Pädagogen des 19. Jahrhunderts*, p. 136; Paul Natorp, *Sozialpädagogik, Theorie der Willenserziehung auf der Grundlage der Gemeinschaft*; Karl Holl, 'Das nationalsoziale Schulprogramm; eine Schuldebatte aus den Jahren 1896 und 1897'.

146. *Die Deutschen Lehrerkonferenzen* (1892), pp. 61–83.

147. August Messer, *Das Problem der staatsbürgerlichen Erziehung historisch und systematisch behandelt*, p. 53; Georg Kerschensteiner, *Staatsbürgerliche Erziehung der deutschen Jugend.*

of importance with religion', said one of the speakers.[148] Or, as a Dr Neubauer wrote a few years later, the need was for a 'history instruction that is concerned with the soul of the pupil and not merely with his powers of recollection'.[149]

Illustrative of the sentiments being generated were those expressed by Hugo Göring in his book, *The New German School*, published in 1890. Göring was a former Gymnasium teacher in Basel who during the 1880s became a spokesman for radical school reform and the founder of what he called a 'New German School Movement'.[150] Göring's main objective was to provide a nationalist (*vaterländisch*) education at all levels of schooling. For the Gymnasium this would mean the abandonment of the classical curriculum; at the lower schools it would mean a comprehensive *Volksschule* for children of all social classes.[151] At both Gymnasium and *Volksschule*, it was to be German literature and history that would be at the centre of the curriculum.[152] An important influence upon Göring's curricular ideas was the nationalist poet Wilhelm Jordan, who as a young man had gained fame as a firebrand nationalist delegate to the Frankfurt Parliament and, more recently, acclaim for his popular refashioning — and public readings — of the Nibelungen epic.

In 1882, at the age of thirty-three, Göring had resigned his teaching position in Basel to take up the cudgels of school reform. To support himself he began to edit some of the writings of educators like Basedow and Froebel, but his main efforts he directed towards finding financial supporters who would back the publication of a journal and the construction of a demonstration school. He managed in 1886 to obtain an interview with Prussia's Education Minister Gossler, but the meeting led nowhere. His subsequent efforts to gain an interview with the Kaiser were unsuccessful. Göring's big break came in 1889 when an anonymous benefactress granted him 50,000 marks. This gift made possible the founding of his Society for School Reform and the publication of its journal, the *Neue Deutsche Schule*.[153]

148. *Die Deutschen Lehrerkonferenzen* (1891), pp. 197–8.
149. Dr Neubauer, 'Geschichtsunterricht und staatsbürgerlicher Unterricht', p. 155.
150. On Göring, see Beyer, *Deutsche Schulwelt*, p. 89.
151. Hugo Göring, 'Die "Deutsche Schule" als Förderung unserer Zeit', p. 444.
152. Hugo Göring, 'Die Entstehung des Allgemeinen Deutschen Vereins für Schulreform "Die Neue Deutsche Schule"', pp. 65–72.
153. Hugo Göring, *Die neue deutsche Schule*, pp. viii–xi, 57.

Although Göring's plans were never implemented, the thinking that underlay them was bearing fruit in the efforts of the Kaiser and the Education Ministry to vitalise history as the spiritual force behind nationalism. New texts and readers glorifying the Kaiser and the Fatherland had been introduced. The great deeds of the wars of liberation and unification, of Prussia's kings, of Bismarck, and of the Kaiser were being offered as the fundamental elements of a new national consciousness.[154] Teachers must be 'socially-minded' and, 'at the same time, nationally-minded', wrote Adolf Damaschke, a young teacher in Berlin. 'The body of *Volksschule* teachers, politically influential and powerful, must help to bring these two streams [social and national] into the same course'.[155] The Kaiser had never said it better.

The eagerness with which teachers had responded to the call to be socially- and nationally-minded was certainly nurtured by the efforts of Bosse during the 1890s to improve their material situation. Salaries, which had declined during the 1880s, after having risen so rapidly the decade before, once again began to rise after 1891. By 1896 they had risen by ten per cent. By 1897 the minimum annual salary of a Prussian *Volksschule* teacher was 1,444 marks; by 1901 it was 1,835 marks.[156]

Of comparable importance to teachers was their elevation in status that accompanied William II's order in January 1895 allowing them to take their military service as one-year volunteers. A privilege since 1814 of the educated classes, the one-year volunteer paid for his own food, clothing, and shelter, and after one year of service automatically became a reserve officer candidate. The Kaiser's order stipulated that *Volksschule* teachers would be allowed a similar, though not the same, privilege. Obviously a *Volksschule* teacher could not be a commissioned officer, but, as the Kaiser said, they 'can be prepared for later usefulness as non-commissioned officers in the reserves'.[157] Although the grade of non-commissioned officer accorded no élite status, it did allow the *Volksschule* teacher to approach the fringes of that status, which in the militarised society of Wilhelmian Germany was dominated by the ranks of the

154. Jürgen Heinl, *Die deutsche Sozialpädagogik des 19. Jahrhunderts im Spiegel der Schulgeschichtsbücher*, p. 25.
155. Adolf Damaschke, *Der Lehrer und die Soziale Frage*, p. 8.
156. Tews, *Ein Jahrhundert*, pp. 206, 208; *Das Volksschulwesen*, ed. Lexis, p. 12.
157. Order of 27 January 1895 quoted in Meyer, *Schule der Untertanen*, p. 96; see also *Die Preussische Volksschule*, ed. E. von Bremen, pp. 385–6.

officer corps.

The Kaiser's order marked elevation to a status to which *Volksschule* teachers had long aspired. Their association with the army had been a tenuous one. In the 1840s they had been required to serve in the military for a six-week, rather than for the regular three-year, term. The shorter term was a concession to the teacher shortage of the *Vormärz* and had, in a day before the militarisation of social values, little effect upon the *Volksschule* teachers' social standing. In the early 1890s the term of service was extended to ten weeks, but by then such abbreviated service could only be seen as a source of humiliation. Bosse was among those pushing hard for the one-year volunteer status, a fact that made him even more popular with the vast majority of teachers.

When the Seminar graduates of 1896 were designated eligible for the new status, a manual for teachers celebrated their full entry into 'civil society' (*bürgerliche Gesellschaft*) and the attending opportunities for intellectual stimulation and social esteem.[158] Many Seminar graduates could not afford the costs of one-year volunteer service, however. To allow them to take advantage of the new opportunity, teachers' associations offered loans to cover the expenses of providing their own clothing, food, and quarters. During the next few years nearly forty per cent of Prussia's Seminar graduates took advantage of these loans.[159] The entire profession was thereby elevated.

Whatever social elevation accompanied their new military status, it did nothing to erase the identification of the *Volksschule* and its teachers with the lower classes. Except for Süvern and those of his generation there had never been any serious intention to have it any other way, and Bavaria, as Humboldt had noted, had not even had its Süvern. The Prussian *Volksschule* was more the product of Beckedorff's vision than of Süvern's; in Bavaria it was Niethammer's vision that prevailed. Thus it was that the *Volksschule* remained an institution of and for the lower classes. Nothing symbolised this more clearly than the demotion of what Süvern and Wismayr hoped would be an *Elementarschule* to a *Volksschule*, and in Bavaria, its further demotion under Ludwig I to the status of a Work-Day School. Süvern and Wismayr had once hoped that their elementary schools might open avenues upwards to the talented children of the

158. Radkte, *Der schulpolitische Kampf*, p. 159.
159. Meyer, *Schule der Untertanen*, pp. 97 and 256–7, n. 204.

lower classes. Beckedorff and Niethammer, on the other hand, who believed such movement to be the generator of social turmoil, saw as the first function of schooling the redefinition and reinforcement of social divisions. Not even the reform era of the 1870s under Falk and Lutz saw serious revision of this social function of schooling. Not one of the schools bills produced after 1819 attempted to reconstruct the educational ladder that had been dismantled in the 1820s. Süvern's vision would henceforth become the property of reformers standing outside the state apparatus, and of those who, like Hugo Göring, perverted his humane intention. Detlef Müller points out in his recent study of Prussian schools that the reforms that were implemented in the nineteenth century actually served to reduce the number of lower-class children who went on to higher school levels. In 1871 nearly thirteen per cent of Prussia's children were in a school that allowed some upward mobility; by 1891 that number had been cut almost in half to seven per cent.[160]

The Seminar, too, in most respects, served to limit social mobility. Those recruited into it were themselves graduates of the *Volksschule* who were being trained to return to it to teach. The pattern of movement was circular rather than upward. The efforts of teachers to break out of this circle were, with rare exceptions, unsuccessful. Time after time the Seminar curriculum was adjusted to dampen the fire of social or educational ambition. Beckedorff, Eichhorn, and Stiehl in Prussia, and Niethammer and Abel in Bavaria all feared the consequences that would inevitably accompany, they believed, the growing social ambitions of teachers. The fear of over-educated teachers generating social discontent within the masses was to be a constant theme of nineteenth-century conservatism, in Prussia as well as in Bavaria.[161]

Whatever the reality, the image was widespread by the late nineteenth century that *Volksschule* teaching was a rung on the social ladder leading upwards.[162] Teachers were the most ardent believers in this image. What 'made the position of *Volksschule* teacher unique', Adolf Damaschke recalled, 'was that it recruited from the talented children of the labouring ranks'.[163] Damaschke's father had been an

160. Detlef K. Müller, *Sozialstruktur und Schulsystem; Aspekte zum Strukturwandel des Schulwesens im 19. Jahrhundert*, pp. 35–6; Lexis, *Das Volksschulwesen*, p. 10.
161. Anthony LaVopa, 'Status and Ideology: Rural Schoolteachers in Pre-March and Revolutionary Prussia', p. 435.
162. Karl Bungardt, *Die Odyssee der Lehrerschaft*, pp. 92–3.
163. Adolf Damaschke, *Aus meinem Leben*, vol. I, p. 80.

artisan; he a *Volksschule* teacher. The view was held that *Volksschule* teaching was the intermediate stage in a three-generational movement that began with the artisan and peasant classes in the first generation, and led to the highly regarded academic professions in the third.[164] Thus the *Volksschule* teacher in the second generation was believed to be performing a platform function on the way up.

The perception, it must be noted, was a reality of its own, providing shape and hope to teachers and their families. Certainly the vast majority of teachers throughout the century came from the artisan and peasant classes. That was true in the 1820s. It was still true in 1908 when Prussia reported that fifty-nine per cent of its male *Volksschule* teachers were the sons of peasants, artisans, or tradesmen, and another eighteen per cent the sons of teachers themselves.[165] Early in the century, before the economic upswing brought on by industrialisation, teaching may well have served a function of a different sort. Rather than being the platform on the way up, it may have been the holding position against the artisan's or peasant's slide downwards on the social scale. The claim for its being the crucial step in the movement upwards is made only for the latter part of the century.

Hartmut Kaelble's studies of social mobility in Germany since 1850, though not of the three-generational kind, do offer useful glimpses into the relationship between school-teaching and social mobility. Teachers' sons certainly did not become the driving force in German economic expansion. They account for only one per cent of all German entrepreneurs between 1871 and the outbreak of World War I.[166] Growing up with a *Volksschule*-teacher father did not, apparently, foster entrepreneurial spirit. On the other hand, five per cent of Bavaria's high-level bureaucrats for the period from 1851 to 1875 were the sons of teachers; of these, Lutz was obviously the most prominent. Comparable statistics for the Prussian bureaucracy are not available, but in the Province of Westphalia between 1835 and 1914, only two per cent of the high-level bureaucrats were teachers' sons.[167] To be sure, the newly-established educational

164. Hasso v. Recum, 'Soziale Strukturwandlungen des Volksschullehrerberufes: Vom Aufstiegsberuf zum Mangelberuf', p. 574.
165. Hartmut Kaelble, 'Sozialer Aufstieg in Deutschland, 1850–1914', p. 66, Table 6.
166. Ibid., p. 52, Table 1.
167. Ibid., p. 55, Table 2.

bureaucracies offered opportunities of their own, as the cases of Eilers and Stiehl in Prussia demonstrate; none the less, the efforts of teachers to have themselves appointed to the critical positions of country and regional school inspectors were inevitably turned back.

As for the sons of *Volksschule* teachers entering the prestigious academic professions, only four per cent of the teachers in Germany's higher schools (Gymnasium, *Realschule*, etc.) between 1850 and 1919 had *Volksschule* teachers as fathers. On the other hand, eleven per cent of Germany's students of philology during the last decade of the century had such a background.[168] *Volksschule* teachers' sons were also heavily represented among Prussia's clergymen. Between 1887 and 1900, eighteen per cent of its Protestant pastors and fourteen per cent of its Catholic priests were teachers' sons.[169] Of the teachers' sons studying at a university at the turn of the century, over forty per cent were studying Protestant theology.[170] Theology and philology were the fields of study that had the lowest tuition fees, no small consideration for a teacher whose average annual income rarely exceeded 1,800 marks.[171]

Income alone was sufficient to exclude the *Volksschule* teacher from the ranks of the middle classes. To qualify for that status he would, according to an estimate of Gustav Schmoller in 1897, have had to earn at least 2,700 marks a year.[172] In the entire *Volksschule* establishment only the Seminar teachers, who then earned somewhere between 2,100 and 4,500 marks,[173] could aspire to middle-class status. Even so, since Falk's day the *Volksschule* teacher had managed to stay above the factory worker in his income, a position that he maintained up to 1914 when a fully employed labourer could not earn much more than 1,300 marks a year.[174]

After a century, the *Volksschule* teacher could aspire to middle-class status, not for himself, but for his son. For a group that at the beginning of the century had generally been accorded a status somewhere below that of a day labourer, the improvement was considerable. On top of that, a strong professional identity had

168. Ibid., p. 59, Table 4.
169. Ibid., p. 63, Table 5.
170. Meyer, *Schule der Untertanen*, p. 122.
171. Fritz K. Ringer, *Education and Society in Modern Europe*, p. 40, n. 7.
172. Schmoller cited in Meyer, *Schule der Untertanen*, p. 120.
173. Friedrich Buchholz and Gerhard Buchwald, eds, *Die Brandenburgischen Lehrerseminare und die Ihnen Angegliederten Präparandenanstalten*, p. 503.
174. Gerhard Bry, *Wages in Germany, 1871–1945*, p. 51.

clearly emerged during the course of the century, an identity reflected in and nurtured by the common Seminar experience, by membership in teachers' associations, and by the political and social recognition accorded to teachers by, for example, Bismarck and William II.[175]

For women the profession of *Volksschule* teacher took on a different sort of significance. Large numbers of women were recruited into teaching during the last decades of the century. By its end, 10,000 women had entered the Prussian teaching corps, bringing their total to nearly 14,000.[176]

One out of every four teachers recruited during the last three decades of the century were women. Their entry into teaching was greatly facilitated by the new Seminars established for women (two during the 1870s, and a dozen more during the next two decades) and by the regulation of 1874 that allowed women access to the teachers' qualifying examinations.[177] Still, elementary school teaching did not become in either Prussia or Bavaria (or anywhere else in Germany) the predominantly female profession that it did in the United States. In 1900 fifteen per cent of Prussia's teachers were women; in Bavaria the figure was almost twenty per cent;[178] in the United States the figure at the turn of the century was seventy per cent.[179] Only in big cities like Berlin, Düsseldorf, Cologne, and Danzig did women come close to constituting fifty per cent of the total number of *Volksschule* teachers.[180] Even in these cases certain traditional patterns continued to prevail. Whether in Prussia or Bavaria, the largest numbers of women entering teaching came from Catholic families. In Prussia alone, nearly sixty per cent came from the Catholic regions of the Rhineland and Westphalia.

By the 1890s it was women teachers, or former teachers, who were providing the leadership for the German women's movement. The

175. Douglas R. Skopp, 'Auf der untersten Sprosse: Der Volksschullehrer als "Semi-Professional" im Deutschland des 19. Jahrhunderts'; Wolfram Fischer, 'Der Volksschullehrer; Zum Sozialgeschichte eines Berufstandes'. See also Cloer, 'Sozialgeschichtliche Aspekte der Solidarisierung der preussischen Volksschullehrerschaft', p. 61; Manfred Heinemann, 'Der Lehrerverein als Sozialisationsagentur', pp. 50–2.

176. Lexis, ed., *Das Volksschulwesen*, p. 13.

177. Margrit Twellmann, *Die Deutsche Frauenbewegung; Quellen*, p. 306; Ilse Gahlings and Elle Moering, *Die Volksschullehrerin*, p. 27.

178. Sophie Schöfer, *Die wirtschaftliche Lage der bayerischen Volksschullehrerinnen*, p. 12.

179. David B. Tyack, *The One Best System; A History of American Urban Education*, p. 61.

180. Badisches Generallandesarchiv, Karlsruhe, Wisser, 'Die Lehrerinnenfrage', *Frauenfrage*, p. 13.

Seminars had become a kind of *ersatz* university for the female sex. Helene Lange, who had taken her teacher-training in Berlin during the 1870s and stayed on to teach pedagogy at a private girls' school, was one of the founders in 1889 of the *Allgemeine deutsche Lehrerinnenverein* (General German Association of Women Teachers) and in 1902 became the head of the Federation of German Women's Associations.[181] Lange's close associate, Gertrude Baumer, a theologian's daughter, had been a *Volksschule* teacher in Westphalia during the 1890s, and early in the twentieth century became one of the editors, with Lange, of the *Handbuch der Frauenfrage*.[182] The same general pattern applied to women teachers in Bavaria. Even more so than in Prussia, the women's Seminars in Bavaria were the nurseries of a women's movement. The founder in 1898 of the Bavarian Association for Women Teachers, Helene Sumper, was a graduate in 1872 of the new Women's Seminar in Munich. Her compatriot from Nuremberg, Bertha Kipfmüller, became the first Bavarian woman to earn a doctor's degree.[183]

The welcome for women teachers was not always universal. The all-male Bavarian Teachers' Association resented the competition and pressed the Education Ministry to place limits upon the number of women allowed to enter teaching. They were supported by Professor W. H. Riehl, who suggested in the *Allgemeine Deutsche Lehrerzeitung* that the backwardness of southern Germany could probably be traced to the fact that for centuries its lower schools had been in the hands of female teaching orders.[184] Did Bavaria want to remain in this backward state, he asked, by handing its classrooms over to lay women teachers?

Criticisms of women teachers were voiced also in Prussia. The Prussian Teachers' Association, no less than its Bavarian counterpart, was unhappy with female competition. Resentments were often couched in conceptualisations of the woman's unsuitability for the intellectually and physically demanding job of teaching. Education Minister Studt noted that women were known to have weaker nerves than men and a lower intellectual capacity and, moreover, 'are apparently less able to withstand the bad air that develops in a

181. James C. Albisetti, 'Could Separate be Equal? Helene Lange and Women's Education in Imperial Germany', p. 306.
182. Gertrude Baumer, *Im Licht der Erinnerung*, p. 103.
183. Helmut Beilner, *Die Emanzipation der bayerischen Lehrerin*, p. 43.
184. Gahlings and Moering, *Die Volksschullehrerin*, p. 45, n. 33.

classroom'.[185] Professor Johannes Conrad of Halle pointed out that 'Whoever has had the opportunity to observe the effect of a three-year teacher preparation programme on women's bodies knows that a very significant number of students have injured their health for life. . . .'[186]

Others, like Riehl, were more concerned with the ill-effects large numbers of women teachers would have upon society. One fear in particular dominated. 'If teachers are feminine, then education will be feminised, and that our well-being (*Volksleben*) cannot tolerate', wrote Walther Hardt in his book on *Die Lehrerinnenfrage* in 1905.[187] A feminised teaching corps, ran the argument, would inevitably lead to a feminised society, thus rendering Germany helpless in the face of her enemies. The United States was cited as an example of a society gone wrong. 'The Americans are all supposed to be "sentimental,"' wrote Moritz Bartsch, because 'instruction and education there are almost exclusively in the hands of women'.[188]

The view of the woman teacher as the feminiser of society added a new dimension to the image of the German *Volksschule* teacher. Teachers had begun the century viewed as useless beings who ranked somewhat lower than day labourers, but from that point forward their image began to change. Süvern and Montgelas saw them as agents who would restore to society the bonds that held it together; Ludwig I and Stiehl as agents of those who would have those bonds torn asunder. William I and von Roon saw them as the heroes of Königgrätz and Sedan; William II as bulwarks against the spread of social democracy.

185. Ibid., pp. 39, 41–2.
186. George Bernstein and Lottelore Bernstein, 'Attitudes Toward Women's Education in Germany, 1870–1914', p. 477.
187. Gahlings and Moering, *Die Volksschullehrerin*, p. 45.
188. Ibid.

8
Protecting Old Worlds Through Schooling

In July 1898, William Torrey Harris, the United States Commissioner of Education, went before the convention of the American Education Association to solicit support for his proposal to send a delegation of American educators to the World's Fair scheduled two years hence in Paris. It was in Paris, he hoped, that American educators, by examining 'educational exhibits side by side with the industrial exhibit', might have impressed upon them the connection between education and economic modernity. Particularly was Harris eager that the Americans see the German exhibits, both educational and industrial, because, as he told the convention, 'Germany is the leading country since the time of Frederick the Great in using the school as a great instrument of political progress. Prussia was before all nations in directing its national housekeeping by the systematic results of intelligence'. Therein lay the source, he said, of German military power and of the extraordinarily productive capacity of German industry. The lesson he wanted drawn was clear. 'The conceited nations who are not anxious to adopt new inventions nor to educate their people . . .soon find themselves lagging behind in power of national defense'.[1]

Harris' encomium was merely the latest example of what in America was nearly a century-long tradition of admiration for German education. But whether the robust, powerful, productive world of William II was as much a product of its schools is not as demonstrably obvious as Commissioner Harris supposed it to be.

1. W. T. Harris, 'Our Educational Exhibit at the International Exposition in Paris in 1900', pp. 130, 131.

Peter Lundgreen's recent detailed analysis of the relationship between education and industrialisation in Prussia during the first half of the nineteenth century concludes that a direct correlation is impossible to establish.[2] Certainly neither the industrial nor military capacities of Germany in 1898, nor its cultural achievements or national enthusiasms, would be intelligible without the mass literacy that was the most immediately measurable effect of a century of schooling. Yet it is equally clear that the society of Wilhelmian Germany was so profoundly different from the one envisioned by those who a century before had initiated schooling that had any one of them — Süvern, Wismayr, Beckedorff, or Niethammer — been set down in late nineteenth-century Prussia or Bavaria, it is unlikely that he would have seen in the schools, or in the society surrounding them, very many components of his educational or social vision. That which he had helped to set into motion had taken on a life of its own.

The idea of schooling was, as we have seen, initiated in the late eighteenth century in response to the fear that society was coming apart and then actually implemented a generation later by those who were charged, so they thought, with putting that society back together. Never again, after this implementation, were the politics of schooling seriously concerned with the question of whether or not schooling should be continued. As Beckedorff said in the 1820s, society would henceforth have to be created, like a work of art, and schools would be the basic instruments making such a creation possible. Or, as Guizot said when he sanctioned French investigation into Prussia's schooling practices: 'The greatest problem of modern societies is the governance of men's minds'. What more effective way to govern those minds than through schooling? Only through such governance could a post-revolutionary society be given coherence and cohesiveness. For that reason control over schooling was vital to those who believed they understood what shape that coherence and cohesiveness should take.

There were those who wanted a world shaped by the terms of modernity, namely liberalism, constitutionalism, social mobility, and, later in the century, by industrialism. These were the Süverns, the Wismayrs, the Falks and the Lutzes. Had they been present in

2. Peter Lundgreen, 'Education, Expansion and Economic Growth in Nineteenth-Century Germany: a Quantitative Study', p. 47. See also Christa Berg, 'Volksschule im Abseits von "Industrialisierung" und "Fortschritt"', p. 257.

1900 they would have recognised in Wilhelmian Germany certain elements of their vision; yet much of what they would have seen they would have regarded as foreign. The same would have to be said for the Beckedorffs, the Eilers, or the Stiehls whose dissatisfaction with the Germany of the late nineteenth century would have been no less striking. Schooling, obviously, was never as precise an instrument for shaping society or for the governance of men's minds as many of them believed.

An important reason for that lack of precision was the politics of schooling itself. Neither liberals nor conservatives, modernisers or traditionalists, had ever succeeded in establishing and maintaining full control over the schools for more than a few years. At the very core of the politics surrounding schooling was the conflict between Church and state. This conflict, at least as it relates to schooling, is obviously not adequately described by traditional accounts of the steady decline of Church influence. Schools more than any other institution were the battlefields of the Church–state struggles of the nineteenth century, and the Church won its share of the battles. The non-confessional school was as much a rarity at the end of the century as it had been at the beginning. Six different times comprehensive school bills that would have curtailed Church influence failed in Prussia. The single attempt at such a bill in Bavaria resulted in Bavarian liberalism's most ignominious defeat of the century.

One aspect of modernity in Wilhelmian Germany, however, that both Church and state agreed was undesirable, was that the socialist world view seemed increasingly during the century's final decades to be making headway among the urban working classes. Not even agreement of Church and state on this matter was sufficient to arrest the spread of socialist ideas. Neither William's proddings of the schools nor the enthusiastic response of the teaching corps to his call for help was able to interrupt even briefly the spread of socialism. Although schooling was, on the one hand, likely to have been a pre-condition for German industrial might, it was also, because of literacy, a pre-condition for the spread of a socialist world view. It may have seemed an open question in 1890 as to whether schooling could, in fact, undo socialism. A decade later it was clear that it could not.

The most visible failure of schooling came in the Polish regions of Prussia where since the early 1870s schools had been directly and consistently engaged in efforts to Germanise a Polish-speaking population. Nowhere were the limits to schooling's powers more clearly manifested. Rather than Germanise the Poles, Prussia's schooling efforts actually served to help generate a Polish national consciousness, one that had in its self-definition a profoundly anti-German cast.

Among Germans, however, the role of schooling in forging an integrating national consciousness is an estimable one. Literacy alone rendered them, Prussians and Bavarians alike, receptive to and prepared for full participation in the national liturgies that emerged after 1871. The extraordinary role of the vast body of *Volksschule* teachers must be seen as central to any analysis of this process. The success with which the state managed, during the course of the nineteenth century, to harness *Volksschule* teachers to those ideas that represented the core of modern values, secularism, liberalism, and nationhood, is a remarkable one. Caught between the Church, which tried to keep them subordinate, and the state, which encouraged their independence — at least from the Church — teachers overwhelmingly joined with those elements that Riehl in the 1850s identified as belonging to the forces of movement. The contribution of the *Volksschule* teacher to the dissemination of the idea of nationhood would be as difficult to exaggerate as it would be to measure precisely. But in doing so, it should be remembered, they were at the same time enhancing their own material, social, and professional status.

A critical juncture in the relationship between the state and the teaching corps came, however, when William II began to perceive the threat emanating from the growing socialist movement. He might easily have blamed the *Volksschule* teacher for failing to check the spread of socialist ideas; he might have gone even further to blame them for consciously fostering radical sentiments. There was certainly sufficient precedent for assigning to teachers the responsibility for social unrest. For William to have done so would simply have put him in line with Eylert, Eilers, or Stiehl in Prussia, or with the likes of Ludwig I in Bavaria. But William II did no such thing. Instead, he sought, instinctually it seems, to enlist the *Volksschule* teachers as allies in the fight against socialism. We have seen the eagerness with which the teachers answered William's call. As a consequence, during the 1890s, they were able to reinforce their professional roles and status as guardians of the liberal–authoritarian and national German state. The national enthusiasm in the crisis of 1914 would have been impossible without that function having been performed. The state, as Süvern had written in 1819, was an educational institution writ large. It was a lesson William II was still attempting to apply at the end of the century, although to very different ends.

There is a direct link between William's calculations and the circumstances that a century earlier had given rise to the idea of schooling. William's interest in schooling was not fundamentally different from that of his illustrious ancestor, Frederick II. For each of them schooling was to help reinforce social bonds that they feared would break apart. Frederick would eventually be able to back away from a commitment to schooling probably because, in spite of his fear, he could not quite imagine those bonds breaking completely. He lived in a world in which such a thing had never happened. The world in which William II lived, on the other hand, was haunted, as was William himself, by the memory of Frederick's world having broken apart, so much so that it believed that schools should be employed in erasing, at least among the lower classes, even the recollection of what had happened to Louis XVI in France. A *Weltbild* that did not contain that particular image, William believed, would for that reason be more secure, and men's minds thereby rendered more easily governable. Without schools no such things could be accomplished.

Bibliography

Archives and Libraries

Badisches Generallandesarchiv, Karlsruhe.
Bayerisches Hauptstaatsarchiv, Munich.
Bayerisches Staatsbibliothek, Manuscript Division.
Deutsches Zentralarchiv II, Merseburg.
Geheimes Staatsarchiv Preussischer Kulturbesitz, Berlin.
Niedersächsisches Staatsarchiv, Bückeburg.

Published Sources

Abel, Wilhelm, *Agrarkrisen und Agrarkonjunktur; Eine Geschichte der Land- und Ernährungswirtschaft Mitteleuropa seit dem hohen Mittelalter*. 2nd edn. Hamburg: Paul Parey, 1966.

Albisetti, James C., 'Could Separate Be Equal? Helene Lange and Women's Education in Imperial Germany', *History of Education Quarterly* 22 (1982), 301–17.

Albrecht, Dieter, 'Von der Reichsgründung bis zum Ende des Ersten Weltkrieges (1871–1918)'. In *Handbuch der Bayerischen Geschichte*, vol. IV, pt. 1, ed. Max Spindler. Munich: C. H. Beck, 1974.

Allgemeine Deutsche Biographie. 56 vols. 1875–1912.

Allgemeines Landrecht für die Preussischen Staaten von 1794 (Textausgabe), ed. Hans Hattenhauer. Frankfurt a. M.: A. Metzner, 1970.

Alt, Robert, *Bilderatlas zur Schul- und Erziehungsgeschichte*, vol. I. Berlin: Volk und Wissen, 1965.

American Journal of Education 6 (1859), 20 (1870).

Anderson, Lavinia M., and Kenneth Barkin, 'The Myth of the Puttkamer Purge and the Reality of the Kulturkampf: Some Reflections on the Historiography of Imperial Germany', *Journal of Modern History* 54 (1982), 647–86.

Angiolillo, Paul F., *A Criminal as Hero: Angelo Duca*. Lawrence, Kan.: Regents Press of Kansas, 1979.

The Annual Register, or a View of the History of the Year 1844. London: George

Woodfall and Son, 1845.

The Annual Register: A Review of Public Events at Home and Abroad for the Year 1885. New Series. London: Rivingtons, 1886.

Appens, Wilhelm, *Die pädagogischen Bewegungen des Jahres 1848: Ein Beitrag zur Geschichte der Pädagogik des 19. Jahrhunderts.* Elberfeld: Lucas, 1914.

Aretin, Karl Otmar von, *Bayerns Weg zum souveränen Staat: Landstände und Konstitutionelle Monarchie, 1714–1818.* Munich: C. H. Beck, 1976.

Arnold, Matthew, 'The Prussian Schoolmasters, their Training, Examination, Appointment and Payment'. Repr. in *Matthew Arnold: Schools and Universities on the Continent*, vol. IV, ed. R. H. Super. Ann Arbor, Mich.: University of Michigan Press, 1964, pp. 218–35.

——, 'Special Report on Certain Points Connected with Elementary Education in Germany, Switzerland, and France'. Repr. in *Matthew Arnold: The Last Word* (*The Complete Works of Matthew Arnold*, vol. XI). Ann Arbor, Mich.: University of Michigan Press, 1977, pp. 3–53.

Ashmore, Eric, 'Wilhelm von Humboldt's Ideas on the Formation of Character through Education', *Paedagogica Historica* III (1963), 5–26.

Atkinson, C. T., *A History of Germany: 1715–1815.* London: Methuen, 1908.

Ballauf, Theodor, 'Zur Entstehungsgeschichte der Pädagogik als Wissenschaft in der Neuzeit', *Berichte zur Wissenschaftsgeschichte* I (1978), 71–85.

—— and Klaus Schaller, *Pädagogik: Eine Geschichte der Bildung und Erziehung*, vol. III. Freiburg: Karl Alber Verlag, 1973.

Ballhausen, Lucius von, *Bismarckerinnerungen.* Stuttgart: Cotta, 1920.

Bär, Max, *Westpreussen unter Friedrich dem Grossen.* vol. I, 1909; repr. Osnabrück: Otto Zeller, 1965.

Barnard, Howard C., *A History of English Education: From 1760.* 2nd edn. London: University of London Press, 1963.

Bastgen, Beda P., *Bayern und der Heilige Stuhl.* 2 vols. Munich: Leutner, 1940.

Baumer, Gertrude, *Im Licht der Erinnerung.* Tübingen: R. Wunderlich, 1953.

Beckedorff, Ludolph, 'Einzelne vorläufige Notiz über das Berlin Schulwesen', *Jahrbücher des Preuss. Volks-Schul-Wesens* I (1825), 289–95.

——, 'Zur Geschichte des Preuss. Volks-Schulwesens', *Jahrbücher des Preuss. Volks-Schul-Wesens* II (1825), 3–96.

Beetz, K. O., *Die Lehrerbildung: Eine soziale Frage.* Gotha: Emil Behrend, 1891.

Beilner, Helmut, *Die Emanzipation der bayerischen Lehrerin; aufgezeigt an der Arbeit des bayerischen Lehrerinnenvereins (1898–1933).* Munich: R. Wölfle, 1971.

Berg, Christa, *Die Okkupation der Schule: Eine Studie zur Aufhellung gegenwärtiger Schulprobleme an der Volksschule Preussens (1872–1900).* Heidelberg: Quelle & Meyer, 1973.

——, 'Volksschule im Abseits von "Industrialisierung" und "Fortschritt"'. In *Schule und Gesellschaft im 19. Jahrhundert*, ed. Ulrich Hermann. Weinheim: Beltz, 1977, pp. 243–64.

Berkner, Lutz, and Franklin Mendels, 'Inheritance Systems, Family Structure, and Demographic Patterns in Western Europe, 1700–1900'. In *Historical Studies of Changing Fertility*, ed. Charles Tilly. Princeton, NJ:

Princeton University Press, 1978, pp. 209–23.

Bernstein, George, and Lottelore Bernstein, 'Attitudes Toward Women's Education in Germany, 1870–1914', *International Journal of Women's Studies* 2 (1979), 473–88.

Beyer, Otto Wilhelm, *Deutsche Schulwelt des neunzehnten Jahrhunderts in Wort und Bild*. Leipzig: A. Pichler, 1903.

Bissing, W. M. von, *Friedrich Wilhelm II; König von Preussen*. Berlin: Duncker & Humboldt, 1967.

Black, Eugene C., ed., *Posture of Europe, 1815–1940: Readings in European Intellectual History*. Homewood, Ill.: Dorsey Press, 1964.

Blackall, Eric C., *The Emergence of German as a Literary Language, 1750–1775*. 2nd edn. Ithaca, NY: Cornell University Press, 1978.

Blasius, Dirk, *Bürgerliche Gesellschaft und Kriminalität: Zur Sozialgeschichte Preussens im Vormärz*. Göttingen: Vandenhoeck & Ruprecht, 1976.

Blessing, Werner K., 'Allgemeine Volksbildung und Indoktrination im bayerischen Vormärz. Das Leitbild des Volksschullehrers als mentales Herrschaftsinstrument', *Zeitschrift für bayerische Landesgeschichte* 37 (1974), 479–568.

——, 'Zur Analyze politischer Mentalität und Ideologie der Unterschichten im 19. Jh.', *Zeitschrift für bayerische Landesgeschichte* 34 (1971), 768–816.

Bloth, Hugo Gotthard, *Adolph Diesterweg; Sein Leben und Wirken für Pädagogik und Schule*. Heidelberg: Quelle & Meyer, 1966.

Blum, Jerome, *The End of the Old Order in Rural Europe*. Princeton, NJ: Princeton University Press, 1978.

Bock, Alfons, ed., *Lehrplan für die Volksschulen in Baiern, 1804–1811*. Munich: Carl Schnell, 1917.

Bodelschwingh, E. von, *Leben des Ober-Präsidenten Freiherrn von Vincke; nach seinen Tagebüchern bearbeitet*. vol. I. Berlin: George, 1853.

Böhm, J., *Statistisches Handbuch des bayerischen Volksschulwesens I*. Nuremberg: Korn, 1872.

Bosl, Karl, *Bayerische Geschichte*. Munich: Paul List, 1971.

——, 'Die historische Staatlichkeit der bayerischen Lande', *Zeitschrift für bayerische Landesgeschichte* 25 (1962), 3–19.

Böttscher, Kurt, 'Das Bild des deutschen Lehrers in Literatur und Wirklichkeit', *Neue deutsche Literatur* 3 (1955), 72–94.

Bowen, H. Courthope, *Froebel*. New York: Charles Scribner's Sons, 1906.

Braun, Heinrich, *Gedanken über die Erziehung und den öffentlichen Unterricht in den trivial- real- und lateinischen Schulen nach den katholischen Schulverfassungen Oberdeutschlandes*. Ulm: J. C. Wohler, 1774.

——, *Pragmatische Geschichte der Schulreformation in Baiern aus ächten Quellen*. n.p., 1783.

Bremen, E. von, ed., *Die Preussische Volksschule: Gesetze und Verordnungen*. Stuttgart: J. G. Cotta, 1905.

Broszat, Martin, *Zweihundert Jahre deutsche Polenpolitik*. 2nd edn. Frankfurt a. M.: Suhrkamp Taschenbuch Verlag, 1972.

Brunnengräber, Hans, *Ludolph von Beckedorff; Ein Volksschulpädagoge des 19. Jahrhunderts*. Düsseldorf: Pädagogischer Verlag, 1929.

Brunschwig, Henri, *Enlightenment and Romanticism in Eighteenth-Century Prussia.* Trans. Frank Jellinek, 1947; repr. Chicago: University of Chicago Press, 1974.

Bry, Gerhard, *Wages in Germany, 1871–1945.* Princeton, NJ: Princeton University Press, 1960.

Buchholz, Friedrich, and Gerhard Buchwald, eds, *Die Brandenburgischen Lehrerseminare und die Ihnen Angegliederten Präparandenanstalten; Einzeldarstellung ihrer Entwicklung.* Berlin: Selbstverlag, 1961.

Bülow, Bernhard von, *Memoirs.* Vol. I, trans. F. A. Voigt. Boston: Little, Brown, 1931.

Bungardt, Karl, *Die Odyssee der Lehrerschaft; Sozialgeschichte eines Standes.* Frankfurt a. M.: Kern & Birner, 1959.

Buske, Thomas, *Thron und Altar: Die Rolle der Berliner Hofprediger im Zeitalter des Wilhelminismus.* Neustadt an der Aisch: Ph. C. Schmidt, 1970.

Bussenius, Ingeborg Charlotte, and Walther Hubatsch, eds, *Urkunden und Akten zur Geschichte der preussischen Verwaltung in Südpreussen und Neuostpreussen, 1793–1806.* Frankfurt a. M.: Athenäum, 1961.

Busshoff, Heinrich, 'Die preussische Volksschule als sozialer Gebilde und politischer Bildungsfaktor in der ersten Hälfte des 19. Jahrhunderts', *Geschichte in Wissenschaft und Unterricht* 22 (1971), 385–96.

Bussmann, Walter, 'Das Zeitalter Bismarcks'. In *Handbuch der Deutschen Geschichte,* vol. III, pt. 2, ed. Leo Just. Konstanz: Akademische Verlaggesellschaft Athenaion, 1965.

Carsten, F. L., *Princes and Parliaments in Germany; From the Fifteenth to the Eighteenth Century.* London: Oxford University Press, 1959.

Centralblatt für die gesammte Unterrichts-Verwaltung. (Prussia). 1860; 1872.

Clausnitzer, L., *Geschichte des Preussischen Unterrichtsgesetzes; Mit besonderer Berücksichtigung der Volksschule.* 5th edn., vol. I. Hamburg: Henri Grand, 1909.

Cloer, Ernst, 'Sozialgeschichtliche Aspekte der Solidarisierung der preussischen Volksschullehrerschaft im Kaiserreich und in der Weimarer Republik'. In *Der Lehrer und seine Organisationen,* ed. Manfred Heinemann. Stuttgart: Ernst Klett, 1977, pp. 59–79.

Conrad, M. G., 'Die Erziehung'. *Deutsche Schulwart* I (Dec. 1871), 14–26.

Constabel, Adelheid, ed., *Die Vorgeschichte der Kulturkampfes; Quellenveroffentlichung aus den Deutschen Zentralarchiv.* Berlin: Rütten & Loening, 1956.

Conze, Werner, 'Vom "Pöbel" zum "Proletariat", Sozialgeschichtliche Voraussetzungen für den Sozialismus in Deutschland', *Vierteljahrsschrift für Sozial- und Wirtschaftsgeschichte* 41 (1954), 333–64.

Cousin, Victor, 'Report on the State of Public Instruction in Prussia'. In *Reports on European Education,* ed. E. W. Knight. New York: McGraw-Hill, 1930.

Crocker, Lester Gilbert, 'The Problem of Truth and Falsehood in the Age of the Enlightenment', *Journal of the History of Ideas* 14 (1953), 575–603.

Damaschke, Adolf, *Aus meinem Leben.* vol. I. Leipzig and Zurich: Grethlein, 1924.

Dawson, Jerry F., *Friedrich Schleiermacher: The Evolution of a Nationalist.* Austin: University of Texas Press, 1966.

Dettmar, H., and G. Baarke, *Lehr- und Lernbüchlein für den ersten Geschichts-*

unterricht. 3rd edn. Harburg a.d. Elge: Gustav Eklan, 1907.

Die Bewegung der Bevölkerung im Königreich Bayern in der fünf Jahren 1857/58 bis 1861/62 mit Rückblicken auf die 22 Jahre 1835/36 bis 1856/57. Munich: E. Huber, 1863.

Die Deutschen Lehrerkonferenzen des Jahres 1891, 1892, 1893. vols. IV–VI. ed. L. E. Seidel. Langensalza: F. G. L. Gressler, 1892–94.

Die Gesetzgebung auf dem Gebiete des Unterrichtswesens in Preussen: Vom Jahre 1817 bis 1868. Berlin: Wilhelm Hertz, 1869.

Diesterweg, Friedrich Adolph Wilhelm, *Sämtliche Werke*. 12 vols. Heinrich Dieters, et al., eds. Berlin: Volk und Wissen, 1956–74.

Dieterici, W., ed., *Die statistischen Tabellen des preussischen Staats nach der amtlichen Aufnahme des Jahres 1843*. Berlin: Nicolai, 1845.

Dilthey, Wilhelm, 'Süvern'. *Allgemeine Deutsche Biographie*. vol. XXXVII, pp. 206–45.

Dobmann, Franz, *Georg Friedrich Freiherr von Zentner als bayerischer Staatsmann in den Jahren 1799–1821*. Kallmünz: Lassleben, 1962.

Doeberl, Michael, *Entwicklungsgeschichte Bayerns*. vols. II and III. Munich: Oldenbourg, 1912–31.

——, 'Zur Geschichte der bayerischen Schulpolitik im 19. Jahrhundert'. In *Sitzungsberichte der philosophisch-philologischen und der historischen Klasse der K. B. Akademie der Wissenschaften*. Munich: Verlag der Königlichen Bayerischen Akademie der Wissenschaften, 1912.

Dörpfeld, F. W., 'Die Schulkonferenz im preuss. Unterrichtsministerium', *Evangelisches Schulblatt und Deutsche Zeitung* 16 (1872), 297–314.

Du Moulin Eckart, Richard von, *Geschichte der deutschen Universitäten*. 1924; repr. Hildesheim: Georg Olms, 1976.

Dunkel, Harold B., *Herbart and Herbartianism*. Chicago: University of Chicago Press, 1970.

Eilers, Gerd, *Meine Wanderung durchs Leben: Ein Beitrag zur innern Geschichte der ersten Hälfte des 19. Jahrhunderts*. vols III–V, Leipzig: F. A. Brockhaus, 1858–60.

——, *Zur Beurtheilung des Ministeriums Eichhorn*. Berlin: Ferd. Dümmler's, 1849.

Ellis, George E., 'Benjamin Thompson — Count Rumford', *American Journal of Education* 27 (1877), 561–92.

Emminghaus, A., ed., *Poor Relief in Different Parts of Europe*. Trans. from the German. London: Edward Stanford, 1873.

Endres, Franz Carl, *Georg Hirth. Ein deutscher Patriot*. Munich: Walther C. F. Hirth, 1921.

Engelsing, Rolf, *Analphabetentum und Lektüre; Zur Sozialgeschichte des Lesens in Deutschland zwischen feudalen und industrieller Gesellschaft*. Stuttgart: J. B. Metzler, 1973.

——, *Sozial- und Wirtschaftsgeschichte Deutschlands*. Göttingen: Vandenhoeck & Ruprecht, 1973.

Epstein, Klaus, *The Genesis of German Conservatism*. Princeton, NJ: Princeton University Press, 1966.

Ergang, Robert, *The Potsdam Führer; Frederick William I, Father of Prussian Militarism*. New York: Columbia University Press, 1941.

Ergebnisse der Unterrichts-Statistik im Königreich Bayern für das Schuljahr 1884/85. Königl. statistischen Bureau, ed. Munich: Kgl. Hof-Buchdruckerei von E. Mühlthaler, 1887.

Eulenburg, Philipp, *Politische Korrespondenz.* Vol. II, ed. J. C. Röhl. Boppard am Rhein: Harold Boldt, 1979.

Evans, Ellen Lovell, *The German Center Party 1870–1933: A Study in Political Catholicism.* Carbondale and Edwardsville: Southern Illinois University Press, 1981.

Evans, Richard J., 'Liberalism and Society: The Feminist Movement and Social Change'. In *Society and Politics in Wilhelmine Germany*, ed. Richard J. Evans. London and New York: Croom Helm and Barnes and Noble, 1978, pp. 186–214.

Eylert, R. Fr., *Charakter-Züge und historische Fragmente aus dem Leben des Königs von Preussen Friedrich Wilhelm III.* 3 vols. Magdeburg: Heinrichshofen, 1843–46.

Faber, Karl-Georg, 'Görres, Weitzel und die Revolution (1819)', *Historische Zeitschrift* 194 (1962), 37–61.

Fichte, Johann Gottlieb, *Addresses to the German Nation*, ed. George A. Kelley. New York: Harper & Row (Torchbook edn.), 1968.

Fischer, Fritz, *Ludwig Nicolovius: Rokoko, Reform, Restauration.* Stuttgart: Kohlhammer, 1939.

Fischer, Konrad, *Geschichte des Deutschen Volksschullehrerstandes.* vol. II. 1898; repr. Leipzig: Zentralantiquariat der DDR, 1969.

Fischer, Wolfram, 'Der Volksschullehrer; Zur Sozialgeschichte eines Berufstandes', *Soziale Welt* 12 (1961), 37–47.

Flitner, Andreas, *Die Politische Erziehung in Deutschland; Geschichte und Probleme, 1750–1880.* Tübingen: Max Niemeyer, 1957.

Flora, Peter, 'Die Bildungsentwicklung im Prozess der Staaten- und Nationenbildung'. In *Soziologie und Sozialgeschichte*, ed. Peter Christian Ludz. (Sonderheft 16: *Kölner Zeitschrift für Soziologie und Sozialpsychologie*) Opladen: Westdeutscher Verlag, 1972, pp. 294–319.

Frank, Horst Joachim, *Geschichte des Deutschunterrichts: Von den Anfängen bis 1945.* Munich: Carl Hansen, 1973.

Frauendienst, Werner, 'Das Deutsche Reich von 1890 bis 1914 (1909)'. In *Handbuch der Deutschen Geschichte.* vol. IV, pt. 1, ed. Leo Just. Frankfurt a. M.: Akademische Verlagsgesellschaft Anthenaion, 1973, pp. 3–274.

——, 'Preussisches Staatsbewusstsein und polnischer Nationalismus; Preussisch-deutsche Polenpolitik, 1815–1890'. In *Das östliche Deutschland*, Göttinger Arbeitskreis, ed. Würzburg: Holzner Verlag, 1959.

Fricke, Dieter, *Bismarcks Prätorianer; Die Berliner politische Polizei in Kampf gegen die deutsche Arbeiterbewegung (1871–1898).* Berlin: Rütten & Loening, 1962.

Fried, Pankraz, 'Bauerntum und Landvolk (1800–1945)'. In *Handbuch der Bayerischen Geschichte.* vol. IV, pt. 2, ed. Max Spindler. Munich: C. H. Beck, 1975, pp. 747–80.

Fritz, Albert, *Geschichte der Lehrerbildungsanstalt Kaiserslauten von 1818–1918.* Kaiserslauten: Eugen Crusius, 1919.

Gagliardo, John G., *From Pariah to Patriot; The Changing Image of the German*

Peasant, 1770–1840. Lexington, Ky.: University of Kentucky Press, 1969.

Gahlings, Ilse, and Elle Moering, *Die Volksschullehrerin; Sozialgeschichte und Gegenwartslage*. Heidelberg: Quelle & Meyer, 1961.

Gatz, Erwin, comp., *Akten zur preussischen Kirchenpolitik in den Bistümern Gnesen-Posen, Kulm und Ermland, 1885–1914; Aus dem Politischen Archiv des Auswärtigen Amtes*. Mainz: Mathias-Grunewald, 1977.

Gebhardt, Bruno, *Die Einführung der Pestalozzischen Methode in Preussen; Ein urkundliches Kapitel preussischer Schulgeschichte*. Berlin: R. Gaertners, 1896.

Gedike, Friedrich, ed., *Annalen des Preussischen Schul- und Kirchenwesens*. vol. I. Berlin: Johann Friedrich Unger, 1800.

Geiger, Ludwig, *Berlin, 1688–1840; Geschichte des geistigen Lebens der preussischen Hauptstadt*. vol. I. Berlin: Paetel, 1893.

Geistbeck, Michael, *Geschichte des Oberbayerischen K. Schullehrerseminars von 1804–1904*. Freising: Datterer, 1904.

Gerlach, Otto, *Die Nationalerziehung im 18. Jahrhundert, dargestellt in ihrem Hauptvertreter Friedrich Eberhard v. Rochow*. Marienwerder: Wendt Groll, 1929.

Germer, Helmut, *The German Novel of Education, 1792–1805; A Complete Bibliography and Analysis*. Berne: Herbert Lang, 1968.

Giese, Gerhardt, *Quellen zur deutschen Schulgeschichte seit 1800*. Göttingen: Musterschmidt, 1961.

Gimbel, Hans-Dieter, 'Sozialistengesetz und "grosse Depression": Die deutsche Gewerkschaftsbewegung von der Wirtschaftskrise 1873 bis zum Kölner Parteitag der deutschen Sozialdemokratie 1893'. In *Geschichte der deutschen Gewerkschaftsbewegung*, ed. Frank Deppe, et al. Cologne: Pahl Rugenstein, 1977, pp. 44–61.

Gleich, Mechthild, *Die Pädagogik des preussischen Konservatismus in der Epoche seine Entstehung*. Bottrop i. M.: Wilh. Postberg, 1933.

Gollwitzer, Heinz, 'Die politische Landschaft in der deutschen Geschichte des 19./20. Jahrhunderts', *Zeitschrift für bayerische Landesgeschichte* 27 (1964), 523–52.

Gooch, G. P., *Frederick the Great; the Ruler, the Writer, the Man*. New York: Alfred A. Knopf, 1947.

Göring, Hugo, 'Die "Deutsche Schule" als Förderung unserer Zeit', *Die Neue Deutsche Schule* 1, no. 10 (1889), 447–61.

——, 'Die Entstehung des Allgemeinen Deutschen Vereins für Schulreform "Die Neue Deutsche Schule"', *Die Neue Deutsche Schule* 1, no. 2 (1889), 65–72.

——, *Die neue deutsche Schule; Ein Weg zur Verwirklichung vaterländischer Erziehung*. Leipzig: R. Voightländer, 1890.

Gossler, 'Ueber die höchstnothwendige Verbesserung des Zustandes der unteren Volksklassen', *Neue Berlinische Monatsschrift* 15 (1806), 401–29.

Grasser, Walter, *Johann Freiherr von Lutz (eine politische Biographie) 1826–1890*. Munich: Neue Schriftenreihe des Stadtarchiv München, 1967.

Greven-Aschoff, Barbara, 'Sozialer Wandel und Frauenbewegung', *Geschichte und Gesellschaft* 7 (1981), 328–46.

Grimsley, Ronald, *Jean D'Alembert*. London: Oxford University Press, 1963.

Haenchen, Karl, 'Zur revolutionären Unterwühlung Berlins vor dem

Märztagen des Jahres 1848', *Forschungen zur Brandenburgischen und Preussischen Geschichte* 55 (1943), 83–114.

Haller, Johannes, *Philipp Eulenburg; the Kaiser's Friend.* vol. I. Trans. E. C. Mayne, 1930; repr. Freeport, NY: Books for Libraries Press, 1971.

Hamerow, Theodore S., *Restoration, Revolution, Reaction; Economics and Politics in Germany, 1815–1871.* Princeton, NJ: Princeton University Press, 1958.

Hammermayer, Ludwig, 'Das Ende des alten Bayern'. In *Handbuch der Bayerischen Geschichte,* vol. II, ed. Max Spindler. Munich: C. H. Beck, 1966, pp. 985–1102.

Harkort, Friedrich, *Schriften und Reden zur Volksschule und Volksbildung,* ed. Karl-Ernst Jeismann. Paderborn: Ferdinand Schönigh, 1969.

Harnack, Adolf, *Geschichte der Königlichen Preussischen Akademie der Wissenschaften zu Berlin.* Berlin: Reichsdruckerei, 1900.

Harnisch, Wilhelm, *Der jetzige Standpunkt des gesammten Preussischen Volksschulwesens.* Leipzig: August Weichardt, 1844.

Harris, W. T., 'Our Educational Exhibit at the International Exposition in Paris in 1900', *Education* XIX (Nov. 1898), 129–40.

Hauser, Oswald, 'Zum Problem der Nationalisierung Preussens', *Historische Zeitschrift* 202 (1966), 529–41.

Haushofer, Heinz, 'Bauer und Schule in der Geschichte', *Zeitschrift für Agrargeschichte und Agrarsoziologie* 18 (1970), 1–15.

Hausmann, G., 'A Century of Comparative Education, 1785–1885', *Comparative Education Review* XI (1967), 1–21.

Hazard, Paul, *The European Mind; The Critical Years (1680–1715),* trans. J. Lewis May. New Haven: Yale University Press, 1953.

Heer, Friedrich, *The Intellectual History of Europe,* Vol. II, trans. Jonathon Steinberg. New York: Anchor (paperback), 1968.

Heer, Georg, *Geschichte der Deutschen Burschenschaft.* Vol. II. 1927; repr. Heidelberg: Carl Winter, 1965.

Heigenmooser, Joseph, 'Aus der bayerischen Volksschulgeschichte des 19. Jahrhunderts', *Das Bayerland* XXXIII (1922), 406–12.

——, *Ein bayerischer Pestalozzischüler: Franz Joseph Müller.* Munich: Carl Aug. Seyfried, 1911.

—— and Alfons Bock, eds., *Geschichte der Pädagogik; Quellenbuch und Überblick der Geschichte der Pädagogik.* Munich: Seyfried, 1909.

Heinemann, Manfred, '"Bildung" in Staatshand. Zur Zielsetzung und Legitimations-problematik der "niederen" Schulen in Preussen, unter besonderer Berücksichtigung des Unterrichtsgesetzentwurfs des Ministerium Falk (1877)'. In *Bildungspolitik in Preussen zur Zeit des Kaiserreichs,* ed. Peter Baumgart. Stuttgart: Klett-Cotta, 1980, pp. 150–88.

——, 'Der Lehrerverein als Sozialisationsagentur: Überlegungen zur beruflichen Sozialisation der Volksschullehrer in Preussen'. In *Der Lehrer und seine Organisationen,* ed. Manfred Heinemann. Stuttgart: Ernst Klett, 1977, pp. 39–58.

——, *Schule im Vorfeld der Verwaltung; Die Entwicklung der preussischen Unterrichtsverwaltung von 1771–1800.* Göttingen: Vandenhoeck & Ruprecht, 1974.

Heinemann, Manfred, and Wilhelm Rüter, *Landschulreform als Gesellschafts-*

initiative: Philip von Reck, Johann Friedrich Wilberg und die Tätigkeit der "Gesellschaft der Freunde der Lehrer und Kinder in der Grafschaft Mark" (1789–1815). Göttingen: Vandenhoeck & Ruprecht, 1975.

Heinl, Jürgen, *Die deutsche Sozialpolitik des 19. Jahrhunderts im Spiegel der Schulgeschichtsbücher*. Braunschweig: Albert Limbach, 1972.

Held, Heinrich, *Altbayerische Volkserziehung und Volksschule (Geschichtliche Darbeitung und Regesten aus dem Erziehungswesen im Bereiche der Erzdiozese München und Freising)*. 3 vols. Munich: Verlag des Vereins für Erforschung der Geschichte der Erzdiozese München und Freising, 1926.

Heller, Gudrun, *Geschichtsschulbücher im 19. Jahrhundert in Bayern*. Diss. University of Munich, 1944.

Hennes, Edmund, *Die Volkserziehungslehre bei Herder und bei Vertretern des gebildeten Mittelstandes des 2. Hälfte des 18. Jahrhunderts*. Bonn: S. Foppen, 1918.

Henning, Hansjoachim, *Sozialgeschichtliche Entwicklungen in Deutschland von 1815 bis 1860*. Paderborn: Ferdinand Schöningh, 1977.

Herber, Pauline, *Das Lehrerinnenwesen in Deutschland*. Kempton: Jos. Kosel, 1906.

Hermann, F. B. W. von, ed., *Beiträge zur Statistik des Königreichs Bayern II; Leistungen der Sicherheitspolizei und Strafrechtspflege*. Munich: J. G. Cotta, 1853.

Hermann, Ulrich, 'Pädagogische und politische Publizistik zur Zeit der Französischen Revolution in Deutschland', *Pädagogische Rundschau* 28 (1974), 242–48.

Herwegh, Georg, *Werke in drei Teilen*, ed. Hermann Tardel. Berlin: Deutsche Verlagshaus Bong & Co., 1909.

Hindringer, Rudolf, *Das kirchliche Schulrecht in Altbayern von Albrecht V bis zum Erlasse der bayerischen Verfassungsurkunde, 1550–1818*. Paderborn: Ferdinand Schöningh, 1916.

Hintze, Otto, *Die Hohenzollern und Ihr Werk; Fünfhundert Jahre vaterländischer Geschichte*. 1915, 5th edn.; repr. Moers: Steiger Verlag, 1979/80.

Hirth, Georg, 'Über Culturpolizei und Rechtsgleichheit zur Lösung der sozialen Frage'. In *Annalen des Deutschen Reiches*, ed. Georg Hirth. Leipzig: Verlag von G. Hirth, 1873, pp. 795–862.

Hodges, A., *The Philosophy of Wilhelm Dilthey*. London: Routledge & Kegan Paul, 1952.

Höfele, Karl Heinrich, 'Sendungsglaube und Epochenbewusstsein in Deutschland 1870/71', *Zeitschrift für Religions- und Geistesgeschichte* XV (1963), 265–76.

Hofmann, Franz, *Karl Friedrich Wilhelm Wander*. Berlin: Volk und Wissen, 1961.

Hohenlohe-Schillingsfürst, Clodwig, *Memoirs*. vol. I, ed. Fr. Curtius. New York: Macmillan Co., 1906.

Hojer, Ernst, 'Das Problem der demokratischen Erziehung bei Schleiermacher', *Pädagogische Rundschau* 27 (1973), 1–13.

Holl, Karl, 'Das nationalsoziale Schulprogram; eine Schuldebatte aus den Jahren 1896 und 1897', *Pädagogische Rundschau* 23 (1969), 434–41.

Hollack, Emil, and Friedrich Trommau, *Geschichte des Schulwesens der*

Königlichen Haupt- und Residenzstadt Königsberg mit besonderer Berücksichtigung der niederen Schulen; Ein Beitrag zur Kulturgeschichte Altpreussens. Königsberg i. Pr.: J. H. Bon, 1899.

Holstein, Friedrich von, *Papers*. vol. II, N, Rich and M. H. Fisher, eds. Cambridge: Cambridge University Press, 1957.

Howitt, William, *The Rural and Domestic Life of Germany*. London: Longman, Brown, Green, and Longmans, 1842.

Hubatsch, Walther, *Frederick the Great of Prussia: Absolutism and Administration*, trans. Patrick Doran. London: Thames and Hudson, 1973.

Huber, Ernst R., *Deutsche Verfassungsgeschichte seit 1789*. vol. I. Stuttgart: Kohlhammer, 1957.

——, *Dokumente zur deutschen Verfassungsgeschichte*. vol. I. 2nd edn. Stuttgart: Kohlhammer, 1961.

Humboldt, Wilhelm von, *Briefe*. Heinz Gollwitzer, intro. Munich: Carl Hanser, 1952.

——, *Werke*. vol. IV, Andreas Flitner and Klaus Giel, eds. Stuttgart: J. G. Cotta, 1964.

Jarausch, Konrad H., *The Enigmatic Chancellor; Bethmann Hollweg and the Hubris of Imperial Germany*. New Haven and London: Yale University Press, 1973.

Jefferson, Thomas, *Papers*, vol. XIII, ed. Julian P. Boyd. Princeton, NJ: Princeton University Press, 1956.

Jeismann, Karl-Ernst, *Das preussische Gymnasium in Staat und Gesellschaft; Die Entstehung des Gymnasiums als Schule des Staates und der Gebildeten, 1787–1817*. Stuttgart: Klett Verlag, 1974.

——, 'Die "Stiehlschen Regulative." Ein Beitrag zum Verhältnis von Politik und Pädagogik während der Reaktionszeit in Preussen'. In *Schule und Gesellschaft im 19. Jahrhundert*, ed. Ulrich Hermann. Weinlein and Basel: Beltz Verlag, 1977, pp. 137–61.

——, ed., *Staat und Erziehung in der preussischen Reform, 1807–1819*. Göttingen: Vandenhoeck & Ruprecht, 1969.

——, 'Volksbildung und Industrialisierung als Faktoren des sozialen Wandels im Vormärz', *Zeitschrift für Pädagogik* 18 (1972), 315–37.

Jensen, Gwendolyn Evans, 'Official Reform in *Vormärz* Prussia: The Ecclesiastical Dimension', *Central European History* VII (1974), 137–58.

Joll, James, *The Second International, 1889–1914*. New York: Praeger, 1956.

Kade, Franz, *Schleiermachers Anteil an der Entwicklung des preussischen Bildungswesens von 1808–1818*. Leipzig: Quelle & Meyer, 1925.

Kaelble, Hartmut, 'Sozialer Aufstieg in Deutschland, 1850–1914', *Vierteljahresschrift für Sozial- und Wirtschaftsgeschichte* 60 (1973), 41–71.

Kant, Immanuel, *On Education*, trans. Annette Churton, 1803; repr. Boston: D. C. Heath, 1900.

Kantzenbach, Friedrich Wilhelm, 'Adolf Stählin und das Landeskirchentum', *Zeitschrift für bayerische Kirchengeschichte* 40 (1971), 206–26.

Keck, K., and Chr. Johannsen, eds, *Vaterländisches Lesebuch für die mehrklassige evangelische Volksschule Norddeutschlands*. 15th edn. Halle a. S.: Verlag der Buchhandlung des Waisenhaus, 1899.

Kehr, Eckart, 'The Social System of Reaction in Prussia under the Puttkamer Ministry'. In Eckart Kehr, *Economic Interest, Militarism, and Foreign Policy*, ed. Gordon Craig. Berkeley: University of California Press, 1977, pp. 109–31.

Kerschensteiner, Georg, *Staatsbürgerliche Erziehung der deutschen Jugend*. 4th edn. Erfurt: Karl Villaret, 1909.

Keyser, Erich, *Bevölkerungsgeschichte Deutschlands*. Leipzig: G. Hirzel, 1938.

Kiehn, Ludwig, 'German Education and Economy in the Nineteenth Century'. In *The Yearbook of Education, 1956*, ed. Robert K. Hall and J. A. Lauwerys. New York: World Book, n.d., pp. 485–94.

Klessmann, Christoph, 'Zur Sozialgeschichte der Reichsverfassungskampagne von 1849', *Historische Zeitschrift* 218 (1974), 283–337.

Klewitz, 'Geschichte und Darstellung des Südpreussischen Schulwesens', *Neue Berlinische Monatsschrift* 14 (Sept. 1805), 161–92.

Klinke, Willibald, *Kant for Everyman*, trans. Michael Bullock. London: Routledge and Kegan Paul, 1951.

Kluckhohn, August, *Beiträge zur Geschichte des Schulwesens in Bayern vom 16. bis zum 18. Jahrhundert*. Munich: Verlag der Akademie, 1875.

Knodel, John, 'Law, Marriage and Illegitimacy in Nineteenth Century Germany', *Population Studies* 20 (1966–67), 279–94.

Kober, Adolf, 'Jewish Communities in Germany from the Age of Enlightenment to their Destruction by the Nazis', *Jewish Social Studies* IX (1947), 195–238.

Koch, M. J., *Die Bergarbeiterbewegung im Ruhrgebiet zur Zeit Wilhelms II (1889–1914)*. Düsseldorf: Droste Verlag, 1954.

Koehl, Robert Lewis, 'Colonialism Inside Germany: 1886–1918', *Journal of Modern History* 25 (1953), 255–72.

König, Helmut, 'Der Kaiser-Erlass vom 1. Mai 1889', *Jahrbuch für Erziehungs- und Schulgeschichte* 12 (1974), 53–103.

Korth, Rudolf, *Die preussische Schulpolitik und die polnischen Schulstreiks; Ein Beitrag zur preussischen Polenpolitik der Ära Bülow*. Marburg: Holzner Verlag, 1963.

Koselleck, Reinhart, *Preussen zwischen Reform und Revolution; Allgemeines Landrecht, Verwaltung und soziale Bewegung von 1791 bis 1848*. Stuttgart: Klett Verlag, 1967.

——, 'Staat und Gesellschaft in Preussen, 1815–1848'. In *Staat und Gesellschaft im deutschen Vormärz, 1815–1848*, ed. Werner Conze. Stuttgart: Ernst Klett, 1961.

Kreppel, Friedrich, 'Der Lehrer in der Zeitgeschichte'. In *Das Wilhelminische Zeitalter I*, ed. Hans-Joachim Schoeps. Stuttgart: Ernst Klett, 1967, pp. 199–218.

Krieger, Leonard, *Kings and Philosophers, 1689–1789*. New York: W. W. Norton, 1970.

Krueger, Bernhard, 'Die Rede Friedrich Wilhelms IV. vor den Teilnehmern der Seminarlehrerkonferenz 1849', *Pädagogische Rundschau* 24 (1970), 845–56.

Küther, Carsten, *Raüber und Gauner in Deutschland*. Göttingen: Vandenhoeck & Ruprecht, 1976.

Landé, Walter, ed., *Preussisches Schulrecht*. 2 vols. Berlin: Carl Heymanns

Verlag, 1933.

Lange, Helene, and Gertrud Baumer, eds, *Handbuch der Frauenbewegung*. Parts I and II. Berlin: W. Moeser, 1901.

Langer, Adam, *Erinnerungen aus dem Leben eines Dorfschullehrers*. Landeck: Selbstverlag, 1900.

Langer, William L., 'Infanticide; A Historical Survey', *History of Childhood Quarterly* 1 (1974), 353–65.

LaVopa, Anthony, *Prussian Schoolteachers: Profession and Office, 1763–1848*. Chapel Hill: University of North Carolina Press, 1980.

——, 'Status and Ideology: Rural Schoolteachers in Pre-March and Revolutionary Prussia', *Journal of Social History* 12 (1979), 430–56.

Lee, W. R., 'Bastardy and the Socioeconomic Structure of South Germany', *Journal of Interdisciplinary History* VII (1977), 403–25.

——, *Population Growth, Economic Development and Social Change in Bavaria, 1750–1850*. New York: Arno Press, 1977.

——, 'Tax Structure and Economic Growth in Germany (1750–1850)', *Journal of European Economic History* 4 (1975), 153–78.

Leipold, Eugen, *Erinnerungen aus meinem Leben*. Regensburg: G. J. Manz, 1912.

Lenk, Leonhard, 'Revolutionär-kommunistische Umtriebe im Königreich Bayern. Ein Beitrag zur Entwicklung von Staat und Gesellschaft 1848–1864', *Zeitschrift für bayerische Landesgeschichte* 28 (1965), 555–622.

Lenz, Max, *Geschichte der Königlichen Friedrich-Wilhelms-Universität zu Berlin*. Vol. IV. Halle a. d. S.: Verlag der Buchhandlung des Waisenhauses, 1910.

Lewisohn, Ludwig, ed., *Goethe: The Story of a Man*. Vol. II New York: Farrar, Strauss & Co., 1949.

Lexis, W., ed., *Das Volksschulwesen und das Lehrerbildungswesen im Deutschen Reich*. Berlin: Verlag von A. Asher & Co., 1904.

Lichtenstein, Ernst, 'Aus dem Krisenjahr der Pestalozzischulreform in Preussen', *Zeitschrift für Pädagogik* 1 (1955), 83–108.

Lidtke, Vernon, *The Outlawed Party; Social Democracy in Germany, 1878–1890*. Princeton NJ: Princeton University Press, 1966.

Liedtke, Max, *Pestalozzi*. Hamburg: Rowohlt Taschenbuch Verlag, 1968.

Liermann, Hans, 'Staatsgedanke und Kirchenpolitik in Bayern seit der Reichsgründung 1871', *Zeitschrift für bayerische Kirchengeschichte* VI (1931), 129–41.

Lotz, Albert, 'Die Kosten der Volksschule in Preussen', *Schmollers Jahrbuch* 22 (1898), 251–68.

Lüdicke, Reinhard, *Die Preussischen Kultusminister und ihre Beamten im ersten Jahrhundert des Ministeriums, 1817–1917*. Stuttgart: J. G. Cotta, 1918.

Ludwig, J. F., *Ein Lehrerleben; Selbstbiographie*. Augsburg: Verlag des bayerischen Lehrervereins, 1876.

Lundgreen, Peter, 'Education, Expansion and Economic Growth in Nineteenth-Century Germany: A Quantitative Study'. In *Schooling and Society*, ed. Lawrence Stone. Baltimore: Johns Hopkins University Press, 1976, pp. 20–66.

Luthardt, August Emil, *Mein Werden und Wirken im öffentlichen Leben*. Munich: C. H. Beck, 1901.

Lüttgert, Gottlieb, *Preussens Unterrichtskämpfe in der Bewegung von 1848*. Berlin: Trowitzsch, 1924.
McClelland, Charles E., *State, Society, and University in Germany, 1700–1914*. Cambridge: Cambridge University Press, 1980.
Mächler, Anita, 'Aspekte der Volksschulpolitik im 19. Jahrhundert; Ein Überblick über wichtige gesetzliche Grundlagen im Hinblick auf ausgewählte Gesichtspunkte'. In *Bildungspolitik in Preussen zur Zeit des Kaiserreichs*, ed. Peter Baumgart. Stuttgart: Klett-Cotta, 1980, pp. 224–41.
Maenner, Ludwig, *Bayern vor und in der Französischen Revolution*. Stuttgart: Deutsche-Verlags-Anstalt, 1927.
Malthus, Thomas Robert, *An Essay on the Principle of Population*. 7th edn., 1872; repr. New York: Augustus M. Kelley, 1971.
Mann, Horace, *Annual Reports of the Secretary of the Board of Education of Massachusetts for the Years 1839–1844*. Boston: Lee and Shephard, 1891.
Manuel, Frank E., *Shapes of Philosophical History*. Stanford, Calif.: Stanford University Press, 1965.
Marcks, Friedrich, *Oskar Jäger, Das Leben eines deutschen Schulmannes*. Leipzig: Teubner, 1930.
Mattheisen, Donald J., 'Voters and Parliaments in the German Revolutions of 1848: An Analysis of the Prussian Constituent Assembly', *Central European History* V (1972), 3–22.
Matthias, Adolf, '*Die Pädagogischen Bewegungen des Jahres 1848* by Wilhelm Appens: A Review', *Zeitschrift für Geschichte der Erziehung und des Unterrichts* VI (1916), 125–33.
Mayhew, Alan, *Rural Settlement and Farming in Germany*. New York: Barnes & Noble, 1973.
Messer, August, *Das Problem der staatsbürgerlichen Erziehung historisch und systematisch behandelt*. Leipzig: Otto Nemnich, 1912.
Methseider, Joh. Friedr., *Erinnerungen aus meinem Leben nach einem 53-jährigen Dienste in der Schule*. Nuremberg: Korn, 1905.
Meyer, Folkert, *Schule der Untertanen; Lehrer und Politik in Preussen, 1848–1900*. Hamburg: Hoffman and Campe, 1976.
Ministerialblatt für Kirchen- und Schul-Angelegenheiten im Königreich Bayern. 1860; 1866; 1871; 1873; 1876; 1877; 1879; 1880.
Mirabeau, Honoré Gabriel Riqueti, Comte de, *Memoirs of the Courts of Berlin and St. Petersburg*. New York: P. F. Collier & Son, 1910.
Möckl, Karl, 'Gesellschaft und Politik während der Ära des Prinzregenten Luitpold. Ein Beitrag zur Vorgeschichte der Revolution in Bayern'. In *Bayern im Umbruch; Die Revolution von 1918, ihre Voraussetzungen; ihr Verlauf und ihre Folgen*, ed. Karl Bosl. Munich: R. Oldenbourg, 1964, pp. 5–36.
——, *Die Prinzregentenzeit; Gesellschaft und Politik während der Ära des Prinzregenten Luitpold in Bayern*. Munich: R. Oldenbourg, 1972.
Moffat, Mary M., *Queen Louisa of Prussia*. New York: E. P. Dutton, 1907.
Moody, Joseph N., *French Education Since Napoleon*. Syracuse: Syracuse University Press, 1978.
Mooser, Josef, 'Soziale Mobilität und familiale Plazierung bei Bauern und Unterschichten; Aspekte der Sozialstruktur der ländlichen Gesellschaft im

19. Jahrhundert am Beispiel des Kirchenspiels Quernheim in östlichen Westphalen'. In *Familie zwischen Tradition und Moderne; Studien zur Geschichte der Familie in Deutschland und Frankreich vom 16. bis zum 20. Jahrhundert*, eds W. Bulst, et al. Göttingen: Vandenhoeck & Ruprecht, 1981.

Mosse, George L., *The Nationalization of the Masses*. New York: Howard Fertig, 1975.

Müller, Artur, *Die Deutschen; Ihre Klassenkämpfe, Aufstände, Staatsstreiche, und Revolutionen*. Munich: Kurt Desch, 1972.

Müller, Detlef K., *Sozialstruktur und Schulsystem: Aspekte zum Strukturwandel des Schulwesens im 19. Jahrhundert*. Göttingen: Vandenhoeck & Ruprecht, 1977.

Müller, F. J., ed., *Beyträge zur Berichtigung der Urtheile über Pestalozzi, seine Methode und sein Institut*. Passau: Niklas Ambrost, 1804.

Müller, Günther, *König Max II und die soziale Frage*. Munich: Olzog, 1964.

Müller, Karl, 'Lehrer in der Revolutionsbewegung des Jahres 1848', *Preussische Lehrerzeitung* 1929, No. 92–98.

Murtfeld, Rudolf, *Der Weg der preussischen Volksschullehrerschaft zum Dienst am deutschen Volke, 1815–1871*. Frankfurt a. M.: M. Diesterweg, 1934.

Müsebeck, Ernst, *Das Preussische Kultusministerium vor hundert Jahren*. Stuttgart: J. G. Cotta, 1918.

Natorp, B. C. L., *Andreas Bell und Joseph Lancaster; Bemerkungen über die von denselben eingeführten Schuleinrichtung, Schulzucht und Lehrart*. Essen: G. D. Bädeker, 1817.

Natorp, Paul, *Sozialpädagogik: Theorie der Willenserziehung auf der Grundlage der Gemeinschaft*. 4th edn. Stuttgart: Fr. Frommans, 1920.

Neubach, Helmut, *Die Ausweisungen von Polen und Juden aus Preussen, 1885–86*. Wiesbaden: Harrassowitz, 1967.

Neubauer, Dr, 'Geschichtsunterricht und staatsbürgerlicher Unterricht', *Deutsche Schulerziehung* I (1907), 152–72.

Neue Deutsche Biographie. vols. I–XIII. 1953–1982.

Neukum, Josef, *Schule und Politik. Politische Geschichte der bayerischen Volksschule, 1818–1848*. Munich: Ehrenwirth, 1969.

Neumann, Sigmund, *Die Stufen des preussischen Konservatismus; Ein Beitrag zum Staats- und Gesellschaftsbild Deutschlands im 19. Jahrhundert*. Berlin: Emil Ebering, 1930.

Nichols, J. Alden, *Germany After Bismarck; The Caprivi Era, 1890–1894*. Cambridge, Mass.: Harvard University Press, 1958.

Niedergesäss, F. W., ed., *Das Elementarschulwesen in den Königlich Preussischen Staaten; Eine Zusammenstellung der gültigen Gesetze, Verordnungen, Erlasse und Verfügungen das Elementarschulwesen betreffend*. Crefeld: Funcke & Müller, 1847.

Niemeyer, A. H., *Grundsatze der Erziehung und des Unterrichts für Eltern, Hauslehrer und Erzieher*. 1796: repr. Paderborn: F. Schöningh, 1970.

Niethammer, Friedrich Immanuel, *Der Streit des Philanthropinismus und Humanismus*. Jena: Friedrich Fromann, 1808.

Nipperdey, Thomas, 'Volksschule und Revolution im Vormärz'. In *Politische Ideologien und nationalstaatliche Ordnung*, ed. Kurt Kluxen and Wolfgang J. Mommsen. Munich: R. Oldenbourg, 1968, pp. 117–42.

Nissl, Josef, *Die Schulpolitik in Bayern von 1850–1914 im Volksschulwesen*. Staffelstein: n.p., 1919.

Noyes, P. H., *Organization and Revolution; Working-Class Associations in the German Revolutions of 1848–1849*. Princeton, NJ: Princeton University Press, 1966.

Nüchter, Fr., 'Die geschichtliche Entwicklung der Lehrerbildung'. *Schule und Gegenwart* 9 (1951), 41–43; 44–47.

Obenaus, Walter, *Die Entwicklung der preussischen Sicherheitspolizei; Bis zum Ende der Reaktionszeit*. 1940; repr. Berlin: Walter de Gruyter, 1978.

O'Boyle, Lenore, 'Klassische Bildung und soziale Struktur in Deutschland zwischen 1800 und 1848', *Historische Zeitschrift* 207 (1968), 584–608.

——, 'A Possible Model for the Study of Nineteenth-Century Secondary Education', *Journal of Social History* 12 (1978), 236–47.

Oer, Rudolfine von, *Die Säkularisation, 1803*. Göttingen: Vandenhoeck & Ruprecht, 1970.

Paulsen, Friedrich, *The German Universities and University Study*. Trans. F. Thilly and W. E. Elwang. New York: Charles Scribner's, 1906.

Pestalozzi, J. H., 'The Method, a Report'. In J. H. Pestalozzi. *How Gertrude Teaches Her Children; An Attempt to Help Mothers to Teach their own Children and an Account of the Method*. Trans. L. E. Turner and F. C. Turner. Syracuse: C. W. Bardeen, 1898.

——, *Sämtliche Briefe*. 13 vols. eds., Emanuel Dejing, et al. Zurich: Orell Füssli Verlag, 1946–71.

Pflanze, Otto, *Bismarck and the Development of Germany; The Period of Unification, 1815–1871*. Princeton, NJ: Princeton University Press, 1963.

Phayer, J. Michael, 'Lower-Class Morality: The Case of Bavaria', *Journal of Social History* 8 (1974), 79–95.

Pinson, Koppel S., *Modern Germany; Its History and Civilization*. 2nd edn. New York: Macmillan, 1966.

——, *Pietism as a Factor in the Rise of German Nationalism*. New York: Columbia University Press, 1934.

Raack, R. C., 'Schleiermacher's Political Thought and Activity, 1806–1813', *Church History* 28 (1959), 374–90.

Rach, Alfred, *Biographien zur deutschen Erziehungsgeschichte*. Berlin: Beltz, 1968.

——, *Sachwörter zur deutschen Erziehungsgeschichte*. Weinheim: Julius Beltz, 1964.

Radtke, Manfred, *Der schulpolitische Kampf in Preussen-Deutschland*. Diss. Universität Greifswald, 1954.

Rall, Hans, 'Ausblicke auf Weltentwicklung und Religion im Kreise Max' II und Ludwigs II', *Zeitschrift für bayerische Landesgeschichte* 27 (1964), 488–522.

——, *Kurbayern in der letzten Epoche der alten Reichsverfassung, 1745–1801*. Munich: C. H. Beck, 1952.

——, 'Die politische Entwicklung von 1848 bis zur Reichsgründung 1871'. In *Handbuch der Bayerischen Geschichte*. vol. IV, pt. 1, ed. Max Spindler. Munich: C. H. Beck, 1974, pp. 224–82.

Rameckers, J. M., *Der Kindesmord in der Literatur der Sturm- und Drang Periode*. Rotterdam: Nijgh & van Ditmar, 1927.

Ramm, Agatha, *Germany, 1789–1919*. London: Methuen, 1967.

Raumer, Kurt von, 'Zum geschichtlichen Hintergrund und europäischen Kontext der preussischen Bildungsreform'. In *Das Vergangene und die Geschichte*, eds. R. von Thadden et al. Göttingen: Vandenhoeck & Ruprecht, 1973, pp. 42–62.

Reble, Albert, 'Das Schulwesen'. In *Handbuch der Bayerischen Geschichte*. vol. IV, pt. 2, ed. Max Spindler. Munich: C. H. Beck, 1975, pp. 950–90.

Recum, Hasso v., 'Soziale Strukturwandlungen des Volksschullehrerberufes: Vom Aufstiegsberuf zum Mangelberuf', *Kölner Zeitschrift für Soziologie* 7 (1955), 574–79.

'Reichsgesetzgebung', *Deutsche Schule* (1907).

Rich, Norman, *Friedrich von Holstein*. vol. I. Cambridge: Cambridge University Press, 1965.

Richter, Kurt, *Der Kampf um den Schulgesetzentwurf des Grafen Zedlitz-Trützschler vom Jahre 1892*. Halle: Eduard Klinz, 1934.

Rieder, Max, *Geschichte der politischen Bildung in den Volksschulen Bayerns von der Zeit der Braunschen Reform bis zur Restauration*. Diss. Universität München, 1968.

Riehl, W. H., *Die bürgerliche Gesellschaft*. 5th edn. Stuttgart: J. G. Cotta, 1861.

Ringer, Fritz K., *Education and Society in Modern Europe*. Bloomington: Indiana University Press, 1978.

Rissmann, Robert, *Deutsche Pädagogen des 19. Jahrhunderts*. Leipzig: Julius Klinkhardt, 1910.

——, *Geschichte des Deutschen Lehrervereins*. Leipzig: Julius Klinkhardt, 1908.

Rittershausen, Dietrich, 'Beiträge zur Geschichte des Berliner Elementar-Schulwesens; Von der Reformation bis 1836', *Märkische Forschungen* IX (1865), 178–317.

Roberts, J. M., *The Mythology of Secret Societies*. New York: Charles Scribner's Sons, 1972.

Rochow, Friedrich Eberhard von, 'Geschichte meiner Schulen (1795)'. In *Rochow; Schriften zur Volksschule*, ed. Rudolf Lochner. Bad Heilbronn, Austria: Julius Klinkhardt, 1962, pp. 39–64.

——, *Sämtliche Pädagogische Schriften*. 4 vols., eds. Fritz Jonas and Friedrich Wienecke. Berlin: Georg Reimer, 1907–1910.

——, *Versuch über Armen-Anstalten und Abschaffung aller Betteley*. Berlin: Friedrich Nicolai, 1789.

——, 'Vom Nationalcharacter'. In *Rochow: Schriften zur Volksschule*, ed. Rudolf Lochner. Bad Heilbronn, Austria: Julius Klinkhardt, 1962.

Röckl, Joseph, *Paedagogische Reise durch Deutschland*. Dillingen: Gedruckt auf Kosten des Verfassers bey Leonard Vrdauer, 1808.

Roeder, Peter Martin, 'Gemeindeschule in Staatshand. Zur Schulpolitik des Preussischen Abgeordnetenhauses'. In *Schule und Gesellschaft im 19. Jahrhundert*, ed. Ulrich Hermann. Weinheim: Beltz, 1977, pp. 212–42.

Roessler, Wilhelm, 'Bildung von Modellen in der Schulgeschichtsschreibung', *Zeitschrift für Pädagogik* 16 (1970), 467–81.

——, *Die Entstehung des modernen Erziehungswesens in Deutschland*. Stuttgart: Kohlhammer, 1961.

——, 'Pädagogik'. In *Geschichtliche Grundbegriffe*, vol. IV, eds. Otto Brunner,

et al. Stuttgart: Klett, 1978, pp. 623–47.
Röhl, J. C. G., *Germany without Bismarck: The Crisis of Government in the Reich, 1890–1900*. London: B. T. Batsford, 1967.
Rönne, Ludwig von, ed., *Das Unterrichts-Wesen des Preussischen Staates*. vol. I. Berlin: Veit, 1855.
Rosenbaum, L., *Beruf und Herkunft der Abgeordneten zu den Deutschen und Preussischen Parlamenten, 1847 bis 1919; Ein Beitrag zur Geschichte des deutschen Parlaments*. Frankfurt a. M.: Frankfurt Societäts-Druckerei, 1923.
Rosenthal, Harry Kenneth, 'The Election of Archbishop Stablewski', *Slavic Review* 28 (1969), 265–75.
——, 'Poles, Prussians, and Elementary Education in Nineteenth-Century Posen', *Canadian-American Slavic Studies* VII (Summer 1973), 209–18.
Roth, Rainer, *Politische Bildung in Bayern. Eine historisch-politische Untersuchung um politische Bildung an den Volksschulen Bayerns in der Zeit der Monarchie von Ludwig I bis zur Gründung des Deutschen Reiches*. Munich: Ernst Vogel, 1974.
Rousseau, Jean Jacques, *Émile*. Trans. Allan Bloom. New York: Basic Books, 1979.
Rudhart, Ignatz, *Ueber den Zustand des Königreichs Baiern nach amtlichen Quellen*. vol. I. Stuttgart: J. G. Cotta, 1825.
Sacher, Werner, *Die zweite Phase in der Lehrerbildung: Ihre Entwicklung seit 1800 aufgezeigt am Beispiel Bayerns*. Bad Heilbronn, Austria: Julius Klinkhardt, 1974.
Sachs, Berta, *Pläne und Massnahmen der Regierung des Königs Max I. Joseph im Mädchenschulwesen Altbayerns*. Munich: Duncker & Humboldt, 1914.
Schärl, Walter, *Die Zusammensetzung der bayerischen Beamtenschaft von 1806 bis 1918*. Kallmünz: M. Lassleben, 1955.
Schieder, Theodor, *Vom Deutschen Bund zum Deutschen Reich, 1815–1871*. 3rd edn. Munich: Deutsche Taschenbuchverlag, 1978.
Schissler, Hanna, *Preussische Agrargesellschaft im Wandel: Wirtschaftliche, gesellschaftliche und politische Transformationsprozesse von 1763 bis 1847*. Göttingen: Vandenhoeck & Ruprecht, 1978.
Schleiermacher, Friedrich, *Ausgewählte pädagogische Schriften*, ed. E. Lichtenstein. Paderborn: Ferdinand Schöningh, 1959.
——, *Pädagogische Schriften*. 2nd edn., ed. C. Platz. Langensalza: Hermann Beyer & Söhne, 1876.
Schleunes, Karl A., 'Enlightenment, Reform, Reaction: The Schooling Revolution in Prussia', *Central European History* XII (1979), 315–42.
Schmidt, Otto, *Die Frage der Reichsschulgesetzgebung*. Berlin: Julius Klinkhardt, 1907.
Schmidt-Volkmar, Erich, *Der Kulturkampf in Deutschland, 1871–1890*. Göttingen: Musterschmidt, 1962.
Schnabel, Franz, *Deutsche Geschichte im neunzehnten Jahrhundert*. vol. I. 4th edn. Freiburg i. B: Herder & Co., 1948.
Schneider, Joanne Frances, *An Historical Examination of Women's Education in Bavaria; Mädchenschulen and Contemporary Attitudes about Them, 1799–1848*. Diss. Brown University, 1977.
Schneider, Karl, *Ein halbes Jahrhundert im Dienste von Kirche und Schule; Lebenserinnerungen*. Berlin: Wilhelm Hertz, 1900.

Schoeps, Hans-Joachim, 'Neues zur preussischer Kirchen- und Schulgeschichte des 19. Jahrhunderts'. In *Neue Quellen zur Geschichte Preussens im 19. Jahrhundert*, ed. Hans-Joachim Schoeps. Berlin: Haude & Spener, 1968, pp. 38–84.

——, *Preussen: Geschichte eines Staates*. 7th edn. Berlin: Propyläen, 1967.

Schofer, Lawrence, 'Patterns of Worker Protest: Upper Silesia, 1865–1914', *Journal of Social History* 5 (1972), 447–63.

Schöfer, Sophie, *Die wirtschaftliche Lage der bayerischen Volksschullehrerinnen*. Munich: Carl Herber, 1918.

Scholz, Christian Gottlieb, *Meine Erlebnisse als Schulmann*. Breslau: Maruschke & Berendt, 1862.

Schramm, Paul, *Hundert Jahre bayerische Schulgeschichte: Ein schulpolitischer Versuch*. Diessen: J. C. Huber, 1911.

Schremmer, Eckart, *Die Wirtschaft Bayerns; Vom hohen Mittelalter zum Beginn der Industrialisierung: Bergbau, Gewerbe, Handel*. Munich: C. H. Beck, 1970.

Schroeder, Paul W., *Metternich's Diplomacy at Its Zenith, 1821–1823*. Austin: University of Texas Press, 1962.

Schulthess' europäischer Geschichtskalendar, 1890.

Schultze, Karl, *Aus acht Jahrzehnten: Lebenserinnerungen*. Gotha: Friedrich Andreas Perthes, 1907.

Schumacher, Bruno, *Geschichte Ost- und Westpreussens*. 5th edn. Würzburg: Holzner Verlag, 1959.

Schurz, Carl, *The Reminiscences of Carl Schurz*. vol. I. New York: McClure, 1907.

Schwartz, Paul, *Der erste Kulturkampf in Preussen um Kirche und Schule (1788–1798)*. Berlin: Weidmannsche Buchhandlung, 1925.

——, 'Die Schulen der Provinz Ostpreussen unter dem Oberschulkollegium, 1787–1806', *Zeitschrift für Geschichte der Erziehung und des Unterrichts* 21 (1931), 51–123.

Schweim, Lothar, comp., *Schulreform in Preussen, 1809–1819: Entwürfe und Gutachten*. Weinheim: Julius Beltz, 1966.

Seiler, Gustav, ed., *Schulbedarfsgesetz vom 28. Juli 1902 mit Einleitung, Erläuterungen und den Vollzugsvorschriften*. Munich: C. H. Beck, 1903.

Shorter, Edward, *The Making of the Modern Family*. New York: Basic Books, 1975.

——, 'Sexual Change and Illegitimacy; The European Experience'. In *Modern European Social History*, ed. Robert J. Bezucka. Lexington, Mass.: D. C. Heath, 1971, pp. 231–69.

Silber, Kate, *Pestalozzi, the Man and his Work*. 2nd edn. London: Routledge and Kegan Paul, 1965.

Simon, Matthias, *Evangelische Kirchengeschichte Bayerns*. 2nd edn. Nuremberg: Selbstverlag des Verfassers, 1952.

Skopp, Douglas R., 'Auf der untersten Sprosse: Der Volksschullehrer als "Semi-Professional" im Deutschland des 19. Jahrhunderts', *Geschichte und Gesellschaft* 6 (1980), 383–402.

——, 'The Elementary School Teachers in "Revolt": Reform Proposals for Germany's Volksschulen in 1848 and 1849', *History of Education Quarterly* 22 (1982), 341–61.

Smith, Benjamin M., 'Reverend Benjamin M. Smith's Report on Education in Prussia to Governor David Campbell of Virginia (1839)'. In *A Documentary History of Education in the South Before 1860.* vol. II, ed. Edgar W. Knight. Chapel Hill: University of North Carolina Press, 1950, pp. 410–60.

Spielhagen, Friedrich, *In Reih' und Glied (Volksausgabe).* Leipzig: L. Staackmann, 1910.

Spranger, Eduard, *Zur Geschichte der deutschen Volksschule.* Heidelberg: Quelle & Meyer, 1949.

——, *Wilhelm von Humboldt und die Reform des Bildungswesens.* 1910; repr. Tübingen: M. Niemeyer, 1960.

Srbik, Heinrich von, *Metternich; Staatsmann und der Mensch.* vol. I. 3rd edn. Munich: Bruckmann, 1957.

Stadelmann, Rudolph, *Social and Political History of the German 1848 Revolution.* Trans. J. G. Chastain. Athens, Ohio: Ohio University Press, 1975.

de Staël-Holstein, Anne Louise Germaine, *Germany.* Pt. 1. Boston: Houghton Mifflin, 1887.

Statistisches Handbuch für den Preussischen Staat. Vol. I. Berlin: Verlag des Königlichen Statistischen Bureaus, 1888.

Stenographische Berichte über die Verhandlungen der zur Vereinbarung der preussischen Staats-Verfassung berufenen Versammlung. 3 vols. Berlin: Decker, 1848.

Stieber, Wilhelm J. C. E., *Spion des Kanzlers; Die Enthüllungen von Bismarcks Geheimdienstchef Wilhelm J. C. E. Stieber.* Stuttgart: Seewald, 1978.

Stölzle, Remigius, 'Ein bayerischer conservativer Politiker, sein Werden und Wirken (August Emil Luthardt)', *Historisch-politische Blätter für das katholische Deutschland* 127 (1901), 851–66.

——, 'Pestalozzi und die bayerische Regierung im Jahre 1802', *Zeitschrift für Geschichte der Erziehung und des Unterrichts* VI (1916), 222–24.

Stowe, Calvin E., 'Report on Elementary Public Instruction in Europe'. In *Reports on European Education*, ed. Edgar W. Knight. New York: McGraw-Hill, 1930, pp. 248–316.

Strangeland, Charles Emil, *Pre-Malthusian Doctrines of Population.* 1904; repr. New York: Augustus M. Kelley, 1966.

Straus, Hannah Alice, *The Attitude of the Congress of Vienna Toward Nationalism in Germany, Italy, and Poland.* 1949; repr. New York: AMS Press, 1968.

Stübig, Heinz, *Armee und Nation; Die pädagogisch-politischen Motive der preussischen Heeresreform, 1807–1814.* Frankfurt a. M.: Europäische Hochschulschriften, 1971.

Sweet, Paul R., *Wilhelm von Humboldt; A Biography.* 2 vols. Columbus: Ohio State University Press, 1980.

Taddey, Gerhard, ed., *Lexikon der Deutschen Geschichte.* Stuttgart: Alfred Kroner, 1977.

Tews, Johannes, *Der achte deutsche Lehrertag und seine Gegner.* Leipzig: J. Klinkhardt, 1890.

——, *Aus Arbeit und Leben; Erinnerungen und Rückblicke.* Berlin: Walter de Gruyter, 1921.

——, *Ein Jahrhundert preussischer Schulgeschichte.* Leipzig: Quelle & Meyer, 1914.

Thiele, Gunnar, *Die Organisation des Volksschul- und Seminarwesens in Preussen 1809–1819. Mit besonderer Berücksichtigung der Wirksamkeit Ludwig Natorps*. Leipzig: Dürr, 1912.

——, *Geschichte des Preussischen Lehrerseminare*. Pt. 1. Berlin: Weidmann, 1938.

Thielen, Peter Gerrit, *Karl August von Hardenberg, 1750–1822; Eine Biographie*. Cologne: Grote, 1967.

Tims, Richard Wonser, *Germanizing Prussian Poland, 1894–1919*. New York: Columbia University Press, 1941.

Titze, Hartmut, *Die Politisierung der Erziehung*. Frankfurt a. M.: Fischer Taschenbuchverlag, 1973.

Tracey, Michael, *Agriculture in Western Europe*. New York: Frederick A. Praeger, 1964.

Treitschke, Heinrich von, *Der Entwurf des Preussischen Volksschulgesetzes*. Stuttgart: J. G. Cotta, 1892.

Trzeciakowski, Lech, 'The Prussian State and the Catholic Church in Prussian Poland, 1871–1914', *Slavic Review* 26 (1967), 618–37.

Twellmann, Margrit, *Die Deutsche Frauenbewegung: Quellen, 1843–1889*. Meisenheim am Glau: Anton Hain, 1972.

Tyack, David B., *The One Best System: A History of American Urban Education*. Cambridge, Mass.: Harvard University Press, 1974.

'Ueber das Betteln auf dem platten Lande und in kleinen Städten', *Berlinische Monatsschrift* 9 (1787), 3–23.

Ullwer, Sigrid, *Der Geschichtsunterricht in der Volksschule nach den Vorstellungen der bayerischen Regierung und der bayerischen Lehrervereine von der Gründung des Bayerischen Lehrervereins 1861 bis zum Ende des Zweiten Weltkrieges*. Bern: Lang, 1976.

Valentin, Veit, *Geschichte der deutschen Revolution von 1848–49*. vol. II. Berlin: Ullstein, 1930.

Valjevic, Fritz, 'Das Woellnerische Religionsedikt und seine geschichtliche Bedeutung', *Historisches Jahrbuch* 72 (1953), 386–400.

Vedeler, Harold C., 'The Genesis of the Toleration Reforms in Bavaria under Montgelas', *Journal of Modern History* 10 (1938), 473–95.

Verhandlungen. Kammer der Abgeordneten (Bavaria). *Stenographische Berichte*. 1871/72; 1875/76; 1877/78; 1879/80; 1881/82.

Volksschulwesen und Kirche in Bayern. Sammlung allgemeinen Actenstücke zur Darstellung des Verhältnisses zwischen Volksschule, Staat und Kirche in den letzten zwanzig Jahren vom Jahre 1848 bis zum Schlusse des Jahres 1867. Regensburg: F. Pustet, 1868.

Vollmar, Ferdinand, *Die preussische Volksschulpolitik unter Friedrich dem Grossen*. Berlin: Weidmann, 1918.

Wächtershauser, Wilhelm, *Das Verbrechen des Kindermordes im Zeitalter der Aufklärung*. Berlin: Erich Schmidt, 1973.

Wallace, Lillian Parker, *The Papacy and European Diplomacy, 1869–1878*. Chapel Hill, NC: University of North Carolina Press, 1948.

Wandycz, Piotr S., *The Lands of Partitioned Poland, 1795–1918*. Seattle, Wash.: University of Washington Press, 1974.

Weber, Eugen, *Peasants Into Frenchmen; The Modernization of Rural France, 1870–1914*. Stanford, Calif.: Stanford University Press, 1976.

Weinlein, Christian, *Der Bayerische Volksschullehrer-Verein*. Nuremberg: Friedrich Korn, 1911.

Weis, Eberhard, *Montgelas, 1759–1799; Zwischen Revolution und Reform*. Munich: C. H. Beck, 1971.

Westenrieder, Lorenz, 'Warum man mit Aufklärung der Bürger und Bauern noch so weit zurück, und wie weit man gleichwohl gekommen ist'. In *Beyträge zur vaterländischen Historie, Geographie, Staatistik, (sic) und Landwirtschaft, samt einer Uebersicht der schönen Literatur*, ed. Lorenz Westenrieder. Munich: Joseph Lindauer, 1790, pp. 352–70.

Wisser, 'Die Lehrerinnenfrage', *Frauenfrage* IV (1905), 13.

Wolfram, Ludwig, 'Heinrich Braun, Ein Beitrag zur Geschichte der Aufklärungsepoche in Bayern', *Historische Abhandlungen aus dem Münchner Seminar* 3 (1892), 1–99.

Wrigley, E. A., *Population and History*. New York: McGraw-Hill, 1969.

Zedlitz, K. A. von, 'Vorschläge zur Verbesserung des Schulwesens in den Königlichen Staaten', *Berlinische Monatsschrift* 10 (1787), 97–116.

Zimmermann, Wilhelm, *Die Anfänge und der Aufbau des Lehrerbildungs- und Volksschulwesens am Rhein, 1814–1840 (1846)*. vol. III. Cologne: B. Pick, 1963.

Zorn, Wolfgang, 'Gesellschaft und Staat im Bayern des Vormärz'. In *Staat und Gesellschaft im deutschen Vormärz, 1815–1848*, ed. Werner Conze. Stuttgart: Klett, 1962, pp. 113–42.

——, 'Sozialer Wandel in Mitteleuropa, 1780–1840', *Kölner Zeitschrift für Soziologie und Sozialpsychologie* 16 (1972), 343–56.

——, 'Die Sozialentwicklung der nichtagrarischer Welt (1806–1970)'. In *Handbuch der Bayerischen Geschichte*. vol. IV, pt. 2, ed. Max Spindler. Munich: C. H. Beck, 1975, pp. 846–82.

——, 'Staatliche Wirtschafts- und Sozialpolitik und öffentliche Finanzen 1800–1970'. In *Handbuch der deutschen Wirtschafts- und Sozialgeschichte*. vol. II, eds Hermann Aubin and Wolfgang Zorn. Stuttgart: Ernst Klett, 1976, pp. 148–97.

Zwick, Hermann, 'History and Development of the Common-School System of Berlin'. In *Report of the Commissioner of Education for the Year 1893–94*. vol. I. Washington, DC: Government Printing Office, 1896, pp. 245–97.

General Index